Disabilities

Disabilities
Insights from across Fields and around the World

Volume 2

The Context:
Environmental, Social, and Cultural Considerations

Edited by

CATHERINE A. MARSHALL, ELIZABETH KENDALL,
MARTHA E. BANKS, AND REVA MARIAH S. GOVER

Foreword by Thomas Bornemann

Praeger Perspectives

PRAEGER

Westport, Connecticut
London

Library of Congress Cataloging-in-Publication Data

Disabilities / edited by Catherine A. Marshall ... [et al.].
    v. cm.
  Includes bibliographical references and index.
  Contents: v 1. The experience : definitions, causes, and consequences—v. 2. The context : environmental, social, and cultural considerations—v. 3. Responses : practice, legal, and political frameworks.
    ISBN 978-0-313-34604-0 ((set) : alk. paper)—ISBN 978-0-313-34606-4 ((vol. 1) : alk. paper)—ISBN 978-0-313-34608-8 ((vol. 2) : alk. paper)—ISBN 978-0-313-34610-1 ((vol. 3) : alk. paper)
  1. People with disabilities. 2. Disabilities. I. Marshall, Catherine A.
  HV1568.D54 2009
  362.4–dc22   2008045497

British Library Cataloguing in Publication Data is available.

Copyright © 2009 by Catherine A. Marshall, Elizabeth Kendall, Martha E. Banks, and Reva Mariah S. Gover

All rights reserved. No portion of this book may be reproduced, by any process or technique, without the express written consent of the publisher.

Library of Congress Catalog Card Number: 2008045497
ISBN: 978-0-313-34604-0 (set)
      978-0-313-34606-4 (vol. 1)
      978-0-313-34608-8 (vol. 2)
      978-0-313-34610-1 (vol. 3)

First published in 2009

Praeger Publishers, 88 Post Road West, Westport, CT 06881
An imprint of Greenwood Publishing Group, Inc.
www.praeger.com

Printed in the United States of America

The paper used in this book complies with the
Permanent Paper Standard issued by the National
Information Standards Organization (Z39.48-1984).

10 9 8 7 6 5 4 3 2 1

Contents

Foreword *Thomas Bornemann*		ix
Preface *Paul Leung*		xiii
Introduction		xix
Chapter 1.	Creating Mental Health Disability through Inadequate Disaster Response: Lessons from Hurricane Katrina *Paula A. Madrid, Roy Grant, and Rachel Rosen*	1
Chapter 2.	Autonomy and Disability: A Quest for Quality of Life *Bedarius Bell Jr., Shelley R. Henthorne, Doris Adams Hill, Jane W. Turnbull-Humphries, and Stephanie T. Zito*	17
Chapter 3.	Children Who Care for Their Parents: The Impact of Parental Disability on Young Lives *Kenneth I. Pakenham*	39
Chapter 4.	The Digital Town Square: Information and Communication Technology as an Opportunity and a Barrier to Social Relations for Disabled Youth *Sylvia Söderström*	61

Chapter 5.	Understanding the Experience of Parenting a Child with Autism *Samantha Bursnall, Eilis Kennedy, Rob Senior, and Jo Violet*	81
Chapter 6.	Through My Rose-Colored Glasses: When Disability Strikes a Health Professional *Melissa Kendall*	99
Chapter 7.	Australian Indigenous Health and the SIPES Model of Well-Being: The Legacy of Lauraine Barlow *Leda Barnett and Dianne Barnett*	111
Chapter 8.	"Surely Someone Can Support Me": A Caregiver's Perspective *Tara Catalano and Debra Domalewski*	129
Chapter 9.	Navigating Societal Norms: The Psychological Implications of Living in the United States with Disability *Jennifer Gibson*	139
Chapter 10.	Disabilities and Employment in the United States, Kenya, and the Philippines: A Race and Class Perspective *Elaine A. Burke and Patricia Denise Lopez*	151
Chapter 11.	Youth with Intellectual Disabilities in Foster Care: Examining Accompanying Risks and Service Outcomes *Crystal L. Cederna, Melissa Palguta, Jacqueline Remondet Wall, and Steven M. Koch*	169
Chapter 12.	Mental Disorder, Disability, and Society *David Pilgrim and Anne Rogers*	185
Chapter 13.	Parental Perspectives on Disability: The Story of Sam, Anna, and Marcus *Heather Douglas and Sally Borbasi*	201
Chapter 14.	Bullying of Children with Developmental Disabilities: An Ecological Approach to Program Development *Rocky Liesman*	219
Chapter 15.	Mosaic Reflections of American Muslims on Disability: Challenges and Solutions *Mobin Tawakkul, Isra Bhatty, and Mohammed Yousuf*	239
Chapter 16.	Voices of People with Disabilities (PWD) in Vietnam *David N. Morrissey*	257

Chapter 17.	Substance Use Disorders and Disability: An Examination of Co-occurring Disorders in Nigeria *Stephanie L. Lusk and Teresia M. Paul*	275
Chapter 18.	Chasing Your Dreams *Connie Susa*	289

Afterword: Reclaiming Globalization for Disability—Further Insights	301
Index	311
About the Advisory Board Members	319
About the Editors and Contributors	323

Foreword

Mental health and physical health are as inextricably linked as their counterparts, mental illness and physical illness. The latter can result in various short- and long-term disabilities. But there is a growing trend, especially outside the United States, to focus attention more on health than illness, with an emphasis on enhancing people's capabilities rather than just mitigating disability. This movement toward social inclusion is an exciting advance, promoting people's talents and assets so that they can live the healthiest, most fulfilling lives possible. For this to be implemented broadly, however, it is important that policies be put in place that demand inclusion of people with all disabilities as fully contributing members of society. These policies must be enacted in all areas of society, not just health. Ensuring that all citizens have access to the myriad services they need to live in society requires that social inclusion policies be adopted in housing, transportation, employment, and other areas that impact all our lives.

The editors of these three volumes hope to engage readers in thinking about the ways in which different frameworks lead to different practices and how these practices then affect people's lives. For example, they hope to engage the reader in thinking about how political and legal frameworks affect people with disabilities. Believing that "collaboration and the creation of partnerships are necessary components of a global strategy for enhancing the lives of persons with disabilities and the professionals who serve them" (Marshall et al., 2004, p. 20), the editors have embarked on a process reminiscent of the work of The Carter Center.

The mission of The Carter Center Mental Health Program is to increase public knowledge of and decrease stigma associated with mental illnesses.

The program does this via strategies such as the annual Rosalynn Carter Symposium on Mental Health, which brings together diverse and multidisciplinary mental health care professionals, government agencies, consumer groups, and advocacy organizations (Palpant, Steimnitz, Bornemann, & Hawkins, 2006). One chapter in these volumes, authored by Paula Madrid and colleagues, addresses how depression and psychological distress can be created within the context of response (or lack thereof) to a national disaster. The editors tapped Madrid's expertise based on the presentation of her work during the 22nd Annual Rosalynn Carter Symposium on Mental Health Policy, "Disaster Mental Health in the Wake of Hurricane Katrina," in 2006.

The editors first came together during the forum "Participatory Action Research and Indigenous Ways of Knowing: Women as Researchers and Partners in Community-Based Disability and Rehabilitation Research," held in Honolulu, Hawai'i, in 2004. Over 30 Indigenous and non-Indigenous women from the United States and the Asia-Pacific region participated in this forum, including a member of the Carter Center Mental Health Task Force. Attendees were women with and without disabilities, researchers, grassroots community members, and community activists. The purpose of the forum was to engage a global community in articulating and redressing disparities in accessing health care and human services via culturally appropriate research methods and networking—networking that would support action outcomes taking place within local communities. The stories of some of the participants formed the underpinnings of these volumes.

In a preliminary conversation about this forum in 2003, I suggested that understanding Indigenous issues and disability might have implications for world peace. One of the more interesting undercurrents that drove the forum in Hawai'i was the question of community and the various levels one's community can encompass. Can community really exist at an international level? The Indigenous women at the forum certainly comprised one community. All participants, all Indigenous and non-Indigenous women, motivated and perhaps personally shaped by chronic illness and disability, comprised another level of community. It is important that we recognize our relationships to one another in these various levels of community, whether they are explicit or more subtle. These relationships are fluid but can be surprisingly strong. The Carter Center representative, Ethleen Iron Cloud-Two Dogs, concluded that support for such efforts "can potentially lead to greater workforce development, self-sustenance, and greater health and productivity for Indigenous women with disabilities, their families, and communities." Surely that is a key component for world peace.

Community is built of multiple layers of identity, interaction, and understanding. Where community begins with the world—with global networking and international collaborations—our work, whether it be understanding disability, supporting disability, or finding resources that address disability, continues in the towns, villages, streets, and suburbs where people with disabilities and their families reside. These volumes began with a few women who wanted to share lessons learned by reaching out to other countries and the world's Indigenous people who had chronic conditions or disabilities—a relatively small number of people given the global population. Yet such a model of interaction can add to our understanding of cultural differences and cultural similarities, highlight the role such understanding can play in reducing health and economic disparities, increase international respect for one another, and set the stage for more effective local intervention. The publication of these volumes is a step forward as part of a movement that can lead to a better understanding of those who are different from us, a movement that can contribute to world peace.

REFERENCES

Marshall, C. A., Burross, H. L., Gotto, G., McAllan, L., Vásquez Martínez, P., García Juárez, et al. (2004). The United States and Mexico: Creating partnerships in rehabilitation. *Rehabilitation Psychology, 49*(1), 14–20.

Palpant, R. G., Steimnitz, R., Bornemann, T. H., & Hawkins, K. (2006). The Carter Center Mental Health Program: Addressing the public health crisis in the field of mental health through policy change and stigma reduction. *Preventing Chronic Disease, 3*(2):A62. Retrieved from www.cdc.gov/PCD/issues/2006/apr/05_0175.htm.

Thomas Bornemann
Director, Mental Health Program, The Carter Center

Preface

Paul Leung

We know that disability is a relative construct. Individuals and countries describe disability in different ways. Disability may be the result of war, malnutrition, environmental pollution, disease, genetic conditions, domestic violence, accidents, and aging. It affects individuals in different ways. At the same time, disability is not just an individual issue, for it affects the whole community. Community, national, and cultural norms all define disability, and do so within contexts that are often idiosyncratic. We also know that disability can be seen as a function of environmental obstacles. Further, there are cultural differences in the perception of disability. We know that in some ethnic groups and cultures, the word *disability* itself has very little meaning. The functional limitations of some people are simply addressed as part of everyday life. Finally, legal frameworks are enacted in different ways in different countries, resulting in different experiences. The International Classification of Functioning, Disability and Health (ICF) is a global attempt to provide a universal definition of what constitutes disability, but this is yet to be fully accepted. This series explores many of these issues. However, a number of chapters in this series allude to the link between poverty and disability, often highlighting the lack of resources available to persons with disabilities and their families. It is evident that the breadth and seeming durability of the connection between poverty and disability requires that issues of poverty be given much more attention.

The preamble to the United Nations Convention on the Rights of Persons with Disabilities (2006) noted "that the majority of persons with disabilities live in conditions of poverty, and in this regard [we recognize] the critical need to address the negative impact of poverty on persons with disabilities."

This recognition only reinforced what Elwan (1999) and the World Bank concluded: "despite the dearth of formal analysis, it is clear that in developing countries, as in more developed areas, disabled people (and their families) are more likely than the rest of the population to live in poverty" (p. i).

We all understand that poverty affects a large proportion of our world today, including those who live in more developed areas, albeit in less severe ways than those living in what is often called the developing world. Adding some urgency to this issue is the likelihood that we may be facing what Josette Sheeran (2008) of the World Food Program calls a "silent tsunami." This comment refers to the rapid worldwide increase in food prices along with food shortages. Those who are most likely to be inundated by this tsunami will be the world's poor, including persons with disability.

As result, the global community adopted the Millennium Development Goals (United Nations, 2007), with a commitment to reduce poverty by 50 percent by 2015. Issues related to class (which usually involves income, education, and occupation) further complicate the equation (Banks & Marshall, 2004). There is some evidence that families with higher incomes in the United States have lower disability rates than families with lower incomes (Yang, 2006). There have been limited efforts directed toward reducing poverty among persons with disabilities and their families (World Bank, 2002). For example, Kiva (www.kiva.org) is a person-to-person micro-lending scheme and although persons with disabilities are not prevented from applying, none of the field partners specifically encourage them to do so.

Certainly we know that being poor is also relative in the United States. The U.S. Department of Health and Human Services (DHHS) (2008) poverty guidelines for determining eligibility for programs vary in terms of numbers of persons within a household and geographic location. For one individual, the amount of income meeting the poverty threshold in the United States is $10,400 per year. Obviously, this is vastly different from the more common measure of absolute poverty that is used globally of $1 a day (Sheeran, 2008).

Common sense suggests, and available evidence has confirmed, that there is a link between disability and poverty in both developed and developing countries (Sum, Khatiwada, & Palma, 2006). Sum et al. indicated that limited employment options and lower earnings result in poverty and poverty, in turn, leads to poor health, poor nutrition, and greater exposure to unhealthy lifestyles and working conditions. Disler (2008), in a presentation on the need for rehabilitation, pointed out that more than 50 percent of males with disability and their families moved into poverty. Jeffrey Sachs (Chen, 2006), the economist perhaps most well known for poverty reduction, has noted the impact of disability in his work. Clearly, the relationship is, at a minimum, a two-way one. As Elwan (1999) pointed out, "disability adds to the risk of poverty and the conditions of poverty increase the risk of disability."

Although a relationship between disability and poverty obviously exists, little is known about the interaction of what may be useful strategies to address this situation. In reality, the relationship is most likely to be highly complex, but without systematic analysis or research, we will be hard pressed to understand it at all. Marshall (2006) found a tendency in the literature to avoid discussion of socioeconomic status in relationship to disability, perhaps partly due to expediency. However, this situation may also be due to the fact that the American disability experience has focused on middle-class European American values to the exclusion of other populations. Marshall's research and experience suggests the need for renewed attention on the importance of socioeconomic factors, especially poverty, in the lives of persons with disabilities. Poverty presents challenges to persons with disabilities in many ways and often is the primary reason they are unable to participate actively in their communities.

For instance, micro-financing is a poverty reduction strategy that is often mentioned in the literature. Yet micro-financing appears to be underutilized by persons with disabilities. As with many mainstream programs, persons with disabilities and their families find themselves on the outside. Although an expectation of equal access to provider services is accepted, difficulties occur when providers themselves continue to harbor doubts about persons with disabilities. How persons with disabilities and their families are perceived within the larger community and how they view themselves continue to be barriers to full inclusion and participation, especially in economic programs that may offer real opportunity to move out of poverty.

Similarly, those who have disabilities are often denied education and training options, based on false assumptions about their learning abilities. These barriers limit their potential for income generation in the future, and also restrict the contributions that persons with disabilities can make within the larger community. Thus, these inherent barriers have a doubly negative impact, both for the individuals/families involved as well as for their communities.

It is important to remember that having a disability as an individual, or its presence within the family, increases costs. There are economic costs created by the fact that having a disability or a family member with a disability requires additional resources and accommodations or modifications. These costs are not always recognized formally or informally and, except in certain forensic situations, are not factored into expense equations. There are also psychic costs consisting of anxiety, worry about inability to provide for the family, discrimination, and the potential exclusion from being able to make choices. The corresponding loss of control can contribute to the development of a fatalistic worldview, where one's actions have little impact. Thus, persons with disabilities or their families who are living in poverty have additional liabilities further preventing them from moving out of poverty.

Ethnicity and race also complicate issues of discrimination beyond disability, further adding to poverty status. Persons with disabilities from minority racial/ethnic populations in the United States have historically found themselves to be more disadvantaged economically than their peers who have no reported disability (National Council on Disability, 1993). Some consider poverty to be a culture, having a value system that impacts on behavior, but others believe this a myth that allows for lower expectations both among those affected and the larger society. Perhaps what is important is the mindset that people have about themselves and their family in relationship to the larger society. Regardless, being poor or being of a particular race or ethnicity has an impact on how disability is perceived and, thus, on how a person acts or behaves.

Ethnicity and race have different implications dependent on context. In American society, issues around race have historically been about African Americans and the legacy of 400 years of slavery. American blacks led a civil rights struggle for equality culminating in the 1960s with the passage of the Civil Rights Act. The success of the civil rights movement expanded to include other racial and ethnic groups and then beyond race to sexual orientation and disability. The civil rights movement was a precursor to the passage of the Americans with Disabilities Act in 1990, which provided persons with disabilities civil protections similar to those related to race.

However, disparities for persons with disabilities continue to exist based on racial and ethnic membership within the American context. Ottenbacher and colleagues (2008) found disparities in postacute rehabilitation outcomes, with non-Hispanic whites having higher functional ratings at discharge than minority populations. Issues of access to rehabilitation programs based on race continue to exist (Leung, Marshall, & Wilson, 2007).

Looking beyond the American scene, discrimination and conflict related to race and ethnicity is not uncommon. We have only to remember how genocide has occurred, whether it was in Rwanda, Bosnia, or Cambodia. Add the experience of disability to race and/or ethnicity and issues of equity and discrimination are magnified. This double disadvantage has been debated in Great Britain for some time (Vernon, 1997). Even in situations where race may not be the most obvious basis for discrimination and unequal treatment, discrimination may occur on the basis of skin color (Wilson & Senices, 2005). In some contexts, these nuances may also reflect long-standing cultural attitudes. For instance, the Chinese perceive light skin in a more positive way because lighter skin suggests a person with wealth who has not worked outside (i.e., not a peasant). The impact of these variables, while relatively unresearched, may nevertheless be significant and cannot easily be ignored.

The content of these volumes is particularly significant given the "post-American world" (Zakaria, 2008) of this 21st century. No longer are issues of disability found to be only relevant in the Western context where, because of available resources, nations have had the luxury of developing systems and programs to intervene and have had the ability to explore what disability means within the human experience. We are now a part of a global society where nations, societies, and cultures are linked in ways we do not always understand, realize, or even recognize.

Elwan (1999) alluded to disability within developing countries as "preventable" consequences of conditions that are no longer found in more developed nations. What kind of global response ought there be to these preventable conditions? Disability will continue to occur in ever-increasing numbers with the global population getting older as a result of increasing life expectancy. At the same time, disability, regardless of definition, has the potential of having lesser impact on the individual and family than in the past. Better health care and the advent of assistive technologies bring a potential for a better quality of life and full inclusion into society for persons with disabilities, regardless of their socioeconomic status or race/ethnicity. Unfortunately, the benefits of such advances will occur only in nations where appropriate policies and programs place priority on their citizens who have disabilities.

Given that there are finite resources in most countries, maybe the issue is one of social justice. Clearly, we must develop a context of resource allocation that will ensure equity for those who are most marginalized or disadvantaged in the world. This series is a much needed exploration and examination of disability on a global scale, but within a personalized human context. The voices in these volumes speak to our need for a common agenda that allows everyone to be able to participate and to choose who we wish to be or what we wish to do. No matter whether we live in wealthy, industrialized nations or poor, struggling economies, we have much more in common than we often realize.

REFERENCES

Banks, M. E., & Marshall, C. (2004). Beyond the "triple-whammy": Social class as a factor in discrimination against persons with disabilities. In J. L. Chin (Ed.), *The psychology of prejudice and discrimination: Combating prejudice and all forms of discrimination. Volume 4: Disability, religion, physique, and other traits* (pp. 95–110). Westport, CT: Praeger.

Chen, I. (2006). Jeffrey Sachs stresses economics to reduce poverty. *Brown Daily Herald*. Reprinted in Poverty News Blog, retrieved from povertynewsblog.blogspot.com/2006/12/jeffrey-sachs-stresses-economics-to.html.

Department of Health and Human Services. (2008). Poverty guidelines. Retrieved July 18, 2008, from aspe.hhs.gov/poverty/08poverty.shtml.

Disler, P. (2008). Tertiary prevention: Rehabilitation in the management of chronic disease. Retrieved July 18, 2008 from www.pictureit.co.il/jerusalemconf/Media/tuesdayhall1/peter%20disler.pps#12.

Elwan, A. (1999). *Poverty and disability, a survey of the literature*. World Bank Social Protection Discussion Paper. Washington, DC: Work Bank.

Leung, P., Marshall, C., & Wilson, K. (2007). Rehabilitation research from a multicultural perspective. In P. Leung, C. Flowers, W. Talley, & P. Sanderson (Eds.), *Multicultural issues in rehabilitation and allied health* (pp. 240–265). Linn Creek, MO: Aspen Professional Services.

Marshall, C. (2006). SES factors influencing the definition of disability. Presented at the American Psychological Association Annual Convention, New Orleans, LA.

National Council on Disability. (1993). *Meeting the unique needs of minorities with disabilities: A report to the president and the Congress*. Washington, DC: Author.

Ottenbacher, K. J., Campbell, J., Kuo, Y., Deutsch, A., Ostir, G., & Granger, C. (2008). Racial and ethnic differences in postacute rehabilitation outcomes after stroke in the United States. *Stroke, 39*, 1514–1519.

Sheeran, J. (2008). The silent tsunami. *Economist*, 13.

Sum, A., Khatiwada, I., & Palma, S. (2006) The links between poverty and disability. *Commonwealth Corporation Research and Evaluation Brief, 4*(6), 1–4.

United Nations. (2007). The millennium development goals report. Retrieved July 30, 2008, from www.un.org/millenniumgoals/docs/UNSD_MDG_Report_2007e.pdf.

United Nations Convention on Rights of Persons with Disabilities. (2006). Retrieved July 18, 2008, from www.un.org/disabilities/default.asp?id=260.

Vernon, A. (1997). Fighting two different battles: Unity is preferable to enmity. In L. Barton & M. Oliver (Eds.), *Disability studies: Past present and future* (pp. 255–262). Leeds: Disability Press. Retrieved August 11, 2008, from www.leeds.ac.uk/disability-studies/archiveuk/vernon/chapter17.pdf.

Wilson, K. B., & Senices, J. (2005). Exploring the vocational rehabilitation acceptance rates of Hispanics and non-Hispanics in the United States. *Journal of Counseling and Development, 83*(1), 86–96.

World Bank. (2002). Disability and poverty reduction strategies. Retrieved August 20, 2008, from web.worldbank.org/WBSITE/EXTERNAL/TOPICS/EXTSOCIALPROTECTION/EXTDISABILITY/0,,contentMDK:20193783~menuPK:419389~pagePK:148956~piPK:216618~theSitePK:282699,00.html.

Yang, S. (2006). New study links higher income with lower disability rates. Retrieved December 5, 2007, from http://www.berkeley.edu/media/releases/2006/08/16_disability.

Zakaria, F. (2008, May 12). The rise of the rest. *Newsweek.*

Introduction

There is no one definition for disability. Initially, this set took its direction from definitions found in the Americans with Disabilities Act (ADA)—U.S. legislation that has had far-reaching impact both in its home country and as a model for legislation internationally.

The ADA provides comprehensive civil rights protections for "individuals with disabilities." An individual with a disability is a person who:

- has a physical or mental impairment that substantially limits one or more *major life activities*, or
- has a record of such an impairment, or
- is regarded as having such an impairment (www.usdoj.gov/crt/ada/t3hilght.htm).

However, as these volumes emerged from the chapters submitted by people who have experienced disability personally, as family members, as health professionals, and as members of the academic community, it became clear that indeed an entire volume was needed just to present and explore definitions of disability. These volumes present contemporary viewpoints of the issues that confront people with disabilities or those who are concerned with disability in some way.

Who are those of us concerned with disability? We are "flawed people." In *Getting to Maybe: How the World is Changed* (Westley, Zimmerman, & Patton, 2006), the authors begin by declaring, "This book is not for heroes or saints or perfectionists. This book is for flawed people . . . who are not happy with the way things are and would like to make a difference. This book is for ordinary people who want to make connections that create extraordinary outcomes."

We are flawed people writing for and with ordinary people. We were brought together as coordinators of, supporters of, and participants in the 2004 international forum Participatory Action Research and Indigenous Ways of Knowing: Women as Researchers and Partners in Community-Based Disability and Rehabilitation Research. We have come to know each other a bit more through the process of coediting these volumes. We have been surprised and pleased to hear from several of the chapter authors that their writing—coming together with coauthors—was also an opportunity to grow and learn from each other.

These volumes explore current understandings of disability from different perspectives and highlight different approaches and philosophies around the world regarding disability. It is our goal to stimulate global communication and exchange of knowledge on these topics among, again, ordinary people. The three volumes in this set include contemporary examinations of disability using psychological, cultural, social, legal, and political frameworks. The chapters describe unique and important aspects of a given country or system that help the reader not only understand a particular place or approach but also all enable a conversation about global exchange and utilization of information, perspectives, and models.

The chapters also include reviews of the literature, conceptual or theoretical work, research studies, descriptions of innovative approaches to disability, experiential narratives, and poetry that reflects personal reactions to disability. We trust that the reader is not confused by the change in genre among chapters, but rather embraces the diversity of presentation as we embrace the diversity of experiences from which they were created. We do not live in an "either/or" world: "Utility and beauty join to form the world of immediate experience. Utility and beauty feed off of each other. Each without the other leads nowhere. Together they transform the world of immediate experience into a new world of unlimited possibilities" (Ittelson, 2007, p. 283). In each volume, we have combined scholarly texts with those written from personal experience—narratives that reflect reality from the perspective of those who are living with disability—or from the perspective of choosing not to identify as having a disability. We have combined the power of personal narratives and the rigor of academic research in a series that highlights how the value of a community voice is as important as the empirical word. Disability is a complex experience—in these volumes, poetry is juxtaposed against theory. Uniformity, which may be considered the antithesis of diversity and disability, is avoided.

In compiling these volumes, we encouraged contributions from diverse cultures and are grateful to those Indigenous women whose stories formed the initial framework for these volumes. We sought to represent the world, but despite our international networks and our capacity to mobilize those networks rapidly in this age of technology and globalization, there are large regions missing from the text. Indeed the world is huge—and, ironically, the very technology that we now depend on to bring us closer and to bring information to us quickly, led us to systematically exclude chapters that would have been submitted handwritten on paper or perhaps painted on canvas.

These volumes would only ever represent those who were able and interested to respond to our call for chapters—in English and submitted electronically. We are pleased with the diversity of authors, including people with disability, family members, advocates, health professionals, research professors, and nonprofit organizations. However, the selection of final chapters is an ironic reflection of the world of disability itself—despite our intentions, some voices are never heard, excluded by language, medium, access, inequitable standards around knowledge production, time, and cost.

We have organized the chapters into three volumes that reflect the themes that emerged from the chapters we received. Volume 1 contains chapters that explore the way disability is defined in different countries and within different populations. In examining disability, it quickly became apparent that regions of the world and different cultural contexts were associated with different stereotypes, criteria, experiences, and consequences. It also became apparent that all views are equally important and all perspectives added something vital to our knowledge. This volume aims to explore these different approaches to disability and the impact of different definitions of both disability and health.

Volume 2 builds on the social aspect of disability, containing chapters that explore the impact of disability on families, and more important, the impact of environment and context on disability. This volume seeks to describe disability as it is experienced in a range of social settings.

Volume 3 focuses on responses to disability, including services, policies and legal approaches. This volume contains some interesting chapters about different legislation around the world, service delivery models, and innovative ways of supporting individuals with disabilities. The volume highlights linkages between definitions of disability, contexts or cultures within which disability occurs, and the legal or service responses that often define people's lives.

A most notable global influence in the past few years has been the United Nations Convention on the Rights of Persons with Disabilities—a global statement about the rights of people with disabilities irrespective of their country of origin. At the UN General Assembly marking the adoption of the convention, Secretary-General Kofi Annan stated: "Today promises to be the dawn of a new era—an era in which disabled people will no longer have to endure the discriminatory practices and attitudes that have been permitted to prevail for all too long." The convention has been heralded as the embodiment of a "paradigm shift" away from a social welfare response to a rights-based approach (Kayess & French, 2008), rejecting the "view of persons with disabilities as objects of charity, medical treatment and social protection" and affirming them as "subjects of rights, able to claim those rights as active members of society" (UN High Commissioner for Human Rights, 2006, as cited in Kayess & French, 2008, p. 3). Most important, the convention provides disability-specific interpretations of existing human rights and, in so doing, transforms (for instance) "negative" rights, such as the right not to be discriminated against, into positive obligations, such as the right to an accessible environment (Kayess & French, 2008). We are grateful that our work can be a small part of such an important global conversation.

The efforts of many people have come together to make these volumes possible. We thank our families for their supportive understanding while we ignored them to focus on this work. Our Advisory Committee is listed in the back of each volume. Their kindness in supporting us and willingness to read chapters, providing both us and the authors with constructive feedback, is much appreciated—we are humbled by these actions. Among those on our Advisory Committee, we are especially grateful to the guidance provided to us by Jean Lau Chin, an accomplished psychologist, educator, writer, and leader. Jean shepherded the process of our proposal and led us to Deborah Carvalko at Praeger. Perhaps needless to say, we are also grateful for Deborah's interest in our project, direction regarding the work, and patience with our seemingly endless questions. We are indebted to Stephanie Prout, Griffith Abilities Research Program, for her accuracy, promptness, and enthusiasm while assisting the editors in this endeavor.

Ultimately, we are most grateful to the authors. It is their words that you will read and their experiences that will bring about desired change, increased understanding, and continued communication among us.

REFERENCES

Ittelson, W.H. (2007). The perception of nonmaterial objects and events. *Leonardo, 40*(3), 279–283.

Kayess, R., & French, P. (2008). Out of darkness into light? Introducing the Convention on the Rights of Persons with Disabilities. *Human Rights Law Review, 8*(1), 1–34.

Westley, F., Zimmerman, B., & Patton, M. Q. (2006). *Getting to maybe: How the world is changed.* Mississauga, Ontario: Random House Canada.

CHAPTER 1

Creating Mental Health Disability through Inadequate Disaster Response: Lessons from Hurricane Katrina

Paula A. Madrid, Roy Grant, and Rachel Rosen

In this chapter, we discuss the widespread and long-term psychosocial impact of Hurricane Katrina in New Orleans in 2006. By exploring the impact of this devastating event, we show how an inefficient and inadequate government response to community disasters can needlessly create psychological disability. The states most affected by Hurricane Katrina—Louisiana and Mississippi—had the worst health and school performance indicators in the United States prior to the storm (Annie E. Casey Foundation, 2008). These states already had an inadequate supply of medical and mental health professionals, especially in the highest risk communities, leaving them ill-prepared for the devastating impact of Katrina.

However, in the years following Katrina, these already disadvantaged communities have demonstrated an alarming increase in new-onset depression, anxiety, and other emotional, behavioral, and school-related problems among children. Two weeks following the hurricane, the first author began a clinical appointment in Mississippi and Louisiana. This chapter builds on the accounts of ongoing desperation and mental health deterioration heard by the first author during this time. The vignettes presented illustrate the profound psychosocial needs and mental health distress we encountered in the aftermath of Hurricane Katrina. Although much of this illness could be attributed to the impact of a serious natural disaster, here we show how the inadequate response of disaster services played a critical role in exacerbating mental health disability.

Hurricane Katrina has been called the greatest disaster in the United States in nearly a century, displacing more than 400,000 people in the New Orleans area and the Gulf Coast of Mississippi (Whoriskey, 2006). Whole communities were wiped out; families were uprooted, homes were destroyed, jobs and schools were lost. The devastation caused by the disaster, including the destruction of the region's health care infrastructure, was unprecedented in our history. The damage wreaked by the storm aggravated the existing lack of infrastructure and inadequate resources in the region. In the immediate aftermath in New Orleans, over 1,100 people were killed. More than 215,000 homes were destroyed, 785,000 people were displaced, 835 schools were damaged, and 18,700 businesses were destroyed, with more than 220,000 jobs lost (Louisiana Recovery Authority, 2006). Entire families were lacking housing and stable schools for their children and were desperate to return to their homes or find loved ones.

DISASTERS AND MENTAL HEALTH

In the wake of natural disasters, mental illness has been documented at rates up to 40 percent higher than typical (Galea et al., 2007). It is generally accepted that posttraumatic stress symptoms emerge relatively soon after a disaster or traumatic event and dissipate during the first year after the disaster (Harrison, 2007; Noji & Sivertson, 1987). It can also be expected that some people with existing symptoms not only will continue to have symptoms but their conditions might be exacerbated by further trauma. Those who appear to recover after the disaster may later experience a recurrence of symptoms (Andrews, Brewin, Philpott, & Stewart, 2007). Sometimes symptoms may be delayed in onset, meaning that they will display no signs of distress in the first three months posttrauma (Carty, O'Donnell, & Creamer, 2006).

However, as described by Redlener (2006), the impact of Katrina and the subsequent hurricane, Rita, on the mental health of the community, was unprecedented:

> Four months after Hurricanes Katrina and Rita, evidence had begun to emerge of a situation that few could have imagined and virtually no one had predicted. Nearly 80,000 people, mostly poor, who had been evacuated from New Orleans were still languishing in federally subsidized shelters, including trailers, mobile homes, and hotels throughout the United States. . . . A chaplain I met told me that he had never seen anything like this. . . . He said, "I have spoken to many of the young men who are begging for someone to talk to. They are overly depressed and have no idea of what the future holds. . . . It's just unbearable." (p. 12)

Psychological distress has proven one of the most enduring of Hurricane Katrina's effects. For instance, the U.S. Centers for Disease Control and Prevention (CDC) found that six months after the hurricane, 13 percent of households had at least one family member with a new-onset mental health problem (Madrid et al., 2008). An astounding 68 percent of the female caregivers surveyed from a group of 665 randomly selected adults who had lost their homes and were living with their families in Federal Emergency Management Agency (FEMA)-subsidized trailers or hotels six months after the hurricane reported symptoms of depression, anxiety, or another psychiatric disorder. Their children were two and a half times more likely to have psychological issues than children of their counterparts who displayed low levels of mental health problems, illustrating the impact of a caregiver's mental health on that of her children in this postdisaster environment (Abramson & Garfield, 2006; Weisler, Barbee, & Townsend, 2006).

Five to seven months after the hurricane, another group of researchers surveyed adults who were living in communities in Alabama, Mississippi, and Louisiana deemed by FEMA as directly impacted by Katrina. The researchers measured for various psychological disorders, most notably posttraumatic stress disorder (PTSD). The prevalence of PTSD alone within the full sample was estimated at 16.3 percent, and in the New Orleans metro area the rate was estimated at 30.3 percent (Galea et al., 2007). One year after the hurricane, 62 percent of parents and other caregivers in families dislocated by the hurricane and in transitional housing in Mississippi reported symptoms consistent with psychiatric diagnoses of anxiety, depression, or PTSD (Abramson, Garfield, & Redlener, 2007).

The Hurricane Katrina Advisory Group followed the mental health of 815 prehurricane residents, and found that prevalence rates of PTSD, suicidality, and anxiety-mood disorders increased during the year following Katrina: PTSD from 14.9 percent (five months post-Katrina) to 20.9 percent (one year post-Katrina), serious mental illness from 10.9 percent to 14.9 percent, suicidal ideation from 2.8 percent to 6.4 percent, and suicide plans from 1.0 percent to 2.5 percent. The increase in these rates was due largely to "unresolved hurricane-related stresses," with 89.2 percent of the serious mental illness, 31.9 percent of PTSD, and 61.6 percent of suicidality present in this cohort caused by the hurricane. These changes are indicative of the deleterious effect of the storm on mental health (Kessler et al., 2008).

CASE VIGNETTES

John

Before the storms, John was an 11-year-old high-achieving student who was well adjusted in his interpersonal relationships. He spent the first night after Hurricane Katrina with his mother on a bridge near his home, where, in the high waters that followed the breach of the levees in New Orleans, he witnessed dead bodies floating by as he tried to sleep. For the next five days, he and his mother found shelter in the New Orleans Superdome, where he witnessed people using IV drugs and was exposed to incidents of violence. Conditions in the Superdome were chaotic: a 50-foot by 10-foot hole was torn in the roof, there was no running water at all, sewage was everywhere, garbage was piled two stories high, and the shelter population grew to at least 25,000 (Jenkins, 2006). After a short stay at the Superdome, John and his mother were placed by FEMA in a short-term shelter. Several weeks later, the family was again moved by FEMA into a trailer in front of their destroyed home in a devastated neighborhood. At this time, John was able to resume school. Also about this time, he presented symptoms of a serious anxiety disorder. Although his symptoms improved over time, more than a year later, when the city of New Orleans was celebrating the return of their home team, the Saints, to play at the Superdome, John's anxiety symptoms returned suddenly and his school work suffered.

Dolores

Dolores, age 60, had raised her 6-year-old grandson, Richard, since he was a baby. Prior to the hurricanes, Dolores had been receiving psychiatric care for depression and psychosis and was prescribed a psychotropic medication. After Katrina, she and her grandson were placed in a FEMA shelter in Baton Rouge, where psychiatric care was not available. Dolores' highest priority was finding permanent housing so she could have a safe home for Richard. She was unable to contact her own psychiatrist, and she attempted to use the public mental health system but was unable to access appointments because of the lack of transport from the geographically isolated location of the shelter. Eventually, she was psychiatrically hospitalized. By this time, she had been without her medication or psychosocial intervention for a full year. Due to the lack of resources, Dolores was discharged quickly with only short-term plans for psychiatric care.

These case vignettes were modified from actual events to protect the privacy of those involved. They illustrate the profound impact of the hurricane on the lives and mental health of residents and demonstrate how the impact of Katrina was exacerbated by the protracted difficulty the public health and mental health infrastructure had in accommodating the predictable level of need among those who remained or returned to the New Orleans area and those who were relocated to temporary shelters.

Katrina represented a complex mix of factors that intensified its impact on mental health disability. The region was already significantly disadvantaged and poorly serviced, with high rates of illness or disability and large groups of marginalized people. However, due to inadequate emergency planning and poor preparation for disasters of this magnitude, the recovery and rebuilding process was protracted, postacute services were overloaded, and people became disconnected from their support systems for excessive periods of time. Each of these issues is discussed further next.

THE GULF COAST: A REGION OF DISADVANTAGE

In discussing the creation of mental health disability following the disaster, it is critical to discuss the predisaster social and economic status of those affected and how this status places them at elevated risk for adverse postdisaster stress reactions (Norris, 2007; Norris et al., 2002; Norris, Friedman, & Watson, 2002). The storm laid bare the problems that had been endemic in the Gulf region for some time. Even prior to Katrina, almost 20 percent of 12th-graders enrolled in Louisiana schools from 2004 to 2005 dropped out prior to graduation (Louisiana Department of Education, 2005). Of the 39,407 families with children under the age of 18 living in New Orleans in

2004, it was estimated that 20,626 (over 50 percent) of these were single mother–headed households (U.S. Census Bureau, 2004).

In 2004, Mississippi and Louisiana were among the states with the highest rates of unemployment (ranked 6th and 10th, respectively) and general poverty (17.7 percent and 17 percent, respectively, compared with the national average of 12.4 percent) (U.S. Census Bureau of Labor Statistics, 2004; U.S. Census Bureau, Housing and Household Economic Statistics Division, 2004). Additionally, 4,467 violent crimes were reported in the city of New Orleans, representing a staggering rate of a 948.3 violent crimes per 100,000 population, compared to the national rate of 463.2 per 100,000 (Federal Bureau of Investigation, 2004). Given the high level of susceptibility that was prevalent in the region, it should have been imperative that additional resources were devoted to the management of mental health in the aftermath of the disaster.

Nonetheless, surveys conducted in the temporary shelters immediately following Hurricane Katrina found in need a disproportionate representation of African Americans, people with very low income, and those without adequate means of transportation (which led to their inability to evacuate in a timely fashion). Nearly 90,000 people with health insurance provided by the state of Louisiana were evacuated to other states, which led to considerable confusion about how their coverage would be maintained and how their health care needs would be met. Most affected by the loss of public health insurance and health services were those who were elderly, chronically ill, and disabled (Rudowitz, Rowland, & Shartzer, 2006). More than 2,500 hospital patients in one county, Orleans Parish, were evacuated. Dialysis centers throughout Louisiana, each of which had caseloads in excess of 3,000 patients, were destroyed. Weeks after the disaster, the whereabouts of half these people remained unknown (Zuckerman & Coughlin, 2006). Medical records were lost, and many doctors in private practice had to evacuate and did not return. During the first year after Hurricane Katrina, the New Orleans death rate increased by nearly 50 percent (Stoddard, 2007).

DEPLETED HEALTH SERVICES

This complex mix of poverty, race, and preexisting illness was complicated even further by the lack of services in the regions and in the areas to which people were evacuated. The extent of the damage to New Orleans' health infrastructure was profound. According to the director of the New Orleans Health Department, the public health workforce for the city was cut in half after the storm. Professionals who provided assistance to disaster victims were, more often than not, themselves victims of the disaster. It was estimated that 70 to 80 percent of helpers had also lost their homes and were living in transitional housing (Osofsky, 2007). A report by the U.S. Government Accountability Office (2006) noted that the city's hospital bed capacity was reduced by 80 percent. The only Level I trauma center available to this area was closed, as were nearly all facilities for uninsured and low-income people, clinics, and hospital emergency rooms.

Community health centers, a critical element of the health and mental health safety net for the poor and uninsured, suffered $65 million in damage. This has had a direct impact on the continued restricted access to health and mental health care by those most in need of services (Lambrew & Shalala, 2006). For instance, when health facilities eventually reopened, it was at a significantly reduced capacity (U.S. Government Accountability Office, 2006). A 2006 survey found that 23 percent of individuals who had a psychiatric disorder prior to Katrina still reported receiving no or restricted mental health services. In situations of inadequate access to mental health services, postdisaster psychological distress can be exacerbated. Indeed, nearly 19 percent of those who met the diagnostic criteria for a psychiatric disorder in 2006 had not had a disorder prior to Katrina (Wang et al., 2008). For several years following Katrina, the Gulf Coast continued to experience a situation of increased need with decreased resources. This need and demand for mental health services for those impacted by the hurricane is likely to be present for many years to come (Madrid & Grant, 2008).

SOCIAL DISCONNECTION

For those who remained or returned to Louisiana, transitional housing (shelters) was provided by FEMA. These shelters typically consisted of travel trailers and at their peak housed up to 70,000 families who had no other choice but to remain in circumstances that were deemed by many as unlivable (Harrison, 2007). The trailers were clustered in FEMA trailer parks, which were usually located in isolated areas, geographically distant from shops, devoid of safe play opportunities for children, and crime-ridden (Aldrich, 2006).

Renaissance Village was an isolated trailer park that opened its doors to evacuees on October 6, 2005 (Singer, 2006). Located on the outskirts of Baton Rouge, the village consisted of 573 travel trailers surrounded by a 12-foot steel fence and guarded by private security officers, many of whom were former military personnel. In many of these trailer parks, the situation became so dire that it was likened to the humanitarian crises more commonly found in the developing world (Nieburg, Waldman, & Krumm, 2005). Four months after Katrina, approximately 80,000 people were still living in federally subsidized shelters including trailers, mobile homes, and hotels throughout the United States (Redlener, 2006). Almost two months post-Katrina, the first author found children and adults with preexisting mental health conditions who had been unable to reconnect with their previous mental health care providers.

Children are particularly vulnerable to trauma, stress, and the repercussions of disasters when social systems break down, leaving them disconnected from the support of those who care for them. School attendance is also critical in maintaining the daily routine and stability of children old enough to attend; educational services were catastrophically disrupted by Hurricane Katrina. The U.S. Department of Education estimates that 372,000 children and their families were displaced by the hurricane and relocated. The children enrolled in new schools across 49 states plus the District of Columbia.

Nine states enrolled more than 1,000 displaced students (U.S. Department of Education, 2005).

Nearly two years after the hurricane, 31.5 percent of displaced children from Louisiana and Mississippi met criteria for a diagnosis of depression, anxiety, or a behavior disorder (Abramson, Redlener, Stehling-Ariza, & Fuller, 2007). Many of the school-age children who remained in Louisiana were moved from school to school. By the end of the school year, approximately 10,000 of the 61,000 displaced school-age children who remained in Louisiana were not enrolled in school. Two and a half years after the hurricane, between 46,000 and 64,000 children remained at risk because of their continued displacement and the uncertainty of their immediate future.

Even those children who returned to their homes were also at risk because of the quality of the housing to which they returned, including unsafe communities and continued inadequate access to health and mental health care. More than half (55 percent) of the 55,000 displaced children in Louisiana and nearly half (47 percent) in Mississippi experienced a decline in academic achievement; lost access to health care because of either geographic access problems or economic ones, such as loss of health insurance; or developed a psychiatric disorder, principally depression, anxiety, and behavior disorders (Abramson, Redlener, et al., 2007).

PROTRACTED RECOVERY AND RETRAUMATIZATION

Redlener (2006) described how, as late as seven months after the hurricane, the most devastated communities of New Orleans remained as destroyed as the day the floodwaters had retreated. This protracted exposure to the traumatic stimuli associated with the disaster—including markings on buildings indicating when they were searched for dead bodies and how many cadavers were found there—made recovery difficult if not impossible for people whose lives were already devastated by the storm.

Events that reawaken memories of the traumatic event are associated with the continuation of posttraumatic stress symptoms. People with a history of trauma and loss are at greater risk for recurring anxiety, problems sleeping and concentrating, and anger and other behavioral manifestations postdisaster (Madrid & Grant, 2008). For example, in Oklahoma City, a site of domestic terrorism in the United States, issues arose or were reawakened when trials for the perpetrators began three years after the bombing (Pfefferbaum, Call, & Sconzo, 1999). Children were exposed to extensive television and other media coverage of the Oklahoma City bombings, resulting in geographically widespread psychological impact characterized by posttraumatic stress symptoms or "posttraumatic distress" (Pfefferbaum et al., 2003).

Although this phenomenon occurred prior to the World Trade Center attack of September 11, 2001, there was no attempt to prevent the continual broadcasting of the plane crashing into the second World Trade Center tower and its collapse. Though viewing a disaster or other traumatic event on television does not constitute exposure in terms of a clinical diagnosis (Pfefferbaum, Pfefferbaum, North, & Neas, 2002), it nonetheless adds to the experience of stress and may be especially disturbing for young children because of their cognitive and developmental level. Similarly, the extremely slow pace of recovery following Hurricane Katrina meant that residents were continually exposed to the trauma of the original event. For instance, on a highway near the city, the hull of a boat remained for two years after the storm.

DISASTER RESPONSES IN THE UNITED STATES OVER THE LAST DECADE

Perhaps the most disturbing feature of Katrina was the preventable nature of psychiatric disability in the aftermath of this devastating natural disaster. The lack of effective disaster planning resulted in the inability of so many evacuees to leave the city safely, to live in safe and well-serviced temporary accommodation, and then return to a restored city as soon as possible following the disaster. Although some local areas did have adequate evacuation plans, people with disabilities, including hospitalized psychiatric patients, were often overlooked (McClain, Hamilton, Clothier, & McGaugh, 2007).

Despite the incidence of disability in the United States, the National Response Plan—issued by the Department of Homeland Security in 2004, which was intended to be an "all-discipline, all-hazards" approach to domestic disasters of any type—did not acknowledge the special needs of the disabled. Following Hurricane Katrina, this lack of preparedness for the disabled was evidenced by the lack of assistive devices or assistive technology and the lack of accessible entrances at shelters and restrooms. This situation often resulted in the separation of people with disabilities from their families at shelters and deprived them of a major source of support (Waterstone & Stein, 2006).

There is no doubt that Hurricane Katrina revealed the extent to which the nation's health care and public health systems were inadequately prepared to deal with a disaster, even with advance warning. By the time of Hurricane Katrina, however, the country had already experienced multiple natural disasters and terrorist attacks, making the lack of effective disaster planning in New Orleans particularly surprising. In his book *Americans at Risk* (2006), Redlener described the extent to which the United States was ill-prepared for megadisasters. Other researchers have also commented on the failure to learn and apply lessons from prior disasters, such as Hurricane Andrew in Florida in 1992 (Landesman, 2007).

Two years after the hurricane, steps were finally taken to develop a consensus framework for preparedness and response in the national public health system (Lyznicki, Subbarao, Benjamin, & James, 2007), including development of core competencies for health care professionals (Subbarao et al., 2008). Following Katrina, the issue of disability has been addressed by the National Center for Disaster Preparedness, Columbia University, at the National Consensus Conference on Emergency Preparedness: Addressing the Needs of Persons with Disabilities (2005). This conference developed recommendations on disaster planning for people with disabilities (Markenson, Fuller, & Redlener, 2007), but too late for those affected by Katrina.

However, the presence of frameworks and legislation do not guarantee adequate responses. At the time of Katrina, intervention focused on the psychological impact of a disaster was provided under a federal law, the Stafford Act (most recently amended June 2007). Section 416 of the Stafford Act reads in its entirety:

> The President is authorized to provide professional counseling services, including financial assistance to state or local agencies or private mental health organizations to provide such services or training of disaster workers, to victims of major disasters in order to relieve mental health problems caused or aggravated by such major disaster or its aftermath.

This very broad range of allowable services is mirrored in the applicable code of federal regulations (42 U.S.C. 5183) and constitutes the statutory and regulatory definition of federally funded postdisaster mental health services known as "crisis counseling" (FEMA, 2007). Stringent restrictions have nevertheless been imposed on crisis counseling services. The FEMA-sponsored psychological intervention programs created in response to Oklahoma City (Project Heartland), post-9/11 in New York City (Project Liberty), and most recently post–Hurricane Katrina in Louisiana and Mississippi (Louisiana Spirit and Project Recovery, respectively) failed to meet the needs of the population because they misinterpreted the Stafford Act (Pfefferbaum et al., 1999).

For instance, funding was time-limited and could not be used for comprehensive mental health assessment and intensive treatment. Many of the counseling staff lacked experience in trauma intervention. The programs tended to focus on restoring predisaster levels of functioning, rather than psychotherapeutic intervention. Thus, the programs offered little more than a screening and referral program. Given the extensive damage incurred by the mental health infrastructure in affected Katrina communities, compounded by the predisaster capacity inadequacies, the FEMA response was ineffective.

Funds that were not spent were returned to the federal government despite the continued need for mental health services. In Mississippi, the FEMA-funded crisis counseling program (Project Recovery) was underspent by $4.5 million when the federal government declared the program over, despite continuing mental health needs and inadequate community-based services to meet those needs. According to published reports at the time, "FEMA refused to assist the institutions that those people were referred to and it has not explained why" (Associated Press, 2007).

The difficulties associated with providing mental health services following Hurricanes Katrina and Rita were exacerbated by interruptions of Medicaid coverage for low-income people. In May 2006, nine months after the hurricanes, the mail service was still sufficiently affected to make receipt of Medicaid eligibility renewal papers unreliable, resulting in termination of coverage for those people who could still be reliably reached at their former address. For the many displaced by the storms, who also had lost documents (birth certificates, Social Security cards, etc.) needed to establish or reestablish eligibility, the problems were still more severe. A Medicaid hotline was set up to capture new addresses by evacuees, but this was not enough to prevent termination of benefits because of nonresponse to renewal papers sent to the wrong address or not delivered at all (Advocacy Center Louisiana, 2006).

For the many hurricane evacuees who had temporarily relocated to other states, there were predictable problems with the lack of interstate portability of Medicaid coverage. There was no consensus as to whether these individuals should bear the fiscal responsibility and be subjected to the Medicaid regulations of their home state or the state in which they currently resided. To the extent that the home state retained responsibility to pay for services in the state where the family had temporarily relocated and sought care, there was no clear mechanism by which the host state would be reimbursed by the home state. Establishing eligibility for evacuees was especially difficult because of lost documentation. A precedent for dealing with establishing emergency Medicaid eligibility following a disaster had already been developed in New York City following the events of 9/11, the Disaster Relief Medicaid Program, but it was not implemented post-Katrina. This failure to apply lessons learned from one disaster to another had the unfortunate impact of delaying access to health and mental health services (Center for Medicare & Medicaid Services, 2007; Christopher, 2005).

Partisan disagreements about the nature of Medicaid waivers delayed and ultimately limited the relief that affected people needed to establish or reestablish financial access to health and mental health services. The congressional waiver approach would have covered low-income individuals in need of health care wherever they were after the storm and would have financially protected the affected states for a period of time after storm. The administration countered with a much more limited and less flexible policy proposal, and it was the administration position that prevailed. Matters were made worse by delays making funding available and eventually allocating only $1.5 billion of the $2 billion appropriation. In their analysis, Lambrew and Shalala (2006) found that this federal response was inadequate to meet both immediate and ongoing needs, the response ignored the needs of newly Medicaid-eligible individuals whose circumstances had been altered by the hurricane, and hospitals and other health care providers who did treat affected individuals were not adequately compensated. In fact, even if the full $2 billion was made available, it would have been inadequate to meet the cost of care for the roughly 3 million people in need. The result was not only delayed or denied care but also a deleterious impact on the safety net providers in the storm affected areas. This may have serious ongoing consequences with respect to access to care for vulnerable populations as they recover from the hurricane and its aftermath.

RECOMMENDATIONS FOR A BETTER RESPONSE

Social factors are associated with risk and resilience following a disaster. Family and other sources of social support mediated the psychological effect of Hurricane Andrew on adolescents in Florida (Khoury et al., 1997) and Hurricane Georges on college students in the Virgin Islands, Puerto Rico, the Dominican Republic, as well as the United States (Sattler et al., 2002).

Consistent with these findings, following Hurricane Katrina, social factors as well as preexisting health and mental status were found to be more closely associated with psychological outcomes than were individual demographics (e.g., race/ethnicity, age, gender). This has important implications for pre-disaster risk assessment and postdisaster intervention (Abramson, Stehling-Ariza, Garfield, & Redlener, 2008).

Since the disaster, strategies have been recommended for promoting a sense of control, empowerment, and normalcy, as well as rapid family reunification following disasters (Madrid, Grant, Reilly, & Redlener, 2006). Of utmost importance is providing individuals and families the opportunity to feel empowered to make decisions and to return to their communities of origin if that is what they wish to do. Children, adults, families, and communities are resilient but need to have the opportunity to resume the roles that are most meaningful to them. Protracted helplessness leads to hopelessness, depression, anxiety, and other manifestations of mental health distress. As such, ensuring that the basic needs of all affected are met is a priority. Once this is the case, it is important to offer opportunities to share, engage in previously important roles, and participate in activities that provide meaning and a sense of belonging.

For those who are most impacted by a disaster and who require mental health intervention, the process of obtaining help should be facilitated by community leaders and those that are trusted by the impacted populations. We have also recommended that when planning interventions and developing programs, disaster response must take into account cultural and socioeconomic aspects of the community and region.

The availability of medical, mental health, and financial support is essential. State and local government, as well as health care and community-based agencies, should develop lists of clinicians and professionals who specialize in disaster and trauma and who are familiar with community resources, in addition to those who can provide short-term treatment and recognize long-term needs. Financial barriers to care must be addressed by government policies that recognize the need for continuous coverage and ongoing access to care, interstate portability of coverage following disaster-related evacuation, and adequate reimbursement to all parties associated with the delivery of health care.

Silove, Steel, and Psychol (2006) proposed a model for conceptualizing, implementing and evaluating psychosocial and mental health programs in postconflict countries. Although the ADAPT framework was developed on the basis of experiences with East Timorese populations and refugees in Sydney, Australia, the paradigm is relevant. It provides ways of thinking about appropriate psychosocial responses that reduce the stress and lack of support experienced and perceived by individuals postdisaster. The model calls for an approach that considers individuals, families, and communities as a whole and emphasizes the role of the community in helping its own members, as the best comfort comes from people who are known and share their experiences and cultural beliefs.

Strategic assistance from outside, for example, in supporting grieving, memorial and healing rituals should be carefully designed to avoid intrusion, cultural insensitivity, or disempowerment of local leadership systems. ADAPT proposes the establishment of an emergency community mental health service that bases treatment on urgency of individual and family need, which leads to advanced or supportive interventions. This approach means that trauma is not ignored, but that the emphasis in the postemergency phase is shifted toward caring for those whose traumatic reactions are impeding their (and/or their family's) immediate capacity to survive and adapt, rather than on attempting to resolve all traumatic reactions across the community as a whole.

SUMMARY AND CONCLUSION

Disasters, whether natural or man-made, can be traumatic and life-changing events for those who directly and indirectly experience their impact. Among those most vulnerable to experiencing postdisaster traumatic distress are people with preexisting psychiatric disorders and/or prior histories of traumatic exposure, immigrants, and other high-risk populations. Children are at heightened risk for postdisaster psychological problems, especially if their daily routine is disrupted and their parents experience posttrauma distress, unemployment, perceived lack of support, or an ongoing sense of helplessness. As such, the psychosocial needs of individuals must be taken into account in disaster preparedness as an essential aspect of appropriate recovery. This is particularly true for at-risk populations.

More than a decade after the Oklahoma City bombing, six years after the terrorist attacks in New York City and Washington of September 11, 2001, and almost three years after the protracted devastation of Hurricane Katrina on the Gulf Coast, the United States is still not adequately prepared to respond to the next natural or human-created disaster. This lack of preparedness and inadequate response have created serious and long-term consequences for populations both directly and indirectly impacted by disasters. It is also interesting to note that among individuals and families, there is a continuing gap between a high perception of risk and low level of personal preparedness in the context of a worsening decline in confidence in government (Redlener, Abramson, Stehling-Ariza, Grant, & Johnson, 2007).

The deleterious impact of failing to meet the mental health needs of people directly and indirectly affected by disaster—especially those with preexisting vulnerabilities—has been repeatedly demonstrated over the past two decades in the United States. Nonetheless, the same fundamental errors in government response have continued to be made. Instead of adequately available, readily accessible community-based mental health services that remain available as long as need persists, restrictive time-limited services are offered and some communities, typically those in greatest need, get no services at all. The predictable result is the needless creation of psychiatric disability—as has been the case in the aftermath of the worst natural disaster in U.S. history, Hurricane Katrina.

NOTE

1. The authors acknowledge the important input from Rita Domnitz, Deputy Director for Mental Health Services, the Children's Health Fund, and from the

Louisiana Children's Health Projects mental health providers: Antoinette A. Bankston from the Baton Rouge Children's Health Project and Donna Usner from the New Orleans Children's Health Project.

REFERENCES

Abramson, D., & Garfield, R. (2006, April 17). *On the edge: Children and families displaced by Hurricanes Katrina and Rita face a looming medical and mental health crisis.* National Center for Disaster Preparedness, Mailman School of Public Health, Columbia University and Operation Assist, Children's Health Fund. Retrieved from www.ncdp.mailman.columbia.edu/files/On%20the%20 Edge%20L-CAFH%20Final%20Report_Columbia%20University.pdf.

Abramson, D., Garfield, R., & Redlener, I. (2007, February 2). *The recovery divide: Poverty and the widening gap among Mississippi children and families affected by hurricane Katrina.* National Center for Disaster Preparedness, Mailman School of Public Health, Columbia University, and Children's Health Fund. Retrieved from www.ncdp.mailman.columbia.edu/files/recovery_divide.pdf.

Abramson, D., Redlener, I., Stehling-Ariza, T., & Fuller, E. (2007, December 7). *The legacy of Katrina's children: Estimating the numbers of at-risk children in the Gulf Coast states of Louisiana and Mississippi.* National Center for Disaster Preparedness, Research Brief 2007:12. Mailman School of Public Health, Columbia University, New York. Retrieved from www.ncdp.mailman.columbia.edu/files/ legacy_katrina_children.pdf.

Abramson, D., Stehling-Ariza, N. A., Garfield, R., & Redlener, I. (2008). The prevalence and predictors of mental health distress post-Katrina: Findings from the Gulf Coast child and family health study. *Disaster Medicine and Public Health Preparedness*, in press.

Advocacy Center Louisiana. (2006, May 12). Important Medicaid information: Hurricane Katrina Louisiana Medicaid program. Retrieved on August 7, 2008, from www.advocacyla.org/news/flyers/Medicaid2.pdf.

Aldrich, D. P. (2006). Strong civil society as a double-edged sword: Siting trailers in post-Katrina New Orleans. Weatherhead Center for International Affairs, Working Paper No. 06-11. Retrieved from papers.ssrn.com/sol3/papers. cfm?abstract_id=960497.

Andrews, B., Brewin, C. R., Philpott, R., & Stewart, L. (2007). Delayed-onset posttraumatic stress disorder: a systematic review of the evidence. *American Journal of Psychiatry, 164*(9), 1319–1326.

Annie E. Casey Foundation. (2008). Kids count data center. Retrieved from www .kidscount.org/datacenter.

Associated Press. (2007). FEMA takes back $4.5M Mississippi wanted for mental health facilities. Retrieved from aminthemorning.blogspot.com/2007/08/ fema-takes-back-45m-mspi-wanted-for.html.

Carty, J., O'Donnell, M. L., & Creamer, M. (2006). Delayed-onset PTSD: A prospective study of survivors. *Journal of Affective Disorders, 90*(2–3), 257–261.

Center for Medicaid and Medicare Services—Center for Medicaid and State Operations. (2007, March). Summary of state reports for Medicaid and the State Children's Health Insurance Program—Hurricane Katrina Section 1115 demonstrations. Retrieved from www.cms.hhs.gov/MedicaidStWaivProgDemoPGI/ downloads/Hurricane%20Katrina%20Final%20Summary%20Report.pdf.

Christopher, G. (2005, November–December). Post-Katrina health policy decisions can be informed by 9/11. *Focus Magazine, 33*(6). Retrieved from www.jointcenter .org/index.php/publications_recent_publications/focus_magazine/2005/

novemer_december_2005/post_katrina_health_policy_decisions_can_be_informed_by_9_11.

Federal Bureau of Investigation. (2004). Uniform Crime Reports. Retrieved from www.fbi.gov/ucr/cius_04/documents/CIUS2004.pdf.

Federal Emergency Management Agency. (2007). Robert T. Stafford Disaster Relief Act and Emergency Assistance Act, as amended, and related authorities. FEMA 592. Retrieved from www.fema.gov/pdf/about/stafford_act.pdf.

Galea, S., Brewin, C., Gruber, M., Jones, R., King, D., King, L., et al. (2007). Exposure to hurricane-related stressors and mental illness after Hurricane Katrina. *Archives of General Psychiatry, 64*(12), 1427–1434.

Harrison, E. (2007). Suffering a slow recovery. *Scientific American, 297*(3), 25.

Jenkins, L. (2006, August 6). Superdome stars: Everyday people confronted chaos. *New York Times, 8*(1), sports desk, 1.

Kessler, R. C., Galea, S., Gruber, M. J., Sampson, N. A., Ursano, R. J., & Wessely, S. (2008). Trends in mental illness and suicidality after Katrina. *Molecular Psychiatry, 13*(4), 374–384.

Khoury, E., Warheit, G., Hargrove, M., Zimmerman, R., Vega, W., & Gil, A. (1997). The Impact of Hurricane Andrew on deviant behavior among a multi-racial/ethnic sample of adolescents in Dade County, Florida: A longitudinal analysis. *Journal of Traumatic Stress, 10*(1), 71–91.

Lambrew, J. M., & Shalala, D. E. (2006). Federal health policy response to Hurricane Katrina: what it was and what it could have been. *Journal of the American Medical Association, 296*(11), 1394–1397.

Landesman, L. Y. (2007). Editor's choice: Improving preparedness by incorporating lessons learned. *American Journal of Public Health, 97*(Suppl 1), 6.

Louisiana Department of Education. (2005). 12th grade enrollment and graduation counts 2004–2005. Retrieved from www.doe.state.la.us/lde/pair/2396.html.

Louisiana Recovery Authority. (2006). 2006 initial quality report. Retrieved from lra.louisiana.gov/assets/docs/searchable/reports/FINAL_QP2006_FEB_06_revised.pdf.

Lyznicki, J., Subbarao, I., Benjamin, G. C., & James, J. J. (2007). Developing a consensus framework for an effective and efficient disaster response health system: A national call to action. *Disaster Medicine and Public Health Preparedness, 1*(Suppl 1), 51–54.

Madrid, P., Garfield, R., Jaberi, P., Daly, M., Richard, G., & Grant, R. (2008). Mental health services in Louisiana school-based health centers post-hurricanes Katrina and Rita. *Professional Psychology: Research and Practice, 39*(1), 45–51.

Madrid, P., & Grant, R. (2008). Meeting mental health needs following a natural disaster: Lessons from Hurricane Katrina. *Professional Psychology: Research and Practice, 39*(1), 86–92.

Madrid, P. A., Grant, R., Reilly, M. J. & Redlener, N. (2006). Short-term impact of a major disaster on children's mental health: Building resiliency in the aftermath of Hurricane Katrina. *Pediatrics, 117*(5), 448–453.

Markenson, D., Fuller, E., & Redlener, I. (2007). *Emergency preparedness: Addressing the needs of persons with disabilitiesa national consensus conference: Executive summary and final report.* National Center for Disaster Preparedness, Mailman School of Public Health, Columbia University. Retrieved from www.ncdp.mailman.columbia.edu/files/DISABILITIES.pdf.

McClain, T., Hamilton, F., Clothier, J., & McGaugh, J. (2007). Opportunity missed: A lesson learned from evacuating mentally ill patients following hurricanes Katrina and Rita. *Academic Psychiatry, 31*(3), 188–189.

National Center for Disaster Preparedness, Mailman School of Public Health, Columbia University. (2005). *Considerations in emergency preparedness: A two track conference.* Available by request from www.ncdp.mailman.columbia.edu.

Nieburg, P., Waldman, R., & Krumm, D. (2005). Evacuated populations—lessons from foreign refugee crises. *New England Journal of Medicine, 353*(15), 1547–1549.

Noji, E. K., & Sivertson, K. T. (1987). Injury prevention in natural disasters: A theoretical framework. *Disasters, 11*(4), 290–296.

Norris, F. (2007). *National Center for PTSD fact sheet: Psychosocial consequences of major hurricanes and floods: Range, duration, and magnitude of effects and risk factors for adverse outcomes.* National Center for Posttraumatic Stress Disorder. Retrieved from www.ncptsd.va.gov/ncmain/ncdocs/fact_shts/fs_range_hurricane.html?opm=1&rr=rr141&srt=d&echorr=true.

Norris, F. H., Friedman, M. J., & Watson, P. J. (2002). 60,000 disaster victims speak: Part II. Summary and implications of the disaster mental health research. *Psychiatry, 65*(3), 240–260.

Norris, F. H., Friedman, M. J., Watson, P. J., Byrne, C. M., Diaz, E., & Kaniasty, K. (2002). 60,000 disaster victims speak: Part I. An empirical review of the empirical literature, 1981–2001. *Psychiatry, 65*(3), 207–239.

Osofsky, H. (2007). In the eye of Katrina: Surviving the storm and rebuilding an academic department of psychiatry. *Academic Psychiatry, 31*(3), 183–187.

Pfefferbaum, B., Call, J., & Sconzo, G. (1999). Mental health services for children in the first two years after the 1995 Oklahoma City terrorist bombing. *Psychiatric Services, 50*(7), 956–958.

Pfefferbaum, B., Pfefferbaum, R., North, C., & Neas, B. (2002). Does television viewing satisfy criteria for exposure in posttraumatic stress disorder? *Psychiatry, 65*(4), 306–309.

Pfefferbaum, B., Seale, T. W., Brandt, E. N. Jr., Pfefferbaum R. L., Doughty D. E., & Rainwater, S. M. (2003). Media exposure in children one hundred miles from a terrorist bombing. *Annals of Clinical Psychiatry, 15*(1), 1–8.

Redlener, I. (2006). *Americans at risk: Why we are not prepared for megadisasters and what we can do now.* New York: Knopf.

Redlener, I., Abramson, D., Stehling-Ariza, T., Grant, R., & Johnson, D. (2007). *The American Preparedness Project: Where the US public stands in 2007 on terrorism, security, and disaster preparedness.* Retrieved from www.ncdp.mailman.columbia.edu/files/NCDP07.pdf.

Rudowitz, R., Rowland, D., & Shartzer, A. (2006). Health care in New Orleans before and after Hurricane Katrina. *Health Affairs, 25*(5), 393–406.

Sattler, D., Preston, A., Kaiser, C., Olivera, V., Valdez, J., & Schlueter, S. (2002). Hurricane Georges: A cross-national study examining preparedness, resource loss, and psychological distress in the U.S. Virgin Islands, Puerto Rico, Dominican Republic, and the United States. *Journal of Traumatic Stress, 15*(5), 339–350.

Silove, D., Steel, Z., & Psychol, M. (2006). Understanding community psychosocial needs after disasters: Implications for mental health services. *Journal of Postgraduate Medicine, 52*(2), 121–125.

Singer, P. (2006). FEMA works to keep trailer parks temporary. *National Journal.* Retrieved from www.govexec.com/dailyfed/0306/031306nj1.htm.

Stoddard, E. (2007). Post-Katrina New Orleans death rate shoots up. Reuters Foundation. Retrieved from www.alertnet.org/thenews/newsdesk/N21396585.htm.

Subbarao, I., Lyznicki, J. M., Hsu, E. B., Gebbie, K. M., Markenson, D., Barzansky, B., et al. (2008). A consensus-based educational framework and competency set for the discipline of disaster medicine and public health preparedness. *Disaster Medicine and Public Health Preparedness, 2*(1), 57–68.

U.S. Census Bureau. (2004). General demographic dharacteristics. Retrieved from factfinder.census.gov/servlet/ADPTable?_bm=y&qrname=ACS_2004_EST_G00_DP1&-geo_id=16000US2255000&-ds_name=&-redoLog=false.

U.S. Census Bureau Housing and Household Economic Statistics Division. (2004). Poverty. Retrieved from www.census.gov/hhes/www/poverty/poverty04/table8.pdf.

U.S. Census Bureau of Labor Statistics. (2004). Unemployment rate. Retrieved from www.census.gov/statab/ranks/rank25.html.

U.S. Department of Education. (2005). Testimony of Assistant Secretary Johnson on Hurricane Katrina and elementary and secondary education. Retrieved from www.ed.gov/news/speeches/2005/09/09222005.html.

U.S. Government Accountability Office. (2006). Status of the health care system in New Orleans. Retrieved from www.gao.gov/new.items/d06576r.pdf.

Wang, P., Gruber, M., Powers, R., Shoenbaum, M., Speier, A., Wells, K., et al. (2008). Disruption of existing mental health treatments and failure to initiate new treatment after Hurricane Katrina. *American Journal of Psychiatry, 165*(1), 34–41.

Watersone, M. E., & Stein, M. A. (2006). Emergency preparedness and disability. *Mental & Physical Disability Law Reporter, 30*(3), 338–339.

Weisler, R., Barbee, J., & Townsend, M. (2006). Mental health and recovery in the Gulf Coast after Hurricanes Katrina and Rita. *Journal of the American Medical Association, 296*(5), 585–588.

Whoriskey, P. (2006, June 7). Katrina displaced 400,000, study says: New Orleans becomes whiter, Mississippi coast more diverse. *Washington Post*, A12.

Zuckerman, S., & Coughlin, T. (2006). *Initial health policy responses to Hurricane Katrina and possible next steps.* Urban Institute. Retrieved from www.urban.org/publications/900929.html.

CHAPTER 2

Autonomy and Disability: A Quest for Quality of Life

Bedarius Bell Jr., Shelley R. Henthorne, Doris Adams Hill, Jane W. Turnbull-Humphries, and Stephanie T. Zito

Autonomy in the United States is embedded in a set of principles deeply rooted in equality—principles which have defined our nation and given way to both civil and human rights. These basic ideas were written to be a blueprint of our country and are part of one of the most well-known documents in American history. The Declaration of Independence, written by Thomas Jefferson in 1776, declared: "We hold these truths to be self-evident, that all men are created equal, that they are endowed by their Creator with certain unalienable Rights that among these are Life, Liberty, and the pursuit of Happiness." From a historical perspective, however, the autonomy alluded to in these high ideals remains unrealized for far too many disenfranchised members of society.

The purpose of this chapter is to examine the concept of autonomy, especially as it applies to people with disabilities. First, the chapter presents a foundation for understanding the nature and meaning of autonomy, and its related constructs of self-determination and choice making, from definitional, disabilities, and legislative perspectives. In addition, several issues are introduced that provide cause for reflection. Second, a life span perspective is presented on supporting autonomy at the preschool age, the school age, and throughout adulthood. Finally, relevant research is summarized: comparative studies, or findings between individuals with and without disabilities; the relationship between motivation and self-determination, and the positive impact of self-determination.

A FRAMEWORK

Definitions

The *Shorter Routledge Encyclopedia of Philosophy* (Craig, 2005) defines the core idea of autonomy as "that of sovereignty over oneself, self-governance or self-determination: an agent or political entity is autonomous if it is self-governing or self-determining" (p. 75). It continues to explain that the ancient Greeks applied the term to city-states and in the later modern period, Immanuel Kant extended it to persons. Kant is typically regarded as one of the most influential thinkers of modern moral philosophy and the age of Enlightenment. He believed that the possession of both will and reason was necessary to be considered a person in the moral sense.

The Western cultural values and priorities that shape the definition of autonomy have fallen short in addressing the ethics of other cultures (Cardol, deJong, & Ward, 2002; Carver & Scheier, 2000; Wehmeyer, 2004). The Western ideal of autonomy, for example, is equated with independence and freedom of choice. The relevance of such concepts, however, may be questioned by cultures that are more centered on loyalty to groups, interdependence in and within families, or respect for traditions.

Autonomy is one of four essential characteristics of a self-determined individual. Autonomous functioning (or behavioral autonomy), self-regulation, psychological empowerment, and self-realization all have a direct relationship to the concept of self-determination (Clapton & Kendall, 2002). Autonomous functioning can be seen as either decisional (making choices, problem solving) or executional (performing behavior that results from choice making, independent living, and risk taking). Within this framework, "a behavior is autonomous if the person acts according to his or her own preferences, interests, and/or abilities and in an independent manner, free from undue external influence or interference" (Wehmeyer, Agran, & Hughes, 1998, p. 7). Conversely, learned helplessness and programmed dependence have been used to describe the consequence of the absence of choice and control: the failure to develop a sense of self-efficacy and direction.

The elusiveness of autonomy in American society is compounded by a lack of clarity and consistency in its meaning. *Self-determination* is a term often used interchangeably with *autonomy* within the field of disability. However, the somewhat variant meanings tend to add some ambiguity to the equation (Turnbull & Turnbull, 2006). One of the earliest introductions to the concept of self-determination in the field of disabilities was in the early 1970s. Nirje (1972) equated self-determination with respect and dignity and identified several of its significant features, such as choice and autonomy. A contemporary of Nirje, Robert Perske (1972), called for the opportunity for people with disabilities to experience "the dignity of risk": "The world in which we live is not always safe, secure and predictable. . . . We must work to develop every human resource within us in order to prepare for these days. To deny any person their fair share of risk experiences is to further cripple them for healthy living" (p. 199).

In 1989, the term *self-determination* and its meaning became a federal initiative (Ward, 1992). Specifically, the Office of Special Education and Rehabilitative

Services, U.S. Department of Education, sponsored a national conference on self-determination. The first of 29 recommendations resulting from that conference was: "The enabling of people with disabilities to determine their own futures to be seen as the top priority in all government policy-making functions" (p. 4). Wehmeyer and Garner (2003) identified two factors that constituted self-determination. The first was the ability of an individual to act in a self-determined manner, and the second was the opportunities the environment produced for individuals to be in control of their lives.

Numerous definitions of self-determination appear in the literature (e.g., Browning, 1997; Halloran, 1993). Serna and Lau-Smith (1995) stated that "Self-determination refers to an individual's awareness of personal strengths and weaknesses, the ability to set goals and make choices, to be assertive at appropriate times, and to interact with others in a socially competent manner" (p. 144). Wehmeyer (1992) defined self-determination as "the attitudes and abilities required to act as the primary causal agent in one's life and to make choices regarding one's actions free from undue external influence or interference" (p. 305). Deci and Ryan (1985), leading social psychologists on motivation and self-determination, defined self-determination as the capacity to choose and to be the determinants of those actions. Choice, the central factor in all three definitions, becomes a critical feature in the development of autonomy. Unfortunately, individuals with disabilities are still often viewed as being unable to make choices about their lives (Clark, Olympia, Jensen, Heathfield, & Jenson, 2004).

Choice making, which is a decision-making process, involves the expression of needs, desires, and preferences, as well as implies the ability to select among options. Some attempts have been made to design curricula for teaching this self-determination skill. As one such example, Martin and Marshall (1995) developed a curriculum for high school students with disabilities titled ChoiceMaker Self-Determination Transition Planning.

Choice is a term and concept that has been especially embraced in the field of rehabilitation (Patterson, Patrick, & Parker, 2000). In the Rehabilitation Act Public Law 103-73) Amendments of 1992 (section 100(a)), it is stated that "individuals must be active participants in their own rehabilitation programs, including making meaningful and informed choices about the selection of their vocational goals, objectives, and services." Choice is also directly related to the Code of Professional Ethics for Rehabilitation Counselors (Commission on Rehabilitation Counselor Certification [CRCC], 2002). The first of five principles is *autonomy*, which is the right to individual decisions. Likewise, a position statement has been adopted on self-determination by the Council for Exceptional Children's Division on Career Development and Transition (Field, Martin, Miller, Ward, & Wehmeyer, 1998).

Some research on self-determination and individual choice has compared individuals with disabilities to those without. Wehmeyer and Kelchner (1995) reported that adults with mental retardation, when compared to their peers without disabilities, experience limited opportunities to make choices and have control in their lives. They also noted that adolescents with learning disabilities, as compared to adolescents without disabilities, differed significantly in their autonomous functioning in self-management activities and the use of community resources. In sample of 408 adolescents and adults with mental retardation, Wehmeyer and Kelchner (1995) found 32 percent reported that they never prepared food that required cooking and 56 percent indicated that they rarely made minor repairs to the home, such as changing a light bulb. These findings suggest that individuals with disabilities are not provided the opportunities to act autonomously or do things for themselves. Perhaps these results are suggestive of society's belief that individuals with cognitive disabilities are unable to make their own life choices.

In preparation for this chapter, one of the authors interviewed the assistant attorney general for the state of Alabama and a consultant to the Alabama Department of Rehabilitation Services. Although much of the interview centered on the legal aspects of autonomy and disability, probably the simplest, yet most profound words expressed by Attorney Graham Sisson, who has a physical disability, in regard to defining autonomy, were:

> Making your own choices and directly making all the major decisions for your life. I decided who I was going to marry, where I was going to go to school, where I was going to live and work, and what I was going to eat every day . . . making the very simplest choices to the most complex choices. . . . Autonomy with limited choices is meaningless. . . . Your life is a product of choices. . . . Why not be the person that makes those choices? (personal conversation, April 4, 2007)

In summary, the nature and importance of having choices and being able to make them among alternatives is a highly valued human condition (Guess, Benson, & Siegel-Causey, 1985). As noted by Parent (1993), "If individuals are to experience personal satisfaction and quality of life, regardless of whether or not they have a disability, it is critical for them to have the right to make choices, express preferences, and exercise control over their lives" (p. 20).

Disabilities

Prior to the 1960s, many people did not enjoy full legal protections as "autonomous persons," including people with disabilities. Once an individual was labeled incompetent or "feeble-minded," for example, access to the inalienable rights afforded by the Declaration of Independence could be controlled through guardianship or paternalism. Institutionalization and forced sterilization became tools for preserving racial purity, and the eugenics movement gained momentum in American society. Court decisions upheld the constitutionality of forced sterilization of people with disabilities (*Buck v. Bell*, 274 U.S. 200; 47 S. Ct. 584, 1927), and by 1938 some 33 states had sterilization laws in place; sterilization was considered to be as commonplace as vaccinations.

Our society has advanced from viewing individuals with disabilities as people who are incapable of making choices. Since the early 1960s, the concept and practice of autonomy and self-determination for people with disabilities has become paramount as an outgrowth of landmark legislative enactments, as well as many movements, including the consumerism movement (Browning, 1997), the civil rights movement (Martin, 2001), the independent living movement (DeJong, 1979), the self-advocacy movement (Rhoades, 1986), and the self-determination movement (Field et al., 1998). One important new philosophy underlying these movements was "normalization," which stressed the principle that the pattern of life for people with disabilities should be as close as possible to that of regular societal environments and circumstances (Wolfensburger, 1972).

The definition of disability itself has implications for how people with disabilities are viewed by others as autonomous functioning, self-determined, choice-making individuals. Until recently, the field of medicine has been more interested with the disease than in the person with the disease (e.g., Cardol et al., 2002; Vehmas, 2004). Such thinking and practice falls under the paternal or deficit model (Pfeiffer, 2002) and focuses on the individual deficits, functional limitations, and impairments. It suggests that something is wrong with the individual. The model states that a person with a disability is insufficient in some area that must be "fixed" before they can be normal, and since most disability cannot be corrected, it suggests there is never a prospect of them becoming normal. This definitional viewpoint encourages the practice of handicapism by treating people with disabilities as children with the tendency to speak for them (Biklen & Bogdan, 1976). Such a framework is inhibiting to the value and practice of autonomy.

According to Cardol et al. (2002), there are several principles that must be applied for the field of medical rehabilitation to employ a focus on the person rather than the disease. These principles include autonomy, involvement in life situations in relation to disability (or participation), self-awareness, interdependence, and an "ethic of care." There is a strong recognition of the importance of the concept of autonomy to participation and even an acknowledgment that it should be the ultimate goal of the field. However, the concept of autonomy as financial or physical independence continues to limit consumer involvement.

In an attempt to define autonomy in the context of a disabling condition, Cardol et al. (2002) distinguished decisional autonomy (the ability to make decisions without external restraint or coercion) from executional autonomy (the ability or freedom to act on the basis of decisional autonomy). Both of these definitions can create major limitations for people with disabilities, due to restricted physical, cognitive, and psychological abilities. Even with this dual definition, autonomy would remain unachievable for some people because the tendency is to equate it with independence.

An alternative to the deficit model is to view disability as a sociopolitical condition that is characterized by the interaction between the individual and society. In this sense, rather than tracing the consequences to one's personal defects, they are traced primarily to the features of the disabling physical, social, political, and economic environment (Bogdan, 1986; DeJong, 1979; Hahn, 1991). This ecologically based disability belief suggests that "we should increase our efforts to assess the community's prothesis, change community attitudes, engage in job redesign and modification, remove inhibiting quality-of-life barriers, and enforce civil rights about access to housing, transportation, education, and employment opportunities" (Browning, 1997, p. 76). Such a viewpoint provides a viable foundation for autonomous functioning.

Legislation

Since 1973, four pieces of U.S. landmark legislation or amendments to legislation have had a profound effect on the rights, dignity, and quality of life for persons with disabilities. The legislation is replete with language that values autonomy, independence, self-determination, equal opportunity(ies), personal interests and preferences, and making choices and decisions.

Collectively, this legislation represents sweeping civil rights acts that target the elimination of discrimination and guarantee equal rights protection in all areas of life, including education, employment, transportation, housing, public services, public accommodation, voting, services operated by private entities, and telecommunications for individuals with disabilities. The legislation provides an infrastructure from which autonomy can be fully promoted and ensured for people with disability.

The Individuals with Disabilities Education Act (IDEA) (Public Law 108-446) addressed the need for special education teachers to include their students' preferences and interests into their individualized plans and programs. The mandate to involve students in the discussion of their future goals and plans reflects the values of self-determination, enablement, and shared responsibility. The Americans with Disabilities Act (ADA) (Public Law 101-336) provided the unique opportunity to enhance "self-determination, choice, and greater freedom for all persons with disabilities in the United States" (Ward, 1993, p. 8). The Developmental Disabilities and Bill of Rights Act (Public Law 106-402) promotes self-determination, independence, productivity, and integration and inclusion in all facets of community life. The Rehabilitation Act (Public Law 103-73) promoted self-determination, independent living, choice making, and full inclusion, especially in the context of work (e.g., career goals, job preferences, community employment) (West, 1995). A major piece of legislation in the United States concerning people with disabilities, the Rehabilitation Act, stated "disability is a natural part of the human experience and in no way diminishes the right of individuals to—(a) live *independently*; (b) enjoy *self-determination;* (c) *make choices;* (d) *contribute* to society; (e) pursue meaningful careers; and (f) enjoy *full inclusion* and *integration* in the economic, political, social, cultural, and educational mainstream of American society" (emphasis added).

The United States and Canada were among the first countries to adopt antidiscrimination laws and other human rights legislation for persons with disabilities (Degener, 2000). Since the beginning of the 1990s, however, more than 20 nations have enacted disability discrimination laws. According to Degener, a significant number of countries seem to have modeled their modern disability discrimination legislation on the ADA and its predecessors. This interest and legal framework for autonomy in the lives of people with disabilities has extended well beyond the borders of the United States. On March 30, 2007, the United Nations' first Convention on the Rights of Persons with Disabilities was held. In a UN press conference held March 13 of that year, it was stated:

> the convention ensures that persons with disabilities enjoy the same human rights as everyone else, and are able to lead their lives as fully-fledged citizens

who can make valuable contributions to society if given the same opportunities. It covers rights such as equality, non-discrimination and equal recognition before the law; liberty and security of the person; accessibility, personal mobility and independent living; right to health, work and education; and participation in political and cultural life. The treaty will enter into force when ratified by 20 countries.

Eighty-one member states and the European Community, a record for the first day of signature of any UN convention, signed a landmark new treaty that was the first comprehensive human rights treaty of its kind in the 21st century. One of the eight guiding principles underlying the convention that aims to improve the lives of the world's estimated 650 million people with disabilities is "Respect for inherent dignity, individual autonomy including the freedom to make one's own choices, and independence of persons."

Reflecting on How Disability Is Defined

How disability is defined has implications for how people with disabilities are viewed by others as autonomous, self-determined, choice-making individuals. For example, too often, the fields of special education and rehabilitation have been married to the medical or "fix-'em-up" disability definition model, which has focused our vision and attention to the individual's clinical needs related to his or her functional limitations, impairments, and skill deficits (Browning, 1997). It suggests that the problem(s) under consideration is mainly the result of something wrong within the individual, which often leads to negative consequences. In all, limitations of choice and control may not only be directly related to disability but to society's interpretation of that disability (Clark et al., 2004).

Major attention has been given to the nature and significance of autonomy as a legal human right and supporting it for its contribution to one's quality of life. Federal legislation has now fully embraced it for people with disabilities, and research has positively supported the concept and practice of self determination and choice making in terms of one's human performance, motivation, and self-esteem. Therefore, the essentialness of autonomy in the lives of these individuals is fully endorsed. Perhaps another way to underscore the significance of this valued human condition is to acknowledge and discuss the alternative (and its consequences) of not allowing individuals to control their own lives! What happens to them if we do not foster their autonomy? What is the relationship between one's state of "helplessness" (Seigleman, 1975) and autonomy?

Professional Support

The discussion of autonomy as an ethical issue means that professionals must be obligated to uphold individual choice. The concept of autonomy is not just providing individuals with the opportunity to be in control of their lives, it is about a belief system that professionals must adopt to foster the development of autonomy (Phemister, 2001). The Commission on Rehabilitation Counselor Certification has taken the step of listing *autonomy* as one of five principles of ethical behavior that guide the construction and development of the CRCC Code of Ethics (preamble). All certified rehabilitation counselors subscribe to a code of professional ethics, which directs the practice of rehabilitation counseling. The code is based on (a) *autonomy*: to honor the right to make individual decisions; (b) beneficence: to do good to others; (c) nonmaleficence: to do no harm to others; (d) justice: to be fair and give equally to others; and (e) fidelity: to be loyal, honest, and keep promises to others (Rasch, 1996). It is essential that rehabilitation counselors demonstrate adherence to ethical standards and ensure the standards are enforced vigorously.

Ability to Act Autonomously

Unfortunately, we are still too often conveying the message that individuals with disabilities are unable to make choices about their lives (Clark et al., 2004). Yet professionals (and parents) may at times wonder whether individuals are capable of understanding the decisions they are making and the potential consequences or dangers regarding those personal decisions (Meininger, 2001). There may be certain situations, for example, when individuals with significant cognitive disabilities lack the necessary skills to make an informed decision. The issue is couched in the questions: When should one's right to make self-determined choices be halted, due to one's level of intellectual functioning? When does a disability affect ones ability to act autonomously?

Providing Opportunities to Function Autonomously

For children and adults to learn how to function autonomously, they must be provided opportunities and environments that allow them to make choices and decisions (Deci & Chandler, 1986). Unfortunately, some parents of children with disabilities provide very few opportunities for their children to make choices or decisions and often display much control over the future of their children with disabilities (Zhang, 2005). Deci and Chandler (1986) recommended using little control in the classroom, allowing children to solve their own problems, encouraging students to create and act on their own plans at their own speed. It is clear that individuals with significant disabilities should be taught directly and provided opportunities to develop autonomy. Are there some essential opportunities that should be afforded to everyone across the life span? Are there some essential (and unique) opportunities that should be especially afforded to people with disabilities across their life spans?

Summary

The definition and expression of autonomy has evolved and, in some cases, devolved over the years. Although the academic means and terms vary and can be confusing to both professionals and consumers, the application is generally unchanged. Autonomy is having some level of control over the decisions and actions made in one's life. We are all dependent on others to varying degrees. The Western societal notion of a self-made individual is false. Just as autonomy need not necessitate total independence, dependence on other people need not be oppressive (Clapton & Kendall, 2002). With the concept of interdependence properly placed within the natural framework of human existence, people with disabilities who have dependence needs would be seen no differently than other members of society. According to Browning (1997), we are now "moving from viewing people with disabilities as being 'passive recipients' of education and services, to that of 'active participants' who are capable of making their own choices, and mapping-out and steering their own future" (p. 85).

SUPPORTING AUTONOMY: A LIFE COMMITMENT

Developing autonomy is important for individuals with disabilities (Crittenden, 1990); autonomy plays a significant role in life's activities such as choice making, goal setting and attainment, problem solving, and self-evaluation (Clark et al., 2004). Federal legislation has mandated adherence to this human condition across the life span for people with disabilities. In spite of these legal safeguards, it remains a major responsibility of families and professionals to create and nurture environments that promote and support autonomy at home, at school, and in the community.

Supporting autonomy, according to Black and Deci (2000), is "the idea that an individual in a position of authority takes the other's perspective, acknowledges the other's feelings, and provides the other with pertinent information and opportunities for choice, while minimizing the use of pressures and demands" (p. 742). Nevertheless, it is not enough to merely provide choices to individuals with disabilities. Rather, families, professionals, and significant others in the lives of these persons must also acknowledge, respond, and discuss those choices in terms of their appropriateness and consequences.

Supporting autonomy can be achieved through the teaching of cognitive-behavioral skills. It can be promoted by teaching self-enabling, self-determination skills such as choice making, goal setting, self-knowledge and awareness, self-advocacy, and positive perceptions of control and efficacy (e.g., Browning, 1997; Shogren & Turnbull, 2006). The teaching of these skills to achieve a more autonomous life must be an ongoing and collective undertaking between key persons in the home, school, and post-school setting (e.g., families, teachers, rehabilitation counselors).

Self-management is another trend in which autonomous functioning can be supported and/or taught. Self-management is a state in which individuals have control over events and actions that affect their lives (Kendall, Muenchberger, & Clapton, 2007). This control may be a collaborative or individual effort. In Australia, self-management is being supported through a peer-led programs to help individuals share in decision making about treatment and gain self-control over the events in their lives despite their illness.

Achieving autonomy requires more than the teaching of self-determination skills. In addition, it calls for the learner to believe that he or she can perform a behavior and have the expectation of achieving the desired result (Thoma & Sax, 2003). Individuals must be provided with opportunities to develop perceptions of their behavior performance efficacy and their ability to maintain control of their lives (Wehman, 2006). This latter consideration is an essential part of the equation in that one must have the opportunity to apply the self-directed skills and a supportive environment in which to do so (Browning, 1997). The autonomous related skills are meaningful only insofar as the environment is open to their application, and herein lies this section's focus. As such, emphasis is placed on the environment for promoting autonomy at the preschool age, school age, and postschool age.

Supporting Autonomy at the Preschool Age

A typical behavior exhibited by toddlers is the testing of their independence. This early age is a time for creating opportunities whereby the toddlers can explore, make decisions, and ask questions (Cook, Klein, & Tessier, 2004). Toddlers are "naturally inquisitive and enjoy self-directed exploration of a new environment" (Bondurant-Utz & Luciano, 1994, p. 37).

These earlier years have been recognized as the "declaration of independence" (Brazelton, 1974), or a stage for developing healthy autonomy (Erikson, 1963). Children at this earliest stage of development are ready to develop a sense of initiative if they have developed a basic trust in their environment and in themselves, and have experienced a growing self-confidence in their ability to explore and experiment (Cook et al., 2004, p. 190). The parent will help the child gain a sense of autonomy if there is a positive, reinforcing, and patient attitude on the parent's part (Turner, 2000). Parents need to be the initiators and supporters for developing autonomy in their children by creating home environments that allow for and nurture autonomous functioning (Shevin & Klein, 2004).

During the preschool years, children develop self-determination skills and attitudes that can be fostered with both physical and social contexts (Turner, 2000). The physical contexts include rooms within the home, the furnishings, and toys, whereas the social contexts include family, culture, and social interactions (Shogren & Turnbull, 2006). The development of autonomy can be promoted when parents permit their children to explore and engage with materials and activities that hold their attention, such as toys and clothing. Having the option to choose activities and materials that are interesting allows children to develop preferences that further define their personal identity (Shogren & Turnbull, 2006). Parents can also help support autonomy within the physical area of the home. It is important for children to have their own space to keep their things or retreat to when they want to be alone. The idea of having their own space aids in the development of perception of control and autonomy.

Within the social realm of the home environment, the parent–child relationship plays a critical role in the development of autonomy. According to research, infants that are securely attached to their parents, or caregivers, tend to have more confidence, curiosity, and self-reliance (Cassidy & Shaver, 1999; Waters, Wippman, & Stroufe, 1979). There are parenting styles, for example, that create a balance between demand and responsiveness, lead to more self-reliance, responsibility, independence, and autonomy (Baumrind, 1972; Baumrind & Black, 1967). Finally, as children get older, they move toward more self-awareness and independence (Field & Hoffman, 1999). Accordingly, families must adapt and make changes to the physical and social contexts in the home as their children grow, since these changing needs effect the home's autonomy supporting environment.

In summary, parents have a significant role to play in helping develop autonomous behavior in their children. The initiation of this quality of life condition should begin at the child's infant–toddler age and continue to be developed across the individual's life span. The home setting provides an important climate for initiating, nurturing, and promoting its development.

Supporting Autonomy at the School Age

Opportunities for autonomous development in the school setting are essential. Underlying its importance is the premise that an autonomous environment within the school will have a positive impact on the motivational climate for students (Lundberg, 2007). Almqvist and Granlund (2005) found participation in school activities to be related to autonomy. The more autonomous the student, the more likely he or she is to participate both in the classroom and in various school sponsored activities. Students with disabilities who are in their least restrictive environment (LRE) have more autonomous opportunities with their typical peers in general education programs. Briefly, LRE is the right to learn in an inclusive environment. The IDEA mandates and ensures that all students with disabilities have the right to learn in an environment that is consistent with their academic, social, and physical needs, and "to the maximum extent appropriate," be educated with children who are not disabled (IDEA, 20 U.S.C. 1412 [5] (B)). An LRE in the educational setting provides an environmental climate that is highly conducive to the development and promotion of self-directed skills (e.g., social problem solving, goal setting). It also ensures them of their right to learn in a setting that is consistent with their needs.

Autonomy within the classroom setting is the students' need for control over decisions in the school regarding "initiation, inhibition, maintenance, and redirection of activities" (Connell, 1990, p. 65). A major strategy to support autonomy is to provide a responsive environment in the classroom by providing situations in which individuals share control, express preferences, and choose activities in which to participate (Wall & Dattilo, 1995). Again, students' perception of control increases when they are given choices and allowed to make decisions based on those choices (Stefanou, Perencevich, Di-Cintio, & Turner, 2004). In turn, their engagement increases in the learning process (e.g., Deci, 1980; Deci & Ryan, 1987). Thus, teachers must provide autonomy supportive environments that aid in the learning process. Three classroom dimensions can be changed to facilitate self-determination, which in turn leads to autonomous functioning (Whaley & Bennett, 1991). These dimensions are physical environment, social environment, and instructional practices.

Whaley and Bennett (1991) suggested setting up the physical environment in such a way that allows for learning zones that make learning materials available to all students. It is important to provide a large variety of materials and to use manipulative toys, which will affect the physical environment, as well as have an effect on the classroom's social environment. Disputes between children can be avoided since there are many more options from which to choose. Finally, this consideration of the physical and social environment allows children to make choices and enhances social interaction among the students.

The third modifiable dimension is instructional practices. One such practice for teaching to self-determination is the Foxfire democratic approach to learning (Ensminger & Dangel, 1992). Through this learner-centered approach to teaching, students have the responsibility for making decisions about the activities they choose. This democratic style of instruction also allows students to guide their learning and leisure. The Foxfire approach is one method that leads to ownership and allows individuals to become engaged participants in their own education (Wall & Dattilo, 1995).

Since the early 1990s, there has been a plethora of curricula designed to teach students self-determination skills. Consider, for example, some of the following programs:

1. Choice-Maker and Self-Determination Series (Martin, Marshall, Maxson, & Jermann, 1997),
2. Steps to Self-Determination (Field & Hoffman, 1996),
3. Skills for Independent Living (1997),
4. Whose Future Is it Anyway? (Wehmeyer & Kelchner, 1995),
5. Self-Advocacy for People with Developmental Disabilities (Browning & Rhoades, 1986),
6. A Practical Guide for Teaching Self-Determination (Field et al., 1998).

The integration of these instructional materials into the students' larger curricula program will underscore the educational system's value and commitment to promoting self-determination in their students. The learning environment becomes one that is directed toward the students' ability to embrace an autonomous lifestyle.

Instead of self-determination instruction, Stefanou and colleagues (2004) focused on the learning opportunities that students have within the classroom and proposed three features of autonomy support: (a) organizational autonomy support, (b) procedural autonomy support, and (c) cognitive autonomy support. Organization autonomy support allows students to have ownership over the environment and make choices about classroom rules and due dates for assignments (Stefanou et al., 2004). Within organizational autonomy support, students are allowed to choose group members, evaluation procedures, and the seating arrangement.

Procedural autonomy support promotes student ownership of form. One teaching strategy might be to allow students to decide how to present a project, whether it is by poster or written report. Students are also given the opportunity to choose materials to use in class projects, discuss their wants, and handle materials. Finally, cognitive autonomy support promotes student ownership of the learning and can consist of teacher behaviors such as asking students to evaluate their own work and that of others (Logan, DiCintio, Cox, & Turner, 1995). Cognitive autonomy support also gives students the opportunity to discuss multiple approaches and strategies, find multiple solutions to problems, and reevaluate errors. There is no perfect mixture of organizational, procedural, and cognitive autonomy support that leads to true learning and motivation.

The high school years are an especially critical time for preparing students to assume the demanding responsibilities of adulthood. The development of their transition plan, which is mandated by law at age 16, is an important tool. Furthermore, the student should be involved in the planning and implementing of his or her own transition; by doing so, he or she will learn self-advocacy, decision making, self-evaluation, and goal-setting skills (Field et al., 1998). As young students prepare for a more independent and autonomous life, it is imperative they be taught self-determination skills in the classroom and community through choice making with regard to academics, independent living, and leisure activities. Self-determination skills are especially important for transition-age students to develop to aid in their becoming young empowered adults. For students to be actively involved in the process, they should learn how to make decisions, advocate for themselves, and set goals. Because of its relevance, self-determination for high school students with disabilities was earmarked as one of five major issues for the 90s (Halloran, 1993).

Most leaders in the field would agree that the concept and practice of autonomy is an essential element in preparing them for a successful transition from school to community life. In addition to the enabling skills, research has shown that enhanced choice opportunities for these young students leads to better outcomes in vocational services and placements (Brooke, Green, Revell, & Wehman, 2006). Through the Individuals with Disabilities Act, legislation states that services must be based on "the individual child's needs, taking into account the child's *strengths, preferences, and interests*" (IDEA; emphasis added).

Even though mandated by law, demanded by individuals, and proven to deliver better outcomes, professional perceptions may not always align with the student's choices or preferences, even when they claim to support behavioral and decisional autonomy (Martin, Woods, Sylvester, & Gardner, 2005). Using a Choose and Take Action software program, eight individuals with severe cognitive disabilities who participated in a school-to-work employment program were surveyed, along with their parents, teachers, and residential and vocational staff. The purpose of the study was to compare what caregivers believed the students with disabilities preferred to what the eight students actually chose. The match ranged between 18 to 35 percent across an array of variables (e.g., setting, activity, choices) (Martin et al., 2005). These findings suggested that it is not enough to simply acknowledge support autonomous functioning. Actions must promote it!

High school students must be provided the opportunity to learn and practice self-advocacy skills. As Halloran (1993) stated, "It is unrealistic to expect students to become well adjusted and active members of their community if they are not also afforded opportunities to become active members in decisions that affect their future" (p. 215). Self-advocacy and group advocacy are highly regarded strategies for preparing students to assume a more autonomous life. At the personal level, self-advocacy involves individuals speaking for and acting on their own behalf, making decisions, and influencing situations that affect their lives, and reaching their highest possible level of independence. It is a matter of stating one's own preferences and interests, setting one's own goals, mapping out one's own plans, and acquiring resources for one's own cause.

Group advocacy provides a viable opportunity for secondary students with disabilities to engage in autonomous experiences outside the classroom. In fact, such experiences may serve as the empowering bridge they cross from school to young adult life. Through self-advocacy groups, students have the opportunity to better learn the right to speak out and be heard, to make choices, and for consumer control. In this regard, the close relationship between advocacy, self-determination, and autonomy is evident (e.g., Beckwith, 1993; *Impact*, 1994; Martin, Marshall, & Maxson, 1993; Turner, 1995; Ward, 1993; Wehmeyer & Berkobien, 1991).

When discussing individual and group self-advocacy for high school students with disabilities, Gould (1986) stated, "The opportunity to be trained and act as advocates, alone or in consumer groups, helps to ensure that transition-age youth will actively participate in giving direction to their own lives" (p. 42). In addition to teaching them their human and legal rights, the very process itself would "sensitize" them to their "responsibilities, to their unique problem-solving and decision-taking skills, to their planning skills, to their communication skills, to their own capacity for assertiveness, [and] to their own areas and interests in community involvement" (p. 41).

In summary, students who learn in the least restrictive environment are more likely to have the opportunity to express their autonomy through choice-making, goal-setting, and decision-making experiences. This normalized educational experience provides an extended developmental foundation that is especially conducive to encouraging and promoting autonomous behavior. Not only is it an especially appropriate setting for teaching them self-determination skills, but also one where the students are able to apply those skills repeatedly, and over multiple years, in a supportive learning environment.

Supporting (and Maintaining) Autonomy throughout Adulthood

Self-determined, autonomous behavior is a central ingredient for enhancing the quality of life for persons with disabilities as they transition from school to community, to employment, and to independent living. Most definitely, adulthood is a time of change and spans many decades. As these changes, transitions, and interventions occur, there should be a focus on maintaining personal control of change to facilitate individual independence and autonomy (Szymanski, 1993).

Congress, in recent years, has enacted legislation that ensures people with disabilities the full civil rights of all citizens in terms of their freedoms and liberties at all levels of life, including an inclusive education, inclusive employment, and inclusive community and residential living. The presence (and legal enforcement) of these inclusive and nondiscriminatory environments serve as a permanent foundation that allows and promotes the autonomy of people with disabilities throughout their lives. The ADA (Public Law 101-336) provides an infrastructure for the promotion of autonomy of all people with disabilities in their adult age. It is a comprehensive mandate to guarantee all people with disabilities equal opportunity in employment, public accommodations, transportation, state and local government services, and telecommunications relay services. At the time of the signing, President George Bush (Sr.) said, "Every man, women and child with a disability can now pass through once closed doors into a bright new era of equality, independence and freedom." Later, President Bill Clinton stated: "Together we've begun to shift disability in the USA away from exclusion, towards inclusion; away from dependence, towards independence; away from paternalism, towards empowerment." Clinton's strong comment illustrated the need for change, but implementation of these changes calls for a partnership in service delivery.

The ADA, in addition to its companions, the Rehabilitation Act and the Developmental Disabilities Assistance and Bill of Rights Act (DD Act), serve as a firm and lasting foundation on which autonomy may be promoted and ensured for all people with disabilities. The DD Act places special emphasis on the practice of community integration for people with developmental disabilities through community-based services, case management, supported employment, and systems advocacy, whereas the Rehabilitation Act promotes the full inclusion in employment and independent living for all people with disabilities.

Postschool Environments

Working in real jobs in typical communities is recognized as a significant quality of life indicator. Halpern (1993) reviewed 41 follow-up studies with regard to postschool outcomes of students with disabilities regarding quality of life dimensions. All 41 studies reported findings that highlighted the importance of employment. Choosing to work, and, just as important, choosing the job, task, or location of job, promotes behavioral autonomy, self-determination, and an enhanced quality of life.

Choice has been mandated since the Rehabilitation Act of 1992, which required consumers to be active participants in their own rehabilitation program, including making meaningful, informed choices regarding vocational goals, objectives, and services (Patterson et al., 2000). The foundation of services provided to help the consumer obtain and maintain gainful employment was spelled out in the individualized plan for employment. This plan of service is an opportunity for the counselor and the consumer to work together as partners to develop successful program for employment. Informed consent of all decisions made, along with the opportunity to appeal those decisions, is provided. The services increase autonomy of the person with a disability, or consumer, by stressing joint involvement and responsibility with the rehabilitation counselor throughout the entire process. Care must be taken to ensure that the process of ensuring choice does not become part of the paperwork.

Understanding the importance of choice and work as a part of autonomous functioning is often a challenge for individuals with significant disabilities. The good news is that there now exists convincing evidence that these individuals can achieve increased autonomy through training in the work setting (Wehman, Inge, Revell, & Brooke, 2007).

For persons with more severe developmental disabilities, supported employment has focused attention on the central premise of work-related preferences to identify potential jobs. Matching work to work preferences is one of the primary components of a behavior analytic approach for preventing/reducing challenging behavior that can occur among some workers with significant disabilities. Generally, individuals show less problem behavior when they enjoy the task in which they are engaged (Wehman et al., 2007). Therefore, it can be said when individuals make their own choices, they move closer to an autonomous, self-determined life.

Adult Roles

Central to the literature on adulthood is the finding that life *in* the community is preferred to life *near* the community (Bierne-Smith, Ittenbach, & Patton, 2002). This message is clear for people with disabilities, as well as those without. As people with disabilities become more self-determined and express behavioral autonomy, the shift must continue toward greater independent and supported living arrangements within their chosen communities.

Today's contemporary movement in independent living, a concept born in the mid-1960s, is legislatively based and promotes the philosophy that "people with disabilities have the right to control their own lives and have access to the same options as people without disabilities. This philosophy is based upon the concepts of disability, esteem and personal value, consumer control and self-determination, self-help and peer support, and political activism" (Rice & Thayer, 1990, p. 17). In a paper prepared by the National Council on Disability (2005), it was written that the "goal is for people with disabilities is to *live independently in the community* with others; this does not preclude family living or other communal arrangements. It is about choice, autonomy, and participation, not separation from families" (pp. 4–5; emphasis added).

Life experiences may differ by person and by disability, but there are several consistent stages that all people encounter as they move through life. *Young adulthood* represents a time when goals are pursued, friendships are established and maintained, and career and residence is established, regardless of functioning level. For young adults with disabilities, with limited or restricted social opportunities, special occasions such as birthdays, promotions, and family events take on an even larger significance as they help define adult roles and greatly affect the quality of one's early adult life (Bierne-Smith et al., 2002). If young adults with disabilities are supported in their self-determined, autonomous choice making, risk taking, and independent living, then enhanced living quality will be experienced for many years.

Middle adulthood is loosely determined as the years between 40 and 60. During this period, achievements can be at their maximum for some while others turn toward introspection. Readjusting to life with aging parents is potentially easier for someone who is self-determined and demonstrates behavioral autonomy (making choices and decisions, solving problems, demonstrating independent living skills). The same logic holds true for *older adulthood* for persons with disabilities. Behavioral autonomy, a lifetime of problem solving and decision making, and an internal locus of control can only make it easier to adapt to these years. Creating a new lifestyle pattern is easier for someone who has not been dependent on others to make choices for them (Bierne-Smith et al., 2002).

The final decision to which an individual might exercise self-determination and autonomy is related to end of life. For individuals making this final transition, paternalism by family, caregivers, doctors, and the legal system may override this last autonomous act. This end of life event can be framed within the context of "quality of life" versus "sanctity of life." Another confounding circumstance to maintaining autonomy might involve physicians who have prejudices involving disabilities or by family members who do not want to let go (Asch, 2005).

Advanced directives and informed consent with regard to individuals with disabilities are dependent on definition of capacity to make and communicate choices. For those with mental retardation, Alzheimer's disease, mental illness, and other forms of compromised cognitive ability, choices regarding end of life care can be problematic and complex. Assessment of decision-specific capacity, assisted capacity, and in-context capacity are being developed to give this population greater input (Botsford & King, 2005).

A lack of oversight regarding withdrawal and withholding treatment, as well as the practice of assisted suicide, is a concern for people with disabilities (Werth, 2005). Efforts by disability rights advocates, consumer direction of long-term care, and the demand that will occur as the baby boomers age will dramatically affect populations needing long-term care as they move toward the end of life phase (Batavia, 2002). To this end, the complexity of end of life care for persons with disabilities with regard to autonomy, self-determination, and legal ramifications for those who provide support must be addressed, as these issues are destined to increase in intensity (Botsford & King, 2005).

CONCLUSION

Whether we are talking about the home, the school, or the adult-aged environment, it is evident that individuals with disabilities must have the opportunity to make choices and express preferences. The benefits of autonomy-supportive environments are numerous, ranging from increased motivation, learning, and sense of self-control and worth. It is critical for families, school personnel, and professionals to provide the environment in which individuals with disabilities can act autonomously. It is now imperative that people with disability be provided supportive autonomous environments across their life span.

Through the evolution of disability rights, it is clear to see how time and events have changed the thinking of our society. Moving from institutionalization to participating as active citizens has shown that the issue of autonomy has developed and changed views. People with disabilities have fought for their own rights with their own voices and have made things happen. Although there has been much progress, there continues to be a need for self-determined individuals to constantly make things happen. The greatest challenge perhaps in the development of control over one's life for individuals with disabilities is the idea that professionals must believe that individuals have the ability to function autonomously (Phemister, 2001). Without this belief, what chance do people with disabilities have to control their own destiny?

Fostering autonomy in individuals with disabilities clearly provides a better quality of life for these individuals. Research supports the need for instruction in choice and self-determination, as well as looking into what happens if we do not develop autonomous individuals. Most individuals develop autonomy as they move through their lives. Part of the human development cycle involves moving from dependence on others to self-direction (Wehmeyer & Kelchner, 1995). However, for some people with developmental disabilities, such skills are not just acquired through life and must be explicitly taught.

Perhaps the greatest implication of autonomy is that allowing individuals to be in control of their own lives is the not only a good thing to do, but it is an absolute right of people with disabilities to be given that opportunity.

REFERENCES

Almqvist, L., & Granlund, M. (2005). Participation in school environment of children and youth with disabilities: A person-oriented approach. *Scandinavian Journal of Psychology, 46*, 305–314.

Asch, A. (2005). Recognizing death while affirming life: Can end of life reform uphold a disabled person's interest in continued life? *Hastings Center Report Special Report, 35*(6), 531–536.

Batavia, A. (2002). Consumer direction, consumer choice, and the future of long-term care. *Journal of Disability Policy Studies, 13*(2), 67–73.

Baumrind, D. (1972). The development of instrumental competence through socialization. In A. D. Pick (Ed.), *Minnesota symposia on child psychology, Oxford, UK*. Minneapolis: University of Minnesota Press.

Baumrind, D., & Black, A. E. (1967). Socialization practices associated with dimensions of competence in preschool boys and girls. *Child Development, 38*(2), 291–327.

Beckwith, R. (1993). People First facilitates student self-determination. *Impact, 6*(4), 11.

Bierne-Smith, M., Ittenbach, R., & Patton, J. (2002). *Mental retardation* (5th ed.). Saddle River, NJ: Merrill Prentice Hall.

Biklen, D., & Bogdan, R. (1976). *Handicapism in America*. Syracuse, NY: WIN.

Black, A. E., & Deci, E. L. (2000). The effects of instructors' autonomy support and students' autonomous motivation on learning organic chemistry: A self-determination theory perspective. *Science Education, 84,* 740–756.

Bogdan R. (1986). The sociology of special education. In R. J. Morris & B. Blatt (Eds.), *Special education: Research and trends* (pp. 344–359). New York: Pergamon.

Bondurant-Utz, J. A., & Luciano, L. B. (1994). *A practical guide to infant and preschool assessment in special education.* Boston: Allyn and Bacon.

Botsford, A., & King, A. (2005). End-of-life care policies for people with and intellectual disability. *Journal of Disability Policy Studies, 16*(1), 22–30.

Brazelton, T. B. (1974). *Toddlers and parents: A declaration of independence.* New York: Dell.

Brooke, V., Green, J., Revell, W., & Wehman, P. (2006). Transition planning in the community: Using all of the resources. In P. Wehman (Ed.), *Life beyond the classroom: Transition strategies for young people with disabilities* (4th ed., pp. 115–116). Baltimore: Brookes.

Browning, P. (1997). *Transition in action for youth and young adults with disabilities.* Montgomery, AL: Wells Printing.

Browning, P., & Rhoades, C. (1986). *Self-advocacy for people with developmental disabilities: Teachers resource book and five-part video series.* Santa Monica, CA: Stanfield.

Cardol, M., de Jong, B. A., & Ward, C. (2002). Autonomy and participation in rehabilitation. *Disability and Rehabilitation, 24*(18), 970–974.

Carver, C. S., & Scheier, M. F. (2000). Autonomy and self-regulation. *Psychological Inquiry, 11*(4), 284–291.

Cassidy, J., & Shaver, P. R. (Eds.). (1999). *Handbook of attachment: Theory, research, and clinical applications.* New York: Guilford.

Clapton, J., & Kendall, E. (2002). Autonomy and participation in rehabilitation: Time for a new paradigm? *Disability and Rehabilitation, 24*(18), 987–991.

Clark, E., Olympia, D. E., Jensen, J., Heathfield, L. T., & Jenson, W. R. (2004). Striving for autonomy in a contingency-governed world: Another challenge for individuals with developmental disabilities. *Psychology in the Schools, 4*(1), 143–153.

Commission on Rehabilitation Counselor Certification. (2002). Code of professional ethics for rehabilitation counselors. Retrieved February 15, 2009, from http://www.crccertification.com/pages/code_of_ethics/10.php.

Cook, R. E., Klein, D., & Tessier, A. (2004). *Adapting early childhood curricula for children in inclusive settings.* Columbus, OH: Pearson/Merrill, Prentice Hall.

Connell, J. P. (1990). *Self in transition. Infancy to childhood.* Chicago: University of Chicago Press.

Craig, E. (Ed.). (2005). *The shorter Routledge encyclopedia of philosophy.* London: Routledge.

Crittenden, P. M. (1990). Toward a concept of autonomy in adolescents with a disability. *Children's Health Care, 19*(3), 162–168.

Deci, E. L. (1980). *The psychology of self-determination.* Lexington, MA: Heath.

Deci, E. L., & Chandler, C. L. (1986). The importance of motivation for the future of LD field. *Journal of Learning Disabilities, 19*(10), 587–594.

Deci, E. L., & Ryan, R.M. (1985). *Intrinsic motivation and self-determination in human behavior.* New York: Plenum.

Deci, E. L., & Ryan, R. M. (1987). The support of autonomy and the control of behavior. *Journal of Personality and Social Psychology, 53,* 1024–1037.

Degener, T. (2000). International disability law—a new legal subject on the rise: The interregional experts' meeting in Hong Kong, December 13–17, 1999. *International Law, 18*(1), 180–195.

DeJong, G. (1979). Independent living: From social movement to analytic paradigm. *Archives of Physical Medicine and Rehabilitation, 60*(10), 435–436.

Ensminger, E. E., & Dangel, H. L. (1992). The Foxfire approach: A confluence of best practices for special education. *Focus on Exceptional Children, 24*(7).

Erikson, E. (1963). *Childhood and society.* New York: Norton.

Field, S. & Hoffman A. (1996). *Steps to self-determination.* Austin, TX: ProEd.

Field, S., & Hoffman, A. (1999). The importance of family involvement for promoting self- determination in adolescents with autism and other developmental disabilities. *Focus on Autism and Other Developmental Disabilities, 14*(1), 36–41.

Field, S., Martin, R., Miller, R., Ward, M., & Wehmeyer, M. (1998). Self-determination for persons with disabilities: A position statement of the division on career development and transition. *Career Development for Exceptional Individuals, 21*(2), 113–128.

Gould, M. (1986). Self-advocacy: Consumer leadership for the transition years. *Journal of Rehabilitation, 52*(4), 39–42.

Guess, D., Benson, H., & Siegel-Causey, E. (1985). Concepts and issues related to choice-making and autonomy among persons with severe disabilities. *Journal of the Association for the Severely Handicapped, 10,* 79–86.

Hahn, H. (1991). Alternative views of empowerment: Social services and civil rights. *Journal of Rehabilitation, 57*(4), 17–19.

Halloran, W. D. (1993). Transition services requirement: Issues, implications, challenge. In R. C. Eaves & P. J. McLaughlin (Eds.), *Recent advances in special education and rehabilitation* (pp. 210–224). Boston: Andover Medical.

Halpern, A. S. (1993). Quality of life as a conceptual framework for evaluating transition outcomes. *Exceptional Children, 59,* 486–498.

Impact. (1994). Special feature on self-advocacy. *Impact, 7.*

Kendall, E., Muenchberger, H., & Clapton, J. (2007). Trends in Australian rehabilitation: Revising its humanitarian core. *Disability and Rehabilitation, 29*(10), 817–823.

Logan, C. R., DiCintio, M. J., Cox, K. E., & Turner, J. C. (1995, October). *Teacher and student perceptions of classroom practice.* Paper presented at the annual meeting of the Northeastern Educational Research Association, Ellenville, NY.

Lundberg, N. R. (2007). Research update: Creating motivational climates. *Parks & Recreation, 42*(1), 22–26.

Martin, E. D. Jr. (2001). *Significant disability: Issues affecting people with disabilities from a historical, policy, leadership and systems perspective.* Springfield, IL: Thomas.

Martin, J. E., & Marshall, L. H. (1995). Choicemaker: A comprehensive self-determination transition program. *Intervention in School and Clinic, 30,* 147–156.

Martin, J. E., Marshall, L. H., & Maxson, L. (1993). Transition policy: Infusing self-determination and self-advocacy into transition programs. *Career Development and Exceptional Individuals, 16,* 53–61.

Martin, J. E., Marshall, L. H., Maxson, L., & Jermann, P. (1997). *ChoiceMaker and Self-Determination Series.* Longmont, CO: Sopris West Educational Services.

Martin, J., Woods, L., Sylvester, L., & Gardner, J. (2005). A challenge to self-determination: Disagreement between the vocational choices made by individuals with severe disabilities and their caregivers. *Research & Practice for Persons with Severe Disabilities, 30* (3), 147–153.

Meininger, H. P. (2001). Autonomy and professional responsibility in care for persons with intellectual disabilities. *Nursing Philosophy, 2,* 240–250.

National Council on Disability. (2005). *Living independently and in the community: Implementing lessons from the United States.* Washington DC: Author.

Nirje, B. (1972). The right to self-determination. In W. Wolfensberger (Ed.), *Normalization: The principle of normalization in human services* (pp. 176–200). Toronto: National Institute on Mental Retardation.

Parent, W. S. (1993). Quality of life and consumer choice. In P. Wehman (Ed.), *The ADA mandate for social change* (pp. 19–44). Baltimore: Brookes.

Patterson, J. B., Patrick, A., & Parker, R. M. (2000, Summer). Choice: Ethical and legal rehabilitation challenges. *Rehabilitation Counseling Bulletin, 43*(4), 203–208. Retrieved March 7, 2007 from www.worksupport.com/documents/proed9.html.htm.

Perske, R. (1972). The dignity of risk. In W. Wolfensberger (Ed.), *Normalization: The principle of normalization in human services* (pp. 194–200). Toronto: National Institute on Mental Retardation.

Pfeiffer, D. (2002) The philosophical foundations of disability studies. *Disabilities Studies Quarterly, 22*(2), 3–23.

Phemister, A. A. (2001). Revisiting the principles of free will and determinism: Exploring conceptions of disability and counseling theory. *Journal of Rehabilitation, 67*(3), 8–12.

Rasch, J. (1996) World wide web review guide for the CRC examination: principles of ethical practice. Retrieved April 5, 2007, from luna.cas.usf.edu/~rasch/ethics.html.

Rhoades, C. M. (1986). Self-advocacy. In J. Wortis (Eds.), *Mental retardation and developmental disabilities* (vol. 14, pp. 312–319). New York: Elsevier.

Rice, B. D., & Thayer, T. (Eds.). (1990). *Vocational rehabilitation services in independent living centers.* 17th Institute on Rehabilitation Issues. Fayetteville, AR: Research and Training Center in Vocational Rehabilitation, University of Arkansas.

Seigleman, M. (1975). *Helplessness.* San Francisco: Freeman.

Serna, L., & Lau-Smith, J. (1995). Learning with purpose: Self-determination skills for students who are at risk for school and community failure. *Intervention in School and Clinic, 30*, 142–146.

Shevin, M., & Klein, N. K. (2004). The importance of choice-making skills for students with severe disabilities. *Research and Practice for Persons with Severe Disabilities, 29*(3), 161–168.

Shogren, K. A., & Turnbull, A. P. (2006). Promoting self-determination in young children with disabilities: The critical role of families. *Infants & Young Children, 19*(4), 338–352.

Stefanou, C. R., Perencevich, K. C., DiCintio, M., & Turner, J. C. (2004). Supporting autonomy in the classroom: Ways teachers encourage student decision making and ownership. *Educational Psychologist, 39*(2), 97–110.

Szymanski, E. M. (1993). Transition: Life span and life space considerations. *Exceptional Children, 60*, 402–410.

Thoma, C. A., & Sax, C. L. (2003). Self-determination: What do rehabilitation counseling students know and where do they learn it? *Journal of Vocational Rehabilitation, 19*, 89–94.

Turnbull, A. P., & Turnbull, R. (2006). Self-determination: Is a rose by any other name still a rose? *Research & Practices for Persons with Severe Disabilities, 31*(1), 83–88.

Turner, E. (1995). Self-advocacy: A key to self-determination. *Journal of Vocational Rehabilitation, 5*, 329–336.

Turner, P. H. (2000). The development nature of parent-child relationships: The impact of disabilities. In E. D. Fine & R. L. Simpson (Eds.), *Collaboration with parents and families of children and youth with exceptionalities* (pp. 103–130). Austin, TX: Pro Ed.

Vehmas, S. (2004). Ethical analysis of the concept of disability. *American Association on Mental Retardation, 42*(3), 209–222.

Wall, M. E., & Dattilo, J. (1995). Creating option-rich learning environments: Facilitating self-determination. *Journal of Special Education, 29*(3), 276–294.

Ward, M. J. (1992). OSERS initiative on self-determination. *Interchange, 12*(1), 1–7. Champaign: Transition Institute, University of Illinois at Urbana-Champaign.

Ward, M. J. (1993). Self-determination: A means to an end. *Impact, 6*(4), 8.

Waters, E., Wippman, J., & Stroufe, L. (1979). Attachment, positive affect, and competence in the peer group; two studies in construct validation. *Child Development, 50*(3), 821–829.

Wehman, P. (2006). *Life beyond the classroom: Transition strategies for young people with disabilities* (4th ed.). Baltimore: Brookes.

Wehman, P., Inge, K., Revell, W., & Brooke, V. (2007). *Real work for real pay: Inclusive employment for people with disabilities.* Baltimore: Brookes.

Wehmeyer, M. L. (1992). Self-determination and the education of students with mental retardation. *Education and Training in Mental Retardation, 27*, 302–314.

Wehmeyer, M. L. (2004) Beyond self-determination: Causal agency theory. *Journal of Developmental and Physical Disabilities, 16*(4), 337–359.

Wehmeyer, M., Agran, M., & Hughes, C. (1998). *Teaching self-determination to students with disabilities.* Baltimore, MD: Brookes.

Wehmeyer, M. L., & Berkobien, R. (1991). Self-determination and self-advocacy. A case of mistaken identify. *Newsletter of the Association for Persons with Severe Handicaps, 17*(7), 11.

Wehmeyer, M. L., & Garner, N. W. (2003). The impact of personal characteristics of people with intellectual and developmental disability on self-determination and autonomous functioning. *Journal of Applied Research in Intellectual Disabilities, 16*(4), 255–265.

Wehmeyer, M. L., & Kelchner, K. (1995). *Whose future is it anyway?* Arlington, TX: ARC.

Werth, J. L. (2005). Concerns about decisions related to withholding/withdrawing life-sustaining treatment and futility for persons with disabilities. *Journal of Disability Policy Studies, 16*(1), 31–37.

West, M. D. (1995). Choice, self-determination and VR services: Systemic barriers for consumers with severe disabilities. *Journal of Vocational Rehabilitation, 5*, 281–290.

Whaley, K. T., & Bennett, T. C. (1991). Promoting engagement in early childhood special education. *Teaching Exceptional Children, 23*(4), 51–54.

Wolfensburger, W. (1972). *The principle of normalization in human services.* Canada: National Institute on Mental Retardation.

Zhang, D. (2005). Parent practices in facilitating self-determination skills: The influences of culture, socioeconomic status, and children's special education status. *Research and Practice for Persons with Severe Disabilities, 30*(3), 154–162.

CHAPTER 3

Children Who Care for Their Parents: The Impact of Parental Disability on Young Lives

Kenneth I. Pakenham

This chapter addresses an emerging global social priority: the potential adverse impacts on children and adolescents of caring for a family member with a disability. Unpaid caregiving represents an important economic resource and carers a vital labor force. For example, in the United States in 2004, family carers contributed an estimated $306 billion of unpaid caregiving (Becker, 2007). There are no such estimates in any country of the hidden economic or social costs of children's unpaid caregiving. However, the research to date does suggest that many young carers suffer in ways that compromise their well-being. This chapter provides an overview of research, theory, and practice regarding children and adolescents caring for a parent who has a physical or mental disability and/or illness.

DEFINITION

Researchers, policy developers, and service providers have used a wide variety of operational definitions of young carers. Young carers have been defined in accordance with the level, intensity, and type of duties they assume and the associated restrictions they encumber as a result. For example, Becker (2007) argued that the term should be used precisely and deliberately and provided the following definition:

> Children and young persons under 18 who provide or intend to provide care, assistance or support to another family member. They carry out, often on a regular basis, significant or substantial caring tasks and assume a level of responsibility that would usually be associated with an adult. (p. 378)

In this definition the terms *regular*, *significant*, and *substantial* are not operationalized and what constitutes caring tasks and adult levels of responsibility is not defined. Becker (2007) suggested a continuum of young caregiving with the caregiving at one end being typical of what most children contribute in family life and at the other end characterized by more substantial and regular caregiving. However, it is not clear at what point on this continuum caregiving warrants the designated label of "young carer."

In contrast to this position, others have defined young carers more broadly and argued that restrictive definitions limit the exploration of young people in different caregiving situations and risk excluding those who may be providing care and who may benefit from services (Newman, 2002). In support of this approach, some studies have not required potential participants to self-identify as carers and have not imposed definitions on what constitutes a young carer. For example, one such study found that Australian children of a parent with a disability/illness reported significantly greater adverse caregiving impacts and poorer adjustment than children of healthy parents regardless of level of caregiving (Pakenham, Bursnall, Chiu, Cannon, & Okochi, 2006). In another study, Siskowski (2006) surveyed 12,681 students in grades 6 to 12 in Florida and did not require participants to self-identify as carers. She found that students with a family health situation[1] (6,714) outnumbered those without a family health situation by 20 percent. Most (92 percent) of the students with a family health situation indicated that they engaged in caregiving, and almost a quarter of those with a family health situation indicated that it adversely affected their learning. Hence, given the very large number of children exposed to family health situations who report involvement in caregiving and corresponding adverse educational impacts, it is important not to have a definition of young carers that is too restrictive.

Although young people may care for any family member or friend with a disability/illness, the majority of care recipients are parents, particularly mothers (Dearden & Becker, 2004; Gays, 2002). In a national UK survey of known young carers, Dearden and Becker (2004) found half of all conditions requiring care were of a physical health nature, 29 percent were mental health concerns, 17 percent were learning difficulties, and 3 percent were sensory impairments. Therefore, the majority of young carers are caring for parents with either a physical or mental disability/illness.

Research has typically focused on young carers aged from 5 to 18 years with the average age of young carers being approximately 12 or 13 (Carers Australia, 2002). However, there is a growing interest in the 18- to 25-year-old group of young adult carers. Levine and colleagues (2005) argued that this group is particularly important because they are at a critical developmental stage. For many of them, life plans are not solidified, education will extend into their twenties, and marriage and child-rearing is likely to occur later.

KEY RESEARCH TRADITIONS IN THE YOUNG CARER FIELD

There are three key bodies of research that are relevant to young caregiving. First, one body of research has examined the impact of a specific parental disability/illness (e.g., Compas, Worsham, Ey, & Howell, 1996) without taking into account the caregiving roles of these youngsters (e.g., Fals-Stewart, Kelley, Fincham, Golden, & Logsdon, 2004). Reviews of research in this field have suggested that parental disability/illness is associated with moderate psychological distress and maladjustment in children (Armistead, Klein, & Forehand, 1995; Pedersen & Revenson, 2005; Worsham, Compas, & Sydney, 1997). There is also evidence from this body of research indicating that parental disability/illness disrupts family roles and functioning, and those children who take on more of the family's responsibilities are more likely to experience higher psychological distress (Grant & Compas, 1995). However, in what Aldridge and Becker (1993b) have termed a "literature of omission," the research has tended to ignore young people's caregiving responsibilities.

A second body of research has specifically examined young caregiving and is largely rooted in the medical sociology literature. Most studies in this area are anecdotal, descriptive, and rely on focus group and/or interview data (Aldridge & Becker, 1994; Becker, 1995; Dearden & Becker, 2000). Within this body of research, there are many qualitative studies that have given important insights into young carers' experiences and the outcomes for these children (e.g., Bolas, Van Wersch, & Flynn, 2007). There are also a number of large-scale surveys that have provided extensive descriptive biographical data on young carers (Dearden & Becker, 1995, 1998, 2004; Siskowski, 2006). However, many of these studies have failed to include appropriate comparison groups and have been conducted in the United Kingdom by Becker and colleagues with samples that have been recruited from young carer support services (Dearden & Becker, 1995, 1998, 2004).

A third body of research has approached young caregiving from a disability rights perspective. According to these researchers, young caregiving is not exclusively the result of disability/illness in families but occurs fundamentally due to a lack of support for families who live in these circumstances (Blackford, 1999; Olsen, 1996). When family members with chronic health problems are inadequately supported, children will often stand in as a natural response to family need (Gopfert, Webster, & Seemen, 2004).

PREVALENCE OF YOUNG CARERS

It is estimated that there are 8.4 million parents with disabilities in the United States with children under 18 years living at home, and there are more mothers than fathers with disabilities (McNeil, 1993). The combined prevalence of serious physical or mental illness in parents of children between the ages of 4 and 18 years in a population-based study in Germany was 6.4 percent (Barkmann, Romer, Watson, & Schulte-Markwort, 2007). Taking a global perspective on young carers, Becker (2007) reviewed the research evidence from the United Kingdom, Australia, and the United States and from developing countries in Sub-Saharan Africa. Becker (2007) claimed that in every group of 100 children in the three developed countries, up to 4 will be young carers, whereas in developing countries, especially those with extensive health problems (e.g., HIV/AIDS), there are likely to be many more. Becker

(2007) showed that 2 percent to 4 percent of all children in Australia, the United Kingdom, and the United States can be referred to as young carers. Estimates of the number of young carers increase if 18- to 25-year-olds are included. For example, in Australia there are 169,900 young carers under the age of 18 (3.6 percent of all children under 18; Australian Bureau of Statistics [ABS], 2003). This figure rises to 347,700 carers under the age of 25, or 5.2 percent of all people in this age group (ABS, 2003). There are approximately 229,309 young carers in the 18- to 25-year range in the United Kingdom (Office for National Statistics, 2003) and up to 5.5 million in the United States (Levine et al., 2005).

However, in all these countries, these figures are likely to be underestimates because of the hidden nature of young caregiving and the tendency for young people not to self-identify as carers. Furthermore, the incidence of young caregiving is expected to rise over the next decades in many parts of the world due to advances in medical technology, increases in the number of sole-parent households, a growing population of elderly persons, and increases in the number of people living with chronic illnesses and disability (Aldridge & Becker, 1993b; Shifren & Kachorek, 2003).

PARENTING WITH A DISABILITY

Young caregiving needs to be understood in the context of the difficulties of parenting with disability/illness. Many parents with disability face harsh socioeconomic circumstances (Olkin, Abrams, Preston, & Kirshbaum, 2006) with particular needs related to employment, recreation, and transportation.

There are also numerous difficulties associated with parenting that may stem from the disability/illness. Parenting can be disrupted by illness exacerbations or fluctuations in disability (e.g., relapses in multiple sclerosis [MS]), cognitive impairment, fatigue, and mobility problems. These in turn may produce other parenting-related difficulties, including lack of family compatible activities, changes in family roles (e.g., reassignment of parental tasks), and separation from children due to hospitalizations (Deatrick, Brennan, & Cameron, 1998). Hence, it is understandable that many parents with disability/illness are concerned about the impact of their condition on their children and report difficulties associated with parenting (De Judicibus & McCabe, 2004).

Research into parents with disabilities and their children has been criticized for perpetuating a view of parents with disability as incapable and their children as victims (Blackford, 1999; Kirshbaum & Olkin, 2002). An alternative view proposed by the disability rights perspective is that with relevant resources and supports, parental disability in and of itself need not present a significant risk factor. Indeed, parents with disability have been shown to develop parenting practices that help overcome some of the challenges they face (Olsen & Clarke, 2003; Prilleltensky, 2004). Stressors such as financial difficulties and lack of formal supports can compound difficulties related to parental disability. Impairment in parenting capacity is likely to vary considerably and may occur only in extreme cases where disability/illness directly impairs the functioning necessary for parenting.

In dual-parent households, the parenting of the healthy parent should also be considered given that they often take on additional parenting responsibilities (Steck, Amsler, Kappos, & Burgin, 2001). However, most research into parenting and disability has considered the parent with disability, and in most cases only mothers who have disability, whereas fathers with disability are often excluded.

THE NATURE OF YOUNG CAREGIVING

Many parents who live with chronic disability/illness rely on their children for immediate, flexible, and continuous care and support. However, informal caregiving activities are often hidden, immersed in the privacy of family interrelations and fueled by care, attachment, duty, and reciprocity. At one end of the caregiving continuum is the level of caring that all children are involved in to some extent throughout their childhood. Some degree of caring and family responsibility in childhood would be viewed as a reciprocal part of family life and as necessary for healthy development. Thus, children who do not have a parent with a disability/illness may also take on responsibilities at home, which is normal and desirable. At the other end of the caregiving continuum is a small group of children who take on substantial, regular, or significant caregiving roles. There is evidence to indicate that many children who undertake levels of caregiving at this end of the continuum of caregiving are more likely to experience a range of negative impacts. Research shows that most youth who have a parent with a disability/illness are likely to undertake a range of tasks, including domestic care (e.g., cooking, cleaning), general care (e.g., managing finances, dispensing medication), emotional support (e.g., comforting the parent), personal and intimate care (e.g., toileting, showering), and child care (e.g., feeding and supervising siblings) (Dearden & Becker, 1995; Ireland & Pakenham, in press).

There is evidence that even children at the low end or middle of the caregiving continuum may be at risk of adverse outcomes (Pakenham et al., 2006). However, few studies have actually examined whether children of a parent with disability/illness take on greater caregiving responsibilities than children of healthy parents.[2] Pakenham and colleagues compared a mixed sample of 100 youth with a parent who has disability/illness to 145 youngsters who had healthy parents. Results showed that the youths with a parent with disability/illness undertook significantly greater levels of family tasks and responsibilities than those with a healthy parent. This finding was replicated when a subsample of 41 children of parents with MS were compared to the 145 children of healthy parents (Pakenham & Bursnall, 2006). Warren (2007) compared 378 children from the general population who were not living with a parent who had a disability/illness with 12 youths who were identified as young carers by agencies or professionals. Warren reported that compared to other children, the young carers performed a wider range of domestic, emotional, general, nursing care, and intimate care tasks, and they spent longer on these activities. Of all the care tasks undertaken, the provision of personal and intimate care most clearly distinguished young carers from the comparison group. Young carers were more likely to regularly carry out a wide range of personal care tasks, including providing health care (e.g., giving medications and injections), assisting with mobility (e.g., get in and out of bed), dressing and undressing, showering, bathing, and toileting. Ireland and Pakenham (in press) found that young carers with a parent with physical disability/illness were more likely to perform personal and intimate care tasks than those who had a parent with mental disability/illness.

These findings stand in contrast to those obtained by Olkin et al. (2006), who used a survey to compare 246 adolescents of parents with disability to 37 adolescents of parents without disability. Data were also obtained from the parents of the adolescents in each group. The authors found no differences in the number of household chores reported by the adolescents or their parents across the two groups. The differences in findings between Olkin's study and the other two studies may be due to several differences in measurement and sampling. For instance, Olkin et al. limited their sample to parents with disabilities rather than illnesses (75 percent physical or systemic disabilities; 25 percent sensory disabilities). They also used a narrow age range for their children, and used both parent and child data, which might have influenced the reporting of the young carers.

Despite some inconsistencies in the literature, Becker (2007) claimed there is now sufficient evidence to show that young carers do differ from other children in both developed and developing countries. These differences include the extent of their caregiving, its nature, the time spent on caregiving, and the adverse outcomes in social, economic, and developmental areas. However, there is a lack of reliable quantitative data indicating what aspects of caregiving are linked with poorer outcomes for young carers at various ages. For example, Pakenham et al. (2005) found that psychosocial and emotional care tasks (e.g., managing inappropriate behaviors, keeping care recipient occupied) were stronger predictors of distress in a mixed sample of adult carers than activities of daily living (e.g., dressing, bathing) or instrumental care tasks (e.g., transportation, housework). It is possible that similar differences might occur for young carers.

FACTORS THAT PULL AND PUSH CHILDREN INTO YOUNG CAREGIVING

The availability, willingness, and effectiveness of children as carers has been proposed as one reason that children perform these roles (Aldridge, 2006). Additionally, children may adopt caregiving roles as task-oriented ways of coping with worry and stress (Gopfert et al., 2004). Stetz, Lewis, and Primomo (1986) found that role distribution was the most common coping mechanism used by families that experience parental disability/illness. Importantly, when a loved one suffers from a health concern, children and young people reported that they wanted to provide support (Banks et al., 2002) and that doing so was a valued part of their family life (Thomas et al., 2003).

Nevertheless, many young people perceive having little or no choice in taking on the caregiving role. Pakenham et al. (2006) found that approximately one third of children of a parent with disability/illness indicated no choice or little choice, just over a third indicated quite a lot of choice, and one third indicated they were free to choose whether or not they helped their parent. This lack of choice by some may be due to financial difficulties that restrict the family from receiving outside help or election of the child into the caregiving role by other family members (Aldridge & Becker, 1993b). Indeed, a number of social issues like poverty, deinstitutionalization, the aging population, increases in sole-parent households, and the inflexibility of formal support services, and the lack of adequate supports have been highlighted as key factors in limiting children's choice about their engagement in caregiving (Aldridge, 2006; Becker, 2007; Shifren & Kachorek, 2003). The interaction between the lack of support services and financial resources often means that young carers are drawn into caring simply because there is no alternative. Less choice in taking on the caregiving role has been shown to be related to more caregiving responsibilities, greater obligation to care, and more caregiving discomfort (Pakenham et al., 2006).

A child's involvement in caregiving may also be influenced by the nature of the parental disability/illness. For example, greater parental impairment, more than one parental disability/illness, parental mental illness (versus physical illness/disability), and greater unpredictability of parental disability/illness have been shown to be related to adverse caregiving experiences (Pakenham et al., 2006). A range of other factors that may also be related to taking on the caregiving role include co-residency, family structure, gender, and socialization. It is likely that several of these factors interact to pull and push children into caregiving. Further research is required to provide greater understanding of the relative strength of these factors and how they might interact to shape the young caregiving role.

THE EXPERIENCE OF YOUNG CAREGIVING

Descriptive studies in the young carer field have identified numerous themes associated with young caregiving, including the adult roles assumed by young carers; the restrictions on leisure, social, and schooling activities; the impact on the family environment; relentless and inescapable caregiving; isolation; perceived maturity; and distress (Aldridge & Becker, 1993a; Bolas et al., 2007). Pakenham and colleagues (2006) undertook quantitative research that explored these themes. Based on qualitative data and a literature review, these researchers developed a questionnaire called the Young Carer of Parents Inventory (YCOPI). Analyses performed on the YCOPI revealed eight reliable and valid factors that described the diverse experiences of young carers. Overall, the YCOPI factors were representative of the range of young caregiving themes reported in prior research. The eight factors comprising the YCOPI are summarized in Table 3.1. This table provides a summary description of the young caregiving theme reflected by each factor.

The range of YCOPI factors points to the complex nature of young caregiving. Prior research has provided important but largely qualitative data on the experience of young caregiving. The YCOPI "unpacks" this often dense and variable descriptive qualitative data, charts the key components of the

Table 3.1 Young Carer of Parents Inventory (YCOPI) Factors and Themes

YCOPI Factor Label	Theme
Caregiving responsibilities	Reflects the family tasks that young carers may assume and their feeling responsible for performing them due to expectations.
Perceived maturity	Reflects the "adult child" theme and how taking on adult roles within the family can foster a sense of independence and personal growth.
Worry about parents	Reflects worry and hypervigilance about the parent's safety and health, and monitoring of their parent for signs of health changes.
Activity restrictions	Reflects the interference of the caregiving role in many areas (e.g., school, employment, leisure, and socializing).
Isolation	Reflects the "hidden" nature of young caregiving, feelings of aloneness and difficulties in sharing caregiving experiences with others.
Caregiving compulsion	Reflects relentless and inescapable caregiving, how young carers feel compelled to care for their parent and the associated guilt when they engage in noncaregiving activities.
Caregiving discomfort	Reflects the distress and stigma associated with caregiving.
Caregiving confidence	Reflects the positive outcomes of young caregiving; the enhanced self-efficacy through the development of new skills and knowledge.

young caregiving experience, and enables these experiences to be quantified for research purposes.

THE IMPACTS OF YOUNG CAREGIVING AND PARENTAL DISABILITY/ILLNESS

Children pass through many distinct developmental stages, each with a characteristic set of biological, psychological, and social demands and issues. For example, psychological development in adolescence involves tasks such as achieving independence from parents, adopting peer codes and lifestyles, and assigning increased importance to body image (Lerner, 2002). Parental disability/illness and young caregiving can impact on the child's behavioral, emotional, social, educational, and physical development. In general, the research has tended to focus on the negative impacts of parental disability/illness on children (Olkin et al., 2006; Olsen, 1996). Most young carer research has focused on emotional distress as the key indicator of adjustment. More recent research has assessed young carer adjustment in both positive and negative domains. The dimensions of the YCOPI reflect the mix of negative (e.g., caregiving discomfort and caregiving compulsion) and positive (e.g., caregiving confidence and perceived maturity) impacts of young caregiving.

Negative Impacts

Evidence to date has suggested that young caregiving can have an adverse impact on children, which can affect their development and transition to adulthood (Dearden & Becker, 2000). Indeed, there is evidence that for some people the adverse impacts of young caregiving persist well into adulthood (Levine et al., 2005). The negative effects of young caregiving have been reported in numerous areas: psychological, physical, social, family, education, and leisure (Dearden & Becker, 2004).

Overall, reviews of studies that have examined the association between parental disability/illness and the adjustment outcomes of children without examining the role of young caregiving have concluded that parental disability/illness is associated with elevated anxiety and depression and low self-esteem (Armistead et al., 1995; Grabiak, Bender, & Puskar, in press; Pedersen & Revenson, 2005; Worsham et al., 1997). Barkmann et al. (2007) found that children aged 4 to 18 years of parents with serious physical illness were at higher risk for internalizing problems (depression, anxiety, and somatic complaints) than externalizing problems (attention problems and delinquent behavior). Several studies have shown that children of parents with mental disability/illness are at greater risk for adverse adjustment outcomes compared to children of parents with physical disability/illness (Anderson & Hammen, 1993; Barkmann et al., 2007; Roy, 1990).

There are fewer quantitative studies that have examined the negative impact of young caregiving. Several studies have compared young carers to children of healthy parents. Banks et al. (2002) found that young carers reported higher levels of depression and lower self-esteem than children of healthy parents. Pakenham et al. (2006) found that compared to children of healthy parents, young carers reported more adverse caregiving experiences and higher levels of somatic complaints. Young carers may also experience physical health problems related to their caregiving. In particular, young carers are at risk of injuries associated with limited sleep, carrying, lifting, and other physical demands (Carers Australia, 2002).

Regarding social and economic outcomes, young carers compared to other children are more likely to have restricted opportunities for social, recreation, and extra-education participation and be more concerned about their future financial security (Warren, 2007). Siskowski (2006) found that 67 percent of young carers reported their participation in caregiving activities had an effect on their academic performance at school. She also found that students who were black and those who were male were more likely to report adverse impacts on education from either living at home with someone needing special medical care or actively participating in caregiving activities.

Qualitative studies have indicated that young carers experience stigma related to their caregiving role and by association with a family member's disability (Bolas et al., 2007; Gullekson, 1992). This has been described by Goffman (1963) as "courtesy stigma," which occurs when a portion of the stigma experienced by the person with disability is shared with family members by virtue of their proximity. There is some evidence indicating that young carers engage in stigma concealment (Bolas et al., 2007), which is likely to lead to secrecy and withdrawal. Indeed, stigma may play an important role in the isolation and restricted peer relations often reported by young carers and may interfere with important developmental processes that are sustained by peer relations, such as autonomy and individuation beyond the family unit (Bolas et al., 2007).

In ongoing research, Pakenham and colleagues examined stigma in 41 children aged 10 to 20 years (average age 13.6) who had a parent with MS. Results showed that children who perceived stigma related to their parent's disability were more likely to report behavioral difficulties, less prosocial child behavior, and less secure attachment to the parent with MS. The level of stigma perceived by the child was associated with the severity of the parental disability. Stigma appears to be an important aspect of young caregiving with potential detrimental impacts on the child's behavior, socializing, and quality of the relationship with the parent. However, few studies have explored stigma in young carers.

Positive Impacts

Research has been criticized for focusing on psychopathology and the negative impacts of caregiving on children of a parent with disability. However, anecdotal reports (Blackford, 1999) and qualitative data (Bolas et al., 2007) have indicated positive outcomes of caregiving, including perceived maturity and a sense of pride and personal accomplishment about their role as carer. Hence, in recent years there has been a growing interest in the positive outcomes and resilience of young carers. Caring has been conceptualized as both a risk factor and a form of resilient behavior (Evans, 2005; McConnell Gladstone, Boydell, & McKeever, 2006). A resilience approach shifts the focus from vulnerability to understanding the protective factors that help individuals cope in situations of adversity and emphasizes the active role taken by engaging with such factors.

Pakenham and colleagues (2006) found that compared to children of healthy parents, young carers reported higher perceived maturity. Olkin et al. (2006) found that in comparison to parents without disabilities, parents with disabilities reported that their teenage children were more comfortable around people with disabilities. However, in both groups parents did not differ on their reports of other positive characteristics (e.g., empathy, independence, problem-solving abilities, and resilience) attributed to their adolescent children.

Recent research has investigated the benefits of adult caregiving (McCausland & Pakenham, 2003; Pakenham, 2005), and benefit finding has been found to be associated with positive adjustment outcomes (e.g., positive affect and life satisfaction) in both cross-sectional (Pakenham, 2005) and longitudinal studies (Pakenham & Cox, in press). Although qualitative studies have shown that young carers report benefits from their caregiving roles (Beach, 1997), few published quantitative studies have examined benefit finding in young caregiving. One exception is a series of studies by Pakenham and colleagues. These researchers developed an 18-item Benefit Finding Scale (BFS) that was derived from adult carer benefit finding data (Pakenham, 2005). Items that reflected the following benefit-finding themes included insights into illness and hardship, caregiving gains, personal growth, strengthening of relationships, appreciation of life, health gains, spiritual growth, and positive changes in personal goals (Pakenham, Chiu, Bursnall, & Cannon, 2007). Higher benefit finding was related to higher positive affect but was unrelated to life satisfaction and distress. Benefit finding was also related to greater reliance on acceptance, problem solving, and seeking social support coping strategies and less reliance on denial coping. Interestingly, benefit finding was unrelated to age, indicating that children as young as 10 years are able to find benefits associated with caregiving.

Predictors of Outcomes

There is marked variation in the outcomes for young carers, which has led researchers to consider factors that might predict young carer adjustment. Such variations may be due to a range of factors that define the caregiving context, including (a) characteristics of the parent and his or her condition (e.g., type of illness/disability, level of parental impairment, predictability of the parent's illness/disability), (b) characteristics of the young carer (e.g., gender, age), (c) characteristics of the caregiving role (e.g., choice in caregiving, type of care tasks, caregiving duration), (d) characteristics of the parent–child relationship (e.g., frequency of contact with the parent, co-residence), (e) characteristics of the family (e.g., single parent, number of children, extended family), and (f) social factors (e.g., access to services). To date, many of these factors have not been systematically examined as potential predictors of young carer adjustment. However, there is evidence to suggest that poorer young carer adjustment outcomes are related to (a) excessive or long-term caregiving, (b) little or no perceived choice in caregiving, (c) inadequate (informal and formal) supports, (d) higher levels of parental disability or impairment, and (e) presence of parental mental illness. The relative strength of these factors and the interplay among them in predicting young carer adjustment outcomes over time have not been systematically investigated. There are also a range of theoretical constructs that may predict young carer outcomes. Theoretical frameworks that have been used to guide the identification of variables that might predict young carer adjustment are summarized next. However, it should be noted that there is a dearth of theory driven research into young carers.

THEORETICAL FRAMEWORKS FOR UNDERSTANDING YOUNG CARERS

Contextual Process Models

Stress and Coping

Much of the research that has examined the role of coping in adaptation to adult caregiving has been guided by Lazarus and Folkman's (1984) stress and coping theory. Although various stress process models of caregiving have been derived from this theory, most are based on the premise that adjustment to caregiving is determined by the caregiving context and three mediational processes: appraisal, coping strategies, and coping resources. Although there is support for the application of the model to adult caregiving (Goode, Haley, Roth, & Ford, 1998; Pakenham, 2001), only one published study has used it to guide research into young caregiving (Pakenham et al., 2007). Nevertheless, several studies have used the model to explain the process of adaptation to stress associated with having a parent with an illness/disability (e.g., Langrock, Compas, Keller, Merchant, & Copeland, 2002).

Consistent with most stress and coping models of caregiving, appraisal, coping strategies, and coping resources are the key determinants of adjustment to young caregiving. *Appraisal* is an evaluative process that reflects the person's subjective interpretation of the event. The appraisal of an event as stressful will generate stress, which may exceed the coping skills and resources available to the person. *Coping resources* are relatively stable characteristics of an individual's environment (e.g., social support) and disposition (e.g., optimism), and refer to what is available when an individual evaluates a situation and develops his or her coping strategies. Lazarus and Folkman (1984) refer to *coping strategies* as "constantly changing cognitive and behavioral efforts to manage specific external and/or internal demands that are appraised as taxing or exceeding the resources of the person" (p. 141). In general, findings from adult carer studies suggest that better carer adjustment is associated with lower stress appraisals, higher social support, less reliance on avoidant coping and greater reliance on problem-focused coping (e.g., Pakenham, 2001). Many studies that have used the stress and coping model to examine the process of adaptation to stress associated with having a parent with an illness/disability support these findings (e.g., Compas et al., 1996; Langrock et al., 2002). Pakenham et al. (2007) also found support for the model with young carers. Specifically, social support was the strongest predictor of adjustment, whereas coping strategies emerged as weaker predictors and stress appraisal was unrelated to adjustment.

Family Ecology Framework

Pedersen and Revenson (2005) have proposed a family ecology model for understanding adolescents' reactions to parental illness. The framework draws on general systems theory, human ecology, and stress and coping theory. This framework describes a set of pathways through which serious parental illness affects adolescent well-being and family functioning. According to this framework, parental disability/illness characteristics (e.g., type and severity of illness) affect family functioning and adolescent well-being indirectly through various individual factors (e.g., stigma, coping strategies) and family-level factors (e.g., family role distribution). The individual- and family-level factors may also interact with each other; for example, the adolescent's coping strategies may not be congruent with those of other family members. These pathways may also be affected by various contextual variables, including parent's gender, the family's attachment style, and youth developmental stage. While Pedersen and Revenson (2005) review research that provide support for many of the pathways within the framework, because it has only recently been proposed, the framework has not been fully tested.

Family Systems-Illness Model

Rolland (1984) developed the family systems-illness model, which he has applied to parental illness (Rolland, 1999). The model was developed within a broad family systems perspective. The model describes the dynamic interplay of three dimensions: (1) a psychosocial typology of illness and disability (based on onset, course, outcome, incapacitation, and uncertainty), (2) time phases of the illness (crisis, chronic, and terminal), and (3) family system variables (e.g., life cycle phases such as marriage, child-rearing, and children leaving home). The model also includes individual life cycles, multigenerational patterns of behavior, and belief systems that may be influenced by culture, ethnicity, and gender. The model is largely descriptive and is not embedded in empirical research and as such has not been tested in the young carer field. The model appears to have been developed primarily as a framework for practitioners working within a family systems therapy approach with families affected by parental illness.

Pathology and Risk Models

Parentification

Some researchers have conceptualized the caring roles among children as parentification (an attachment disorder) or a pathological role reversal (Chase, 1999; Earley & Cushway, 2002; Thomas et al., 2003). Parentification occurs when children are obligated to care and adopt inappropriate (adult-like) responsibilities for their parent as a direct result of parental incapacity (Gopfert et al., 2004). Though this type of role transfer may occur in extreme cases, for the majority of families, caring does not mean children internalize the concern and sense of responsibility parents have for their welfare (Keith & Morris, 1995). Aldridge and Becker (2003) maintain that all parent–child relationships are reciprocal and interdependent by nature, and regardless of some role adaptation young carers in their research continued to see their parents as parents. Furthermore, as Walmsley (1993) points out, care and dependence are false dichotomies. She argues that caring is a continuum more complex than a linear division between care and dependence and that we are all dependent to a greater or lesser extent on others. Carers are also recipients of care and vice versa and therefore parents may be care recipients but also continue to provide care (Aldridge, 2006). Young caregiving is more accurately conceptualized as a form of functional "adaptive parentification," which results from acute stress rather than a pathological role reversal (Chase, 1999).

Attachment Theory

Attachment is a special bond of substantial emotional intensity between two people and is a necessary precondition of healthy psychosocial development (Gopfert, Webster, Pollard, & Nelki, 1996). A fundamental principle of attachment theory is that quality of care leads to differences in the quality of attachment (Weinfield, Sroufe, Egeland, & Carlson, 1999). Attachment can be characterized as either more or less secure, with mutual care, reciprocal connection, and emotional closeness characterizing secure attachment (Bostik & Everall, 2006). According to Bowlby (1969), it is the sensitive responsiveness of the carer to the child that leads to secure attachment. Therefore, the securely attached child perceives his or her attachment figure as reliably available and effective in responding to his or her needs.

Parental disability/illness has been acknowledged as one factor that can impinge on the carer's ability to sensitively respond to the child's needs (Pedersen & Revenson, 2005). However, only a few studies have examined attachment in children of parents with a disability/illness, and the majority have focused on mothers with mental illness. These studies suggest that many mothers with serious mental disorders report insecure attachments in past or present relationships and that their children are often insecurely attached to them (Beardslee, Versage, & Gladstone, 1998; Hipwell, Goosens, Melhuish, & Kumar, 2000; Manassis, Bradley, Goldberg, Hood, & Swinson, 1994).

Risk and Resilience Framework

Children of parents with disability have been viewed as at risk for adverse outcomes, and those who exhibit good outcomes are viewed as extraordinarily resilient. Resilience is the capacity to respond adaptively in the presence of adversity and is the result of a complex interaction of risk and protective factors, both internal and external to the individual (Waller, 2001). Consistent with this framework, many researchers have attempted to identify both risk and protective factors associated with young caregiving.

Some researchers have criticized the "at risk" versus "extraordinarily resilient" polarized conceptualization of children of parents with disability (Aldridge, 2006; McConnell Gladstone et al., 2006). They claim that the research and discourse that has focused on risk factors has inflated their potency and question whether such factors are true determinants of poor outcomes for children. It is also claimed that such research has pathologized many of the experiences and processes associated with childhood in the context of parental disability. At the at risk end of the risk–resilience continuum, the vulnerabilities of children are emphasized and the child is regarded as a victim rather than an active participant in the lives of their families. In contrast, it is claimed that resilience-focused research is at risk of casting children of parents with disability as super-kids with extraordinary resilience. Some have called for a broadening of the risk/resilience framework that recasts "children as complex young persons who have competencies as well as vulnerabilities linked to their developmental stages" (McConnell Gladstone et al., 2006, p. 2540). They call for researchers to consider the social and interpersonal contexts within which young caregiving occurs, emphasizing the importance of reciprocity and interdependence of caring.

POLICY, SERVICE, AND RESEARCH FUTURE DIRECTIONS

Policy

In recent years, young carers have been recognized by governments in many countries. However, even in those countries where young carers feature highly on the social agenda, policy development varies considerably. With the exception of the United Kingdom, young carers in most countries have no specific legal rights to recognition, assessments, or to support services. In most developing countries, there is a lack of official recognition of the role of young carers at all levels (Becker, 2007). Although making legislative provisions for young carers is important, it is not clear whether a legislative response should be within a carer or child protection framework.

Considerable discussion has focused on the needs and rights of young carers, yet in many countries there is very little local empirical data to inform the development of policy and services. Becker (2007) has observed that in the United Kingdom the local young carer research was "critical in raising awareness among UK policy and practitioner networks of the experiences and needs of young carers and their families" (p. 35). He also claimed that "local context is critical in determining social policy and service development responses at the national level."

The development of workable policies must take into account a number of conflicting paradigms and the complex interplay of numerous factors (Aldridge, 2008). For example, policy makers are challenged with developing workable policies that balance the rights of children and the rights of parents with disabilities and balance the protection of young carers and respect for family autonomy and privacy. Policies need to allow the young person to choose to provide care and thereby receive the benefits associated with the role, while at the same time providing necessary supports that minimize the negative impacts.

Service Provision

Service delivery responses to the needs of young carers vary considerably across countries (Becker, 2007). Moore (2005) has researched the service needs of young carers by reviewing the relevant literature and drawing on findings from his own research in Australia. His report summarizes what young carers want for their families and cared-for relatives (e.g., family-based rehabilitation programs, respite care, and in-home support), what they want for themselves (e.g., recognition, respect, age-appropriate information, personal and peer support), and the barriers to accessing services for themselves and their families (e.g., lack of service delivery flexibility and lack of self-identification as young carers). Service delivery and intervention development may be dealt with on the four levels specified next.

Young Carer Level

Most of the research that has examined the feasibility and/or efficacy of psychosocial interventions for young carers has been carried out with children of parents with mental illness. Fraser, James, Anderson, Lloyd, and Judd (2006) reviewed studies that evaluated interventions for families affected by parental mental illness including those that targeted the child, parent, or family. Most intervention studies in the physical family disability/illness area have focused on siblings of a child with illness or developmental disability (Fraser et al., 2006;

Lobato & Kao, 2002, 2005; Williams et al., 1997); few have targeted children of a parent with physical disability/illness (Coles, Pakenham, & Leech, 2007). Most interventions have employed a group format, and some have included both children and parents (Lobato & Kao, 2002, 2005), whereas others involved only children (Coles et al., 2007; Pitman & Matthey, 2004; Williams et al., 1997). Most interventions provided education about disability/illness, opportunity to share experiences, and training in coping skills. Overall, findings indicated that many of these interventions were effective in producing increased knowledge of the target illness/disability at the end of treatment. Other benefits included increased social connectedness (Lobato & Kao, 2002, 2005) and self-perceived competence (Lobato & Kao, 2005), and decreases in distress, stress appraisals, adverse caregiving impacts (Coles et al., 2007) and behavior problems (Lobato & Kao, 2002). In addition, many interventions were rated as highly satisfactory by both the children (Coles et al., 2007; Pitman & Matthey, 2004) and parents (Lobato & Kao, 2002, 2005; Williams et al., 1997).

Of the studies reviewed by Fraser et al. (2006), over 50 percent were rated as methodologically weak with shortcomings such as the absence of control groups and focus on descriptive rather than empirical results. These and other deficiencies also characterize intervention studies in the parental physical disability/illness domain. Clearly, a gap exists in the current evidence base regarding the effectiveness of psychosocial interventions for children of parents with disability/illness.

In addition to the interventions already reviewed, other young carer–focused services might include (a) delivery of age-appropriate information via advice and referral services (e.g., telephone hotlines and online advice); (b) peer support via mentoring and buddy systems; (c) counseling; (d) respite care; (e) financial recognition and remuneration for caregiving; and (f) advocacy bodies. For these young carer services to result in meaningful improvements and choice for young carers, they need to occur in concert with supports for the parent.

Parent Level

Flexible alternative care and supports for parents with disability/illness are necessary to lessen the load placed on young carers. These should be across a number of areas depending on need (e.g., medical, psychological, practical, and financial). Clinicians do not routinely collect information regarding the parenting status of patients; hence, there is a need for a shift away from the biomedical model focus on the individual to include the family and community.

Family Level

There is growing recognition of the importance of a "whole family approach" to meeting the needs of young carers and the person with care needs (Aldridge & Becker, 2003).

Systemic Level

Disability, health, and community care sectors are likely to offer services relevant to the young carer's caregiving role, and the education and employment sectors are relevant to the needs of carers that fall outside of their caregiving role. To facilitate interventions at the systemic level, professionals in these settings (e.g., nurses, GPs, and teachers) need to be educated about young carers, and standards, guidelines, and procedures for identifying and responding to young carers need to be developed. Finally, community awareness and understanding regarding young carers and people with disabilities is required.

The complexity inherent in responding to young carers is clear. Young carers have needs across many sectors and areas of responsibility. Hence, any response to young carers should ensure that services are highly coordinated. Young carers need to be represented and consulted about how these programs will be designed and delivered to ensure that they are responsive to their needs.

Research

A new challenge for researchers is the balance of inquiry into both the risk and protective or resilience factors in a social and interpersonal context. As such, researchers might be guided by an empowerment framework whereby the strengths, assets, and resources of parents with disability and their children are identified to ensure that these are built on, along with the identification of potential deficits, needs, and barriers. An empowerment approach has the potential to address many aspects of the theories summarized here, as well as provide future service and policy directions.

Most researchers have relied on data from one family member. However, given evidence that children and their parents often have differing perspectives on the impacts of parental disability, it is important to collect data from both (Deatrick et al., 1998; Kirshbaum & Olkin, 2002). In view of findings suggesting that the parent with disability and the healthy parent offer unique parenting contributions (Steck et al., 2001), data should be collected from both parents where available. There is also a lack of research data on young children and fathers with disability/illness.

Research in the young caregiving field has suffered from the lack of contextually sensitive measures. Prior research has relied on the use of generic measures that often lack sensitivity to the young caregiving context. The recent development of a contextually grounded measure of young caregiving (YCOPI) represents a significant foundational step for future research in this field. However, the YCOPI, although showing potential, requires further refinement by way of validation with independent samples of young carers. Another promising measurement development in this field is the use of photographic participation and elicitation methods. Aldridge (2008) in research on children caring for a parent with mental illness gave children cameras to provide photographic diaries of their lives. Preliminary data suggest that this method has the potential to yield valuable in-depth information on the lives of young carers.

Based on the notion that the construction of meaning around stressful situations is an important process in coping with adversity (Taylor, 1983), future research should explore the meaning caregiving holds for youngsters.

While research investigating the meaning of caregiving in adult carers has recently increased, it is a relatively neglected area of inquiry in the young carer field. Studies show that the meaning carers impose on their caregiving experience plays a role in determining carer adjustment outcomes (Pakenham, 2008, 2008).

Further research is also needed to tease out the roles of specific factors that shape young carer well-being, including caregiving activities, role changes, financial burdens, parental disease characteristics, fear of contracting disability/illness, and so on. Given that biological, psychological, and social issues differ across the developmental stages of childhood, research studies tailored to early, middle, and late childhood who have a parent with disability are needed.

Many of the research, policy, and practice challenges discussed here are interrelated. For example, adequately designed research and measures that tap the experiences of young carers is necessary to develop frameworks to inform policy and service provision. Consequently, in many cases policies are not embedded in appropriate paradigms, and services fall short of meeting young carers' needs in all areas of their lives.

NOTES

1. "Family health situation" refers to "someone living in your home or close by who needs special medical care because he/she is sick, has a disability, or can no longer care for him/herself" (Siskowski, 2006, p. 166).

2. The use of the phrase "healthy parents" refers to parents with no overtly diagnosed medical condition or disability.

REFERENCES

Aldridge, J. (2006). The experience of children living with and caring for parents with mental illness. *Child Abuse Review, 15*, 79–88.

Aldridge, J. (2008). All work and no play? Understanding the needs of children with caring responsibilities. *Children and Society, 22*(4), 253–264.

Aldridge, J., & Becker, J. (1993a). Punishing children for caring: The hidden cost of young carers. *Children and Society, 7*, 376–387.

Aldridge, J., & Becker, S. (1993b). *Children who care: Inside the world of young carers.* Loughborough: Loughborough University Young Carers Research Group.

Aldridge, J., & Becker, S. (1994). *My child, my carer: The parents' perspective.* Loughborough: Loughborough University Young Carers Research Group.

Aldridge, J., & Becker, J. (2003). *Children caring for parents with mental illness: Perspectives of young carers, parents and professionals.* Bristol: Policy Press.

Anderson, C. A., & Hammen, C. L. (1993). Psychosocial outcomes of children of unipolar depressed, bipolar, medically ill, and normal women: A longitudinal study. *Journal of Consulting and Clinical Psychology, 61*(3), 448–454.

Armistead, L., Klein, K., & Forehand, R. (1995). Parental physical illness and child functioning. *Clinical Psychology Review, 15*(5), 409–422.

Australian Bureau of Statistics. (2003). *Disability, ageing and carers: A summary of findings.* Canberra: Author.

Banks, P., Cogan, N., Riddell, S., Deeley, S., Hill, M., & Tisdall, K. (2002). Does the covert nature of caring prohibit the development of effective services for young carers? *British Journal of Guidance and Counselling, 30*(3), 229–246.

Barkmann, C., Romer, G., Watson, M., & Schulte-Markwort, M. (2007). Parental physical illness as a risk for psychosocial maladjustment in children and adolescents: Epidemiological findings from a national survey in Germany. *Psychosomatics, 48,* 476–481.

Beach, D. L. (1997). Family caregiving: The positive impact on adolescent relationships. *Gerontologist, 37*(2), 233–238.

Beardslee, W. R., Versage, E. M., & Gladstone, T. R. G. (1998). Children of affectively ill parents: A review of the past 10 years. *Journal of the American Academy of Child and Adolescent Psychiatry, 37*(11), 1134–1142.

Becker, S. (Ed.). (1995). *Young carers in Europe: an exploratory cross-national study in Britain, France, Sweden and Germany.* Loughborough: Young Carers Research Group.Becker, S. (2007). Global perspectives on children's unpaid caregiving in the family. *Global Social Policy, 7*(1), 23–50.

Blackford, K. A. (1999). A child's growing up with a parent who has multiple sclerosis: Theories and experiences. *Disability and Society, 14*(5), 673–685.

Bolas, H., Van Wersch, A., & Flynn, D. (2007). The well-being of young people who care for a dependent relative: An interpretative phenomenological analysis. *Psychology and Health, 22*(7), 829–850.

Bostik, K. E., & Everall, R. D. (2006). In my mind I was alone: Suicidal adolescents' perceptions of attachment relationships. *International Journal for the Advancement of Counselling, 28*(3), 269–287.

Bowlby, J. (1969). *Attachment and loss, Vol. 1: Attachment.* Middlesex: Penguin Books.

Carers Australia. (2002). *Young carers research project: Final report.* Canberra: Author.

Chase, N. D. (1999). *Burdened children: Theory, research, and treatment of parentification.* Thousand Oaks, CA: Sage.

Coles, A. R., Pakenham, K. I., & Leech, C. (2007). Evaluation of an intensive psychosocial intervention for children of parents with multiple sclerosis. *Rehabilitation Psychology, 52*(2), 133–142.

Compas, B. E., Worsham, N. L., Ey, S., & Howell, D. C. (1996). When Mom or Dad has cancer: II. Coping, cognitive appraisals, and psychological distress in children of cancer patients. *Health Psychology, 15*(3), 167–175.

De Judicibus, M. A., & McCabe, M. P. (2004). The impact of parental multiple sclerosis on the adjustment of children and adolescents. *Adolescence, 39*(155), 551–569.

Dearden, C., & Becker, S. (1995). *Young carers—the facts.* Sutton: Reed Business.

Dearden, C., & Becker, S. (1998). *Young carers in the United Kingdom: A profile.* London: Carers National Association.

Dearden, C., & Becker, S. (2000). *Growing up caring: Vulnerability and transition to adulthood—young carers' experiences.* Leicester: Youth Work Press.

Dearden, C., & Becker, S. (2004). *Young carers in the UK: The 2004 report.* London: Carers UK.

Deatrick, J. A., Brennan, D., & Cameron, M. E. (1998). Mothers with multiple sclerosis and their children: Effects of fatigue and exacerbations on maternal support. *Nursing Research, 47*(4), 205–210.

Earley, L., & Cushway, D. (2002). The parentified child. *Clinical Child Psychology and Psychiatry, 7*(2), 163–178.

Evans, R. M. C. (2005). Social networks, migration, and care in Tanzania: Caregivers' and children's resilience to coping with HIV/AIDS. *Journal of Children and Poverty, 11*(2), 111–129.

Fals-Stewart, W., Kelley, M., Fincham, F., Golden, J., & Logsdon, T. (2004). Emotional and behavioral problems of children living with drug-abusing fathers: Comparisons with children living with alcohol-abusing and non-abusing fathers. *Journal of Family Psychology, 18*, 319–330.

Fraser, C., James, E. L., Anderson, K., Lloyd, D., & Judd, F. (2006). Intervention programs for children of parents with a mental illness: A critical review. *International Journal of Mental Health Promotion, 8*(1), 9–20.

Gays, M. (2002). *A lifetime of caring: ACT schools-based young carers survey.* Canberra: Marymead Child and Family Centre.

Goffman, E. (1963). *Stigma: Notes on the management of spoiled identity.* Upper Saddle River, NJ: Prentice Hall.

Goode, K. T., Haley, W. E., Roth, D. L., & Ford, G. R. (1998). Predicting longitudinal changes in caregiver physical and mental health: A stress process model. *Health Psychology, 17*(2), 190–198.

Gopfert, M., Webster, J., Pollard, J., & Nelki, J. S. (1996). The assessment and prediction of parenting capacity. In M. Gopfert, J. Webster. & M. V. Seemen (Eds.), *Parental psychiatric disorder: Distressed parents and their families* (pp. 271–309). Cambridge: Cambridge University Press.

Gopfert, M., Webster, J., & Seemen, M. V. (Eds.). (2004). *Parental psychiatric disorder: Distressed parents and their families* (2nd ed.). Cambridge: Cambridge University Press.

Grabiak, B. R., Bender, C. M., & Puskar, K. R. (In press). The impact of parental cancer on the adolescent: An analysis of the literature. *Psycho-Oncology*.

Grant, K. E., & Compas, B. E. (1995). Stress and anxious-depressed symptoms among adolescents: Searching for mechanisms of risk. *Journal of Consulting and Clinical Psychology, 63*(6), 1015–1021.

Gullekson, M. (1992). Stigma: Families suffer too. In P. J. Fink & A. P. Tasman (Eds.), *Stigma and mental illness*. Washington, DC: American Psychiatric Press.

Hipwell, A. E., Goosens, F. A., Melhuish, E. C., & Kumar, R. (2000). Severe maternal psychopathology and infant–mother attachment. *Development and Psychopathology, 12*, 157–175.

Ireland, M., & Pakenham, K. I. (In press). The nature of young caregiving in families experiencing chronic illness/disability: Development of the Youth Activities of Caregiving Scale (YACS). *Psychology and Health*.

Keith, L., & Morris, J. (1995). Easy targets: A disability rights perspective on the "children as carers" debate. *Critical Social Policy, 44*, 36–57.

Kirshbaum, M., & Olkin, R. (2002). Parents with physical, systemic, or visual disabilities. *Sexuality and Disability, 20*(1), 65–80.

Langrock, A. M., Compas, B. E., Keller, G., Merchant, M. J., & Copeland, M. E. (2002). Coping with the stress of parental depression: Parent's reports of children's coping, emotional, and behavioral problems. *Journal of Clinical Child and Adolescent Psychology, 31*(3), 312–324.

Lazarus, R. S., & Folkman, S. (1984). *Stress, appraisal, and coping*. New York: Springer.

Lerner, R. M. (2002). *Adolescence: Development, diversity, context and application*. Upper Saddle River, NJ: Prentice Hall.

Levine, C., Gibson Hunt, G., Halper, D., Hart, A. Y., Lautz, J., & Gould, D. A. (2005). Young adult caregivers: A first look at an unstudied population. *American Journal of Public Health, 95*(11), 2071–2075.

Lobato, D. J., & Kao, B. T. (2002). Integrated sibling-parent group intervention to improve sibling knowledge and adjustment to chronic illness and disability. *Journal of Pediatric Psychology, 27*, 711–716.

Lobato, D. J., & Kao, B. T. (2005). Brief report: Family based group intervention for young siblings of children with chronic illness and developmental disability. *Journal of Pediatric Psychology, 30*, 678–682.

Manassis, K., Bradley, S., Goldberg, S., Hood, J., & Swinson, R. P. (1994). Attachment in mothers with anxiety disorders and their children. *Journal of the American Academy of Child and Adolescent Psychiatry, 33*(9), 1106–1122.

McCausland, J., & Pakenham, K. I. (2003). Investigation of the benefits of HIV/AIDS caregiving and relations among caregiver adjustment, benefit finding, and stress and coping variables. *AIDS Care, 15*, 853–869.

McConnell Gladstone, B., Boydell, K. M., & McKeever, P. (2006). Recasting research into children's experiences of parental mental illness: Beyond risk and resilience. *Social Science and Medicine, 62*, 2540–2550.

McNeil, J. (1993). *Americans with disabilities: 1991–1992*. Washington, DC: U.S. Bureau of the Census.

Moore, T. (2005). *More than words: Supporting young carers and their families*. Canberra: Youth Coalition of the ACT.

Newman, T. (2002). "Young carers" and disabled parents: Time for a change of direction? *Disability and Society, 11*, 41–54.

Office for National Statistics. (2003). *Census 2001 data*. London: Author.

Olkin, R., Abrams, K., Preston, P., & Kirshbaum, M. (2006). Comparison of parents with and without disabilities raising teens: information from the NHIS and two national surveys. *Rehabilitation Psychology, 51*(1), 43–49.

Olsen, R. (1996). Young carers: Challenging the facts and politics of research into children and caring. *Disability and Society, 11*, 41–54.

Olsen, R., & Clarke, H. (2003). *Parenting and disability*. Bristol: Policy Press.

Pakenham, K. I. (2001). Application of a stress and coping model to caregiving in multiple sclerosis. *Psychology, Health and Medicine, 6*(1), 13–27.

Pakenham, K. I. (2005). The positive impact of multiple sclerosis on carers: Associations between carer benefit finding and positive and negative adjustment domains. *Disability and Rehabilitation, 27*(17), 985–997.

Pakenham, K. I. (2008). Making sense of caregiving for persons with multiple sclerosis (MS): The dimensional structure of sense making and relations with positive and negative adjustment. *International Journal of Behavioral Medicine. 15*, 241–252.

Pakenham, K. I. (2008). The nature of sense making in caregiving for persons with multiple sclerosis (MS). *Disability and Rehabilitation. 30*(17), 1263–1273.

Pakenham, K. I., & Bursnall, S. (2006). Relations between social support, appraisal and coping and both positive and negative outcomes for children of a parent with MS and comparisons with children of healthy parents. *Clinical Rehabilitation, 20*, 709–723.

Pakenham, K. I., Bursnall, S., Chiu, J., Cannon, T., & Okochi, M. (2006). The psychosocial impact of caregiving on young people who have a parent with an illness or disability: Comparisons between young caregivers and non-caregivers. *Rehabilitation Psychology, 51*(2), 113–126.

Pakenham, K. I., Chiu, J., Bursnall, S., & Cannon, T. (2007). Relations between social support, appraisal and coping and both positive and negative outcomes in young carers. *Journal of Health Psychology, 12*(1), 89–102.

Pakenham, K. I., & Cox, S. (In press). Development of the benefit finding in multiple sclerosis (MS) caregiving scale: A longitudinal study of relations between benefit finding and adjustment. *Psychology and Health*.

Pakenham, K. I., Stebbins, P., Cannon, T., & Samios, C. (2005). *Carers in contemporary Australia: Relations among carer illness/disability groups, biographies, caring context, coping & distress*. Brisbane: PsyHealth Media.

Pedersen, S., & Revenson, T. A. (2005). Parental illness, family functioning, and adolescent well-being: A family ecology framework to guide research. *Journal of Family Psychology, 19*(3), 404–409.

Pitman, E., & Matthey, S. (2004). The SMILES program: A group program for children with mentally ill parents or siblings. *American Journal of Orthopsychiatry, 74*, 383–388.

Prilleltensky, O. (2004). My child is not my carer: Mothers with physical disabilities and the well-being of children. *Disability and Society, 19*(3), 209–223.

Rolland, J. S. (1984). Toward a psychosocial typology of chronic and life-threatening illness. *Family Systems Medicine, 2*, 245–263.

Rolland, J. S. (1999). Parental illness and disability: A family systems framework. *Journal of Family Therapy, 21*, 242–266.

Roy, R. (1990). Consequences of parental illness on children: A review. *Social Work and Social Sciences Review, 2*, 109–121.

Shifren, K., & Kachorek, L. V. (2003). Does early caregiving matter? The effects on young caregivers' adult mental health. *International Journal of Behavioral Development, 27*(4), 338–346.

Siskowski, C. (2006). Young caregivers: Effect of family health situations on school performance. *Journal of School Nursing, 22*(3), 163–169.

Steck, B., Amsler, F., Kappos, L., & Burgin, D. (2001). Gender-specific differences in the process of coping in families with a parent affected by a chronic somatic disease (e.g. multiple sclerosis). *Psychopathology, 34*, 236–244.

Stetz, K. M., Lewis, F. M., & Primomo, J. (1986). Family coping strategies and chronic illness in the mother. *Family Relations, 35*(4), 515–522.

Taylor, S. E. (1983). Adjustment to threatening events: A theory of cognitive adaptation. *American Psychologist, 38*(11), 1161–1173.

Thomas, N., Stainton, T., Jackson, S., Cheung, W. Y., Doubtfire, S., & Webb, A. (2003). "Your friends don't understand": Invisibility and unmet need in the lives of "young carers." *Child and Family Social Work, 8*, 35–46.

Waller, M. A. (2001). Resilience in ecosystem context: Evolution of the concept. *American Journal of Orthopsychiatry, 71*(3), 290–297.

Walmsley, J. (1993). Contradictions in caring: Reciprocity and interdependence. *Disability, Handicap and Society, 8*, 129–141.

Warren, J. (2007). Young carers: Conventional or exaggerated levels of involvement in domestic and caring tasks? *Children and Society, 21*, 136–146.

Weinfield, N. S., Sroufe, L. A., Egeland, B., & Carlson, E. A. (1999). The nature of individual differences in infant-caregiver attachment. In J. Cassidy & P. R. Shaver (Eds.), *Handbook of attachment: Theory, research, and clinical applications* (pp. 68–87). New York: Guilford.

Williams, P. D., Hanson, S., Karlin, R., Ridder, L., Liebergen, A., Olson, J., et al. (1997). Outcomes of a nursing intervention for siblings of chronically ill children: A pilot study. *Journal of the Society of Paediatric Nurses, 2*, 127–138.

Worsham, N. L., Compas, B. E., & Sydney, E. Y. (1997). Children's coping with parental illness. In S. A. Wolchik & I. N. Sandler (Eds.), *Handbook of children's coping: Linking theory and intervention* (pp. 195–213). New York: Plenum.

CHAPTER 4

The Digital Town Square: Information and Communication Technology as an Opportunity and a Barrier to Social Relations for Disabled Youth

Sylvia Söderström

The topic of this chapter is social relations among disabled youths in Norway and the opportunities or barriers that are associated with information and communication technology (ICT). This chapter focuses on the significance of personal computers (computers) and mobile phones (mobiles) to inclusion and exclusion processes for disabled youth in relation to their peer group, social capital, and identity negotiations. Specifically, the chapter discusses when, how, for whom, and with what consequences ICT can provide new opportunities or create new barriers for disabled youths to participate in social relations. It illustrates how engagement in digital communication and interaction is vital to social participation by describing the experiences of Norwegian disabled youths between the ages 15 and 20 as they interact with ICT as a form of communication. The chapter concludes that ICT enhances opportunities for social relationships through:

- Communication and interaction with peers on the "digital town square,"
- Participation in shared digital activities, on and around the computer screen,
- Displaying and sharing digital competencies, in real and in virtual contexts,
- Taking part in the permeability of the real and the virtual in everyday life.

However, the chapter also illustrates how ICT can create inhibiting barriers for young disabled people. These barriers are found to emerge in settings where the interactive use and account of ICT is experienced by the young disabled people as:

- Discouraging of social relationships,
- Difficult, confusing, and exerting,
- A risky social setting where ICT becomes a tool for harassment.

Breaking down disabling barriers and the purposeful provision of equal opportunities for participation and development for disabled people is a declared goal in official Norwegian documents (Norwegian Official Report, 2001, p. 22; White Paper no. 40, 2002–2003). The government claims that removal of disabling barriers in society, including those created by technology, and increased accessibility is vital if this goal is to be achieved. In achieving the goal of removing disabling barriers, the Norwegian government points to a need for more social research on the interactions between environments, disabling barriers, and the consequences of social change (Full Participation for All? Development Trends, 2001–2006; Government's Action Plan for Increased Accessibility, 2004; Ministry of Modernisation, 2009; State of Affairs on Accessibility in Norway, 2006). This chapter explores social changes in communication and interpersonal interaction and also illustrates how the increasingly widespread dissemination and utilization of ICT in the population can mediate new opportunities for communication, interaction, and participation for many disabled youths. On the other hand, ICT can also create new barriers for disabled youths.

In the abundant literature on theories guiding the field of ICT and young people in general, Livingstone (2003) found two key questions to be essential. (1) Are young people a special group? (2) Is ICT a distinctive technology? In writing this chapter, I acknowledge three broad assumptions guiding the field. First, I recognize the fact that children and youth play a key role in establishing emerging ICT-related practices. Second, I recognize a need to go beyond the issue of access and contextualize ICT uses and impacts within everyday life. Third, I recognize that new technology not only adds to the existing mix of available technology but also transforms the way in which the latter are perceived and used (Livingstone, 2003). ICT manifests in diverse practices that vary as much as the contexts in which it is used. Thus, ICT, social context, and action are found to be an inseparable phenomena, each influencing each other (Lievrouw & Livingstone, 2006; Valentine & Holloway, 2002).

CURRENT RESEARCH ON YOUTH, ICT, AND SOCIAL RELATIONS

There is a comprehensive body of research on young people in general and the use of ICT. The dissemination of ICT in Norway is among the highest in Europe. In 2006, virtually all young Norwegians aged 16 or older were active computer and Internet users, and all of them owned their own mobile telephone (Kaare, Brantzæg, Heim, & Endestad, 2007; Lorentzen, 2007). Thus, ICT has become a common device in Norwegian society, and Norwegian children and youth are as accustomed to this technology as earlier generations were to television or radio. But how do the young people use ICT, and what significance does it hold in their social relationships?

The most utilized function of computers among Norwegian youth is the Internet. On the Internet, they communicate mainly with friends and acquaintances who are already known in real life, and they surf the Web for fun and leisure (Arnseth, Hatlevik, Kløvstad, Kristiansen, & Ottestad, 2007; Kaare et al., 2007; Torgersen, 2004). Similar findings have emerged from studies conducted in other parts of the world (Baym, 2006; Baym, Zhang, & Lin, 2004; Livingstone, 2003; McMillan & Morrison, 2006; Räsânen & Kouvo, 2007; Rice & Haythornthwaite, 2006; Thulin & Vilhelmson, 2005). Young Norwegians' preferred method of Internet communication has, however, changed during the latest years from e-mail to instant messaging (MSN) (Arnseth et al., 2007; Kaare et al., 2007; Torgersen, 2004). When it comes to the mobile phone, the most popular and utilized function among Norwegian youth is text messages (SMS) (Kaare et al. 2007). The greatest significance of SMS and MSN for young people is the opportunity these communication channels hold in being available and staying in touch with friends and peers (Kaare et al. 2007; Ling, 2004; Oksman & Turtianien, 2004; Wei & Lo, 2006).

A comprehensive body of research has demonstrated that young people's use of mobile phones and online communications is highly integrated in their real-life relationships (Baym, 2006; Baym et al., 2004; Brandtzæg & Stav, 2004; Buckingham, 2006; Kaare et al., 2007; Livingstone, 2003; Madell & Muncer, 2005; McMillan & Morrison, 2006; Peter & Valkenburg, 2006; Thulin & Vilhelmson, 2005; Valentine & Holloway, 2002; Wei & Lo, 2006; Wellman, Hase, Witte, & Hampton, 2001). Buckingham (2006) pointed out that media-based commodities have become a crucial factor in the social construction of young people's peer group cultures. Other researchers have pointed to how the real and the virtual are no longer separate worlds, but are permeable and influential on each other (Livingstone, 2003; Seymour & Lupton, 2004).

Despite this impressive body of evidence, it is not clear how the findings relate to disabled youths. It is difficult to identify whether any disabled youths were included in these studies. Further, the studies have not explored questions about personal functioning level or accessibility and usability of the technologies. Although some studies have been conducted on ICT use among disabled people, these have focused on adults or have sought an adult perspective (Anderberg & Jönsson, 2005; Bowker & Tuffin, 2002; D'Aubin, 2007; Dobransky & Hargatti, 2006; Houlihan et al., 2003; Pell, Gillies, & Carss, 1999; Seymour, 2005; Seymour & Lupton, 2004; Stienstra, 2006; Tobias, 2003). Generally adults and young people use ICT in different ways, just as disabled and nondisabled people may have different preferences in use of ICT. These potential differences make it especially important to additionally investigate the perspectives and uses of ICT among disabled youths.

CURRENT RESEARCH ON DISABLED PEOPLE, ICT, AND SOCIAL RELATIONS

The potential of ICT to facilitate social connection is one of the benefits identified by adult disabled people (Anderberg & Jönsson, 2005; Bowker & Tuffin, 2002; Houlihan et al. 2003; Seymour, 2005; Seymour & Lupton, 2004). Some disabled people have described how "bodiless" communication on the Internet has given them an opportunity to meet online acquaintances as equals and given them the ability to choose whether to disclose their impairment (Anderberg & Jônsson, 2005). However, other researchers have found that impairment and disabling experiences are not concealed in online communication, and in fact, it is the impairment and disabling experiences that remains the principle bond in digitalized relationships (Seymour & Lupton, 2004).

Many researchers point to how ICT can be a great communication tool for those who find it difficult to meet friends and participate in leisure activities (Anderberg & Jönsson, 2005; Bowker & Tuffin, 2002; Houlihan et al. 2003; Rice & Haythornthwaite, 2006; Seymour, 2005; Seymour & Lupton, 2004). Exclusion from the opportunities provided by ICT is perceived as one of the most damaging exclusions in modern society, especially for young people (Livingstone & Helsper, 2006). However, the possibilities ICT may hold in communication and participation need to be studied in its social envelope, which is the sets of expectations, contexts, and social practices that surround ICT.

ICT AND DISABILITY IN A NORWEGIAN CONTEXT

Since World War II, Norway has become a solid welfare state, securing the citizens' material rights by means of official social benefits and health services. A central ideal in this development has been the notion of universalism, accompanied by actions for differentiation (Hjelmtveit, 2005). Whereas universalism is the equal rights to public services and arenas for every citizen, differentiation provides individual adoptions for those who need special adjustment to exploit their rights. Since the 1960s, disability has been a separate field in the Norwegian archives, which means that disability has been addressed in separate governmental documents. The emphasis in these documents is on disabled people's right to equal inclusion and full participation in all parts of society and on the need for universal design and access for all (Government's Action Plan for Increased Accessibility, 2004; Ministry of Modernisation, 2009; Norwegian Official Report, 2001; State of Affairs on Accessibility in Norway, 2006; White Paper no. 40, 2002–2003). In the same period of time, the relational model of disability was introduced in Norway. Tøssebro (2004, p. 3) calls this development an "environmental turn" because it calls attention to the disabling impacts of cultural, social, and environmental barriers (Taustadòttir & Kristiansen, 2004). In Norway, disability is thus defined as a mismatch between a person's capabilities and the functional demands of the environment, or in terms of a gap between an individual and their functioning and societal and environmental demands (Norwegian

Official Report, 2001; White Paper no. 40, 2002–2003). The important point in this perspective is that the social construction of disability takes place both in interpersonal relationships, in encounters between individuals and the environment, and between individuals and society (Gustavsson, Tøssebro, & Traustadòttir, 2005). Considering disability as something relational that displays itself differently in different encounters and relationships, the empirical context in which this takes place becomes of great analytical importance. Thus, disabled is something one becomes in different relationships and encounters, and this chapter uses the term *disabled youths*, which is dominant in the Nordic perspective on disability, to underscore this social and environmental dimension of disability.

For most Norwegian disabled children and youths, the policy of universalism and differentiation implies that they attend their local school and are expected to participate in ordinary settings with their friends and peers, with some individual adaptations if needed. The provision and assignment of assistive technology is an essential part of implementing this policy as evidenced by the national public system of assistive technology center, allocating assistive technology based on discretionary evaluation of the needs of the individual (Halvorsen & Hvinden, 2007). Many disabled children and youths in Norway are allocated computers as an educational assistive technology through these centers. Those with visual impairments are additionally allocated ICT assistive technologies, such as Braille displays and screen readers.

THE ICT EXPERIENCES OF DISABLED YOUTHS

Given the perception that ICT may provide a mechanism for addressing disadvantage in Norway, it is important to investigate this assumption. The rest of this chapter describes the opportunities and barriers experienced by a group of young people with disabilities as described to me in conversations. Major themes were identified through the conversational interviews, each simultaneously representing an opportunity and a barrier.

A Central Meeting Place: The Digital Town Square

The significance of ICT for young people's friendships and social relations might be perceived as an empirical image of a "digital town square." This image displays the social envelope and cultural context in which youths, both disabled and nondisabled, find themselves. This digital town square holds the same significance as the physical local market—a central meeting place for communication, interaction, gossip, and exchanging news. An important difference is, however, that the digital town square is independent of physical location, presence, or mobility.

Iselin is a 17-year-old vision-impaired young woman who attends the local high school and has chosen music as her main subject. Iselin described herself as a friendly and extroverted person who enjoys hanging out with her friends. She was allocated a computer and various ICT assistive technologies in primary school. We talked about friendship, leisure activities, communication, and ICT. When I asked Iselin if she ever uses the MSN, she said:

> I love the MSN. It is a very nice way to keep in touch with my friends. On the MSN I talk to my friends at school, my friends where we used to live and my friends from summer camps and stuff. We talk about every thing at MSN, like how stupid the teachers can be or what you are going to wear to the party this weekend. But it is also a little bit different according to whom I am talking to. Like if it is only an acquaintance then it is just like "Hi how are you doing?" but if it is one of my close friends then we talk about more personal stuff. The MSN is so much better than e-mail, because even though you can write a lot on e-mail you don't get an answer right away like you do on the MSN. And you can always log on to the MSN and meet your friends there.

Like most of the young people I interviewed, Iselin loved to chat with her friends on MSN, and like most other young people, it was with existing friends and already known acquaintances that she communicated (Kaare et al., 2007; McMillan & Morrison, 2006; Thulin & Wilhelmson, 2004). They all described the convenience and efficiency of MSN as the main reason for its popularity. Its efficiency lay in the capability of rapid and simultaneous conversation, and its convenience was based on the fact that they can always meet some friends on MSN. If young people, for some reason, were not able to meet their friends on MSN, then the mobile phone was used. Iselin and most of the other young people used the mobile telephone as a replacement technology when MSN was not available.

Heine is a 20-year-old young man with many interests. He uses a wheelchair and has comprehensive movement difficulties. We talked about technology and communication, friends, and participation in society. When I asked Heine how he used his mobile phone, he answered, "If I for some reason can't use the MSN, like when I am on camps and stuff, it is nice to have the mobile. Because then I can use the mobile to keep in touch with friends and family. Or if I can't get hold of a friend on MSN, I just send am SMS to give a message or something. Usually you can always get hold of people on their mobiles."

Even when Heine did not have access to a computer or his friends were not logged on MSN, he was still able to establish contact with his friends using the mobile phone. He was, therefore, using his mobile phone like most other young people, as a complement to MSN and in establishing contact by means of SMS (Kaare et al., 2007; Madell & Muncer, 2005; Oksman & Turtianien, 2004). The main content of his SMS messages are short notes such as, "What are you doing?," greetings or requests such as, "Can you log on and meet me on MSN?" The mobile phone, and especially SMS, was found to be an important contact establishing channel and an everyday micro-organizational tool. However, the Internet-connected computer, especially MSN, took priority as the most important communication channel (Kaare et al., 2007; Ling, 2004; Oksman & Turtianien, 2004; Wei & Lo, 2006). For teenagers and young adults, the Internet-connected computer and MSN has become a central meeting place for communication, interaction, and just hanging out. This meeting place is independent of geography and mobility because one does not have to travel, dress up, and plan ahead to meet friends there.

Some disabled youths found the properties of the digital medium a bit frustrating and exhausting. Jon is a 16-year-old partially sighted young man. He was allocated a computer in primary school as well as several assistive technology devices, but was not fond of using the latter as they were too bothersome to use. Jon was not fond of reading and writing, as he found it quite exhausting. He was, however, very fond of playing games and talking to friends. In response to my question about how he preferred to communicate with his friends he said, "I have Skype. I think it is easier to talk to people on Skype than on the MSN. It is easier to avoid misunderstandings. You can listen to the voice and correct things right away."

Skype is a software program that is freely downloaded and installed on a personal computer. Using Skype is like making a normal phone call. Jon was thus talking to and listening to his friends instead of writing to them and reading as he would on MSN. Using Skype was a common communication strategy for several young people, both disabled and nondisabled. Like MSN, the fact that Skype is free to use was one of its advantages and contributed to the preferences of young people to make use of this medium.

Digital communication, whether by means of MSN, SMS, or Skype, provided Iselin, Heine, and Jon, as it did most other youths, with the opportunity to be available and stay in touch with friends and acquaintances at all times. The convenience and efficiency of these technologies was emphasized as the greatest benefit for young people with disabilities, as found in relation to most young people (Arnseth et al., 2007; Houlihan et al., 2003; Kaare et al., 2007; McMillan & Morrison, 2006; Torgersen, 2004). McMillan and Morrison (2006) found that young people were expected to be connected, and if they were not connected, they were not able to participate in their community. Young people's use of digital interaction, especially on MSN, had created a digital town square where they met, chatted, made appointments, and exchanged the latest news. This digital town square has become the central meeting place for young people, both with and without disabilities. Through the computer, supplemented by the mobile phone, the digital town square is accessible regardless of time, place, and mobility. Kaare et al. (2007) pointed to how this availability brings about the "always-on" relationships. These relationships are characterized by the need and demand for always staying connected and by the dependency on technology to be able to participate (McMillan & Morrison, 2006). Such always-on relationships, and the consequent dependence on technology, presents both opportunities and barriers for disabled youths as they attempt to participate in the digital town square and build their social relationships.

The Notion of Disability

Opportunities to Make Disability Unessential

When disabled youths experienced ICT as accessible and usable, the most significant impact in relation to social relationships was the opportunity to make disability unessential.

Signe is a 17-year-old young woman who uses a wheelchair. She lives in a rural area and attends the local high school. Signe presented herself as an outgoing girl with many friends and hobbies, but like many other disabled youths, she described a lack of organized leisure activities. When I asked her how she usually socialized with friends, she replied, "Whenever I am at home I am logged on to MSN. I talk to my friends every day on MSN. We share news, discuss hobbies and help each other with school work. Nowadays we are designing a Web site; it's supposed to be a fan club for a local pop artist we like. It is I who knows the most about computers." Signe sounded very proud when she told me that she was the one with the most knowledge about computers. She described how her friends visited her often and together they engaged in browsing the Web, designing Web sites, or watching movies on the computer. Thus, ICT emerged as a tool that brought Signe and her friends together in shared activities around the screen. She was, in this way, demonstrating how digital competence is a valued quality among most young people and that it plays an important role in peer group relationships (Buckingham, 2006; Kaare et al., 2007; McMillan & Morrison, 2006; Valentine & Holloway, 2002). Sharing her digital competence with her friends allowed Signe to achieve a valued status and create a place where she was appreciated and included. The digital town square thus provided Signe, like many other disabled youths, the opportunity to participate in society in a way that made her lack of mobility unessential.

In a digital environment, many disabled youths found themselves freed from prejudice, stigma, and isolation, and empowered by a tool for enhancing their functional and personal abilities (Anderberg & Jönsson, 2005; Dobransky & Hargittai, 2006; Whitley, 1997). Like Signe, other young people experienced ICT as an opportunity to share their digital competencies and reinforce friendships. Maren is a 17-year-old young woman who is visually impaired. She says, "The advantage of Skype is that I can express myself more orally, which is easier than writing. Most of my friends use Skype too." Like almost 25 percent of the young people I spoke with, Maren used Skype in addition to MSN to communicate with her friends. Using Skype provided her with the ability to communicate more freely than she did in writing, and she was thus able to display herself in more favorable ways. Even though Skype is not yet a common property, more young people are adopting this technology. In using it, Maren was part of an initiator group who were shaping a youthful trend based on the rapid incorporation of new technologies. Young people's attitudes toward new technologies are generally characterized by curiosity and enthusiasm. They easily incorporate new technologies and the utilization of these technologies is generally valued in their peer groups (Buckingham, 2006; Kaare et al., 2007; McMillan & Morrison, 2006; Valentine & Holloway, 2002). Similarly, these technologies provide many disabled youths the opportunity to be trendy, communicate with peers on their own terms, and render their disabilities unessential.

Eivind is a 17-year-old young man who is partially sighted. He has finished school and is waiting for an apprentice training place in a bakery. For the time being, he spends his days at home. Eivind told me that he does not use the computer much, except for using Skype and playing computer games. I asked him to tell me about what kind of games he played and he responded,

> I play World of Warcraft. Sometimes I can play it for six hours. I play sometimes together with friends and sometimes together with people from England and the Netherlands. We play and talk at the same time. It is fun to get to know other people. You get to know them quite well when you play and talk with them almost every day. But I haven't met any of them.

Thus, on the digital town square, Eivind meets people who share his interest in computer games. He participates in the game playing and gets to know people from other countries. Eivind is thus building a digital network of his own choice, a network where he is able to control the degree of personal exposure, where his competencies are displayed, and where his visual impairment is made unessential.

On the digital town square, disabled youths have the opportunity to interact without the interference of the stigma of disability getting in the forefront of the interaction. A stigma is a discrediting attribute, like lazy, dull, or unqualified, that is inflicted on people with disabilities. A stigma is derived from stereotypical notions about external and social attributes, and it brings about inflexible and stereotypical anticipations and behaviors toward the person with a disability (Barron, 2005; Goffman, 1963; Grue, 2001). The opportunity ICT might provide to escape a stigma and make disability unessential lies in the properties of digitally mediated interaction. Digitally mediated interaction is not subject to the biases that might arise in face-to-face interactions due to external attributes and physical cues, such as different appearances, gestures, or facial expressions (Brandtzæg & Stav, 2004; Kaare et al., 2007; Whitley, 1997). Even when the digital interaction takes place with well-known friends, potential physical cues are not as prominent, and thus do not interfere with the interaction in the same way as they might in face-to-face interactions. This digital context provides Eivind, Signe, Maren, and other disabled youths an opportunity to escape the interference of stigma in their social relationships, interact on more equal terms, and seize the chance to display digital competencies and personal capabilities and thus make their disability nonexistent.

Barriers to Making Disability Unessential

When the digital town square was inaccessible or unusable, it was found to be a barrier in making disability unessential. Importantly, the digital town square itself neither provided opportunities nor created barriers. The same person found both opportunities and barriers in different parts of the digital town square.

Kristin is a 16-year-old young woman with movement difficulties; she uses a wheelchair to get around. She attends the local high school and described how she loved spending time with her friends. She talked a lot on MSN, listened to music, and did her homework, all at the same time. I asked her what else she did on the computer and she said, "Nothing much. I have never figured out how the other ones download movies or design home pages. It's a little bit annoying actually, because it sounds fun." When Kristin listened to her friends talk about movies they downloaded from the Internet or how they designed their home pages, her lack of digital competencies in this area results in her exclusion from participating not only in her friends' joint online experiences but also in their offline face-to-face interactions about their online activities. Thus, inaccessible ICT weakened Kristin's social ties and relations, illustrating the significance of ICT in sustaining and reinforcing young people's social relationships and the social consequences of not being able to engage in valued activities on the digital town square. In facing this ICT-mediated barrier, which in Kristin's case is a lack in digital competencies, her difference from her peers was highlighted. It is not uncommon for every behavior, limitation, or appearance to be linked to the person's impairment (Barron, 2005; Goffman, 1963; Grue, 2001). Given the extent to which people's attitudes toward and expectations of a person who has an impairment generally guide their interpretation and understanding of that person, it is plausible to assume that Kristin's peers ascribed her lack of digital competencies to her impairment. She thus encountered ICT-mediated barriers that not only hampered her effort to make disability unessential in her social relations with friends and peers but also impacted on her ability to engage in non-ICT relationships.

Some young disabled people described how they found parts of the Internet inaccessible, confusing, and complicated. Despite being allocated assistive technology to make the Internet accessible, most of the young people found that this technology only made some parts of the Internet accessible, and very often not the popular sites or interactive parts, like MSN, chat rooms, or interactive computer games. By not engaging in these digital interactivities, young disabled people were excluded from the digital town square and thus from participating in a central meeting place for young people. Consequently, they did not meet the demand associated with always-on relationships, namely, to be connected and available at all times. Further, these ICT-mediated barriers to social relationships with friends and peers are likely to be ascribed to disability, and not to the technology or its properties and practices.

The Experience of Solitude

An Opportunity to Escape the Solitude

When young disabled people found ICT accessible and usable, this allowed them to attend the digital town square, it also provided them an important opportunity to break a potential solitude. Young people with disabilities may not have the same opportunities to socialize and participate in leisure activities as other young people. Although most disabled Norwegian youths attend the local school and are able to participate in social settings, it has been found that they participate less in such settings, and that they have fewer friends than nondisabled Norwegian youth (Grue, 1998, 2001). Similar findings have emerged from studies in other countries (Aitchison, 2003). Many of the young disabled people I interviewed told me that they did not have many friends, nor did they attend organized leisure activities. ICT offered an opportunity for these young people to overcome this solitude. For example Maya, an 18-year-old partially sighted young woman, stated, "Thank God for MSN! You see, I don't have like many friends around here. I have one friend, a neighbor who I grew up with." All the young people spoke about their utilization of computers and mobile phones as a way of relieving solitude. Harald, an 18-year-old young man with some movement difficulties, stated, "The best part with the computer is to have something to do. There is not always a lot to do you know . . . like social activities and stuff."

The lives of young people are typically characterized by multiple and complex social networks, defined by more than one way of relating to their friends. As they meet in different social settings, their roles and relationships change accordingly, but the boundaries between these arenas are permeable, with events from one arena being discussed in other arenas (Grue, 2001). For young people, friends are an important source of feedback and represent a unique closeness that involves sharing of personal experiences and opinions. Friendships are a vital part of the development and foundation of self-esteem and personal identity (Frønes, 2003). The Internet-connected computer has been found to play an important part in these processes by facilitating relationships (Valentine & Holloway, 2002).

For disabled youths, friends and peers are not guaranteed. Indeed, many young disabled people face the challenge of becoming marginalized. To be marginalized is to be put aside and made insignificant in social relationships (Grue, 2001), as might happen by being shut out of common meeting arenas, such as the digital town square, and from engaging in mutual communication and participating in shared activities. One consequence of marginalization is solitude, which can already be problematic in a country such as Norway, where the population is scattered and many people live in rural areas without a wide range of potential friends. The diversity in small local communities is often limited, increasing the likelihood of being marginalized. Harald and Maya confronted this challenge, like many other disabled youths, by engaging in digital interactions and activities. On the digital town square, they do not encounter the same obstacles as in the local physical environments because they are provided an opportunity to socialize, participate, and interact with other youths. At the digital town square, disabled youths can meet people and interact independently of characteristic, geography, time, or mobility. As found by other researchers, the Internet provided these young people who have a hard time meeting people with a great communication tool (Dobransky & Hargittai, 2006; Rice & Haythornthwaite, 2006; Seymour & Lupton, 2004; Valentine & Holloway, 2002).

Tore, a 16-year-old young man with comprehensive movement difficulties, makes the significance of the computer quite clear. In response to my question about what he would miss the most if he did not have a computer, he promptly answers, "Without the computer I have no friends." For all these young people, the computer brings the digital town square into their homes, and they are provided an opportunity to communicate and interact with friends and peers. Thus, ICT contributes to the process of breaking their solitude.

A Barrier to Escaping the Solitude

Some of the disabled youths were unable to address their solitude through ICT. Øyvind is a 19-year-old young man with movement difficulties. He stated that he enjoyed swimming, horseback riding, and listening to audio books. Both swimming and horseback riding are activities he attended accompanied by professional helpers as part of a training program. Øyvind told me about how he spent his days. He has dropped out of school and is receiving disability income support benefits. At school, he was bullied a lot, and even though he found it a little boring spending so much time at home, he was reluctant to go back to school. He used his computer solely for e-mail and reading news on the Internet, whereas he used his mobile phone to SMS his parents and his cousin. When I asked Øyvind if he had tried the MSN he said, "Well, I have tried to use the MSN but I don't use it a lot . . . I don't have like so many . . . but of course there is my cousin. Recently it has been so nice weather that I have been too occupied with other things." The stories Øyvind told me and the manner in which he responded to my questions confirmed that he did not have many friends but that it was hard for him to admit this. Thus, because he did not have any friends with whom to communicate on the MSN, this technology did not provide him any opportunity to escape his solitude. Øyvind therefore illustrated the importance of an offline social group to facilitate the social potential provided by ICT, a conclusion that is supported by a comprehensive body of research (Arnseth et al., 2007; Baym, 2006; Baym et al., 2004; Kaare et al., 2007; Livingstone, 2003; McMillan & Morrison, 2006; Räsånen & Kouvo, 2007; Rice & Haythornthwaite, 2006; Thulin & Vilhelmson, 2005; Torgersen, 2004).

For those young people who have literacy, concentration, or cognitive difficulties, the use of ICT is even further complicated. Several young people talked about the confusion and exertion they experienced in using ICT. Christine is a 19-year-old young woman who had just moved to the city to attend college and was living alone for the first time. She is using a wheelchair, and as a result of the difficulties she experienced in getting around outside her apartment, special transport had been organized for her to get back and forth to college. So far, she had only one friend in the city, a young man with an impairment living in the same building. She spent her spare time in the apartment, something she found a little annoying. Talking about friends and communication she said, "I think it is easier to discuss things face-to-face than on the MSN. On the MSN I easily get confused. It is a little bit difficult to keep track of every thing, so I don't have the habit of chatting on the MSN. But I use the e-mail quite regularly." During the conversation, it was revealed that Christine's use of email was her tool for organizing her daily life. She used e-mail "for purposes regarding my situation, which I will never get rid of." These purposes included planning meetings with her support group, organizing transportation, or making appointments with professional helpers.

Although most Norwegian young people use the MSN as their highway to communication and interaction with friends and peers, Christine found the speed and heavy traffic on this highway confusing and overwhelming. Thus, she restricted her ICT activity to e-mail, a road traveled by very few Norwegian young people. Consequently, Christine does not meet any friends or peers on this road. Most young people described e-mail as being too slow and inefficient for communication purposes because it is not capable of immediate exchanges. They do, however, use e-mail for public contacts, as Christine did, and for schoolwork. Some evidence has confirmed that e-mail is utilized more by Norwegian youth at school and for school-related work than at home, where MSN is the preferred communication channel (Arnseth et al., 2007). Thus, for Christine the speed and complexity of the MSN, the central meeting place for young people, created a barrier for her in her efforts to escape potential solitude.

The properties of ICT are experienced differently by different users and in different contexts. For some young people, ICT is associated with sociability and communication and for others with academic use (Valentine & Holloway, 2002). For some of the young people in the current study ICT was associated with difficulties, confusion, and exertion. In addition, because ICT constitutes such a central meeting place for young people to develop and maintain their social relationships, young disabled people who encounter ICT-mediated barriers are particularly disadvantaged in their social relations with friends and peers.

Permeability of the Real and the Virtual

The conceptions and experiences about what is real, social, and interpersonal are changing contemporaneously with the expansion of the arenas within which communications, interactions, and relationships occur. Thus, the real world and the virtual world are no longer separate entities but are permeable, mutually constituted, and embedded within everyday life (Anderberg & Jönsson, 2005; Baym, 2006; Baym et al., 2004; Brandtzæg & Stav, 2004; Buckingham, 2006; Houlihan et al., 2003; Kaare et al., 2007; Oksman & Turtianien, 2004; Peter & Valkenburg, 2006; Seymour & Lupton, 2004; Thulin & Vilhelmson, 2005; Wellman et al., 2001). Young people typically experience this permeability of the real and the virtual, but little is known about how it affects the social relationships of young disabled people.

However, three girls, Henny, Mette, and Karin, illuminate the common experience among young people of the significance of this permeability. Henny, a 17-year-old nondisabled young woman, says, "Because all the others have a computer I would have been completely lost without my computer. I would have felt like totally outside everything." Mette, a 16-year-old nondisabled girl, puts it this way: "I don't know how I would have managed without the computer. Being on the computer is to be social. I would have missed it a lot." Karin, another 16-year-old nondisabled girl, gives a clear expression: "If you can sit and chat with someone on the computer then it means that you also have a relationship to them in your leisure time."

An Opportunity to Enhance Social Relationships

For most disabled youths, the permeability of the real and the virtual enhanced their opportunities in social relations. The most common opportunity taken up by young people in general, and by the young people I interviewed, was to continue to communicate with schoolmates and other already known friends after school hours (Baym et al., 2004; Brandtzæg & Stav, 2004; Kaare et al., 2007; McMillan & Morrison, 2006; Thulin & Vilhelmson, 2005; Valentine & Holloway, 2002).

Ingrid is a 15-year-old blind young woman. She shared, "On the MSN I talk to my friends from school and other blind youths I have met on camps and stuff." Almost all of the disabled youths described how they attended summer camps and gatherings, and then used ICT to remain in touch with the friends they made at such camps and gatherings. Despite distances and the lack of face-to-face interactions with these friends, they communicated and interacted on the digital town square by means of ICT. Here, they talked about joint experiences and common acquaintances from the camps or gatherings, they discussed their everyday local life at school and in the neighborhood, and they planned meeting at the next camp or gathering. When they again met in person, they knew each other even better than the last time, which is congruent with many other studies on how young people engage in ICT (Baym et al., 2004; Brandtzæg & Stav, 2004; Kaare et al., 2007; McMillan & Morrison, 2006; Thulin & Vilhelmson, 2005; Valentine & Holloway, 2002).

Many young disabled people seek the company of other young disabled people. Close friends share interests and experiences and understanding. Given the complexity of experiences of young disabled people, it is likely that they may require a great deal of empathy and understanding from close friends. As a result, young people may be forced to make careful selection of friends, partially accounting for the fact that young people with disabilities have fewer friends than other young people (Aitchison, 2003; Grue, 2001). For many disabled youths, the permeability of the real and the virtual provided them an opportunity to maintain friendship with their friends regardless of geographical distance. It also provided them an enhanced opportunity to choose their affiliation, their close and intimate relationships, and their distant acquaintances. The extended dissemination and use of ICT in the population has provided many young people a freedom of choice in this area, which was not an option earlier. In this way, the young disabled people integrate the real and the virtual to enhance their social relationships.

Many of the young people with movement difficulties discussed problems getting around in the local community. Jacob is a 16-year-old young man with comprehensive movement difficulties. He uses an electric wheelchair. He lives in a small town and attends the local school. Jacob stated that he enjoyed school and he told me about his three friends, "I have three friends at school. We are all into computers and computer games. Every other weekend they visit me at home and then we play games, surf the Web, and discuss computer stuff. And if I need help with anything [on the computer], I can just ask them." Like Signe and her friends, Jacob and his friends gather around the computer screen in shared activities, thus blending the real world and the virtual world as a way of facilitating social relationships. The implementation of ICT by young people has turned it into a tool that brings friends together in face-to-face activities around the computer screen. The virtual has become an important element in the real interactions and relationships of many young people. Gatherings around the computer screen can take place almost anywhere and do not demand much mobility or physical efforts. Such settings provide many disabled youths, who experience difficulty attending leisure activities or social gatherings, with enhanced opportunities in social relationships and activities with friends and peers. In these settings, the real and the virtual are combined, and communications about digital commodities and virtual experiences have become an important aspect of social engagement.

A Barrier in Establishing Social Relationships

The permeability of the real and the virtual also created barriers for disabled youths, even when the digital town square was accessible.

Christopher is an 18-year-old young man with some movement and visual difficulties. He told me that he used his computer to read news and watch movies, whereas he used his mobile phone to SMS his parents, siblings, and other relatives. Christopher attends the local school. When I asked him how long he spent on the computer in an ordinary day, he answered, "Not so long, maybe half an hour. The reason why I don't use it more is because I don't chat on the MSN. I don't think it is very nice. Some people are quite rude, and they say things they would never have said face to face. I like it better to get to know people in the ordinary way." Christopher had experienced harassment on the Internet, confirming that digital-mediated communication and face-to-face communication may differ in both content and in style. The opportunity to communicate on the computer without face-to-face contact has been found to promote a lower social threshold for unrestricted, creative, and unreserved communication than would be found in traditional offline communication. This lower threshold leads to a richer emotional communication, sometimes in the shape of emotional support or intimate messages, but sometimes in the shape of hostility and harassments (Brandtzæg & Stav, 2004; Kaare et al., 2007; Oksman & Turtianien, 2004; Peter & Valkenberg, 2006; Whitley, 1997). Christopher did not have any close friends to facilitate his safe introduction to the Internet, and when he accessed MSN, he had come into contact with casual acquaintances, making him vulnerable to ICT-related abuse.

Livingstone (2003) and Buckingham (2006) pointed to the need for more knowledge about how technology enters into the peer group. As described by Valentine and Holloway (2002), this chapter has shown how ICT emerges and is utilized differently by young disabled people.

Although ICT is generally experienced positively by young disabled people, for some it has been a source of negative experiences. Only a few young people told stories about being harassed through ICT, but many admitted to knowing about someone who has experienced negative interactions. When negative interactions occurred, it was mostly on home pages on the Internet or by SMS.

Lars is a 17-year-old young man who has some movement difficulties. He talked about his experience with a home page on the Web:

> One time, my friends and I designed a home page. But it was just nonsense, just for fun to tease people. But I know many, especially girls, who have made their own home page and then someone has written a lot of rubbish about them in the guest book. At school some teachers try to reprimand those who write such things. But it is not always easy to know who this is, and I personally don't bother. I would never be offended by such things.

Negative experiences such as this resulted in young people's withdrawal from engaging in interactions on the Web. This experience made young people reluctant to seek contact with strangers on the Web. Although the permeability of the real and the virtual enhanced social relationships for most of the young people, such as Mari, Jacob, and Lars, it diminished social relationships for a few young people.

Most of the young people expressed their skepticism regarding contact with unknown people via the Web. They advocated only communicating with already known friends and acquaintances. The few young people who admitted to chatting with unknown people noted that this communication was superficial and that they were careful about what they disclosed as well as what they believed about others' disclosures.

A few of the young people did not communicate on the Web at all, particularly those who did not have any close friends at school, in the neighborhood or elsewhere, like Christopher. For these young people who did not have any close friends or trusted acquaintances to chat with, and did not wish to expose themselves to interactions with strangers or to the risk of being harassed, ICT represented a barrier to social interactions. Thus, those young people who did not have any friends in the real world were less likely to access friends via the virtual world.

Research on disabled adults has found that many of them visited disability-related Web sites to establish contact with other people with disabilities (Anderberg & Jönsson, 2005; Houlihan et al., 2003; Seymour & Lupton, 2004). This was, however, not the case for the disabled youths I interviewed. Those who chatted with other young disabled people did so by means of MSN and only chatted with people they already knew. They chatted about common experiences, but not explicitly about disability. Thus, the online life of these young disabled people mirrored their offline relationships, as found in many other studies on youth in general (Arnseth et al., 2007; Baym, 2006; Baym et al., 2004; Kaare et al., 2007; Livingstone, 2003; McMillan & Morrison, 2006; Räsänen & Kouvo, 2007; Rice & Haythornthwaite, 2006; Thulin & Vilhelmson, 2005; Torgersen, 2004). ICT therefore sustained and reinforced already existing social ties for young people (Brandtzæg & Stav, 2004; McMillan & Morrison, 2006; Thulin & Vilhelmson, 2005). This conclusion challenges the common assumption that ICT radically transforms the contact behavior of young people and that they seek new friends on the digital town square. Although some young disabled people did seek new contacts on the Internet, most did not. The majority chatted and interacted with already known offline friends and used ICT as a means of sustaining those relationships. At school and in face-to-face settings, they discussed and exchanged digital experiences and activities with their offline friends. For those young people who had no friends in their everyday offline lives, this permeability of the real and the virtual created barriers in their social relationships.

CONCLUSION

This chapter has explored the significance of ICT on the social relationships of Norwegian disabled youths using examples provided by a group of young disabled people. It has illuminated how their use of ICT as a form of communication has created a digital town square or a central online meeting place that featured prominently in the social relationships of young disabled people. This chapter has shown how accessible and usable ICT can provide opportunities for young disabled people to engage in social relationships, but it can also create barriers for some of these young people. When disabled youths engaged in ICT, disability is made unessential, a potential solitude is escaped, and already existing social relationships are sustained and reinforced. However, barriers also emerge, emphasizing disability and solitude. As a result, opportunities to create social relationships are inhibited.

The increasing permeability of the real and the virtual in young peoples' lives was found to have the most significant impact on the possibilities for social relations mediated through ICT. On the digital town square, young people interacted and discussed joint physical and local experiences and events, such as what happened at school or at shared leisure activities. Just as they did in face-to-face settings, they discussed and shared virtual experiences, such as what Web sites to visit or how to download movies. To engage in these settings, young people are required to be digitally connected to offline friends with whom they can discuss joint experiences on the digital town square. Similarly, they need some mutual online digital experiences to discuss and share in face-to-face settings.

For young people who have offline friends, accessible ICT can sustain and reinforce those relationships, provide enhanced inclusion and participation, and may even create opportunities for new offline friendships. However, for those young people who have no close offline friends, even accessible ICT was found to create inhibiting barriers to social relationships, to promote exclusion and alienation, and thus even weaken the potential offline friendships.

The permeability of the real and the virtual has generated a dependency on the technologies (McMillan & Morrison, 2006). This dependency is a double-edged sword inasmuch as it embraces more and more of young people's everyday lives. Consequently, the use of this technology is vital for inclusion. Further, withdrawal from ICT or inability to engage in digital forms of communication is perceived to be one of the most damaging forms of exclusion. Thus, it is vital to closely examine who is not using ICT, why, and with what consequences (Livingstone & Helsper, 2007; McMillan & Morrison, 2006). The ICT-mediated barriers described by the young disabled people in this chapter testifies to the importance of adequate engagement in ICT.

REFERENCES

Aitchison, C. (2003). From leisure and disability to disability leisure: Developing data, definitions and discourses. *Disability & Society, 18*(7), 955–969.

Anderberg, P., & Jönsson, B. (2005). Being there. *Disability & Society, 20*(7), 719–733.

Arnseth, H. C., Hatlevik, O., Kløvstad, V., Kristiansen, T., & Ottestad, G. (2007). *ITU Monitor 2007 Skolens digitale tilstand 2007.* Oslo: Universitetsforlaget.

Barron, K. (2005). I am, and I am not: Identity, a multifaceted concept and social phenomenon. In A. Gustavson, J. Sandvin, R. Traustadòttir, & J. Tøssebro,

(Eds.), *Resistance, reflection and change* (pp. 163–176). Lund, Sweden: Studentlitteratur.

Baym, N. K. (2006). Interpersonal life online. In L. A. Lievrouw & S. Livingstone (Eds.), *The handbook of new media updated student edition* (pp. 35–54). London: Sage.

Baym, N. K., Zhang, Y. B., & Lin, M. C. (2004). Social interactions across media: Interpersonal communication on the Internet, telephone and face-to-face. *New Media & Society, 6*(3), 299–318.

Bowker, N., & Tuffin, K. (2002). Disability discourses for online identities. *Disability & Society, 17*(3) 327–344.

Brandtzæg, P. B., & Stav, B. H. (2004). Barn og unges skravling på nettet Sosial støtte i cyberspace? *Tidsskrift for ungdomsforskning, 4*(1), 27–47.

Buckingham, D. (2006). Children and new media. In L. A. Lievrouw & S. Livingstone (Eds.), *The handbook of new media updated student edition* (pp. 75–91). London: Sage.

D'Aubin, A. (2007). Working for barrier removal in the ICT Area: Creating a more accessible and inclusive Canada: A Position Statement by the Council of Canadians with Disabilities. *Information Society, 23*, 193–201.

Dobransky, K., & Hargittai, E. (2006). The disability divide in Internet access and use. *Information, Communication & Society, 9*(3), 313–334.

Frønes, I. (2003). *De likeverdige Om sosialisering og de jevnaldrendes betydning* Oslo: Gyldendal Akademisk.

Full Participation for All? Development Trends 2001–2006. Oslo: DOK and HS-Dir.

Goffman, E. (1963). *Stigma notes on the management of spoiled identity.* New Jersey: Penguin.

Government's Action Plan for Increased Accessibility. (2004). Oslo: Arbeids- og Sosialdepartementet og Miljøverndepartementet.

Grue, L. (1998). *På terskelen En undersøkelse av funksjonshemmet ungdoms sosiale tilhørighet, selvbilde og livskvalitet.* Oslo: NOVA Rapport 6/1998.

Grue, L. (2001). *Motstand og mestring Om funksjonshemming og livsvilkår.* Oslo: Abstrakt Forlag.

Gustavsson, A., Tøssebro, J., & Traustadòttir, R. (2005). Introduction: Approaches and perspectives in Nordic disability research. In A. Gustavsson, J. Sandvin, R. Traustadòttir, & J. Tøssebro (Eds.), *Resistance, reflection and change Nordic disability research* (pp. 23–44). Lund, Sweden: Studentlitteratur.

Halvorsen, R., & Hvinden, B. (2007). Accessibility and participation for people with disabilities—unsolved issues in the Nordic welfare states. In *The Nordic Development Centre for Rehabilitation Technology Report* 2007 (pp. 7–15).

Hjelmtveit, V. (2005). Sosialpolitikk i historisk perspektiv. In M. A. Stamsø (Ed.), *Velferdsstaten i endring Norsk helse- og sosialpolitikk ved starten av et nytt århundre* (pp. 24–57). Oslo: Gyldendal Akademisk.

Houlihan, B. W., Drainoni, M. L., Warner, G., Nesathurai, S., Wierbicky, J., & Williams, S. (2003). The impact of Internet access for people with spinal cord injuries: A descriptive analysis of a pilot study. *Disability and Rehabilitation, 25*(8), 422–431.

Kaare, B. H., Brantzæg, P. B., Heim, J., & Endestad, T. (2007). In the borderline between family orientation and peer culture: The use of communication technologies among Norwegian tweens. *New Media & Society,* 9(4), 603–624.

Lievrouw, L. A., & Livingstone, S. (2006). Introduction to the updated student edition. In L. A. Lievrouw & S. Livingstone (Eds.), *The handbook of new media updated student edition* (pp. 1–14). London: Sage.

Ling, R. (2004). *The mobile connection: The cell phone's impact on society.* San Francisco: Elsevier.

Livingstone, S. (2003). Children's use of the Internet: Reflections on the emerging research agenda. *New Media & Society*, 5(2), 147–166.
Livingstone, S., & Helsper, E. (2007). Gradations in digital inclusion: Children, young people and the digital divide. *New Media & Society*, 9(4), 671–696.
Lorentzen, K. (2007). *Nøkkeltall om informasjonssamfunnet 2006 IKT i husholdningene*. Oslo: Statistisk Sentral Byrå. Retrieved from www.ssb.no/ikthus.
Madell, D., & Muncer, S. (2005). Are Internet and mobile phone communication complementary amongst young people? A study from a "rational actor perspective." *Information, Communication & Society*, 8(1), 64–80.
McMillan, S. J., & Morrison, M. (2006), Coming of age with the Internet: A qualitative exploration of how the Internet has become an integral part of young people's lives. *New Media & Society*, 8(1), 73–95.
Ministry of Modernisation. (2009). e-Norway—*the digital leap*. Oslo: Author.
Norwegian Official Report. (2001). *Fra bruker til borger En strategi for nedbygging av funksjonshemmende barrierer*. Oslo: Statens forvaltningstjeneste, informasjonsforvaltning.
Oksman, V., & Turtianien, J. (2004). Mobile communication as a social stage meanings of mobile communication in everyday life among teenagers in Finland. *New Media & Society*, 6(3), 319–339.
Pell, S. D., Gillies, R. M., & Carss, M. (1999). Use of technology by people with physical disabilities in Australia. *Disability and Rehabilitation*, 21(2), 56–60.
Peter, J., & Valkenburg, P. M. (2006). Research note: Individual differences in perceptions of Internet communication. *European Journal of Communication*, 21(2), 213–226.
Råsånen, P., & Kouvo, A. (2007). Linked or divided by the Web? Internet use and sociability in four European countries. *Information, Communication & Society*, 10(2), 219–241.
Rice, R. E., & Haythornthwaite, C. (2006). Perspectives on Internet use: Access, involvement and interaction. In L. A. Lievrouw & S. Livingstone (Eds.), *The handbook of new media updated student version* (pp. 92–113). London: Sage.
Seymour, W. (2005). ICTs and disability: Exploring the human dimensions of technological engagement. *Technology and Disability*, 17, 195–204.
Seymour, W., & Lupton, D. (2004). Holding the line online: Exploring wired relationships for people with disabilities. *Disability & Society*, 19(4), 291–305.
State of Affairs on Accessibility in Norway. (2006). Oslo: Statens råd for funksjonshemmede og DOK.
Stienstra, D. (2006). The critical space between access, inclusion and standards in information technologies. *Information, Communication & Society*, 9(3), 335–354.
Thulin, E., & Vilhelmson, B. (2005). Virtual mobility of urban youth: ICT-based communication in Sweden. *Tijdschrift voor Economische en Sociale Geografie*, 96(5), 477–487.
Tobias, J. (2003). Information technology and universal design: An agenda for accessible technology. *Journal of Visual Impairment & Blindness, October*, 592–601.
Torgersen, L. (2004). *Ungdoms digitale hverdag: bruk av PC, internett, TV-spill og mobiltelefon blant elever på ungdomsskolen og videregående skole*. Oslo: NOVA-rapport 8/2004
Tøssebro, J. (2004). Introduction to the special issue: Understanding disability. *Scandinavian Journal of Disability Research*, 6(1), 3–7.
Traustadòttir, R., & Kristiansen, K. (2004). Introducing gender and disability. In K. Kristiansen & R. Traustedòttir (Eds.), *Gender and disability research in the Nordic countries* (pp. 31–48). Lund, Sweden: Studentlitteratur.

Valentine, G., & Holloway, S. L. (2002). Cyberkids? Exploring children's identities and social networks in on-line and off-line worlds. *Annals of the Association of American Geographers, 92*(2), 302–319.

Wei, R., & Lo, V. H. (2006). Staying connected while on the move cell phone use and social connectedness. *New Media & Society, 8*(1), 53–72.

Wellman, B., Haase, A. Q., Witte, J., & Hampton, K. (2001). Does the Internet increase, decrease or supplement social capital? Social networks, participation and community commitment. *American Behavioral Scientist 45*(3), 436–455.

White Paper no. 40. (2002–2003). *Nedbygging av funksjonshemmende barrierer Strategier, mål og tiltak for personer med nedsatt funksjonsevne.* Oslo: Det Kongelige Sosialdepartement.

Whitley, E. A. (1997). In cyberspace all they see is your words: A review of the relationship between body, behaviour and identity drawn from the sociology of knowledge. *Information, Technology & People, 10*(2), 147–163.

CHAPTER 5

Understanding the Experience of Parenting a Child with Autism

Samantha Bursnall, Eilis Kennedy, Rob Senior, and Jo Violet

It has long been recognized that a disability impacts not only the children involved but the entire family system. Among the plethora of research exploring the impact of disability on family members is a body of research examining the impact of childhood autism on the family. There is a general recognition in this literature that "living with a person with autism can have a devastating impact on all other family members" (Reid, 1999, p. 63). Studies have observed that parents of children with autism typically experience greater levels of stress when compared to parents of normally developing children, children with chronic illness, or other types of disabilities (Sivberg, 2002; Sounders, DePaul, Freeman, & Levy, 2002; Tunali & Power, 2002).

Examining the experiences and perceptions of parents who have a child with autism through in-depth interviews is useful because it provides participants with the opportunity to fully describe their experiences and needs as opposed to limiting their responses to predetermined questionnaire categories. Thus, using a thematic analysis, this chapter explores the views of 12 parents of children with autism.[1] The findings were presented back to the parents, who confirmed and approved the themes that now form the basis of this chapter.

RESEARCH ON PARENTS OF CHILDREN WITH AUTISM

Parents of children diagnosed with autism are likely to experience anxiety, fear, guilt, and emotional stress (Gray, 1994) as well as a sense of loss and despair at their child's lack of ability to emotionally reciprocate and connect to them (Reid, 1999). In a grounded theory study, Midence and O'Neill (1999) found that prior to receiving a diagnosis, lack of understanding and confusion about their child's difficulties increased parental distress and despair. Particularly distressing was the child's "different" development, including problems with language, awareness, behavior, eye contact, sleep, pointing, and rituals (p. 277).

A lack of adequate resources (e.g., education facilities, appropriate community support agencies), delay in receiving a diagnosis (Fleischmann, 2005), limited access to professionals with knowledge of autism (Sivberg, 2002), and information and support to guide them in the care of their children (Huws, Jones, & Ingledew, 2001) have also been observed to exacerbate family stress.

The stress has also been observed to impact negatively on marital relationships (Rivers & Stoneman, 2003) and on siblings who, when compared to other groups of siblings of children with disability, have shown elevated levels of behavioral problems (external and internal) and lower levels of social interaction with the child with autism (Fisman et al., 1996). Siblings have also been observed to get less parental attention and adopt more of an adult role in the family (Reid, 1999).

Not surprisingly, parents with better support have been found to report less stress (Weiss, 2002). Obtaining a correct diagnosis of autism has also been shown to help parents understand, accept, and adapt to their child's condition and form realistic expectations of their future (Midence & O'Neill, 1999). Other research has focused on identifying coping strategies (e.g., Gray, 2003, 2006; Hastings, Kovshoff, et al., 2005; Sivberg, 2002) and the more positive outcomes of parenting a child with special needs (Hastings & Taunt, 2002; Hastings, Beck, & Hill, 2005).

Although these studies have made enormous contribution to the disability literature, further exploration on the emotional experience of parenting a child with autism is warranted. In addition, many of the studies exploring the impact of autism on parents and other family members have used standardized questionnaires, which limit the identification of process issues and experiences (Hastings & Taunt, 2002).

THE EXPERIENCE OF PARENTING A CHILD WITH AUTISM

Parenting is one of the most important, rewarding, and challenging roles one may be fortunate enough to experience. However, parenting a child with autism often involves additional challenges that take the role of parenting to a higher level of intensity. The interviews provided insight into the experiences and difficulties that the parents of children with autism encountered and the reasons this experience was so intense. As one parent described, the uniqueness of having a child with autism was difficult to understand by anyone other than parents in the same situation.

> [All parents experience trials and tribulations, it] happens to everybody but it is difficult to get across the twist of the disabled child which is really different [to having normally developing children]. It's a step up in the kind of thing that you

do and I think . . . having a disabled child is the same as having a [normally developing] child except that it's got a lot of extra responsibility and twists and that's what people don't really understand. . . . [The emotions you feel and the experiences you have] are a darker, deeper shadow altogether. . . . Everything is just much, much more intense . . . people with ordinary children just don't get it.

This chapter describes the context in which parenting a child with autism often takes place (within and external to the family). It is important to note that although presented sequentially and separately, the themes that follow usually occurred simultaneously. This section gives insight into the experiences, stresses, and difficulties that parents of children with autism encounter. These stresses coexist with a range of positive experiences associated with raising a child with autism. Experiencing difficulties does not necessarily mean a lack of positive experiences.

SEARCHING FOR ANSWERS

The most emotionally charged time described by parents was when they realized that something was different about their child. The processes associated with discovering a diagnosis of autism and accessing support for their child undermined parents' sense of control in their parenting role and often left them feeling disempowered and disenfranchised. Trying to gain a sense of control to protect and provide for their child was a major source of stress for parents, which involved them having to search for answers and support.

Discovering a Diagnosis

Parents described feeling confused and unsupported when they sought answers for a condition they knew little about. As would be expected, parents said they were unaware, particularly in the initial stages of their child's diagnosis, of what services were available and what they needed to do to access them. Most said they did not even know what they needed in the initial stages of their child's diagnosis. One parent observed "how ignorant parents are about what is available and how difficult it is to find out what is available."

Before a formal diagnosis was given, many of the parents perceived their child's unusual behaviors and differences to reflect their "bad parenting." This self-doubt was magnified when the child with autism was their first born and parents had no prior experience from which to compare their child. Not surprisingly this left them feeling confused and insecure.

> I knew something was wrong from about 18 months. . . . First of all I had a feeling like "How come I can get along with all my friends' children but like my one I couldn't?" . . . "Why can't I talk to my own daughter? Why can't I play with my own daughter?" I thought "Is it me?"
>
> [My child with autism] was beginning to cause me problems in playgroups . . . there was just something different about the way he was relating to other babies and other children. . . . I . . . used to go to baby groups and just sit there and sometimes cry. I think things weren't right, and I couldn't understand it. Life was very hard.

Although the time of diagnosis was emphasized as a time of intense stress and confusion, it was just one of many hurdles that required parents to seek answers and support for their child. Some parents searched for years before they were given a diagnosis.

Negotiating the Hostile System

One of the major hurdles parents had to overcome in finding a diagnosis and accessing support for their child was negotiating the "hostile system." The systems of health, education, and social services set up to help parents were perceived to be difficult to negotiate and further exacerbated their confusion, self-doubt, and loss of control. They had countless appointments with professionals (once appropriate professionals were identified), during which time many parents felt their concerns were not acknowledged or were questioned.

For children whose special needs were less obvious, finding support was particularly difficult. "The delay you can have from diagnosis . . . finding the right people then getting a diagnosis . . . that's a huge pressure on people to manage." Parents described how everything was a battle, how services were often suboptimal, and how there was little regard for their role as carers.

Everything's a Battle

To access support for their children, parents felt they had to fight for everything. "No one's actually told you what you need or you feel like you've had to find everything out and then, once you've found it out, you have to fight to get it." Parents described this process as "traumatic," "the whole looking into schools and that, I think, was perhaps absolute trauma. Very, very difficult and I think that the way the system is set up is horrific." Parents felt their views were dismissed and that budget constraints, rather than their child's actual needs, dictated what supports their child eventually received. Parents perceived the battles for securing support would continue as their child grew: "[I will be fighting] for the rest of my life and, assuming that I go first, I hope that someone will be in place to do it for [him]".

To access the support required, parents noted that one needs many resources, including, energy, time, financial resources, education, and a good command of English. The time and energy required to fight the system for support meant that the role of a parent became blurred and reflected more that of an advocate. "I have the time and the wherewithal and the energy to fight it. If I hadn't have done, it wouldn't have come about and I know parents who don't have that energy and you know sometimes you just want to be a parent? You don't want to be their advocate so it is hard."

Many parents were concerned about other parents who did not have English as a first language, who themselves had vulnerabilities, or who did not have the internal or external resources to negotiate the hostile system.

Suboptimal Services

Many services were of enormous help to parents, especially given the constraints of the hostile system. However, most found at some point in their child's rehabilitation continuum they were confronted with the trauma of having to deal with services that fell short in some way.

First, the services were considered to be scattered geographically in that the parents had to attend appointments, sometimes on the same day, at clinics in different parts of the city. Communication was scattered between services, and parents found they had to repeat themselves on seeing new consultants. They did not always know why they were sent to appointments, and the information did not always get passed between relevant professionals.

Second, appointments were often difficult to secure with long waiting lists and long waiting times. Also, many helpful services remained unknown to parents because they were not available on a centralized database, not highlighted by other professionals, or not well advertised. Parents said that knowing about the existence of services could potentially save them time and money. "I've had to find everything myself you know? Like getting her diagnosed, it's like 'How do I do that?' I had to find out and then I had to go and see the doctor and ask her to refer me. . . . Whereas really I think [we should be told] 'Well this is how it is, I'll refer you to these people.'"

Finally, once parents were connected to services, they highlighted that a lack of consistency between professionals within some services (often as a result of high staff turnover and low levels of communication between old and new staff) was particularly unhelpful and upsetting.

Parents also spoke of their experience with services in which there appeared an apparent lack of expertise and knowledge of autism and/or the use of professional jargon, which made it difficult to understand the professional feedback (in reports and at appointments), further isolating them. Often in conjunction with the professional jargon, parents had to deal with professionals who appeared insensitive and unsympathetic.

Unfortunately, much of what parents found unsatisfactory in services was mirrored in many schools ill equipped for children with autism (many children of the parents interviewed attended mainstream schools, at least for some time). Particularly unhelpful in relation to schools were teachers who lacked training and an understanding of children with autism. As a result, the children often struggled to make progress in mainstream school and were expected to behave and abide by the same rules as other pupils, which were inappropriate to their needs. This was exacerbated when a child's difficulties were more "hidden" (e.g., children with high-functioning autism). "I am sick and tired of [the school] saying, 'yes he has ASD, but he must behave like everyone else.' It doesn't make sense. It is like saying to a blind person 'you should see red, you need to know the difference between red and blue' and I'm sick of it!"

A lack of communication between staff and parents, a general experience of not being listened to and of being misunderstood, judged with no sense of sympathetic listening contributed to the "me against them" feeling between parents and school staff. It seemed many children were left to struggle as did the teachers without training.

> The most unhelpful thing is the lack of understanding in the school and having to go up there and fight against them all the time. Because they don't

understand the nature of her needs whereas if they did I wouldn't have to go and explain things and you know? . . . Because they're not trained, they're not aware, they're not bothered.

No Regard for Carers

Parents believed that the hostile system took advantage of their role as competent parents and failed to acknowledge the hard work that being a full-time carer involved.

> I don't think [the services/system] recognize how hard it is for us, like you're carers and having to do a hundred and one things. . . . I'm a lone parent . . . I'd love to go to work . . . but I need to get my [child's needs sorted out] . . . there is enough for me to do . . . if I got paid for everything I do as a carer I would be very rich.

JUGGLING EVERYDAY DEMANDS

In addition to coming to terms with their child's autism and negotiating the necessary supports and services, parents had to juggle the often competing everyday family demands. Although these everyday demands were not unique to these parents, they appeared to be more intense and concentrated due to the added pressure of the child's autism. The parents juggled the ongoing changes in their child, their own relationship, and the issues raised by siblings.

Changeable Child

Many parents described the process of getting to know, understand, and parent their child as requiring considerable patience and acceptance. They described their children as unique individuals with different personalities, characters, and needs, who still remained a mystery at times. Most parents indicated that their child was unpredictable and that his or her behavior and mood was changeable and difficult to manage on a continual basis. "He's great fun. He's very hard work because he's so up and down. And it's quite an up and down experience being the parent of him . . . you're never really sure what you're dealing with. . . . It's a rollercoaster. . . . He is very hard to control."

Many parents described their child with special needs as demanding and requiring constant support and attention. "Children [with ASD] are very self-centered and if you're on your own with a child like that you can sort of get sucked into that." For some parents, the unpredictability of their child's condition also related to their vulnerable health condition and the possibility that they could become physically ill at any time. It was common for parents to report that the child's behaviors were relentless, requiring them to be vigilant at all times.

This constant focus and attention required parents to sacrifice many of their own needs. "I could never [work full-time] because I feel I have to be so alert at home . . . and [hypervigilant] about so many things . . . emotionally I could never do that." As a result of their child's behavior, parents also described having to manage their own discomfort in social and public situations. Social situations provided little respite for the parents as they were required to focus on the child and continually predict their next move. "I feel embarrassed with her and I don't like people looking at me. . . . But you go to the theater and it's you know, you don't know how it's going to go. If she's bored by it, it's going to be really difficult and people are looking around all the time. She starts making a lot of noise and you might have to leave."

Relationship Stress

Parents described being drawn into the child's world by necessity, which made it difficult to share their time and emotional resources equally around the family. Although one parent acknowledged, "It's a matter of balancing your life," many times the child's needs dictated and influenced the entire family system. "The strain on the family is huge and it continues to be huge and it goes through these ups and downs and when he isn't at his best, everybody feels it and it feeds into everyone has their own ways of managing it or not managing it."

Given the enormous stresses endured by the parents, it is not surprising that parental relationships were placed under enormous pressure. Although some parents said that their child's condition brought them closer together—"we found it strengthening"—others felt it had added strain. Some parents were no longer in relationships, and many of the other parents described how the pressures surrounding their child's autism (particularly around the time of diagnosis) led to difficulties in their relationships.

Often a lack of information and support led parents to argue about what was best for the child and what they needed. In addition the high level of care many children required meant that much of the parents' focus was on the child, and thus little time and energy was left for the relationship. One parent recalled, "There used to be a time when me and my husband . . . [had] terrible arguments just because of her because I was really concerned." Another parent shared the challenges of her relationship,

> At that same time [I] was finding out Lenny's diagnosis, his dad left as well. So it was a very, very traumatic experience at the time. . . . You feel incredibly isolated . . . even within a relationship. . . . [Our child needed support] and more time . . . [which] meant that, within a relationship, I wasn't available to give any time to my partner any more.

Relationship pressures were further complicated by differences in opinion between parents about their child's condition, often due to one parent spending more time with the child and having a different awareness of their needs. Different levels of interpretation and acceptance about the child's condition, in addition to the delay often involved in acquiring a diagnosis, also played a role in further perpetuating the stress and relationship breakdown.

> If you've got a child who's doing something that the mother sees [and] the dad doesn't . . . and the mom is saying there is something wrong with this child and no one else is backing her up, that puts a huge strain on the marriage. . . . [At

the special needs school my child attends] nearly all the divorces went through at the time of diagnosis. So I think it's that strain, you know . . . they sort of end up growing apart.

Professionals working with families of children with autism also noted the strain on the parental couple relationship due to the ongoing nature of the child's needs.

> To deal with an autistic child . . . parenting takes on a whole new [meaning]. Essentially, you are parenting an adult . . . [when other children leave the nest] parents themselves are thinking 'can I go back to work? Can I have a relationship with my husband? Can I have the house to ourselves?' These things don't happen [for parents of children with autism], they're huge obstacles. And there's a huge correlation with marriages that break down, with children with autism after the age of 12.

Although it is common for relationships to breakdown in such a situation, many parents explained how they were grateful that they had a partner with whom they could share the stress and burden. Even though some had received professional help for their relationship, many of the parents' relationships were surviving despite the additional stress. "I'm very grateful that I have [my partner] because there's some mother's with children with [autism spectrum disorder] and they're on their own. My goodness! And to me that would be a hundred times harder. So I like it that [my partner] is there."

Sibling Stress

Parents were particularly concerned that siblings often missed out on quality and equality of time with their parents. Most parents noted that siblings' needs were compromised on a daily basis due to the demanding nature of the needs of the child with autism. Less obvious but as important was the lack of emotional energy parents seemed to have for siblings. Parents tried to juggle their children's competing demands, but siblings often missed out because "My daughter [with autism] is my priority now. . . . He [sibling] is in a loser in a way." Other parents described trying to manage competing interests fairly.

> She [sibling] is still not old enough, emotionally, to digest all the differences but knows there's massive differences. . . . So she is a big thing for me. To make sure that emotionally and psychologically, she's as well balanced as possible. Something that she feels, to this day, and will probably always feel, is the imbalance of time spent. . . . I have had periods where I have actually spent far more time with her than with her brother [with autism] but she doesn't feel that . . . she still felt it to be the reverse. . . . She fits in with us and what [my child with autism] needs . . . rather than what she needs and I know that that is a permanent balancing act.

Despite parents' best efforts, siblings still noticed the inequality of time and energy between them and the child with autism. Parents expressed concern and anxiety about who would be available to take care of their child when they were no longer able to do so and for many families, the child's sibling(s) appeared to be the obvious choice to take on the carer role. "She [sibling] will have to be responsible. Even though I don't want her to feel responsible, you know, there isn't anyone else. . . . We hope she continues to want to do it. . . . So that's always a pressure."

These concerns extended to siblings, who naturally assumed responsibility for the carer role despite no formal expectations from the family. "I think you underestimate how much they have to take on board. . . . My [nondisabled] son is taking on that burden and saying . . . 'Well I'll obviously have to look after [child with disability] for the rest of my life,' which is very sweet but not right, really. It's not his burden."

Another issue some parents found challenging was juggling family rules when different rules applied to the children with autism and their siblings. Siblings would witness their brother or sister "getting away with" behavior that was considered unacceptable for them. Siblings were also hidden casualties of school and community ignorance and as a result were often expected to carry on with everyday activities (e.g., school) despite having their daily lives disrupted by the needs of their brother or sister. For instance, one mother emotionally recalled,

> Siblings often don't get any acknowledgment from anywhere of the stress that they have to bear. If they've been kept awake all night by their [sibling with ASD] banging on their door, or being very aggressive or snatching their toys or mom and dad not having time for the siblings because they've had it up to here [points to head]—all these types of things. And the sibling has to come into school where [teachers think] "there's nothing wrong with them!" They are expected to get their heads down and get through their working day and have the best results. . . . They've got no voice, they've got nothing, but they can have as much stress and it's hidden.

On a positive note however, siblings were also acknowledged as being more responsible, mature, and empathetic. "One blessing that I would never, ever have anticipated has been the development of more generosity in the teenage years . . . and it's gone on from that into their adult lives. . . . They talk about it as if he has taught them so much, so there is great good there." This theme indicates that like parents of children with ASD who experience intensity in parenting, siblings also endure a magnification of typical sibling rivalries and competition that are likely to span into adulthood. Juggling these sibling issues placed another extraordinary demand on the everyday experience of parents.

EMOTIONAL ROLLERCOASTER

From the time they noticed that something was different with their child, parents described experiencing a rollercoaster of emotions that varied in intensity and duration. Some emotions were stronger than others at different times, and some were experienced simultaneously or not at all. These emotions were a common and natural part of the adjustment process for parents but, if left unchecked, contributed to parents' sense of lack of control. The rollercoaster included emotions such as devastation, denial, grief and loss, guilt, depression, stress and exhaustion, and a sense of mixed blessings.

Devastation

All parents responded to their child's diagnosis differently, but it was common for them to feel devastation and shock as they processed what the official diagnosis could mean for their child's future and ultimately the family system. One parent recalled, "I know some parents just sort of shut down completely for a while. . . . One father said that for six weeks he stared at a brick wall and didn't sleep. He just couldn't communicate with anybody. He couldn't speak, when his son was diagnosed."

Devastation and shock over the period of the diagnosis (and sometimes for a while after) had implications for how much information parents were able to process and understand because "over a diagnosis period . . . you feel so raw, and it's so horrible, and actually perhaps you can't take things in that are being said to you." Indeed, most parents did not expect to have a child with autism and therefore information to the contrary required time to process. Their sense of control and predictability about the future was threatened and left them feeling vulnerable.

Denial

Given this devastation and shock, it is not surprising that parents reported experiencing denial, particularly (but not exclusively) in the early stages of their child's condition and diagnosis. Denial seemed to be a common (unconscious) defense mechanism to reduce their anxiety by denying thoughts feelings or facts that were consciously intolerable at the time. Parents acknowledged denial to be a natural and necessary process but, if left unchecked, described it as unhealthy and unhelpful for moving forward and gaining access to help.

> You do go into denial because you think "this can't be happening, this can't be happening to my child" and so on. . . . Virtually anybody whose given any sort of diagnosis, even though in the long term it will be a relief [to have answers], the immediate effect might be denial because you need that period of time to come to terms with it. . . . It's when it gets five years down the line and you're still stuck . . . that's when problems start and there needs to be some [help] where people are given time to grieve about it but then they need to be asked to move on if that child's going to make any progress.

Interestingly, some parents believed that fathers tended to stay in a state of denial for longer than most mothers, perhaps due to the mother generally having more time with the child (e.g., taking child to appointments, therapy, etc.) and openly discussing the child's condition with others. "I felt very unsupported because I think men, in some ways, don't know how to process it all when their child is diagnosed with a disability."

Grief and Loss

Naturally, most parents have hopes, dreams, and expectations for how their children are going to grow up and live their lives. When a child is diagnosed with a condition that may prevent the actualization of these hopes and dreams, however, an unexpected life course is usually presented to parents requiring them to reevaluate their own and child's futures.

> There's grieving, because when you have a child and you think "Oh I'm going to do this with this baby, and that with that baby and I'm gonna . . . school uniform and take them to school" and then all of a sudden you're landed with that official "there's something wrong or not right." . . . It's a loss . . . You have this thing where you've forecast what you think your life is gonna be and then, all of a sudden, that's taken away from you and you don't know what it's gonna be.

Parents expected that they would be likely to grieve at every milestone or life change that represented their previous expectations and hopes for their child's future.

Guilt

One of the strongest emotions many parents felt was guilt. The child's diagnosis came with many questions for parents who searched for answers and reasons for their child having special needs. They often turned the blame inward.

> I wanted a natural birth, I was brainwashed into wanting a natural birth and I feel very much that I might have hung on for too long . . . although the hospital is "in denial" [and says] it has no effect on it, it is still in the back of my mind—if I hadn't have hung on for so long . . . would he have been autistic? It does cross your mind.
> First of all I thought it's maybe something that I did in my pregnancy or maybe it was something that, things I'd fed him or maybe just anything. Clutching at straws completely! . . . You can't stop somebody feeling those elements of guilt or responsibility for it. As long as you're supported in that space and time, to understand that that is quite normal and natural.

Parents recognized that their guilt, like denial, was a common and natural emotion. They also recognized that if left unaddressed, guilt could cause extreme anxiety and depression.

Isolation

All parents identified feeling emotionally isolated and alone at times, even from family and close friends. Parents felt as though they were alone in that no one else could know what it felt like to have a child diagnosed with autism. "I remember thinking 'everyone's children are normal' and that was a huge sense of isolation." Some parents even felt isolated within their relationship, particularly when there was communication breakdown and stress. "I did feel so unsupported and very, very isolated and I still do. . . . You do feel incredibly isolated and also even within a relationship, I think." "Initially I felt alone because [my partner was away a lot] . . . and he was so out of it that he couldn't connect even when he was home so consequently I did find the early years much more about drawing on whatever resource I did have. . . . I was very unhappy and very isolated, very isolated, just got through each day."

Although extended family and friends are often described as important sources of support for families who have a child with autism (indeed, they were acknowledged in these interviews as good supports), many parents highlighted that the opposite was also often the case, especially in the early stages of a child's diagnosis. In fact, it was suggested that extended family and friends were often sources of great stress and isolation. For example, family members in denial of the child's autism challenged the parents' concerns and maintained unrealistic expectations of the child. They often gave inappropriate advice about how to help the child and for some parents, relatives or friends simply withdrew from spending time with them and their child, which increased their sense of isolation and feeling judged as bad parents. "I really don't think people understand . . . [the] prejudice and the stresses that come with it."

> It's very difficult with other parents too, actually. Even your own relations to be honest with you. [They say] "you're making a meal of a perfectly sweet little boy." And it's not meant unsympathetically, but there is an element to it that is . . . it would just be time and again; that sort of reaction. And [family] would say something like, "Is X better yet?" In that sort of slightly peremptory way . . . so you do feel very lonely.

Parents experienced schools, family, friends, and community members to also be unsympathetic and intolerant. It was clear to the parents, however, that these attitudes stemmed from an obvious lack of understanding and education about the child and their needs and reflected an ignorance and fear about how to interact with these children. One parent observed, "You have to live with these children to know what it is like. " "My mum and dad are from a different generation. . . . They try to understand as best they can but I don't know. . . . My friends are there and they say they will be there for [my child] but they just don't get it as well . . . unless I was to give her to them for a month, 24/7, then they might understand it."

Despite feeling isolated, however, one mother was philosophical about the exclusivity of the experience. "That's right, people shouldn't know what you go through because if everybody knows everyone's pain, life would be just too depressing."

Depression, Stress, and Exhaustion

Given the enormity of their pressures, their child's vulnerability, and everyday stresses and long-term worries described so far, it is not surprising that parents experienced depression at times. "The situation I'm in . . . is depressing me."

> [A few months ago] I'd have said that there's no hope. It's just all going to end in blackness and tragedy. I was pretty depressed about it . . . I think [life

was throwing a lot of pressures and] . . . her seizures had reappeared and there seemed to be this very strong, sort of strong feelings about unknown, not anxious exactly, but gloominess about what would happen.

The effort and emotional investment involved in negotiating the hostile system (see following) as well as trying to continually juggle competing demands, led to stress and mental exhaustion for parents. "Stress, stress, stress all the time. Life is not 100 percent." Indeed, the pressures were so stressful that it seemed parents were at risk for mental health difficulties. "Feeling very unsupported and grieving the loss of what I thought my child was gonna be, it was the closest I've ever come to having a mental breakdown."

In addition, parents felt exhausted and emotionally defeated at times, being sapped of their emotional energy and strength. "[I've had] 10 years of no sleep." Not surprisingly this exhaustion made it even more difficult for parents to muster up the strength and energy to fight the hostile system. "I haven't got the emotional strength for people to be confrontational with me . . . I think it's all to do with emotional wear and tear, you've gotten sort of ground down."

Mixed Blessings

Parents experienced conflict between the acknowledgment that their child needed support and their reluctance to fully embrace the support because it made their child's needs real. What they really wanted was for their child to be normal and not need support. The acceptance of support was ultimately the acceptance of their child's disability, which stripped parents of any form of denial they may have been experiencing. One professional described the diagnosis and presentation of a label as a "mixed blessing." On one hand, it empowered parents because they had an answer to their questions that presented them with a pathway. On the other hand, however, it was a realization that this was a label for life and presented many obstacles for which parents had not bargained. This is illustrated in the following experiences.

> We were still hoping . . . that he'd end up in a mainstream school. 'Cause you do, as parents you know, that's what you want. In a way you fight hard to get your child to [a special school] and you really wish he wasn't going to go there.
> Another thing that I have also found difficult . . . I am a bit embarrassed to say it, but I'm going to say it. Part of me doesn't want anything to do with NAS [National Autistic Society] and disability because I don't want him to be like that. I don't want him to be like that. I want him to be normal, you know!? And I find that personally difficult. I find it difficult to belong to that group . . . and I think maybe other people feel like that.

A group of parents reflected on how the hostile system exacerbated their doubts and emotional turmoil.

> [In] relation to denial, partly there is an element of you don't know whether you want the support, so the fact that it may or may not be available is particularly emotionally exhausting because really in an ideal world you don't want

your child to go to a special needs school, you don't want your child to [have to have] OT and S&L, you want your child to get up and be fine. So the fact that it is very difficult to access these things is an added stress in terms of an emotional knife, it makes you think "do I need it if they're not offering it to me?" and you worry about whether it is you being mad! But you're not mad.

It was acknowledged that this feeling did not last, but seemed to once again be a natural and common experience.

LOSS OF CONTROL

A single theme that resonated across all the parents was a real or perceived lack of control in their role as parents. Rather than being able to provide for all their child's needs as they developed, parents often found themselves having to seek answers and supports outside of their own resources because their children required special support which they alone were not always able to provide. On many occasions they were dictated to by services and professionals about what their child needed and not surprisingly felt stripped of their sense of control in their parenting role.

> I think there is a theme of being out of control as a parent. So you go through this huge thing, you process [so much], they say your child needs one-on-one, and needs whatever, whatever, and then they recommend a mainstream school and you sort of think "why am I so out of control, you know?" We're people who are used to making decisions and choosing schools and it's very hard, so somewhere . . . [among the external pressures and] processes I think there is a parent being out of control.

This perceived lack of control took its toll on the parents' confidence, and there appeared to be a fine line between supporting parents and stripping away their perceived responsibility and control. "Why do I feel [guilty]? It's like from mother and toddler group, it's from nursery, it's always been, 'Mrs. X, could you come and have a word because Johnny is not . . . ' I've been told that I am not doing a good job from when he was two, so I feel crushed."

Their parental instincts were to provide for their child and meet their needs, but their capacity to do so was hampered by external systems over which they had little or no control. "[It] . . . is just so awful . . . and it's very out of your control. . . . You're used to making decisions yourself, and following them. But everything's taken away from you really."

A NEVER-ENDING STORY

Unlike parenting a typically developing child, the responsibility for parenting a child with autism is ongoing and is likely to remain intense for the parents' entire lifetime. Parents described how they experienced new challenges as their child developed. They expected that as their children grow, develop, and learn new skills, they would be confronted with new issues. The parents recognized that normally developing children would become independent and eventually "leave the nest," whereas many children with autism would continue to require high levels of emotional and physical support from their parents to ensure their safety and survival. They observed making the transition from being a parent to being a carer as their children aged. Parents described this life-long expectation that lay ahead.

> I think the transition from parent to carer is a big, big, big transition and it occurs around seven to eight years old. It's not that you're no longer a parent but you start to realize that actually you're turning more into a carer, that other eight-year-olds don't require this level of input and that's when I think you start to feel the burden of them growing up. It sort of hits you. When they're little, you're a full-time parent anyway.

Figure 5.1 illustrates a conjugation of the parents' stories and themes described in this study, highlighting the process of the ongoing nature of parenting a child with autism. It must be noted that this experience is not a linear process—it differs in extremity for different people—and the issues identified are not mutually exclusive and may coexist.

The experience of having a child with autism is diverse and complicated. This chapter is based on interviews with parents of children with autism and has provided an in-depth account of the process of parents' emotional experience. We have confirmed that parents find having a child with autism to be more demanding and emotionally intense than having neurotypical children. It was common to experience extreme stress, social isolation, family stress, and exhaustion.

Figure 5.1 shows that when noticing something is different about the way their child is developing, parents tend to begin a quest in search of answers to their concerns. The search for answers resulted in a diagnosis, from which point they sought measures to support their child. However, the search for answers may take years, and for some people a formal diagnosis may never be reached. It was often a diagnosis that helped parents in this

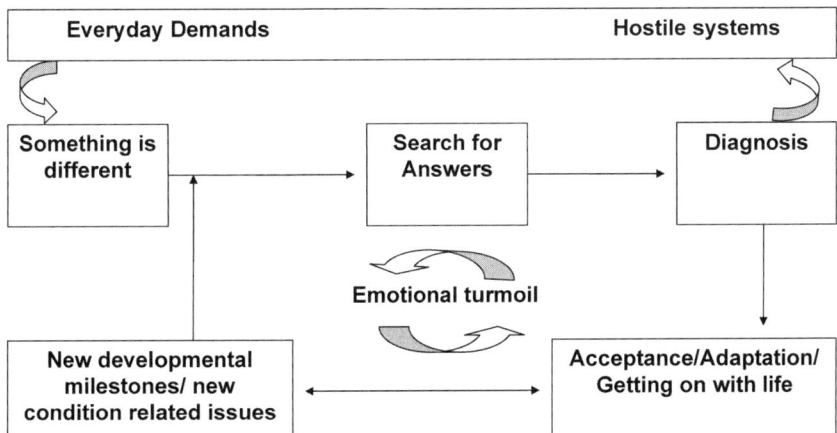

Figure 5.1. Parenting a Child with Autism: The Never-Ending Story.

chapter eventually accept and adapt their life accordingly, but the time and pace of this acceptance differed for everyone.

Autism is variable and the needs of children change as they grow (e.g., puberty), experience new milestones (e.g., change schools, finish school), or develop associated medical/behavioral/emotional issues (e.g., epilepsy, depression). This change may require a further search for answers, diagnosis (of the issues), and acceptance/adaptation for parents. This chapter has highlighted the importance of the ongoing nature of autism and its subsequent relentless impact on the child and their family.

As shown in Figure 5.1, life outside of the world of autism continues for parents, including everyday demands (relationship and sibling demands) and negotiating with services. These daily demands are often magnified due to the additional demands involved with having a child with special needs. Different levels of emotional turmoil accompanied this experience and led to high levels of stress and exhaustion and a perceived loss of control in their parenting role. This feeling of loss of control, to our knowledge, has not yet been formally identified in the literature.

In summary, parents reported that having a child with autism was demanding and emotionally intense and that their role as a carer was likely to continue for their lifetimes. This chapter has provided a rich context for understanding the experience of parents. Without an in-depth insight into the experience, it would be difficult to appreciate the intensity and relentlessness of the parents' everyday life. Only by understanding this experience, from the parents themselves, can services, friends, family, and professionals implement strategies to help and avoid those that negatively impact on their parenting role. Indeed, one of the factors contributing to parents' sense of isolation was ignorance about their experience. Given the isolation and exclusivity many parents feel, and the benefit they can experience through contact with others who understand their experience (Huws et al., 2001), this chapter will hopefully give parents the opportunity to hear others' stories and feel more understood and less isolated.

NOTES

We extend our appreciation to the parents and professionals who gave their time to be interviewed and review feedback, as well as to the Camden LAA for funding the research that formed the basis of this chapter.

1. The children of the parents interviewed were diagnosed with autism. Some of the children in this study also had accompanying developmental delay or learning or physical disabilities. Two parents had children who were not diagnosed with autism but had social and communication difficulties and learning and physical difficulties. These parents were included because the themes in their interviews did not differ in content to the parents of children with autism.

REFERENCES

Fisman, S. N., Wolf, L. C., Ellison, D., Gillis, B., Freeman, T., & Szatmari, P. (1996). Risk and protective factors affecting the adjustment of siblings of children with chronic disabilities. *Journal of American Academy of Child and Adolescent Psychiatry, 35*, 1532–1541.

Fleischmann, A. (2005). The hero's story and autism: Grounded theory study of websites for parents of children with autism. *Autism, 9*(3), 299–316.

Gray, D. E. (1994). Coping with autism: Stresses and strategies. *Sociology of Health and Illness, 16*, 275–300.

Gray, D. E. (2003). Gender and coping: The parents of children with high functioning autism. *Social Sciences & Medicine, 56*, 631–642.

Gray, D. E. (2006). Coping over time: The parents of children with autism. *Journal of Intellectual Disability Research, 50*(12), 970–976.

Hastings, R. P., Beck, A., & Hill, C. (2005). Positive contributions made by children with an intellectual disability in the family. *Journal of Intellectual Disabilities, 9*(2), 155–165.

Hastings, R. P., Kovshoff, H., Brown, T., Ward, N., Espinosa, F. D., & Remington, B. (2005). Coping strategies in mothers and fathers of preschool children with autism. *Autism, 9*(4), 377–391.

Hastings, R. P., & Taunt, H. (2002). Positive perceptions in families of children with developmental disabilities. *American Journal on Mental Retardation, 107*(2), 116–127.

Huws, J. C., Jones, R. S. P., & Ingledew, D. (2001). Parents of children with autism using an e-mail group: A grounded theory study. *Journal of Health Psychology, 6*(5), 569–584.

Midence, K., & O'Neill, M. (1999). The experience of parents in the diagnosis of autism. *Autism, 3*(3), 273–285.

Reid, S. (1999). The assessment of the child with autism: A family perspective. *Clinical Child Psychology and Psychiatry, 4*(1), 63–78.

Rivers, J. W., & Stoneman, Z. (2003). Sibling relationships when a child has autism: Marital stress and support coping. *Journal of Autism and Developmental Disorders, 33*(4), 383–394.

Sivberg, B. (2002). Family system and coping behaviours: A comparison between parents of children with autistic spectrum disorders and parents with non-autistic children. *Autism, 6*(4), 397–409.

Sounders, M. C., DePaul, D., Freeman, K. G., & Levy, S. E. (2002). Caring for children and adolescents with autism who require challenging procedures. *Pediatric Nursing, 28*, 555–564.

Tunali, B., & Power, T. G. (2002). Coping by redefinition: Cognitive appraisals in mothers of children with autism and children without autism. *Journal of Autism and Developmental Disorders, 32*, 25–34.

Weiss, M. J. (2002). Hardiness and social support as predictors of stress in mothers of typical children, children with autism and children with mental retardation. *Autism, 6*(1), 115–130.

CHAPTER 6

Through My Rose-Colored Glasses: When Disability Strikes a Health Professional

Melissa Kendall

Through rose-colored glasses: With an unduly cheerful, optimistic, or favorable view of things: see the world through rose-colored glasses. (Answers.com, 2007)

What causes us to follow certain paths in life? Life presents us with so many intersections, each with so many roads leading in an endless possibility of directions. Yet at each intersection, we select a road to follow, sometimes intentionally with a clear purpose and goal in mind and sometimes unintentionally in a haphazard and chance way. At other times, we are channeled down certain roads by the environmental forces that are surrounding us. In pondering these decisions, what emerges as key is that these roads that we choose or are forced to choose lead us on a journey that is unique. Nobody else will follow these same roads, and there is no definitive map which tells us what will lie ahead. Sometimes our choices prepare us for what lies ahead, and sometimes nothing can prepare us.

THE PROFESSIONAL IN THE MAKING

It is with this thought that I wonder why I chose, so clearly in my mind at the age of 15 years, to study psychology, the study of cognition and behavior, the study of the human mind, that vast array of neural connections and gray matter that remain as mystical today as they were at the beginning of time. I vividly recall sitting in this poky little room at the back of the common area at the school I attended for my entire school life, a school I hold dear for fostering the work ethic I now have. At the time I was in year 9 and in this little room was a career counselor, one of my senior teachers, my parents, and myself. It was our collective task to plan my future vocational path as I had to choose electives for the coming years and these would determine what I could continue to do at university. So here I was pondering the variety of vocational options available to me and time after time, I returned to psychology as a career choice, drawn to the mystic of it as well as the promise of having a life role that meant something.

Did I even truly understand at that time what psychology was or what a psychologist does? Probably not, and although I don't recall with clarity, I suspect that in my naive teenage mind, I thought that by studying psychology, I would learn all the answers. I would know why people behave the way they do, I would know why people think the way they do, I would know why people feel the way they do, I would know exactly what controls what within the human brain and most of all, I would know how to fix it. I would be able to help anybody that had some disturbance in thought or behavior or emotion. I would understand how people act in groups, how children develop, and how we learn. From this early point in my life, I had put on my rose-colored glasses and, in my naiveté, adopted a professional stance. The stance I adopted was of the all-knowing and all-conquering professional. And I didn't waver; not once in the next three years after I chose this life path did I veer off course.

With my mother being a nurse, it is perhaps not surprising that I chose to follow a path in the helping professions, and yet as I enter my 38th year of life, I find that I am nowhere near where I had envisaged. I don't really understand human cognition, behavior, or emotion in the all-knowing way that I expected. I can't predict how people will behave in groups or how people learn and I can't fix people. Indeed, my current world-view is that this is a task that cannot be achieved in the way that I had anticipated or hoped. What appears realistic for me now is to understand some minute aspects of thought, behavior, and emotion as they emerge within my past, current, and future research endeavors.

How I reached this conclusion is as much a journey of discovery as the one I aim to achieve through my research, but it defines who I am and how I came to be at this point. What I describe next is historical. It tells of this journey, from the naive teenager to the assuming professional, with rose-colored glasses. And it tells of how I lost those rose-colored glasses, was left in the dark, blind and fumbling, to understand the simplest of things. It tells the story of how I had to find my way back, to be able to see clearly again, no longer through rose-colored glasses but in the bright light of reality, human suffering, and human experience.

THE WORST DAY OF MY LIFE

A phone call from my mother at 6:45 P.M. on Friday September 12, 1997, less than three months after my daughter was born, changed my life forever and became the catalyst for not only my ongoing career path but also the context within which my passion for research emerged. My brother had been hit by a car crossing the road, and his injuries were numerous. These included a badly broken leg (near the hip), a bruised and damaged left lung, dislocated left shoulder, and deep scars in his right hand. But that wasn't all. The one injury, given my educational background, which I dreaded to hear, emerged shakily through my mother's voice. "He has head injuries, is unconscious and his condition is critical." I was at an intersection, but this time I had no choices. The road that I would follow had been thrust on me by fate.

While I knew that this meant my own life and the life of others around me had forever changed, the coming years would challenge all that I thought I knew about injury, disability, and rehabilitation. No longer would my experience of disability and my notions of rehabilitation be filtered through a textbook. No longer would I be able to reduce the concepts of autonomy, self-determination, social support, and human worth to what was advocated by rehabilitation professionals. The fact is that working with injury and disability through the rose-colored glasses and espoused values of the rehabilitation profession and living it were two different things. The void was larger than anyone who has not been personally touched by this experience could understand.

My previous life experiences and education held opposing functions; they were both good and bad. On one hand, they helped me understand the continuous terminology, jargon, and hidden messages that the medical and allied health professions conveyed and helped me become the conduit through which my parents could understand the enormity of the situation. They helped me call on networks and colleagues and resources that the layperson couldn't possibly hope to have in situations where comprehension failed me. They helped me rationalize, objectify, and distance myself in some instances where the pain was too much. But they failed me miserably in trying to plan and prepare for what lay ahead. The simple fact is that the void was too big between the ideal (as I knew it) and the actual (as I lived it). What should happen (according to rehabilitation philosophy and espoused practice) doesn't. Not all rehabilitation professionals truly value the whole person, not all rehabilitation professionals understand the social construction of disability or believe in social justice, and not all rehabilitation professionals have the capacity for empathy that I believed they did. What happened? Had I been lied to for all this time, or were these rehabilitation professionals still looking through the same rose-colored glasses that I had now lost? This I will probably never really know because I cannot return to the all-knowing professional paradigm within which I previously existed. I now had two hats, one professional and the other personal, but without the capacity to ever truly remove one hat and wear the other. These roles were merged, and it was my challenge to make them complement rather than oppose each other. Not an easy task.

The situation required me to call on all of my resources, both internal and external, to help guide me through that dark tunnel within which my brother nearly died, but from which he survived a traumatic brain injury and emerged changed but triumphant. But a brain injury doesn't just happen to the person that is injured. As Lezak (1988) put it, a brain injury is a family affair. The family is forever changed, not just by the injury itself, or by the remaining impairments to "body structure or function," or by the "activity and participation restrictions" for the injured individual but also by the rehabilitation environment and the way in which each family member's life interacts with and is changed by the rehabilitation experience.

The despair of the intensive care unit, the uncertainty regarding life or death, and the machines that constantly beep and instigate a mini-tornado of anxiety each time can never be forgotten. There is the agitation of your family member in their unconscious state paralleled by the hope that (despite knowing differently) alights each time they open their eyes, or take an independent breath, or squeeze your hand, and the hope that is crushed each time that progress is not noted. There is the bruising that emerges in the most extensive tones of purple, brown, and black, like a patchwork quilt covering the person beneath. There is the feeling of being too scared to touch but needing to, just to make sure that they are still there and it is not just a bad dream. There is the sense of pervading doom that fills the air when other families experience the ultimate loss (despite the best intentions of staff to hide this). There is the "in your face" experience of pain and loss of others around you, which you experience as if it were your own. There is the immersion of yourself in their experience also, although it is a job you never wanted. There is the sickness that you feel deep down inside your stomach that takes your breath away and belies your own deep-seated fear of facing the same loss.

This occurs against the backdrop of the constant activity of the ICU, a place with no night and day. As people constantly buzz around you, you watch the stories of trauma unfold (both your own and others), but you have no script to follow. You cling to every scrap of information you receive as if this will help you understand the plot. Yet the information only comes in dribs and drabs, never really telling you the entire story. You are caught up in a whirlwind with no control and the most overwhelming sense of helplessness. These are pervasive aspects of the family's every living minute during these early few weeks or months and, for some, years. In hindsight, after speaking with my brother many years later, these are experiences that belong with the family. The injured person is usually blissfully unaware (at least this was so in our situation). Thank God for small mercies.

Nothing can prepare you for this. There is no book you can read or class you can take that guides you on how to deal with trauma. Even for those who work with trauma every day, the roles are different, and being on the receiving end is a totally new kettle of fish. While the ICU and hospital experience was something that was not so familiar to me, it was familiar to my mother. As a professional, you may have seen this happen to someone else and their family a million times and, with your professional hat on, maintained a safe distance. But when it is your mother, father, sibling, or child that you see lying helpless, hooked up to a multitude of machines, the intensity of the experience is often all-encompassing. There is no escape, and avoidance is not an option. My mother still tells me stories now of times when she is called to the ICU at the hospital where she works and how she feels sick to her stomach each time, how the flood of memories comes rushing back in torrents of anxiety. As I said, this lives with you forever and changes who you are, but you would do it all over again if the need arose and you would cope, because you have no choice.

But how do you cope? The most certain thing I can say here is that you don't feel like you are. You go into automatic pilot, and coping is not so much a conscious effort as it is trial and error, sheer determination, and unconditional love. The things I found helpful were varied, and my reflections on their effectiveness are only apparent in hindsight. I learned there was a need to recount my experience, to other family and friends, colleagues, and whoever else would listen (even the lady at the canteen who serves you your fifth cup of coffee for the day). It was almost as if by telling others, something would change. Perhaps someone would give you some positive information, some reassurance that this is only temporary and that all will be good in the end. Maybe someone had been in a similar position and they would be able to offer some words of wisdom or reveal some tidbit of knowledge that you hadn't acquired yet. Realistically, of course, this was never going to happen. All people could offer were platitudes. Yet somehow I found them comforting (or as comforting as anything would be at that point in time).

Knowledge is power, and in a situation where all is foreign and nothing is certain, I learned that it was so important to ask questions. It was important to know which drug was being given through the drip, what each sound that emanates from each machine means, what each word written on a chart means, and what every gurgle and movement signified. When I didn't do this for fear of upsetting or annoying the staff, I would truly believe in the movie version of consciousness where my brother would suddenly wake up and ask what was for dinner (despite the fact that I knew deep down this was not the way it happened). Asking questions was my reality check. It kept me grounded in what we could realistically hope for at that point in time, and I am glad I chose to do this. Yet I often wonder even today, how many others don't ask the questions. How often do people continue to hide behind ignorance? How do they cope when the reality of a poorer outcome than they expected occurs?

At other times, my mind would start to race, and catastrophizing thoughts on situations would develop. I call this getting the "what ifs." What if he doesn't wake up? What if he can't talk again? What if he doesn't remember me? What if he can never get a job or a girlfriend or a house? Yet these thoughts only served to heighten my anxiety, and I consciously tried to avoid them, knowing that they were counterproductive. Indeed, the two polar reactions that I experienced (unrealistic hope and the what ifs) emerged from what was my fear of the unknown and my need to have an explanation for everything. Somehow by explaining something, we feel much more in control. Yet the reality is that there is no certainty and there is no control, and whenever I avoided the two extremes and accepted this uncertainty, I was much more able to cope in the here and now.

I must also make mention of what I have called the newly acquired ICU family. As I said earlier, you are inevitably drawn into the lives of those around you, merely because of the close and highly personal nature of the ICU environment. It is this group of people that you see every day, with whom you share progress stories, who hug you when you aren't coping and whom you hug when they are not coping. It is this family that supports you in those moments where you feel most vulnerable (e.g., when you are asked to leave the room for some unknown procedure), and it is this family that gives you the strength to keep going. Although you never asked for this new family, the support offered within those relationships is priceless and cannot be provided by any other family member or friend that you have because they simply don't exist in the same emotional place that you do. One woman we met while my brother was in the hospital lost her husband to a brain tumor during the time that we were there, and despite the gravity of her loss, she still asked about my brother in her moment of grief. This is the type of support that cannot be quantified and will be forever remembered. In fact, we maintained contact with her for years afterward, even if just through Christmas cards, because she was such an important part of our lives at that time.

Yet life could not for me exist solely within the confines of the hospital. Despite the guilt and apprehensiveness I would feel as I left the hospital each day, afraid that this may be the last time I saw my brother alive, I had to go home every night and feed a family, bathe the baby, wash the dishes, and fold the clothes. I had two lives, and the truth is I needed to have two lives. I needed to have my normal life as well. Just to have the mundane was a welcome respite from being at the hospital, to lessen the intensity of emotion, and to maintain a more objective view of reality, without which I am sure would have been extremely detrimental to my mental health. It was essential not to lose these other parts of my life, for they gave me the strength to return the next day with the added advantage of the fact that I have probably never enjoyed these tasks more than I did at that time.

Within these times at home, as I would reflect on the days events, I discovered one of the most helpful things for me was to write about those events and experiences. Writing helped collect my thoughts, process the information that I had managed to garner from interactions with staff, detail progress (or lack thereof), and vent feelings of frustration, anxiety, and overwhelming sadness. It helped objectify a situation that wasn't objective and it helped tell a story—my story. It provided an ongoing record of where we had been and how far we had come, and this was so important, to recognize progress. I found many times I looked back over what I had written the previous week, only to find I wasn't in that place anymore. While everything felt like it moved in slow motion on a daily basis and you would become disheartened at a perceived lack of progress, when you scanned back over writing from the previous week, it seemed like it was an eternity away. It was a place that I had moved on from, a place that I never wanted to return to, but a place that I would never forget.

What I described about my experiences of ICU highlights it to be one of the most life-changing and significant experiences that one could endure. Yet even today, I find it perplexing that this experience is not recognized by rehabilitation professionals within research or at a clinical level for the enormity of its impact. As a professional, when I read literature on the family experience, I read of coping with ongoing behavioral challenges and the burden of providing personal care for a family member with a brain injury and the strategies to help with memory deficits. I find paper after paper written about caregiver burden, their need for social support, and their need for coordinated personal care services. But I never read about the ICU experience, apart from within the personal narratives of those who have lived it. Indeed, the literature is lacking when it comes to recognizing and validating the early hospital experience for families after a loved one sustains a brain injury.

This lack of recognition at a research level is paralleled by a similar lack of recognition in the clinical setting. I remember one time hearing a respected health professional relate to me in a professional context their own frustration with family members of people with brain injury (not knowing that I was one of these people). He said to me he just wished the families would get over the hospital experience because he was sick of hearing about it and they should just move on. At this moment I fully appreciated the great divide between what we know as a professional outsider and the experience of those who live it. Yet you cannot just move on from this experience, you cannot minimize its importance, and you cannot forget; in all honesty, you don't want to forget. In this situation, my personal hat tells my professional hat that I believe it is only when we, as rehabilitation professionals, recognize and respect the importance of this experience for the family that we will truly be able to foster therapeutic relationships with those families.

FRIENDSHIPS

Up to now, I have spoken of what this means to the family as I experienced it as a sibling. Yet even from this early stage, through my own grief, I had moments of awareness of the importance of friends. The importance of their presence for the injured person and the importance of their presence for the family to share the load was something that I recognized very early following my brother's injury. For a single male in his mid-twenties, friends are a larger part of his life than you are as a family member, and this is reflected in your ignorance of what occurs in his life on a day-to-day basis. I didn't know what my brother was doing when that car hit him, and I wasn't with him. But one of his friends was. I didn't have to see him lying unconscious on the road, but his friend did. I didn't have to see the passing doctor and then the ambulance officers fight to stabilize him right there on the asphalt. But his friend did. I didn't know where he was the night before the accident. He was with his friends, the same people he lived with and played sports with and went out with. These people were the most important people in his life at that point in time. And I was acutely aware of this in the early days. They helped fill in the gaps in my knowledge.

What slowly emerged during these early days following my brother's injury was an awareness of not only the importance of friends but also their relative exclusion from the rehabilitation setting. They were never included, apart from being at the end of a Chinese whispers chain that started with the medicos, passed through nurses, the family, and onto them. To be honest, although aware of it as a family member, you hold these notions of mutual exclusivity, almost as if at this point you felt like they had no right to be there. So while I was aware of their exclusion and to some degree supportive of it at the time, I can reflect now on the possible impact that this may have had for these people. No one really considered how this affected them, despite the fact that their friend as they knew him was lying unconscious in a hospital bed. How did they observe and assimilate the image of their friend through the indignity of restraints or the gut-wrenching sound of the nasogastric tube being reinserted after it had been pulled out for the 10th time that day? Nobody stopped to consider how traumatic this must have been for them. No one explained to them that the person who would emerge, after all the rehabilitation and recovery, would probably not be the same person they knew before. No one offered them counseling, or included them in physiotherapy sessions, or invited them to take their friend out for the day. And most of all, nobody explained to them that the injured person would need them, as a friend, more than ever during this period of recovery.

Early on, they came in numbers, waiting patiently outside the intensive care unit for their turn to come. They tried to help and would often sit there talking to my brother, telling him about all the "days of our lives" dramas that permeated their pre-injury conversations, with my brother being a passive recipient. Other times they would apprehensively ask questions of the staff. At other times they would just sit there, the concerned looks on their faces betraying some signs of their inner fears. But as time passed, these moments became fewer. As my brother slowly but surely emerged from unconsciousness, the visits became fewer. There wasn't a time where I could say this changed, perhaps because of my own oblivion or perhaps because it happened so gradually as to escape notice. But in the end, they just seemed to fade away, pursuing their own lives and allowing family the exclusive right to fill the days.

These fleeting early thoughts on the importance of friends were encapsulated in time by the need to live the experience of recovery with my brother. They didn't engender daily thought, they just occurred as momentary glimpses of reality. So day after day, for three months, I drove the 30-plus kilometers with a baby in tow to watch my brother give the fight of his life. The journey from the ICU, to the high-dependency unit across the hall and then to the brain injury rehabilitation unit was a long one, and this experience alone could fill a book. With each transition came a raft of new insecurities and uncertainties and a plethora of new experiences that would inherently change the way I viewed rehabilitation and life.

My most poignant memories of these places will be forever etched in my mind. The move from ICU to high dependency came with its associated decrease in staff ratio that produced such high feelings of anxiety and was characterized by a preponderance of what ifs. What if they don't notice an important change? How can they watch him closely enough when there is not one nurse devoted to watching just him? What if he dies because they aren't paying attention? What if he just gives up? What if they have given up on him? The uncertainty and anxiety associated with the what ifs was paralleled by the deep sadness and despair felt when you see a family member placed in restraints or when you see him propped up in a chair despite the fact that he can't keep himself upright or when you witness him gagging as the nasogastric tube is being reinserted or when you watch him trying to speak with a tracheostomy and you can't make out what he is trying to tell you. The brain injury unit has locked doors that accost any sense of dignity or autonomy. There is the long process of relearning the mundane daily tasks of eating, walking, and going to the toilet. There is overwhelming sadness and despair for others who sit for 24 hours a day with no visits from family or friends and the way in which they never seemed to improve as much as those who were surrounded with support. There is constant mulling over what will happen to them if nobody comes for them. Even the smallest task or goal becomes not only a goal for your family member but a goal for the whole family. Indeed, I remember clearly the weeks as my brother was emerging from posttraumatic amnesia (PTA). His occupational therapist had asked him to remember three items and to have emerged from PTA, he had to have day-to-day recollection of these three items. I don't know how many days he remembered two of the three. I don't know how many days we sat there asking him if he remembered what the third thing was, as if remembering that one item was a pot of gold at the end of the tunnel. This tiny rehabilitation goal had become the whole point around which each day revolved, and we all had so much emotion invested in its achievement. The day that he remembered that third item, anyone would think we had just won the lottery, the relief and sheer excitement was incredible.

What I have discussed so far are but a few of the most prominent memories of this journey. The diary that I have kept of this time is some 150 pages long and may, one day in the future, provide the basis for sharing this experience in its entirety. For the moment, suffice to say this was an extremely difficult and trying time, filled with tears, anger, frustration, anxiety, sadness, and loss. It heralded the fact that my rose-colored glasses existed no more, I was not the all-knowing professional, I was just a little boat in a big sea, drifting aimlessly in the vast expanse of this thing we call rehabilitation.

My journey through these contexts is also filtered through my feelings of shock, disappointment, and sometimes disbelief at the way in which people are managed by the rehabilitation professionals who are charged with their care and who must, by virtue of their role, care for not only the injured person but also their significant others. In my mind, as I entered this experience, I thought all rehabilitation professionals held the same values as me, namely, respect for the individual, care, compassion, and an understanding of the whole person and their environment. I did see many instances where this was the case. But I also witnessed many incidents that seriously challenged my perceptions of healthcare professionals and culminated in the loss of my rose-colored glasses. For instance, I saw a lack of understanding of age-appropriate interactions when a staff member sent a 16-year-old boy to his room because he was being behaviorally disruptive. I saw a lack of care and compassion when an evidently distressed mother was not offered comfort because "she always does this." I saw clients refused psychosocial support and counseling because they "won't remember it anyway." I saw friends turned away if they couldn't make it during visiting hours. I saw friends excluded from therapy sessions where family was allowed. I saw friends offered no explanation or support in situations where they were clearly confused and worried. Therefore I saw friends who didn't come back.

There were times where my own feelings toward my brother's friends were overrun by anger and hurt, and these remain clear memories, signaled by the intensity of the emotion that accompanied them. I recall the female friend who spent so much time in the early days just talking and touching my brother, trying desperately to uncover memories and awareness. I remember when she stopped coming to see him after realizing that recovery in many respects followed its own timeline. I remember the time, while my brother was hospitalized, when the friends he shared a house with prior to his injury decided to move out, leaving the house in a state of disrepair and mess, and simultaneously leaving my brother with the massive bond debt, which my parents covered. I remember the times following his discharge from the hospital when his friends excluded him from involvement in recreational activities because they didn't think they would be able to help him if he got into trouble. I remember the raw emotional pain that was obvious each time he was disappointed, forgotten, or deliberately excluded.

In these early days, my sisterly protectiveness was fierce, and I blamed those friends. Why couldn't they just support him? Why was their friendship no longer a part of their everyday lives? How could they go on with their lives while he struggled to regain some semblance of normality to his own? The immediacy of this situation left me with an overwhelming sense of the unfairness of life, as if he hadn't been through enough already.

FRIENDSHIPS IN HINDSIGHT

Hindsight is a wonderful thing, however, and it was not until many years later that reflection enabled me to let go of these feelings of anger. In more recent years, since commencing my doctoral research, curiosity and contemplation has replaced anger and frustration. What has emerged is an awareness of the fact that friendships are a process unto themselves. Despite what we may see as a family member or as a rehabilitation professional, friendships follow an independent process, a process of maintenance or dissolution in the wake of trauma and injury. Yet nobody truly understands this process, and I would even go as far to say that nobody has really recognized that this process even exists. It is only at the times that this friendship process intersects with the family process or the rehabilitation process that we become aware of it. Yet these intersections are so brief that we fail to understand that friendship is a process rather than a collection of static moments in time. As family members or rehabilitation professionals, we are outsiders in this process, mere spectators. Sometimes, we may throw rubbish on the field that interrupts the game, but in the end, the outcome of the game rests with the major players, namely, the injured person and their friends. Their experiences of injury and friendship are their own, independent of the family experience and maybe at times independent of each other.

What are the motives for their friendship behaviors? How do they feel about friendship? What do they think about friendship? What level of reciprocity exists in maintaining that friendship? What level of awareness do they have of their friendship and the direction that it follows? What is the rehabilitation experience for the friends, as outsiders, as people who stand on the sidelines but don't receive any cues or props to assist them? Would these friendships have stood the test of time without the injury, or did we just attribute a natural course of events to the injury? The simple answer is we don't know, and there is probably no rehabilitation professional or family member who could come close to answering these questions given our current state of knowledge. These are questions for now to be asked of the major players. The importance of friendships has not been recognized, not by the rehabilitation professionals, not by the families, and even in some instances not by the injured individual themselves until it was too late. It was with growing realization of this fact that I returned to work.

A CAREER RETURNED

My return to work following my brother's injury and the birth of my first child took the form of some casual research work with a university and from this emerged a decision to do my master's degree by research, which then developed into a doctoral thesis. From this emerged a position as Research and Development Officer with a community rehabilitation service for people with spinal cord injury. My professional career and my life path as I see it has now emerged, not as a clinician but as a researcher. At last, I felt I had found what I had been looking for. Indeed, it became clear to me at this point in time that I could no longer fulfill the role of the clinician—my personal hat covered too much of my head. My desire to exist in the real world of the clinical setting, rather than in academia, was realized within this position. I wasn't sitting in the ivory tower of academia but in the real world, with real people who had real injuries, real families, and real losses. So I witnessed on a daily basis, whether through personal contact or involvement with a clinical team, the struggle that injured people and families had trying to negotiate the rehabilitation system. Sometimes that system worked extremely well, usually for certain types of people, those whose physical impairment itself represented the major personal aspect of their injury. In other instances, the system failed dismally, for those who didn't fit the norm, for those whose psychological or social needs were of overarching relevance, for those whose cultural backgrounds were different, for those who experienced cognitive impairments as a result of their injury, and for those who were just that little bit rebellious. Research offered me the opportunity to see these personal losses and triumphs, sometimes vicariously and other times personally. It allowed me the space to examine the systems in rehabilitation without being one of the key stakeholders in the process. It allowed me objectivity while still allowing compassion. And it allowed me to realize that our system often fails to provide the support that people need. To develop research agendas that would not only give me publications as a professional but would provide direction for practice, to make real changes that would enhance the lives of people who have been injured and their families. I had found my calling and to this day believe that this is where I can make the largest difference.

Of course, the life stories I see and hear in spinal cord injury rehabilitation offer me a different perspective to those in brain injury rehabilitation, each with their positives and negatives, each with their own idiosyncrasies and philosophies. For people with spinal cord injury, there is an overwhelming focus on the physical, often leaving large gaps in providing adequate psychosocial support. On the other hand, in spinal cord injury rehabilitation, there was greater autonomy provided to the injured person because at least they had insight, something that is often a blight against the reputation of and struggle for autonomy among people with brain injury. For people with brain injury, the psychosocial was often foremost but in many instances attributed merely to the nature of the injury itself and therefore perceived as untreatable. Each rehabilitation system had parallel challenges. Both struggled against the dominance of the medical model, the focus on the individual, the failure to consider the whole person and the entirety of their social circumstances, the inadequacy of the system to facilitate a return to valued social and vocational roles, and in both an overwhelming failure of the system to recognize and value the role of friends. In spinal cord injury rehabilitation, I have experienced this within my professional role alone. In brain injury rehabilitation, I had experienced this on a personal level but would later experience this as a researcher when I took a part-time position in a research and development role with a community rehabilitation service for people with acquired brain injury.

As I write this chapter, I continue to hold both these research roles in spinal cord injury and acquired brain injury rehabilitation. I remain entrenched within the rehabilitation setting, while never truly removing the personal experience that set me on this life path. Therefore I write from a position of inclusion in the clinical rehabilitation arena. Writing is of critical relevance to me, both as a professional and as a person because it is through this medium that I can share these insights. It is true that the roads that we follow lead us in unique directions and I am sure that had it not been for my brother's injury, I would not be where I am today.

Does my personal position and history impact how I see my work and how I write? It surely does, and I would be disappointed if it didn't. Yet it is a point from which I may be and have been criticized or questioned, particularly in the professional arena. I have been asked whether I could maintain objectivity, whether I show too much empathy for clients, whether I act like an advocate rather than a professional. If these are my greatest sins as a professional, then I gladly accept them, because I don't ever want to lose the ability to hear the stories of real people and fight to improve the way in which we help them return to their lives. I don't ever want to be detached from their realities and I don't ever want to hear myself calling a person "the T4 paraplegic." This person is not defined by their injury but by who they are as a person. Through my writing, I hope that I can do justice to the experiences of people who have spinal cord injuries or acquired brain injuries as well as doing justice to the experiences of their friends, the forgotten majority. The truth is I don't ever want to wear those rose-colored glasses again—reality becomes too blurry.

REFERENCES

Answers.com. (2007). Dictionary: Rose-colored. Retrieved February 18, 2007, from www.answers.com/topic/rose-colored.

Lezak, M. D. (1988). Brain damage is a family affair. *Journal of Clinical and Experimental Neuropsychology, 10*(1), 111–123.

CHAPTER 7

Australian Indigenous Health and the SIPES Model of Well-Being: The Legacy of Lauraine Barlow

Leda Barnett and Dianne Barnett

> The dominant Western model of health has continued to marginalize Aboriginal people by impressing Western methods of health education and care, and failing to acknowledge cultural methods of learning and healing. (Davis et al., 2004, p. 108)

The Western medical system is struggling to address the health needs of Australia's Indigenous[*,1] people, particularly those with disabilities or chronic conditions. One reason for this mismatch is the fact that aspects of Indigenous well-being are unable to be incorporated into health interventions that are developed from the dominant Western medical health model. This chapter discusses a model of well-being that incorporates social, intellectual, physical, emotional, and spiritual (SIPES) aspects of health. This model of well-being was derived from a local Murri artist's painting and has emerged in the health literature. The SIPES model of well-being is presented as a foundation from which Indigenous communities can assess well-being and initiate, develop, and deliver culturally appropriate community-based health interventions.

Many of Australia's Indigenous people attribute their ill health to the inability of the medical system to accommodate their needs (Barnett, 2006). Maher (1999) recognized that Aboriginal people have resisted the dominant beliefs and practices that form the basis of the predominant Western health care model. This resistance is based on a history of predominantly negative experiences of

---

* In this chapter the word "Indigenous" will be spelt with a capital "I".—Our use of "Indigenous" in this way is motivated by the need to respect the cultural reference inherent in the capitalised form, rather than subscribe to an act of precedence in accordance with "common" usage.

Indigenous people with the medical model, resulting from the inherent differences between Western health frameworks and Indigenous understandings of health (Kendall, Barnett, & Hunter, 2006). Discord continues when medical services are provided that do not consider the cultural contexts of health issues, for example, some traditional Indigenous health beliefs attribute illness to social and or spiritual dysfunction (Barnett, 2006; Honeyman & Jacobs, 1996). Indigenous systems of health beliefs can also incorporate religion, the interconnectedness with the land, and various obligatory requirements in relation to kin, which for many Aboriginal people is dictated by culture, often taking higher priority than their own health (i.e., social responsibilities are given the highest priority in many communities) (Maher, 1999).

A considerable amount of literature positions holistic health as an alternative to the predominant biomedical model of Western disease and illness. Central to this contrast is the belief that the biomedical model devalues many aspects of health, other than the physical, a stark contrast to the foundational beliefs of holistic health and the understanding of health from an Indigenous Australian perspective (Lutschini, 2005). A holistic concept of health parallels the Indigenous understanding in that they are multidimensional, incorporating "a degree of depth and balance among such diverse elements as physical health, emotional health, intellectual health, social health and spiritual health" (Hawks, 2004, p. 11). The various aspects coexist to form a state of well-being or a level of optimum health in an individual's life (Viner & Macfarlane, 2005). The balance among the various aspects of health determines an individual's holistic well-being.

The purpose of this chapter is to discuss the importance of viewing Australian Indigenous health from a holistic framework. As holistic beings, we cannot separate our emotions, bodily sensations, thoughts, and spiritual experiences into discrete compartments. For this reason, a model of health that is culturally appropriate must recognize and encapsulate the Indigenous worldview as reflected by the complexities of Indigenous understandings of health and its influence within the cultural context. As depicted in the original painting by Murri[2] artist Lauraine Barlow,[3] the SIPES model of well-being provides a holistic model that can illustrate an individual's health more clearly. Many health practitioners are required to utilize a framework for the assessment of clients and communities. The SIPES conceptual framework prepares the health practitioner to assess well-being by following a comprehensive, holistic framework for assessment through the association of the fingers of the hand as illustrated in Barlow's painting.

AN INDIGENOUS MODEL OF HEALTH

The National Aboriginal Community Controlled Health Organisation (2003) defined Aboriginal health as encompassing "mental health and physical, cultural and spiritual health. Land is central to well-being. Crucially, it must be understood that when the harmony of these interrelations is disrupted, Aboriginal ill health will persist" (p. 5). The National Aboriginal and Torres Strait Islander Health Council (2003, p. 2) noted that the improvement of Indigenous health status "must include attention to physical, spiritual, cultural, emotional and social well-being, community capacity and governance." Despite a lack of consensus regarding the aspects of holistic well-being, conceptualizing health within a model that incorporates social, emotional, and spiritual aspects that engage other entities (including family, the community, and the environment) as active participants in the construction and maintenance of health is critical (Barnett, 2006).

Many health services are inappropriate for the needs of Australia's Indigenous communities as they unwittingly disregard the communities ideas of health (Stephens, Nettleton, Porter, Willis, & Clark, 2005). Lutschini (2005) explained that the complex interrelated constructs that facilitate Aboriginal understandings of health, as evidenced in language, cannot be easily translated (if at all) into Western languages. For example, the Ngarigman of the Northern Territory use the word *punyu* as a concept of well-being that "encompasses person and country, and is associated with being strong, happy, knowledgeable, socially responsible (to 'take a care'), beautiful, clean and safe—both in the sense of being within the law/lore[4] and in the sense of being cared for" (Atkinson, Graham, Pettit & Lewis, 2002, p. 286). Here well-being is dependent on the quality of an individual's relationships, which are based on mutual care. Punyu demonstrates that health concepts are developed within the community in which they are used, meaning they may have limited relevance to other Indigenous communities. For this reason, interventions developed on the basis of localized Indigenous contexts have less generalizability, providing an explanation for why such constructs receive little attention in the wider health community (Lutschini, 2005).

THE SIPES MODEL OF WELL-BEING

In 2006, a project was conducted in relation to the management of chronic disease in Murri communities (Kendall et al., 2006). The Indigenous community researcher in this project, Lauraine Barlow, reflected her thoughts about the project in a painting titled "Journeys of Healing" (see Figure 7.1). Barlow used art and her life story as media by which to portray her understanding of health within the cultural context with which she identified. Through this process, she effectively linked the past, present, and future across the interrelated aspects of well-being and embedded these factors within her artistic identity and culture. As shown in Figure 7.1, Barlow's understanding of well-being is based on five aspects of health (i.e., social, intellectual, physical, emotional, spiritual), each creating an equal section of the whole yet inextricably reliant on each other. Barlow wrote on her painting:

> There are five segments to life, each with a meaning about health: Stars = spiritual health Tree = physical health Tears = emotional health Owl = intellectual health Queen Green Ant = social health. These five aspects are essential parts of a healthy existence. The hands signify our need to tell our story and the four figures represent all different people of different sexes. The circles represent the various stories we share and the places we have been. We are all telling the same journey of healing, if people would just stop and listen.

Figure 7.1. "Journeys of Healing," by Lauraine Barlow. Australian Indigenous Health and the SIPES Model of Well-being, Leda Barnett & Dianne Barnett. [Lauraine Barlow]

Barlow's symbolism demonstrates a complex and intimate understanding of the environment and its inhabitants. Her artwork provides an effective, efficient, and comprehensive overview of a Murri woman's understanding of health in a familiar, appropriate and concise medium. The painting has proven to be an effective medium for communicating a health message, as it facilitates transmission of culture, instills cultural pride, and incorporates Murri understandings of learning, healing, living, and other cultural features (Davis et al., 2004).

The diversity of Indigenous culture denotes an expansive conceptual understanding of well-being. The SIPES model provides a foundation on which to construct a health assessment and customize appropriate health interventions that can respond to this model of well-being. "Journeys of Healing" provides a degree of validation for the appropriateness of health practices that incorporate these five aspects of well-being. By extrapolating the illustration of the hands that are central to the painting and associating each of the five aspects of holistic health to the fingers of the left hand, health professionals are well placed to apply an appropriate conceptual framework for assessment of Indigenous holistic health.

Social Health as Represented by the Left Thumb

Social support has a significant role in the implementation of health interventions for various types of cancer, cardiovascular disease, immune function, and women's health (Hawks, 2004). Studies investigating the effect of the social environment on health have identified that the quality of relationships, sense of belonging, mutual obligations to social groups, satisfaction gleaned from societal roles, and feelings of love and acceptance as influential factors

(Bloom, 1990; Hawks, 2004; House, Landis, & Umberson, 1988). The construction and augmentation of an individual's sense of self is facilitated by his or her interactions with others and through the social meaning attributed to an individual's appearance and behavior (Chaney, 2004; Kelly & Field, 1996; Wilson, 2003). Inherent in the social presentation of self are the physical characteristics embodied in gender, age, and ethnicity. These characteristics influence the perception of an individual by others, drawing in the complications of stereotypes and other assumptions that underpin previously formed and socially constructed understandings and expectations (Chaney, 2004). The social identity of a person, as defined by their allegiance to various social groups, influences how one interacts with others. In the case where illness affects one's body, one's self-concept (as dictated by the activities one can participate in) influences that individual's view of him- or herself. Together with other people's perceptions, either an individual's self-concept is reconstructed or a new identity is confirmed (Kelly & Field, 1996).

The quality of environmental interactions and their social meaningfulness facilitates further understanding of an individual's social capacity (Kelly & Field, 1996). Consequently, the efficiency with which an individual interacts with the environment; discrepancies between expectations, obligations, and abilities and the application of stereotypes; and discrimination can all impact an individual's well-being. In a recent study conducted by Kendall et al. (2006), the importance of this social aspect of health to Indigenous people was evident through the conversation about family ties and kinship structures that preceded every interview about health (Barnett, 2006). For many Indigenous people, the lack of culturally competent practices within interpersonal health interactions with nonIndigenous people (e.g., going to a nonIndigenous doctor) is particularly problematic. Discussions about what is needed to improve Indigenous health often focus on the need for Indigenous staff as the first point of contact in health professional positions at medical centers, clinics, or surgeries. This need reflects the significance of the social aspect of well-being (i.e., language, interaction, interpersonal skills) and its role in physical health (Barnett, 2006).

The effect of dysfunctionality in the social dimension of health on a population level is evidenced in the "Bringing Them Home" report (Human Rights and Equal Opportunity Commission, 1997). Alienation from family and culture has been thought to underlie many behavioral and social issues relating to ill health and poor well-being, for example, the presence of domestic violence, assaults, poverty, unemployment, and criminal activities in some Indigenous communities (Brown, 2001; Jackson & Ward, 1999).

It is an individual's history and life connectedness that brings him or her to the current point of life. Social connectedness can be seen as the glue that holds people in place in a community and provides a sense of identity. Family connectedness, involvement in community groups, and physical ability to move about are part of the threads of social assessments. These factors impact individuals' richness of present living and their ability to either maintain or improve their whole self. It is important that health professionals consider the social construct of the Indigenous client's life prior to any further assessment, as other aspects of health could be associated with this social situation.

The impact of the social context of health on individuals requires the health professional to consider his or her approach to the client. The health professional's attitude, verbal and nonverbal communication, and how the client may interpret the approach all affect the responses received by health assessments. Aspects of oral communication, such as the tone of voice used, whether the questioning is open or closed, and the cultural appropriateness of the interaction, should also be considered. The cultural appropriateness of any interaction will be affected by the client's gender and that of the health professional, the presence of family or other persons, and various privacy issues. Taking the time to connect with the client socially can be as simple as smiling, making eye contact when appropriate, and inviting a response to a simple question such as, "How can I help you today?"

Assessment of the client's social life will provide an understanding of his or her lifestyle, support systems, and whole of life infrastructure that affects well-being. Orientation of language and connecting through family or social networks is important to establish a base of respect and openness to gather the information needed for a comprehensive assessment. The need for interpreters or the presence of cultural support persons should also be considered and practiced where necessary, prior to further assessment being undertaken.

It is often not appropriate to ask direct or multiple questions that may leave the client feeling he or she has been interrogated. Rather, asking open questions that allow clients to provide information about themselves and how they fit into their community can include "Tell me about your community and where you have come from," "Tell me about yourself and how your family came to this place," "Tell me how you are feeling," and "How are your feelings affecting your family?" Reflecting the feeling and content of the responses to such questioning should elicit further interaction and provide an initial baseline of the social infrastructure of support that surrounds the client.

Intellectual and Mental Health represented by the Left Index Finger

A person's thought patterns and cognition significantly impact his or her ability to understand, plan, and process information to interact with others (Sharifian, 2001). This skill relates to not only intelligence and cognitive processes but also how an individual makes sense of the world (Sharifian, 2001). For example, people who place a high value on intellectual ability in one culture (e.g., the ability to complete tertiary studies or pursue a career as a lawyer) may not value the intelligence required to understand seasons or patterns of nature in Indigenous culture where this skill impacts on the ability to hunt and fish for survival in a natural and changing environment.

The consequences of not providing formal education for children are well recognized. The effect on the individual, the immediate and extended family, and the wider community is evident in Indigenous communities (Storry, 2006). In some Aboriginal communities, many of the current generation of parents do not have basic English literacy and numeracy skills, meaning the next generation is being raised in low-literacy environments and are ill-prepared for an education in the mainstream school system (Storry, 2006). The need for a community approach to address low educational achievements for Indigenous people living within predominantly English or Western societies is clear and is the basis of several national initiatives at present. However, the relevance of English-based education programs that lack any culturally relevant curriculum (i.e., no teaching of traditional language, Aboriginal history, or cultural traditions) is questionable. Health in Indigenous communities requires access to an education system that facilitates Indigenous ways of knowing.[5]

For many Indigenous people, intellectual health involves knowledge of traditional cultural influences. Thus, good intellectual health (in accordance with what is deemed culturally important) would include learning and practicing cultural ceremonies, traditional language, traditional songs, and cultural beliefs that are predominantly learned from elders (Colomeda & Wenzel, 2000). This learning is of great value within Indigenous culture and is a source of continuity with the past, being knowledge that has been handed down from generation to generation. Intellectual health necessitate not only Indigenous knowledge and ways of knowing but also the process of communicating knowledge. Education within Indigenous culture requires an approach suited to its traditional context, for example, storytelling and participation of kin is critical to a successful education experience for Indigenous people (Colomeda & Wenzel, 2000).

Where intellect has been described as a person's ability to reason, solve problems, understand, and live safely in the world (Sharifian, 2001), mental well-being can be described as psychological functioning, the ability to undertake an activity normal to a human being, and fulfill the social role that is normal for the individual. When assessing the intellectual and mental well-being of an Indigenous person, it is appropriate to consider that the nonIndigenous health professional may be viewed with hostility and could represent part of the colonizing history of white settlement. Thus, simply interacting with nonIndigenous health professionals may exacerbate mental ill health.

Mental illness within a cultural group is influenced by what is considered to be normal, acceptable behaviors or abnormal within that group (Davis, 2003). The norms of broader society may be irrelevant. Understanding of mental disorders in Indigenous people is generally poor, although one study has estimated the prevalence to be between 35 and 54 percent (Clayer & Divarakan-Brown, 1991). There is recognition of mental illness in Indigenous communities through the use of language such as *Womba* to describe abnormal mental states (Davis, 2003). Whereas Western medicine views mental illness as a problem within an individual, for the Indigenous community these abnormal mental states are seen as a community issue and can often be considered as spiritual issues that require spiritual intervention (Davis, 2003). Traditional healers, therefore, continue to have a place in the intervention and management of mental health problems for many Indigenous people.

Risk assessments of mental health for Indigenous clients should occur with culturally appropriate tools and understanding (Couzos & Murray, 2003).

Consideration should always be given to the losses experienced by Indigenous people through colonization and how this has had an ongoing effect on individual and community well-being. It is estimated that up to 1 in 10 Indigenous children were forcibly removed from their family between 1910 and 1970 and that most Indigenous families have been directly or indirectly affected by this process (Couzos & Murray, 2003). The loss of land and family connections caused by this upheaval has had an impact on Aboriginal identity, and the widespread cultural anger can be seen as a response to these events.

Asking questions of Indigenous clients and their families that have no relevance to community life may elicit misleading responses, resulting in incorrect evaluations, misdiagnosis, and inappropriate management plans. It is therefore important to consult with and involve the family of the client in any mental health assessment. If there are symptoms or signs of mental illness, these should be explored within the context of the culture of origin as they may be seen as acceptable behavior within that culture or the local community. For example, hallucinations may not necessarily be a psychotic phenomenon in some communities, as it may be considered acceptable or normal for a person to receive messages or hear voices following a death or traumatic incident. It is therefore essential that cultural differences are considered by the health professional, in all instances where a mental health problem may be present (Davis, 2003).

Physical Health Represented by the Middle Finger of the Left Hand

The physical aspect of the SIPES model refers to the functioning of the physical components of the body, the absence of physical ailments and disease, and other structural indicators of health, such as blood pressure and bone density (Saylor, 2004). The physical dimension of health is the predominant feature of the dominant medical models (i.e., Western approaches to health that address the affects of biological factors in relation to illness and physical health). Physical health is easily defined, operationalized, and measured across disciplines, making it a legitimate goal for health interventions (Hawks, 2004). Physical dimension of health is identified as a well-established component of quality of life (Miller & Thoresen, 2003).

However, its influence on other aspects of well-being and its interrelatedness with the other dimensions of health are less well understood (e.g., as physical health decreases, so do other health dimensions, such as increasing inability to engage in social activities). Natural changes of physicality, as human bodies mature, also impinges on social capacities in a variety of ways (Kelly & Field, 1996). Often, the physical manifestations of an illness precede changes in other dimensions of health, for example, relationship dynamics change when intimate physical care needs transform the roles of family members. Additionally, the symbolic meaning that is inherent in societal roles performed prior to physical ill health can be challenged and cause those involved emotional distress. Thus, identity is reconstructed and further limitations are imposed on socially determined actions (Kelly & Field, 1996).

The physical aspect of well-being includes engagement in daily exercise, eating a diet high in fresh food and vegetables, and maintaining a posture that affects how a body looks and reacts to environmental demands (Berry & Sherman Hansen, 2000). In this regard, health benefits have been attributed to traditional Indigenous lifestyles (McLaughlin, 2006), such as the physical benefits of acquiring bush products (i.e., exercise) and its nutritional content incorporates social and relational dynamics that render each participant an active player in the daily functioning of the community (e.g., people hunting together, infants fed the blood of kangaroos hunted by relatives, and women catching and cooking goannas) (Lagan, 2006). Many of these activities are actively sought by people living in Western urban communities, but for many others, these activities have been completely lost and replaced by unhealthy life habits.

Health professionals observe and make health assessments on the basis of the physical appearance of their clients. This assessment can include, among other things, the person's age, gender, sexuality, stature, physical characteristics, and general appearance. An individual's physical appearance can readily identify some aspects of well-being and identity. Judging of one's character and nature through the features of the face is called physiognomy (Lindhauer, 1986). The face reflects tiredness, fatigue, joy, pleasure, happiness, stress, pain, fear, and other emotions. The face can also reflect personality and mood as well as mental illness. Additionally, signs of disease can be reflected in the individual's facial characteristics, for example the skull enlargement of Paget's disease, the mask like features of Parkinson's disease, and the flat profile and crowded features of Down syndrome (Murtagh, 2003). Other examples—the butterfly mask or rash of lupus —can also be readily seen on a person's face, and so can the bluish tinge of the lips that can reflect cyanosis or oxygen deprivation that is associated with shock or heart failure (Murtagh, 2003).

When assessing well-being, hair and skin can provide a picture of race and help define a cultural group as well as reflect personal hygiene standards and class. The skin can be touched to identify temperature, sores, lumps, and rashes along with hydration and edema that can be associated with heart failure or pregnancy-induced hypertension. Erect stature and muscle definition can provide information on the individual's fitness, self-esteem, and body composition, and movement will show activity and obesity. This often rapid and immediate assessment of individuals provides significant information.

Genetic makeup influences not only biological characteristics but also innate temperament, activity level, and intellectual potential and has also been related to susceptibility to specific diseases such as diabetes and heart disease (Murtagh, 2003). There is significant evidence that both Aboriginal and Torres Strait Islander peoples have a higher incidence of cancer and cardiovascular disease and that their life expectancy is 17 years lower than other Australians (Australian Bureau of Statistics, 2006b). There is evidence to suggest that Aboriginal adults encounter a higher rate of some infectious diseases, which include *Haemophilus* B and bacterial sexually transmittable infections (Australian Bureau of Statistics, 2005). Mortality rates for Indigenous infants are also higher than nonIndigenous infant mortality rates, and there is an increased prevalence of low birth weight babies with infectious illnesses (Menzies, McIntyre, & Beard, 2004; National Centre for HIV Epidemiology and Clinical Research, 2007). A thorough physical assessment that is repeated annually will identify early signs and symptoms of disease and allow for early intervention in relation to harmful behaviors that may affect well-being and longevity.

Physical well-being is the basis for Western medical assessment and interventions. There is evidence that the medical model of health is not providing the necessary interventions that can bring about changes in physical health status and disease processes in Indigenous communities (Bailie, Robinson, Kondalsamy-Chennakesavan, Halpin, & Wang, 2006). Any approach to physical health improvement in Indigenous communities must include respect for emotional and spiritual well-being. Westernized health care systems are slow to learn from Indigenous people that the goal of well-being should be the maintenance of wellness, not the management of illness (van Holst Pellekaan, & Clague, 2005).

Emotional Health Represented by the Fourth (Ring) Finger of the Left Hand

Emotions and emotional support significantly influence a person's well-being (Butler, Koopman, Classen, & Spiegel, 1999). Negative emotions, if left unchecked, can influence self-esteem, relationships, physical health, and disease processes (Butler et al., 1999; Salovey, Detweiler, Steward, & Rothman, 2000). Emotional distress creates a susceptibility to physical illness by affecting the immune system. Importantly, lifestyle activities, such as smoking and the consumption of alcohol and high-fat foods, have been identified as mechanisms that relieve emotional distress, which lends credence to the widely held belief that physical ill health is a manifestation of emotional distress (Stewart-Brown, 1998). The relationship between emotional distress and poor health behaviors necessitates a focus on emotional well-being, emotional supports, and emotional distress to facilitate physical health (Butler et al., 1999; Salovey et al., 2000; Stewart-Brown, 1998).

Emotions and feelings color life. The body experiences feelings and emotions through awareness of the lived experience. The human body responds to stressors by alerting the nervous system. The hypothalamus signals the adrenal glands to release adrenaline, cortisol, and hormones that raise blood pressure, raise respiratory and heart rate, dilate pupils, release stored glucose from the liver for energy, and produce sweat to cool the body. These physical reactions are the body's stress response and clearly demonstrate the body's ability to perform under pressure. The stress response, however, can cause significant health problems when it overreacts (Health and Emotional Wellness, 2004).

Emotional health also incorporates the ability to control one's reactions to the environment. For example, many Indigenous Australians experience strong emotions in relation to past injustices that include the removal of Indigenous children from their families (Human Rights and Equal Opportunity Commission, 1997). Such emotions have been associated with psychological issues such as anxiety, depression, and other serious mental illnesses (Brown, 2001). Allowing the expression of feelings such as the anger, sorrow, and shame associated with these situations allows for the development of emotional health by provoking detachment from past negative experiences and realignment with an Indigenous identity that facilitates a positive outlook to the ongoing process of healing (Brown, 2001).

Financial income is found to positively correlate with health (i.e., poor health and low income correlates with low social status, whereas good health and higher income correlates with high social status) (Chaney, 2004). Indigenous Australia's low social gradient "reflects the material disadvantage and the effects of insecurity, anxiety and lack of social integration" (Chaney, 2004, p. 1). The ongoing process of reconciliation, the quest for a government apology for past wrongs,[6] and the pursuit of the return of stolen wages can be identified as not only attempts to address injustice but attempts to address the emotional trauma of the past to bring about healing (Hermeston, 2005). The prevalence of ill health in Australia's Indigenous people is a product of the emotional distress they have experienced, which facilitates a susceptibility to physical illness, and also of the emotional factors that hinder an individual's ability to proactively manage their health (Australian Bureau of Statistics, 2006a; Metherell, 2002; Stewart-Brown, 1998).

Indigenous clients' feelings are complex and intergenerational. Thus, health professionals need skills to elicit, clarify, and articulate the different elements of emotional well-being. Often multiple and sometimes unspeakable feelings will be experienced at once. Guilt, shame, depression, hurt, anger, fear, and anxiety are inextricably intertwined for Indigenous people.

Cultures differ in the way emotions are expressed, and health professionals should consider that somatic symptoms of illness can be manifested in individuals as a result of psychological distress (Davis, 2003). Skills for assessing feelings include the ability to show respect, sensitivity, and empathy as well as the ability to listen and reflect back feeling messages. Health professionals can use "feeling" questions to encourage the experiencing of and sharing of feelings. By expressing, experiencing, and managing feelings, physical conditions can be positively self-managed (Nelson-Jones, 1992).

Spiritual Health Represented by the Small (Fifth) Finger of the Left Hand

Human beings can be described as the combination of three elements, namely, body (physiological, our relationship with the world), soul (psychological, our relationship with others), and spirit (spirituality, our relationship with God) (Lea, 2004). The human spirit is that part of a person that connects to the supernatural whether for good (e.g., abundant and righteous living) or bad (e.g., occult). The spiritual side of life involves a consciousness of God, which may have different interpretations according to individual beliefs and religion. Each of the three elements interact with each other. A healthy and well-maintained body and psyche that is balanced and able to manage the impact of personal history and development will be well placed to address the spiritual side of life. Each person is born with a deep spiritual need that relates to security or a sense of being loved, self-worth or being valued, and significance or the sense of meaning or purpose in life. This spiritual need occupies a crucial part of culture and well-being for Indigenous people (McLellan & Khavarpour, 2004).

The importance of spiritual well-being is reflected in health outcomes as diverse as recovery from addiction, teen sexual activity, depression, eating disorders, breast cancer, and long-term survival with AIDS (Hawks, 2004). To explain spiritual health, an understanding of the worldview is required. Good spiritual health requires strong commitment to a well-defined worldview that results in personal clarity, understanding of one's purpose in life and one's role in society. Through this worldview one subscribes to a value system and an ethical framework that enables fulfillment of a higher purpose. Aspects of the spiritual worldview encompass relationships with others, the form of a higher power or a larger reality, and a sense of personal worth (Hawks, 2004).

One's worldview encompasses all elements of culture, in fact, it is defined by the culture within which an individual lives (Tuhiwai Smith, 1999). Thus, the community helps create and form the worldview of its people (Colomeda & Wenzel, 2000). The extent to which spirituality features in a culture affects the spiritual health of its members (i.e., in magnitude and direction), resulting in differences across societal groups (Miller & Thoresen, 2003). For example, beliefs associated with miracles, visions, and ritualistic practices (e.g., baptism) have been accepted by many Christians and people of other religions (Brown, 2001). This is also the case for many Indigenous people, who have strong beliefs regarding the spiritual significance of certain practices, including hallucinations (in the form of ancestral visions or voices) and through a belief in the dreaming. These practices are accepted as commonplace (Brown, 2001).

The spiritual aspect of well-being is arguably the most important measure of longevity and health for Australia's Indigenous people (McClain, Rosenfeld, & Breitbart, 2003). The spiritual link with land provides identity, which lies at the core of spirituality and spiritual beliefs for many Indigenous people. Land is often positioned as central to health and well-being (Jackson & Ward, 1999), and the loss of connection with land is seen as a key factor in illness. Connectedness to a supreme being or spiritual beliefs can mean a connectedness to the land, through God and Christian understandings of the world (e.g., the coming of the light festival) and geographically specific beliefs found in the dreaming (National Aboriginal and Torres Strait Islander Health Council, 2003; Reeves Lawrence, 1998; Wilson, 2003). Whatever connectedness involves for individuals, it is incorporated into their reason for living and their view of health.

Many people live in confusion of their identity and have no real meaning of life (Jackson & Ward, 1999). They can become absorbed with the natural life, collecting possessions and prioritizing involvement in superficial human relationships (Belk, 1988). Neither of these activities are wrong in themselves, but they can become the focus of one's life and when this occurs the human spirit suffers. Seeking life's meaning through temporal pleasures does not provide spiritual health for many Indigenous people. Instead, spiritual well-being relates to identity or the sense of who people are and the meaning they ascribe to life. People want to feel secure in their sense of spiritual identity. The spiritual self can be identified when a person is able to answer who they are in relation to other things of the world. The connectedness to land, for Aboriginal people, is evidence of their spirituality and identity (Jackson & Ward, 1999). The loss of that connectedness can result in feelings of rejection, low self-esteem, withdrawal and apathy, hostility, and compulsive-addictive behavior. Thus, the importance of this dimension cannot be overlooked by health professionals.

CONCLUSION

Although the World Health Organization has focused on a definition of health that encompasses more than the absence of disease, Western medicine's focus on disease and disease processes will continue to limit the ability to address the well-being of the whole person (Saylor, 2004). For Australia's Indigenous people, a model of well-being that incorporates broader influences, such as that depicted in Barlow's (2005) painting, would enable identification of the broad influences that impact on well-being. The SIPES model of well-being acknowledges the importance of social, intellectual, physical, emotional, and spiritual aspects of health that occupy equal sections of the whole. Although presented in a compartmentalized fashion, through the linking of each aspect of health to a finger of the left hand, the artist has acknowledged that each aspect will interact with the others in a dynamic and complex way to create an overall status of wellbeing.

Western models of health, on which many health interventions are developed, do not accommodate Indigenous ways of knowing (e.g., punyu health) (Atkinson et al., 2002). Indigenous people's spiritual relationship with the land is central to well-being, the significance of which is not encapsulated in any Western health models. The relationship between health and the physical world is evident in the characters used to depict the different aspects of health in Barlow's painting. The role of the physical world is rarely represented as a theme in health psychology literature (Wilson, 2003), other than in terms of environmental pollution or climate change, which is only just beginning to feature in contemporary research.

Barlow's art also emphasizes the collective nature of Indigenous way of life and how this interacts with health. Indigenous well-being dictates that support needs are addressed through kinship structures and collective processes (Brown, 2001). This approach contrasts with many Western health models, which fail to encompass the health of the community and environment with which an individual is affiliated (Stephens et al., 2005). It is the well-being of the community that influences the well-being of the individual in a intimate way, working from a whole-of-life perspective (Lutschini, 2005). The context of community and environment engender pluralistic solutions and holistic models to address health issues, enabling the use of allopathic and traditional medicines in addition to Western medical practitioners (Lagan, 2006; Lutschini, 2005).

Finally, Barlow's art asks us to hear the stories of Indigenous people. Indigenous health must be approached in the context of Australia's history. Health disorders are firmly encapsulated within a milieu born from a violent history characterized by oppression, racism, and cultural genocide. This history is associated with widespread psychological distress, stress, trauma, and grief (Brown, 2001). According to Davis et al. (2004), understanding about the affects of colonization on spiritual and emotional suffering of Australia's Indigenous people is growing. Health interventions that draw on such cultural awareness provide hope for improving Indigenous health. Cultural pride and self-sufficiency are important products of culturally appropriate service models (Davis et al., 2004), particularly if the interventions also provide for social intellectual, spiritual, and emotional healing in addition to physical health.

The SIPES model of well-being, as depicted in Barlow's painting "Journey's of Healing," could guide the development of a community-based health intervention that is entrenched in Indigenous culture and could facilitate strength, identity, and cultural pride. As a consequence of these improvements, such a model could inherently improve individual and community health (Bond, 2005). The development and incorporation of a model of health that encompasses caring for others within the community context and factors associated with geographic, environmental, and socioeconomic situations is important for Australia's Indigenous populations (O'Donoghue, 1999). In a predominantly Western country such as Australia (if economic and attitudinal barriers could be addressed), a holistic model such as SIPES might address the gaps and inconsistencies that are evident in the current health system.

Although more difficult to measure in terms of their efficacy, interventions that address the multiple pathways and multidimensional aspects of health have been underresearched (Atkinson et al., 2002). Multidimensional health interventions based on the SIPES model would be time- and energy-intensive for medical professionals and clients (Hawks, 2004; Lutschini, 2005). However, as Hawks (2004) noted, "an intensive, comprehensive approach that addresses all dimensions of health is capable of providing lasting, life-altering solutions that can be achieved in no other way" (p. 16). Although the biomedical model is attractive in that a drug prescription or short appointments are likely to be preferred by health professionals, Indigenous people need and demand respect for their right to shape understandings of health in an appropriate way, inform research methods, and influence health policies (Stephens et al., 2005). The SIPES model provides an avenue for developing this understanding by clearly illustrating differences between Western health models and Indigenous understandings of health.

NOTES

We acknowledge the traditional custodians of the areas in which we have conducted research in the past. Lauraine Barlow provided the inspiration and impetus to write about the importance of holistic health for Indigenous people. Our work colleagues and friends, provided valuable feedback throughout the writing process. Our ongoing thanks, admiration, and gratitude to the participants of chronic disease management studies in which we have participated and whose stories continue to develop our understanding of health and our culture. We acknowledge Indigenous Health Workers with whom we have worked in rural and remote areas of Queensland and western Australia. Through their generosity of spirit and acceptance of us, we have grown in our understanding of Indigenous ways of life.

1. *Aboriginal* and *Indigenous* are used interchangeably, we acknowledge the Torres Strait Islander population, but the research referred to here focused on Aboriginal people.

2. The term *Murri* is used to refer to Aboriginal Australians who identify as Queenslanders.

3. A descendant of the Mandingalpa clan, Yidiny tribe, Kulla Kulla clan, and Lama Lama tribe in North Queensland, Lauraine Barlow has the Aboriginal name of Jana-n/Jigiddirri Jigiddirri (standout willy wagtail). Lauraine has lived with several chronic illnesses throughout her life, a situation that influenced her to relocate from her native home to a suburb near the capital city for easier access to appropriate medical treatment.

4. Lore is an important concept in Indigenous communities, where there are recognized and valued ways of behaving in society.

5. The "ways of knowing" concept refers to the cognitive orientation in which members of a cultural group view the world and understand their role within it. This cultural view is based on a subset of shared beliefs, assumptions, presuppositions, theories, and schemata (Turton, 1997).

6. The national government of Australia provided an apology to the Indigenous people in 2008 as one of the first tasks of the newly elected Labour Government under Prime Minister Kevin Rudd. This apology had been sought by Indigenous people for several decades, but had been refused by the prior government.

REFERENCES

Atkinson, J., Graham, J., Pettit, G., & Lewis, L. (2002). Broadening the focus of research into the health of Indigenous Australians: We know the problems—we need to seek solutions rather than more statistics. *Medical Journal of Australia, 177*, 286–287.

Australian Bureau of Statistics. (2005). Deaths in Australia 2004. ABS Catalogue no 3302.0. Canberra: Author.

Australian Bureau of Statistics. (2006a). 4715.0—National Aboriginal and Torres Strait Islander health survey 2004–05. Retrieved September 12, 2006, from www.abs.gov.au/AUSSTATS/abs@.nsf/ DetailsPage/4715.02004-05-?OpenDocument.

Australian Bureau of Statistics. (2006b). Deaths in Australia 2005. ABS Catalogue no. 3302.0. Canberra: Author.

Bailie, R., Robinson, G., Kondalsamy-Chennakesavan, S., Halpin S., & Wang, Z. (2006). Investigating the sustainability of outcomes in a chronic disease treatment program. *Social Science and Medicine, 63*(6), 1661–1670.

Barlow, L. (2005). Journeys of healing [painting].

Barnett, L. (2006). *Chronic disease management for Murris: Culturally appropriate methods.* Brisbane: Griffith University Press.

Belk, R. (1988). Possessions and the extended self. *Journal of Consumer Research, 15*(2), 139–145.

Berry, D., & Sherman Hansen, J. (2000). Personality, nonverbal behavior, and interaction quality in female dyads. *Personality and Social Psychology Bulletin, 26*(3), 278–292.

Bloom, J. (1990). The relationship of social support and health. *Social Science and Medicine, 30*(5), 635–637.

Bond, C. (2005). A culture of ill health: Public health or aboriginality? *Medical Journal of Australia, 183,* 39–41.

Brown, R. (2001). Australian Indigenous mental health. *Australia and New Zealand Journal of Mental Health Nursing, 10,* 33–41.

Butler, L., Koopman, C., Classen, C., & Spiegel, D. (1999). Traumatic stress, life events, and emotional support in women with metastatic breast cancer: Cancer-related Traumatic stress symptoms associated with past and current stressors. *Health Psychology, 18*(6), 555–560.

Chaney, F. (2004). Engagement will do more than a treaty for Indigenous health. On Line Opinion. Retrieved May 23, 2007, from www.onlineopinion.com.au/print.asp?article=2581.

Clayer, J. R., & Divarakan-Brown, C. S. (1991). *Mental health and behavioral problems in the urban Aboriginal population.* Report of a study conducted by the Aboriginal Health Organization and the mental health evaluation centre of the South Australian Health Commission.

Colomeda, L., & Wenzel, E. (2000). Medicine keepers: Issues in Indigenous health. *Critical Public Health, 10*(2), 243–256.

Couzos, S., & Murray, R. (2003). *Aboriginal primary health care; An evidence-based approach.* Melbourne: Oxford University Press.

Davis, B., McGrath, N., Knight, S., Davis, S., Norval, M., Freelander, G., et al. (2004). Aminina Nud Mulumuluna ("you gotta look after yourself"): Evaluation of the use of traditional art in health promotion for Aboriginal people in the Kimberley region of western Australia. *Australian Psychologist, 39*(2), 107–113.

Davis, J. (2003). *A manual of mental health care in general practice.* Canberra: Commonwealth Department of Health and Ageing.

Hawks, S. (2004). Spiritual wellness, holistic health, and the practice of health education. *American Journal of Health Education, 35*(1), 11–16.

Health & Emotional Wellness. (2004). How does stress affect us? APA Help Centre. Retrieved from www.apahelpcentre.org/articles/article.php?id=11.

Hermeston, W. (2005). Telling you our story: How apology and action relate to health and social problems in Aboriginal and Torres Strait Islander communities. *Medical Journal of Australia, 183*(9), 479–482.

Honeyman, P., & Jacobs, E. (1996). Effects of culture on back pain in Australian Aboriginals. *Spine, 21*(7), 841–843.

House, J., Landis, K., & Umberson, D. (1988). Social relationships and health. *Science, 241,* 540–545.

Human Rights and Equal Opportunity Commission. (1997). *Bringing them home: National inquiry into the separation of Aboriginal and Torres Strait Islander children from their families.* Retrieved May 28, 2007, from www.hreoc.gov.au/social_justice/bth/preliminary.html.

Jackson, L., & Ward, J. (1999). Aboriginal health: Why is reconciliation necessary? *Medical Journal of Australia, 170,* 437–440. Retrieved April 12, 2007, from www.mja.com.au/public/issues/may3/jackson/jackson.html.

Kelly, M., & Field, D. (1996). Medical sociology, chronic illness and the body. *Sociology of Health and Illness, 18*(2), 241–257.

Kendall, E., Barnett, L. & Hunter, B. (2006). *Indigenous self-management: Developing a culturally appropriate program.* Meadowbrook: Griffith University and Arthritis Queensland.

Lagan, B. (2006). Utopia—a place where Aborigines live long and prosper. Retrieved May 14, 2007, from www.eniar.org/news/Utopia.html.

Lea, L. (2004). Body, mind, spirit and soul. *Mental Health Today, September*, 35–37.

Lindhauer, M. (1986). Perceiving, imaging and preferring physiognomic stimuli. *American Journal of Psychology*, 99(2), 233–255.

Lutschini, M. (2005). Engaging with holism in Australian Aboriginal health policy—a review. *Australia and New Zealand Health Policy*, 2.

Maher, P. (1999). A review of traditional Aboriginal health beliefs. *Australian Journal of Rural Health*, 7, 229–236.

McClain, C., Rosenfeld, B., & Breitbart, W. (2003). Effect of spiritual well being on end of life despair in terminally ill cancer patients. *Lancet*, 361(10), 1603–1607.

McLaughlin, M. (2006). *Good news on Indigenous health front*. Television show. Australia: Australian Broadcasting Corporation.

McLellan, V., & Kharvarpour, F. (2004). Culturally appropriate health promotion: its meaning and value in Aboriginal communities. *Health Promotion Journal of Australia*, 15(3).

Menzies, R., McIntyre, P., & Beard, F. (2004). Vaccine preventable diseases and vaccination coverage in Aboriginal and Torres Strait Islander communities 1999 to 2002. *Communicable Diseases Intelligence*, 28(2), 127–159.

Metherell, M. (2002). Indigenous health faces bleak future. *Sydney Morning Herald*, p. 6.

Miller, W., & Thoresen, C. (2003). Spirituality, religion, and health. *American Psychologist*, 58(1), 24–35.

Murtagh, J. (Ed.). (2003). *General practice* (3rd ed). Sydney: McGraw-Hill.National Aboriginal Community Controlled Health Organisation. (2003). Overview of the NACCHO Business Plan 2003-2006. Retrieved May 30, 2007, from http://www.naccho.org.au/PolicyReports/Reports/NACCHOBusinessPlan.html.

National Aboriginal and Torres Strait Islander Health Council. (2003). *National strategic framework for Aboriginal and Torres Strait Islander health: Framework for action by governments*. Retrieved May 30, 2007, from www.health.gov.au/internet/wcms/publishing.nsf/Content/health-oatsih-pubs-healthstrategy.htm/$FILE/nsfatsihfinal.pdf.

National Centre for HIV Epidemiology and Clinical Research. (2007). HIV/AIDS, viral hepatitis and sexually transmissible disease surveillance report 2007. AIHW catalogue no. PHE 92. Sydney: Author.

Nelson-Jones, R. (1992). *Lifeskills helping—a textbook of practical counselling and helping skills*. Sydney: Holt Reinhart and Wilson.

O'Donoghue, L. (1999). Towards a culture of improving Indigenous health in Australia. *Australian Journal of Rural Health*, 7, 64–69.

Reeves, L. H. (1998). "Bethlehem" in Torres Strait: Music, dance and Christianity in Erub (Darnley Island). *Australian Aboriginal Studies*, 51. Retrieved May 31, 2007, from find.galegroup.com/itx/infomark.do?&contentSet=IAC-Documents&type=retrieve&tabID=T002&prodId=EAIM&docId=A54479677&source=gale&srcprod=EAIM&userGroupName=griffith&version=1.0>.

Salovey, P., Detweiler, J., Steward, W., & Rothman, A. (2000). Emotional states and physical health. *American Psychologist*, 55(1), 110–121.

Saylor, C. (2004). The circle of health: A health definition model. *Journal of Holistic Nursing*, 22, 97–115.

Sharifian, F. (2001). Schema-based processing in Australian speakers of Aboriginal English. *Language and Intercultural Communication*, 1(2), 120–134.

Stephens, C., Nettleton, C., Porter, J., Willis, R., & Clark, S. (2005). Indigenous peoples' health—why are they behind everyone, everywhere? *Lancet*, 366, 10–13.

Stewart-Brown, S. (1998). Emotional wellbeing and its relation to health: Physical disease may well result from emotional distress. *British Medical Journal, 317*, 1608–1609.

Storry, K. (2006). Tackling literacy in remote Aboriginal communities. *Issue Analysis*, 73. Retrieved May 31, 2006, from www.cis.org.au.

Tuhiwai Smith, L. (1999). *Decolonizing methodologies: Research and Indigenous peoples*. Dunedin: University of Otago Press.

Turton, C. (1997). Ways of knowing about health: An Aboriginal perspective. *Advances in Nursing Science, 19*(3), 28–36.

van Holst Pellekaan, S., & Clague, L. (2005). Toward health and wellbeing for Indigenous Australians. *Postgraduate Medical Journal, 81*(10), 618–624.

Viner, R., & Macfarlane, A. (2005). ABC of adolescence health promotion. *British Medical Journal, 330*, 527–529.

Wilson, K. (2003). Therapeutic landscapes and First Nations peoples: An exploration of culture, health and place. *Health & Place, 9*, 83–93.

CHAPTER 8

"Surely Someone Can Support Me": A Caregiver's Perspective

Tara Catalano and Debra Domalewski

The fact that the family functions as a primary source of care and support for its dependent elderly members and that this role is often burdensome and stressful has been well documented for decades (Barber, 1988; Kasuya, Polgar-Bailey, & Takeuchi, 2000; Shanas, 1980). What is not well established is that the caregiving experience often demands skills that are associated with those held by health professionals. Case management, for instance, is recognized as a skillful method of integrating long-term care services into a seamless continuum of care across time and settings in a way that supports people with disabilities to make the most of their lives (Scharlach, Giunta, & Mill-Dick, 2001). Skills such as assessing needs, planning, client advocacy, monitoring, reassessing, and evaluating the outcomes are common in health professionals who engage in case management (Aliotta, Archibald, Brown, Chen, & Fox, 2000; Case Management Society of Australia, 2005).

Many caregivers assume a role that is similar to that of a case manager, but do so without adequate guidance, support, or education. In 1999, as part of the International Year of the Older Persons, several debates occurred about the shortcomings of adult children taking responsibility for the welfare of elderly parents. These debates focused on questions about social equity between the generations, the parameters of self-reliance in old age (Millward, 1999), the burden of caregiving, the residualization of services, the increased contracting of service provision to charitable private agencies, and the increased reliance on the family for care (Jamrozik, 2001).

Research has shown that one of every two caregivers suffers financial burden, and two out of three caregivers have experienced compromised health as a result of their role (Kasuya et al., 2000). Women continue to be the predominant caregivers, providing care in over 75 percent of cases (Kasuya, et al., 2000; Millward, 1999). This finding supports the "feminization of caregiving" and reinforces the societal expectation that women will provide care for their families (O'Connor, Wilson, & Setterlund, 2003). However, in the current complicated care environment, these primary caregivers are often assuming the role of case manager without the necessary infrastructure of professional and financial support.

It is estimated that informal caregivers who support their ill or disabled family member(s) save the government and taxpayers $171.4 million (Australian dollars, A$; opportunity cost) and A$331.8 million (replacement cost) each year (Dewey et al., 2002). These caregivers are often juggling their supportive role in addition to a range of commitments (i.e., employment, raising a young family, etc.) that result in significant costs to themselves and their families. Although the economic burden is often debilitating, the cost of supporting family members also takes its toll emotionally and physically. The following story of Jennifer illustrates some of the issues faced by informal caregivers as they struggle to provide support to their dependent family member (subjective) while simultaneously fulfilling their usual roles and responsibilities.

Jennifer's story illustrates the qualitative aspects of caregiving within the framework of an informal caregiver's experience as she struggles to provide support to her aging and frail elderly parent, while simultaneously fulfilling her usual roles and responsibilities. As we listen to her story, the unique reality of her caregiving experience becomes apparent, and we begin to gain an understanding of the oppression that is built into the structure of our social and health care systems. This subtle oppression reveals itself when we take the time to listen to the voices of caregivers (Howell & Ellis, 2005; Sorrell, 2003).

JENNIFER: CASE MANAGER OR DAUGHTER?

Jennifer is in her late thirties. She works full-time and is raising her young daughter. She also provides support to her elderly father, Bill, who recently had a stroke. Bill now requires assistance with many of the daily tasks he once took for granted—showering, cooking, cleaning, and shopping. Bill, who lives alone, is no longer able to drive and cannot walk far on his own. Jennifer is uncertain if he will be able to continue living in his own home safely and independently. During the first six months following her father's stroke, Jennifer's major concerns were her "father's safety versus his independence" and "how this change would influence her personal and family life." This was a time of uncertainty for Jennifer, about what the future might hold for her father, herself, and her own immediate family.

From the time of Bill's stroke, Jennifer assumed an active role in supporting her father. Initially, the hospital recommended Bill be sent to a nursing home, but Jennifer advocated for independent living for her father. She was the only supporter of *his* primary goal to maintain his independence in his own home. She was instrumental in organizing the support that would enable her father to make a successful transition from hospital to home.

> When he was in hospital . . . professionals were saying, "you've got to get this organized and that organized and this organized." So I went ahead and did try to get things organized. But it was a catch-22, "you can't organize it until he goes home"; but that's ridiculous because you have to have things in place before they go home. So I'm running around getting things organized and then at the very last minutes they said, "we would have done that for you." But I wasn't told that at the time. And I think that was deliberate in that . . . it will save state money if famil[ies] run around organizing things instead of staff.

Jennifer invested a considerable amount of time and energy in this process and continued to encounter many hurdles that impeded her ability to organize supports in a timely way for her father's return home. "When dad first went home they said, 'oh we've got a wheelchair ordered for you but you won't get it for six weeks. And you'll have a disability-parking permit but you won't get that for so many months.'"

In thinking about how she provided care for her father, Jennifer considered his "self-esteem, dignity, empowerment, adjusting to a different lifestyle and pace, understanding and appreciating his disability," and so on. She believed that her efforts in the first few months were rewarded because he now "has increased his independence and [has taken on more] responsibility." However, she explained that supporting her father, both practically and emotionally, was exhausting and difficult.

Jennifer described the frustration she endured during those early months. She believed that she succeeded because she challenged the authorities despite being advised not to. Her assertive behavior led her to continue "speaking to managers of managers until I got answers about why things are so halted." Her persistence ultimately translated into a positive outcome—"we got everything straight away, but I had to do that, which most people wouldn't do." Jennifer argued that if she had not "antagonized a few people" to get immediate results, her father "would have gone home and failed in the first week in being able to live at home and he would have felt within himself that he was a failure."

Although Bill successfully returned to his own home, the emotional, financial, and physical impact of Jennifer's caregiving role was substantial. Jennifer found it necessary to cut back on her work hours. As a consequence of her reduced hours and the increased costs associated with caring for her father, she experienced a range of financial problems. Jennifer described her financial burden:

> There's no financial assistance . . . for instance, the caregiver's pension, you must be residing with the person over night in order to get that. . . . I think the criteria for that is not practical . . . for me to help him as much as I would like to, it requires me to be able to finance [my] petrol use and he doesn't have this much money as a pensioner. If I was to go over there everyday it would be, say, $5 petrol per day, say $35 per week. Maybe to people who have an income of around $40,000 it probably doesn't mean much. But anybody who's on much lower [like myself] or lower socioeconomic situations, it does make a big difference. I think that if government agencies would like to encourage people to stay at home rather than go into institutions or nursing homes or retirement villages, then they have to look at ways that they can help people to do that.

And if that means helping to support people who support those people with disabilities or aged, then I think that's what they should do.

The emotional and social toll of Jennifer's caregiving role extended to her young family. She described the "effect this experience [caring for my father] has had on my now two-year old daughter":

> She was 18 months old when dad had his stroke. She spent most days at the hospital with me and as a result of this, [she] was often unwell from colds/bugs picked up at the hospital. . . . She had self-initiated toilet training just prior to dad going into hospital, this went by the wayside and we're still waiting for her to return to this stage. . . . She has become increasingly frustrated with my attention being shared elsewhere and we have a lot of behavior problems to deal with now.

Clearly, the impact of Jennifer's caregiving activities were pervasive and intrusive to her family and would continue to be ongoing while her father remained in his own home.

Ten Months Poststroke

At approximately 10 months following Bill's stroke, Jennifer continued to express a great deal of frustration about her caregiving role. However, her frustration mainly stemmed from the systemic issues that she and her father faced as they attempted to navigate the public health care system. Jennifer described how her father's ongoing health concerns were exacerbated by the breakdown of communication between health professionals. Information regarding his health was not shared in a timely fashion between the hospital system and his general practitioner (GP), so following up on this information eventually became her responsibility.

> So it's up to the patient who has had a couple of strokes and who is having difficulty getting around and coping with life in general and is being given the responsibility to do this. . . . Of course [dad] rang me all very worried . . . and when people put things onto him and say that it's his responsibility to do it, I get very annoyed by that. So I rang the hospital and said that the GP wanted the information passed onto her and why hadn't it been. . . . So all of these set processes that are supposedly in place [for information sharing in the health care system] are not working. It's taken dad to get worried and then to ring me and then me to follow-up and make a couple of phone calls.

Advocating on behalf of her father within the health care system was time consuming and frustrating and required a great deal of vigilance on Jennifer's part.

> That [advocating] takes a lot of effort, a lot of time and a lot of assertion. And at times just a simple lot of "front," to be able to put up with the comments that come back at you. Some people who are in the medical profession think that people who are not in the medical profession don't have any right to question their decisions or their judgments. And unless you have the gall to get up

there and confront that [you get nowhere], [but] you're lucky if it's not seen as aggressive.

Jennifer felt responsible for keeping on top of the health care system to obtain answers and ensure continuity for her father. She shared her concern for the future, "I feel that [dad's] health is declining . . . it worries me that he is on his own." Her anxiety was exacerbated when the services (e.g., Meals on Wheels, Home Care) she had organized to support her father to live safely in his own home unexpectedly ceased over the Christmas holidays.

> I was disappointed . . . that over the Christmas break, all of those services stopped and dad didn't tell me that. . . . He doesn't want to put me out so he doesn't tell me. But it puts me out more when he doesn't tell me. He's just making do himself . . . doing all the things that he doesn't normally do like bathing himself.

Jennifer's father had a mini-stroke on the evening of Boxing Day, when he was at home alone. Although Jennifer had taken precautions in case of emergencies, she learned that these techniques were fallible, "I had an [emergency call service] for him—[but] he wasn't wearing his pendant [emergency call button]" at the time of his stroke. This event exacerbated her sense of dread—"in hindsight [it is terrible] to think about what has happened to your father . . . that he has actually had a stroke and he's been lying there on his own, not being able to get anybody to help him."

The unpredictability and uncertainty associated with her father's health condition impacted on Jennifer's ability to decisively plan for the future. She described her concerns for the future and the considerations involved in providing more support to her father in the event that his health continued to deteriorate.

> I'm starting to feel that I'd be more comfortable, and it is selfish . . . that I want him here with me. . . . The possibility is there. But it's something you really need to plan. Unless your house is equipped you'd have to move, which is what I'd have to do. That's what I started looking into selling and buying a place that's easily accessed, another bedroom, all that sort of thing. . . . Everything is just so unpredictable and up in the air . . . we just don't know enough about anything to make any decisions.

Clearly, providing appropriate accommodation for her father would result in an upheaval for Jennifer's entire family.

Fourteen Months Poststroke

Approximately 14 months following Bill's stroke, Jennifer's role in supporting her father had changed substantially. She had relinquished a great deal of her responsibility for supporting Bill to her brother, who had recently returned to Brisbane. Taking a backseat in her father's care was described as a bittersweet process. Jennifer was able to rechannel her energy into the neglected areas of her own life—"I've taken on more work commitments for myself" and, more important, "[my daughter] benefits a lot more from [the change] than anybody because she really was robbed of a lot of time and attention." However, the emotional impact of withdrawing her support was an acute sense of worry and guilt. "I think guilt is a pretty natural response to feel when you withdraw because you feel that not only should you be doing it [supporting dad], but you want to be doing it, but you're not." Jennifer explained that the only reason she felt secure to withdraw her support was because it was family who were taking over from her. "I wouldn't have withdrawn if there hadn't have been family there anyway."

Despite Bill's greater contact with other family members, Jennifer's main concern for her father was his lack of social contact and dwindling support of friends. "I think that sometimes people are very well meaning and put a lot of effort in and then . . . find it exhausting . . . to maintain something that wasn't normally what you would do all the time." She noted that Bill's friends provided important support early on that enabled him to make substantial improvements following the stroke, but the loss of these networks was damaging and was difficult for him to accept. "I think [his friends' support] served a great purpose in that it's helped dad be motivated and get as well as he has. There were great benefits in it but on the other hand, I think it's a bit of a decline [now that is hard] for dad to adjust to. . . . I think he needs that contact."

Jennifer also relinquished her role as her father's case worker within the health care system but for different reasons. She described ongoing concerns with the medical care her father received as a result of poor communication between health professionals, inadequate information management systems, and lack of appropriate discharge planning. She explained:

> We found out recently that dad was being serviced by two consultants at the hospital. . . . [As a result] he had two separate files with information that was important split across two files . . . basically all they were doing was over-servicing dad yet still managing to neglect him because information was still not being communicated to each doctor because there were two files. And in the end, information that was relevant and critical wasn't, and still isn't, getting back to his GP. . . . If you have two files, you don't have any link-up between events and health.

Despite feeling that "I shouldn't have to sort that out!" Jennifer raised the issue with the relevant health professionals. As a result of airing her grievances, she felt that her father was ultimately disadvantaged. She felt compelled to "just shut my mouth, and whatever happens, happens."

> In the end, the public health doctor said, "I won't see him anymore, I'm not going to over service him." . . . So dad went back to see [the second doctor] . . . and he said, "don't come back." I feel like because I complained, that they have said, "well none of us are going to see you now." . . . Basically, if you whinge [complain], you get nothing . . . all of a sudden he's got no doctors and nobody wants to service him. So then it comes back to the loudmouth daughter. . . . So dad is the one disadvantaged in the end. Which makes me . . . want to step back even more.

Implicit in Jennifer's statements was a sense of futility, helplessness, and frustration. "It seems like the only safe option for dad is if I don't say anything. Maybe he'll get better care if I don't say anything at all."

Eighteen Months Poststroke

At the time of the last interview (approximately 18 months following Bill's stroke) Jennifer was resuming the caregiving role for her father. Her brother, who had recently taken on the supportive role, had moved away again. The imminent resumption of caregiving responsibilities resulted in Jennifer "feeling a bit down about the prospects of the near future for me and my little daughter." The situation caused her to reflect about how her caregiving responsibilities impacted on her as an individual.

> Just on a "self" note . . . it's difficult at times to have your own time for yourself or your own goals. And I'm sort of privately a bit sad about that because there are things I want to do. My values . . . help me set my priorities [caring for my father] and I'm not about to reset my values. [But] I don't know what to do about the disappointment I feel.

Jennifer's comments concerning the personal sacrifice she had made to fulfill her caregiving role were indicative of the lived experience of juggling multiple caring responsibilities. She was quick to normalize the experience, acknowledging that this was probably a universal experience—"I think that happens to anybody who has to support other people for whatever reason."

Although Jennifer conceded that her caregiving role equated to a significant personal cost, she was adamant that social policy was in desperate need of attention to support her efforts. The resumption of caregiving responsibilities reignited Jennifer's earlier arguments that "if I'm going to support people and make their life better, surely someone can support me to do that. Not support me—but what I'm trying to do." She felt strongly that the current "all or nothing type policy . . . doesn't fit in with what [governments] publicly state about supporting elderly people and disabled people to live in their home independently."

Jennifer raised cogent and valid criticisms of the rhetoric that surrounds the pressing public health issue of supporting the ageing population to live in their own homes. She had voiced her concerns to her local politicians— "Don't you worry, I do that sort of thing all the time." However, the process of contacting politicians was just one more task that drained her already depleted energy reserves for very little reward.

> One person can make a big difference, but you've only got so much time in your day, and throughout your own life there are so many issues that come up that are unfair or unequal in our society. You can only run with so many of them before you get exhausted. And they're usually prioritized; whatever is causing the most stress for you and your family at the time.

She commented on the relative ignorance of some of the politicians she had contacted for support.

> Two [politicians] that I called [to discuss the caregiver's pension] actually said to me, "of course you can get the caregiver's pension." . . . I said, "no you can't," and I gave them the criteria by which you have to fit to get that [you must live with the person]. They were astonished. So they don't even know in

the first place. And yet . . . here we are in Australia, probably one of the biggest issues is that we have an aging population and you want to look at social policy that supports people to stay at home. You want to look at family and community supporting each other—but we don't even understand what are the structures around us and processes that stop us from being able to do that.

Jennifer experienced a sense of futility when her efforts of advocating for change of social policy and procedure were "to no avail." The negative impact of this dismissal on her sense of self was evident in her comments. "[Politicians] say, "we'll write it down and ring you back," but they never did. . . . I can only make so many phone calls and annoy so many people without feeling like a dickhead myself at the end of the day." Furthermore, she argued, "None of the politicians want to hear about that anyway. . . . They're not really interested. It's not the big issue of the day."

In the end, Jennifer was cautiously hopeful that her involvement in research would expose some of the issues faced by individuals, like her, who provided support so their ill or disabled family member could reside in their own homes. "I don't know whether talking to you makes any difference. You make a note and somebody reads it—hopefully. But even if they do, whether they do anything about it is another matter."

DISCUSSION

Family caregiving still remains a central part of adult children's responsibility to older parents. Effective government policy based on empirical and qualitative research is fundamental to the development of successful strategies to reduce the feelings of burden for caregivers of the aging population. It is imperative to acknowledge that caregivers often assume the role of a case manager and the system is not useful across all settings and professions (Hyde, 2004; Ozanne, 1990). This added responsibility and the consequent loss of a traditional role results in frustration, poor communication, and compromised outcomes for both the dependent elder and the caregiver. Case managers should provide clients with collaboration, continuity, consistency, and coordination of care across clinical settings (National Chronic Care Consortium, 2000). However, without the necessary support and education, "case managers" feel pressured, unsupported, and unable to adequately coordinate existing services.

Another area of concern is caregiver financial burden. McClelland, Austin, and Schneck (1996) found when fiscal concerns displace client focus, outcomes for patients are compromised. Government policy that directs its long-term care to the communities is lacking infrastructure and funding to support the caregivers, their families, and invariably the impaired client. With the length of hospital stays getting shorter and more care being forced on families, the issue of burden is becoming a major concern, and therefore governments must access the psychological, social, economic, and health care costs of caregiving. They must ask the questions, are we reducing the health care costs for the presently ill patient, or are we, as a consequence, creating health problems for the caregivers (Roach, 2005)?

As the 21st century advances, many changes are occurring within family dynamics that can further impact the domain of caregiving. Cohen and Lepkowski (2004) discussed the decline in fertility rates and the impact this will have on the ratio of caregivers available. Over 10 years ago, the National Chronic Care Consortium (1997) warned that the demographics of the increasing elderly population would shape future government health policies. Jennifer's story illustrates that caregivers often want to provide more support, but are sometimes impeded from doing so by social and environmental constraints. Yet if she had been provided with adequate financial support (i.e., via petrol vouchers), she insists that her father would "have a better quality of life in his home." Thus the challenge for service providers, health care workers, and policy makers is to listen and learn from the firsthand experiences of caregivers and take action to find a solution to the situation.

This story also highlights the need for a more collaborative, coordinated system of support from all stakeholders to support caregivers, both financially and holistically. As Rosenthal et al. (2006) stated, the delivery system of care is "fragmented, inefficient, and poorly coordinated, especially considering the interdependency among its parts" (p. 117). The health care system needs to listen to the narratives of caregivers and its elements need to work together so that burden is reduced. It makes good economic sense, as well as ethical and practical sense, to provide caregivers like Jennifer with a responsive system that maximizes their caregiving capacity.

REFERENCES

Aliotta, S., Archibald, N., Brown, R., Chen, A., & Fox, P. (2000). *Best practices in coordinated care.* Princeton, NJ: Mathematica Policy Research.

Barber, C. E. (1988). Correlates of subjective burden among adult sons and daughters caring for aged parents. *Journal of Aging Studies, 2*(2), 133–144.

Case Management Society of Australia. (2005). *National standards of practice for case management.* Victoria: Author.

Cohen, S. B., & Lepkowski, J. M. (2004). *Eighth Conference on Health Survey Research Methods.* Hyattsville, MD: National Center for Health Statistics.

Dewey, H. M., Thrift, A. G., Mihalopoulos, C., Carter, R., et al. (2002). Informal care for stroke survivors: Results from the North East Melbourne Stroke Incidence Study (NEMESIS). *Stroke, 33*(4), 1028–1033.

Howell, D., & Ellis, J. (2005). A story telling approach to case management. Plenary abstract at the Case Management Society of Australia's Eighth Annual Conference, 2005.

Hyde, P. (2004). *Care management, case management and utilization review in a managed care environment. An introduction to terms and concepts.* Boston: Technical Assistance Collaborative.

Jamrozik, A. (2001). *Social policy in the post-welfare state.* Sydney: Pearson Education.

Kasuya, R., Polgar-Bailey, P. P., & Takeuchi, R. (2000). Caregiver burden and burnout. *Postgraduate Medicine, 108*(7), 1–7.

McClelland, R., Austin, C., & Schneck D. (1996). Practice dilemmas and policy implications in case management. In C. Austin & R. McClelland (Eds.), *Perspectives on case management practice* (pp. 257–278). Milwaukee, WI: Families International.

Millward, C. (1999). Caring for elderly parents. *Australian Institute of Family Studies, 52,* 26–30.

National Chronic Care Consortium. (1997). *Case management for the frail elderly: A literature review on selected topics.* Minnesota Senior Health Options.

National Chronic Care Consortium. (2000). *Case management: Methods and issues.* University of Maryland Center on Aging, Robert Wood Johnson Foundation Medicare/Medicaid Integration Program.

O'Connor, I., Wilson, J., & Setterlund, D. (2003). *Social work and welfare practice* (4th ed.). Malaysia: Person Longman.

Ozanne, E. (1990). Reasons for the emergence of case management approaches and their distinctiveness from present service arrangements. In A. Howe, E. Ozanne, & C. Shelby-Smith (Eds.), *Community care policy and practice: New directions in Australia* (pp. 186–194). Victoria: Public Sector Management Institute.

Roach, M. J. (2005).*Caregiving and family burden.* Center to Improve Care of the Dying. Retrieved April 10, 2005, from www.gwu.edu-cicd/toolkit/caregive.htm.

Rosenthal, M. P., Butterfoss, F. D., Doctor, L. J.,Gilmore, L. A., Krieger, J. W., et al. (2006). The coalition process at work: Building care coordination models to control chronic disease. *Health Promotion Practices, 7,* 117–126.

Scharlach, A. E., Giunta, N., & Mills-Dick, K. (2001). *Case management in long-term care integration: An overview of current programs and evaluations.* Berkeley: University of California Press.

Shanas, E. (1980). Older people and their families: The new pioneers. *Journal of Marriage and the Family, 42,* 9–15.

Sorrell, J. M. (August, 2003). The ethics of diversity: A call for intimate listening in thin places. *Online Journal of Issues in Nursing.* Retrieved April 5, 2005, from www.nursingworld.org/ojin/ethicol /ethics_13.htm.

CHAPTER 9

Navigating Societal Norms: The Psychological Implications of Living in the United States with Disability

Jennifer Gibson

The purpose of this chapter is to share my personal experience with disability while highlighting the social constructs and obstacles people with disabilities face in the United States. I begin with a historical account of my parents' being given the diagnosis of my being a "vegetable" as an infant and its impact on my family. I describe specific developmental milestones throughout my life to the present day, when I am actively involved on a national level as a psychologist. The second half of the chapter focuses on disability competency for clinicians and includes a description of the disability identity development model (DIDM) that I have created based on two decades of working with individuals with disabilities. This model provides insight into how people with disabilities perceive themselves within today's society. As a psychologist, writer, and person with a disability, my intent is to demonstrate that disability is an inclusive factor in the life cycle and is a part of the great diversity within our society. Disability should not define a person, but be a contributing trait of an individual just like gender, ethnicity, sexual orientation, and socioeconomic status.

LIFE'S JOURNEY WITH A DISABILITY

As far back as I can remember, I would look forward to Labor Day weekend. This would be the one opportunity of the year to see others who were similar to me. I would remind my mother that the Jerry Lewis Labor Day Telethon would begin on Sunday evening. Though I did not completely understand why I had created this annual family tradition, I knew that for one weekend out of the year, disability could be discussed. I had 2 days out of the 365 a year to explore my thoughts and feelings about strangers with disabilities on television with my family, while minimizing my own disability. This was quite a feat, needless to say!

I began my life's journey in the mid-1960s, being born as a typically healthy baby girl at a hospital in Los Angeles, California. Two days later, I was found not breathing and blue in the hospital's nursery. I had been left unattended on my back. As a result, I choked on my phlegm. It just so happened that the nurse on duty had a grandchild being born during my brief stay. Instead of monitoring the nursery, she was in her daughter's room, paying a visit. This one event set the stage for my life with disability.

Once I had been revived and stabilized, my parents were told that the odds were not in my favor for survival. "At best," they were told, "she will be a vegetable. You will need to consider your options, including placing her in an institution where she can be attended to. There is nothing more that we can do." My parents refused to believe that my short life was over before it had begun. They transferred me to the children's hospital in the area, hoping that I would receive the care and treatment that I would need to have a chance for living life. Following a week of tests and observation, my parents brought me home when I was 10 days old. They were told that I would be "fine" and that they should go home and enjoy their baby girl. My family was thrilled to have the opportunity of hope for the daughter that they had dreamt of the day I had been born. As time passed, my mom had begun to notice struggles as I reached developmental milestones. I would attempt to walk, but my balance would not allow me to take more than two steps. I began to form sounds, but would have difficulty pronouncing words. She discussed her observations with the pediatrician, who thought my 17-year-old mother was exhibiting signs of depression. Thus, the doctor dismissed my mom's concerns and wrote her a prescription for an antidepressant.

My mom did not allow her concerns to be dismissed. After much reading of medical journals, my mom found a description of my symptoms and took it to the pediatrician, who then agreed that I had cerebral palsy. During this same visit, the doctor presented my parents with the decision of having me institutionalized. This had been the common practice for dealing with children with disabilities. My parents thought such a question was absurd. From that day forward, my parents, especially my mom, advocated and sought out services that would increase my chances of living a full and independent life.

With this, I began attending a school for the handicapped immediately to receive early intervention modalities, speech and physical therapies, while receiving a quality education. I enjoyed physical therapy since the therapists made it fun by playing games that increased my coordination. We would often played catch with a big ball, and over a few years time, the ball became a tennis ball as my abilities improved. Swimming was extremely fun! My confidence grew as my coordination increased. My experience with speech therapy was not as positive. In fact, I hated it! It was *real* work. I would have to say things that I just could not say. I would be told to repeat words that began with "l," "s," and "r," which were the most difficult for me to pronounce. I remember crying during many sessions out of frustration. I would attempt to talk my way out of going to speech therapy. In fact, I was so desperate to avoid it, that one day I pretended to be sick and had my dad drive 50 miles to pick me up (normally a school bus would take me to and from school).

In all of my memories surrounding my disability, I must say that the inability to be understood by others as a young child has been the most difficult experience. Repeating myself over and over was not only frustrating but quite embarrassing. I would try to think of words to replace words so that I could be understood. For example, when asked what I would like to have for lunch, I would say, "I want anything good to eat," instead of saying what I actually wanted, "I would like spaghetti." As a result, I often settled for something that I did not want due to my speech. Thus, I must admit that all of the frustration and tears that I had gone through with speech therapy paid off over the years. People besides my parents began to understand what I was saying.

When I was six years old, the doctors who worked through my school offered an experimental corrective hip surgery to one boy and one girl who had displayed promise of excelling academically. I was the girl chosen. This surgery along with hospital costs came to tens of thousands of dollars. It would have been impossible for my family to have paid such a bill. Thankfully, all but $150 had been covered by nonprofit organizations and the hospital. My parents gladly struggled to pay the $150. Yet there was no guarantee of the surgery being successful. My parents asked me if I wanted to have the surgery, I eagerly answered, "yes."

Once the surgery had been completed, I struggled through rehabilitation while learning to walk again. It seemed as if the surgery had been a success. Therefore, when I was eight, I had the second hip surgery. However, this time, I wasn't as eager. I can remember the morning of the operation, looking at and feeling the side of my unblemished thigh, where soon a long incision would be made. I began to cry. My dad asked why I was crying since I had not cried before my first surgery. I said that this time I was aware of what was going to happen as I began to cry harder. He told me that I didn't need to be a crybaby and that I needed to be tough like before. From that moment on, I knew that I couldn't share my thoughts and feelings about my disability with my dad. Believing that my dad was unable to discuss or just listen to me talk about the negative side of having a disability has been painful. Though I could speak more with my mom about my disability, I soon came to learn that my parents could not fully comprehend my life experience with a disability. Once completing rehabilitation for the second time, it became evident that both surgeries had been successful. I no longer walked on my tiptoes with my hands and arms up in the air for balance. There was no comparison to the before and after. Moreover, I had been the first successful patient who had received this procedure. I have been very thankful ever since, yet disturbed that I only had this chance because I had showed intellectual promise and that the surgery had been experimental and virtually free. I had been lucky, though I think of all the other children who could have benefited from the same opportunity.

By age eight, I knew my life's direction. I wanted to be a psychologist. However, I had no role model in my life to guide me toward this lofty goal.

My parents had dropped out of high school, as had all members of my extended family. When I would share my goal with my parents, they would encourage me to follow my dream. They had instilled within me that I would need an education and could not simply rely on my physical abilities as they had. They did not want my disability to limit my life and wanted me to have every opportunity possible. With that, I was given a clear message that I would attend college.

During third grade, a doctor at my school who had known me for five years began to discuss with my parents the possibility of my attending regular school. Dr. Morris told my mom that with the success of my surgeries, it had become evident that my current school was holding me back. However, it would be a very political move on her part to advocate on my behalf and that it could possibly take over a year before it could become actualized. Therefore, Dr. Morris wanted my parents to seriously consider this possibility before she took the risk of making waves within the school district. My parents asked me what I wanted. I did not hesitate to say that I wanted to attend the school right down the street from our home. That had always been one of my fantasies. My dad mentioned that the kids might laugh at me and asked if I would be prepared to handle their ignorance. "Yes, yes . . . I can handle it," I replied without hesitation.

I began regular school in fifth grade after much wrangling from Dr. Morris and my parents. There had been much trepidation from both schools. One did not want to release me because of state monies, the other did not want to accept me fearing that I would not succeed and would create confusion for their students. Though this was a public school in the early 1970s, they had not yet begun a special education program. Thus, students had not experienced a peer with a disability.

I must admit, I have often wondered what my educational career would have been like if in fact they had a special education program. Would I have been presented with the same academic challenges? Needless to say, ultimately I had been allowed to attend the school down the street from home. However, to be considered, I would have to attend summer school. There were two motives in play. One was whether I could effectively academically compete with the other children, and second, whether I would be accepted as a peer. It was a "yes" to both, though I did experience ridicule and being laughed at by many of the children. Once most of them got to know me, they accepted me as a fellow student. Summer school proved to be a success, and onward I proceeded.

During eighth grade, I was fortunate to have one of our state's four-year universities visit my school. My family lived in a lower-middle-income neighborhood, and I and my fellow classmates were not expected to attend a four-year college. I had never heard about the SAT or what class requirements were to be considered for admittance. I had thought as long as I had earned A's and B's in any class that I would be a shoo-in for college. I was a dry sponge soaking up every bit of information about college.

In ninth grade, I had begun to take the required courses. I had to fight with my high school to remain in a qualifying English class due to my physical writing ability. My English teacher thought that because I had difficulty with cursive writing, I should be marked down one grade for all written work assigned. I would spend two hours on written homework that should have taken a half hour, leaving me with calloused fingers from gripping my pen tightly to write as neatly as possible. If I continued to be graded in this manner, in all probability, this would have left me with a C for the class.

I shared my frustration with my mother, who, as always, advocated on my behalf. Though she had wished that I would drop out of this teacher's class, she met with the principal to discuss the inequality in grading. I remember being called into their meeting along with my teacher. When asked for my reason for wanting to remain in this English class, I simply stated that this was the only qualifying college English course offered and I needed to take it. Discussion followed concerning my teacher's grading practices and a decision was made in that whatever grade I earned on assignments was the grade I would receive, regardless of how curly my R's and S's may appear. In time, I grew fond of my English teacher. She graded me fairly from that day on. This is my first memory of advocating for myself. I had taken many lessons from my first mentor, my mother.

I was filled with much excitement as I entered into 12th grade for I knew that in just one short year that I could be attending college. And not just attending college, but living away at college! As do many parents, mine struggled with the thought of their child moving away. They honestly did not realize the differences between community and state college and a four-year university. I applied to the university that had visited my junior high school. I only applied to this one university. It was nearly 50 miles away from home.

By the next fall, I was moving into my dorm room. Lucky for me to have been accepted by the only school I had applied to! I was eager to meet with an academic advisor to select my courses. Unfortunately, the advisor provided inadequate assistance and I was in a statistics class that most students take during their senior year. By the second week of class, I knew that completing this course with any grade higher than an F would be impossible. Crushed with knowing that I would receive my first ever F, I had decided to focus my energies on my other classes and did not return to statistics. It was not until the spring term that somebody told me that students add and drop courses all of the time. I felt so embarrassed and angry knowing that my GPA was going to be impacted due to my ignorance. If only there had been someone who could have given me direction.

Being fearful of having ruined my hopes of becoming a psychologist by having received an F, I sought out a clinician on campus to learn what preparation is required to become a psychologist. I walked into the university counseling center, presuming that I could find someone who could share this information with me. Unknown to me, I was about to meet my first professional mentor. I was introduced to Marikyo Adams, LCSW, and she took the time to assure me that a career in psychology remained quite possible. She explained the need to attend graduate school (I had never known of such schools) and various opportunities within the field of psychology. Throughout the years, our relationship has grown into a true friendship.

After receiving my bachelor's degree in psychology, I attended the one graduate school she had made me aware of. Due to my lack of knowledge, I applied to only this one graduate program. Luck or perhaps fate has been a guiding force in my life. I have fondly termed this phenomenon my "unseen mentor." However, fate did not produce any mentors during my graduate school years, or for that matter, to the current day. I have had some near misses. However, those who I had viewed as mentoring material chose to mentor others. For example, I had introduced my best friend to one of my undergraduate professors who had many achievements within the field of psychology and had gained national acclaim and respect as a founder of multicultural psychology. I had hopes that he would give me direction regarding graduate schools and career opportunities. My hopes did not materialize. Instead, he became a mentor to my friend, guiding her throughout graduate school into her present career. I am very happy for my friend, though I wish that I could have also benefited from my professor's knowledge and national network of psychologists.

Toward the end of graduate school, I married a man that I had met at work. Prior to this, I had dated a few men throughout college. I had fallen in love once, however, the feelings were not mutual. That man had difficulty dealing with my disability. This did not sway my belief that if he had truly gotten to know me, he would love me. We dated on and off for eight years. With time, it finally sank in that the issue was not mine but his. I realized that he would never want to spend his life with me. After much time, I came to terms with loving him without spending my life with him. It was around this time that I met the man who became my husband.

My mother had met my future husband just once before her untimely death. She liked him. She had never liked any man I had dated, so I thought this was a sign that he was the one. The day of her death, he proposed. Without hesitation, I said "yes." We had a modest wedding a month later and moved across the country on my husband's desires. I had known him less than six months. Three months later, we tried to get pregnant. We were successful on the first try. I was so happy! I had always wanted to be a mother. Shortly into the pregnancy, my husband began drinking. It became readily apparent that he had a problem with alcohol. Moreover, his personality was that of Jekyll and Hyde. He would become verbally abusive and physically violent. After witnessing such behavior, I calmly spoke with him the following day and said that if he continued to drink, I would not be able to stay with him. He said that he understood. He did not drink after that, at least until my son was born.

My husband came to pick me and my son up from the hospital in a limousine. I should have been ecstatic. However, as my husband walked into the room, it became apparent that he had been drinking. He knew that I would not have had gotten into a car with him in his condition. So to deflect from his drinking, he rented a limo. My heart sank. What I had hoped to be the start of a beautiful family quickly became terror and a great disappointment. I had hoped that this would be an isolated drinking binge. However, it just was not to be.

Six months later, I left my husband, though he did fight for custody of our son. He claimed that I was an unfit mother due to my disability. The courts were able to see through him. This was such a relief! For once in my life, I did not have to struggle to prove my abilities to a societal institution. However, I could not move back home, to my family and friends, until custody had been finalized. My soon-to-be-ex-husband resolved this matter by kidnapping my son. Thankfully, my son was returned safely within days. With this, the court ruled that I would have sole custody, with him only having court-supervised visitation. He refused such visitation, and my son and I went home to California.

On returning home, I completed my dissertation and received my long awaited doctorate in psychology. My son was nearly four, and he can still recall the event. He is now 14, a high school student, and playing basketball for his school's team. He has been nothing but a blessing in my life! I have instilled within him that he can be and do anything he sets his mind to. Likewise, he has encouraged me to fulfill my dreams of being a psychologist, professor, writer, and community leader. I am currently all of those. And, more important, I am what I had always dreamed of being—a mother!

DISABILITY PSYCHOLOGY

People with disabilities are often overlooked as a part of the tapestry of diversity. However, this population spans every ethnicity, gender, sexual orientation, age, religion, and socioeconomic group ever known. Approximately one of every five Americans has a disability, comprising nearly 20 percent of our nation's population (Waldrop & Stern, 2003). It is evident that people with disabilities, particularly people of color with disabilities, have less access to and availability of mental health services (U.S. Department of Health and Human Services, 1999). Section 2.01(b) of the American Psychological Association (APA) Ethics Code (APA, 2002) supports an affirmative need as a profession to develop disability-related competence.

When working with clients with disabilities, it is vital to recognize the heterogeneity of this population. People with disabilities come from all facets of life. Moreover, they differ vastly from one another, such as lifelong versus acquired disabilities, type of disability (i.e., physical, sensory, learning, and psychological), and variation of level and impact of disability. With such diversity among people with disabilities, being a member of the disability community does not guarantee acceptance by other individuals with disabilities. Unlike other marginalized groups in society who take pride and celebrate their commonalities, people are not eager to become members of the disability population (Gibson, 2008). Families do not celebrate when a baby is born with a disability or when a relative acquires a disability.

Children with disabilities mostly grow up with able-bodied family members who may attempt to understand their daily struggles but fall short of fully grasping the experience of the child with a disability. This is not due to lack of effort by family members but is attributed to not sharing the same life experience. Likewise, individuals with acquired disabilities initially may have family and friends rally around them. However, due to fears and an inability of relating to the individual's experience, there is a tendency of others to withdraw over time. This may explain why the divorce rates among persons who acquire a disability have been reported to be anywhere from 8 percent to 48 percent (Kreuter, 2000).

Those with disability do not differ from others in striving for psychological well-being. However, the mental health of these individuals is often ignored (Vash & Crewe, 2003; Williams & Upadhyay, 2003). In instances when mental health treatment has been sought, clinicians tend to focus on the disability and medical aspects of the person, thus depersonalizing the individual. Sadly, unknown to the clinician, this can lead to the revictimization of the client (Gibson, 2006) and the likelihood that they will not continue treatment. Many people with disabilities have internalized society's perceptions of being just a medical diagnosis and have experiences of marginalization.

Marginalization may also be experienced by a client with a disability when a clinician exhibits a variation of cultural encapsulation. *Cultural encapsulation* refers to the protective capsule or cocoon that some clinicians construct to protect themselves from meaningful engagement with persons from other cultures (Wren, 1962). However, unlike cultural encapsulation where there is no challenge to one's cultural affiliation, clients with disabilities may not only represent a fear of the unknown but also bring about a sense of vulnerability for the clinician. Such vulnerability may include gaining a sudden awareness that disability is an equal opportunity life experience. Thus, perhaps for the first time in their lives, clinicians are being exposed to the concept that they or a loved one could acquire a disability. Similar to how many fear death and dying to avoid thoughts of one's own mortality, working with clients with disabilities may trigger fear and avoidance of disability. This can lead to the concept of disabiliphobia, for lack of a better term. In a clinical setting, disabiliphobia, a fear of people with disabilities or perhaps a fear of what they may represent, might explain why some clinicians depersonalize clients with disabilities. Depersonalization can serve as a protective barrier from meaningful engagement, allowing them to avoid feelings of vulnerability. Disabiliphobia can interfere with the delivery of competent and effective treatment.

The limited exposure to training opportunities may leave psychologists prone to biases and misconceptions about disability (Taliaferro, 2005). The inclusion of disability within clinical training programs would lend exposure to future clinicians and may begin to alleviate disabiliphobia. However, training related to disability has been difficult to attain (Leigh, Powers, Vash, & Nettles, 2004). This oversight might be attributed to our society historically viewing disability from a medical model (Leeds Metropolitan University, 2005). This model states that disability represents a defect or loss of function that resides in the individual. In turn, medical doctors have treated people with disabilities exclusively with surgery and/or medication. These individuals often are viewed as "scientific subjects" and are probed as if they are inanimate objects, communicating an unspoken message that they are not fully human. Moreover, whatever its outcome, this medical treatment is seen as good enough practice and worthy of appreciation by the individual as an attempt to improve one's life.

Recently, a societal shift has emerged away from the medical model to social and minority models (Gallardo & Gibson, 2005). These models view disability as an external problem involving an environment that fails to accommodate the needs of individuals with disabilities. The models shift the responsibility of accommodation from the individual to the society that needs to accommodate them as individuals. Therefore, it is essential when establishing the initial therapeutic alliance to not assume that a client's presenting problem is his or her disability. Individuals are multidimensional and experience life and its struggles in the same manner as others. Clinicians should not assume that disability is or should be the focus of treatment (Gibson, 2008). Disability is an added variable that necessitates a clinician's awareness and sensitivity. It should be noted as with clients without disabilities. Clients with disabilities will seek a clinician based on their area of specialization (i.e., phobias, adjustment issues). For this reason, it is imperative that all clinicians possess disability-related competence to provide services to all persons who could benefit from their expertise (Johnson-Greene, 2006).

To minimize the revictimization of clients, disability-competent treatment is needed and includes:

1. sensitivity toward disability,
2. confronting one's own beliefs and disability-related stereotypes, and
3. knowledge of disability.

Table 9.1 is an introduction to the DIDM (Gibson, 2006). I have developed this model over two decades of working with clients with disabilities by noting common characteristics, issues, and preferences they share. Based on the resources of existing multicultural identity models (Atkinson, Morten, & Sue, 1993; Cross, 1971; Helms, 1990), this disability-specific model is intended to facilitate understanding for persons with lifelong disabilities while increasing the ability of professionals to provide competent treatment to this underserved population.

Table 9.1 Disability Identity Development Model

Stage 1: Passive Awareness: First part of life 0–? Can continue into adulthood	Stage 2: Realization: Often occurs in adolescence/early adulthood	Stage 3: Acceptance: Adulthood
No role model of disability Medical needs are met Taught to deny social aspects of disability Disability becomes silent member of family Codependency/"good boy/good girl" Shy away from attention Will not associate with others with disability	Begins to see self as having a disability Self-hate Anger: Why me? Concerned with how others perceive self Concerned with appearance "Superman/-woman" complex	Shift focus from "being different" in a negative light to embracing self Begins to view self as relevant; no more no less than others Begins to incorporate others with disabilities into life Involves self in disability advocacy and activism Integrates self into majority (able-bodied) world

Source: Gibson (2006).

As with other multicultural identity models of development, the DIDM promotes understanding of a client by giving insight into her or his possible perceptions and struggles. However, one should not assume that all clients with disabilities must fit into a particular stage. Identity development of people with disabilities can be fluid. Thus, a client may have reached Stage 3, Acceptance, but may revert to Stage 2, Realization, when faced with job discrimination or lack of dating partners. The feelings of "Why me?" and anger can resurface, creating much frustration for the client since she or he might have thought that she or he were beyond such feelings.

In contrast to people with lifelong disabilities, people who experience later-onset chronic illness or acquired disability may find their sense of self suddenly and dramatically challenged or altered (Bishop, 2005). Thus, such clients may be faced with significant changes in their social and familial relationships and life roles while dealing concurrently with psychological distress, physical pain, prolonged medical treatment, and gradually increasing interference in or restriction of the performance of daily activities (Livneh & Antonak, 1997). Therefore, disability identity development for people with acquired disabilities may resemble those with lifelong disabilities yet differ because they have a comparison of life with and without disability. Understanding how people navigate this process of adapting to disability-related changes and applying this understanding in the form of effective clinical interventions have been important focuses of rehabilitation research for several decades (Elliott, 1994; Wright & Kirby, 1999).

Common traits that many clients with chronic illnesses and acquired disabilities have been shown to share include the processing of the stages of grief (i.e., denial, anger, bargaining, depression, and acceptance) (Kübler-Ross, 2005). Although a client may reach acceptance of disability, he or she may often have "what if there is a cure?" thoughts and a yearning to achieve the level of functioning he or she once experienced. Though their physical bodies may have acquired disability, they have lived able-bodied lives up until the time of accident or disease. Thus, clients with acquired disabilities may successfully integrate disability into their sense of self while retaining an able-bodied perception of the world.

Moreover, other aspects of the client, for example, ethnicity, gender, sexual orientation, and so forth, should not be ignored. Rather, clinicians should integrate what they know about other cultures and incorporate it into treatment. The APA (2003) Multicultural Guidelines state that "All individuals exist in social, political, historical, and economic contexts, and psychologists are increasingly called upon to understand the influence of these contexts on individuals' behavior."

As clinicians begin to consider the identity development of people with disabilities within practice, the following communication strategies are recommended to assist in providing competent treatment to this population:

- Incorporate all aspects of the individual (e.g., gender, ethnicity, sexual orientation, etc.) into treatment.
- Use person-first language. Language empowers.
- Speak directly to the person rather than through a companion or sign language interpreter. Although at times, the personal assistant needs to be

included in a session/meeting, people with disabilities have the right to expect privacy, confidentiality, and to participate in decision making regarding their mental health care.
- Do not assume a person with a physical disability is either hard of hearing or has a cognitive disability as well. Speaking louder is not typically necessary or more helpful.
- When meeting a person with a visual disability, always identify yourself and others who might be with you. When conversing in a group, remember to identify the person to whom you are speaking.
- Treat adults as adults. Address people who have disabilities by their first names only when extending the same familiarity to all others.
- Listen attentively when you are speaking with a person who has difficulty speaking. Be patient and wait for the person to finish, rather than correcting or speaking for the person. If necessary, ask short questions that require short answers, a nod or shake of the head. Never pretend to understand if you are having difficulty doing so. Instead, repeat what you have understood and allow the person to respond. The response will clue you in and guide your understanding.

CONCLUSION

There were two goals for this chapter. The first was to provide a window into life with a disability in the United States. Yes, there are additional struggles that I have faced because of disability, mostly caused by others' attitudes and beliefs about disability. Yet I feel as if I have experienced life as much as any other person. I have been a daughter, mother, spouse, friend, student, and professional. I have experienced happiness and heartache. I have been given opportunities and have missed out on others. I have experienced life.

The second goal of this chapter was to provide a window into disability competency within clinical work. Disability is a natural part of the life cycle. It is just part of the great diversity within our society. It should not define a person, but should be a contributing trait of an individual, such as gender, ethnicity, sexual orientation, and socioeconomic status. If the reader's awareness of disability and competent treatment has increased as a result of reading my story, then my intention has been realized.

REFERENCES

American Psychological Association. (2002). Ethical principles of psychologists and code of conduct. *American Psychologist, 57*(12), 1060–1073.

American Psychological Association. (2003). Guidelines on multicultural education, training, research, practice and organizational change for psychologists. *American Psychologist*, 58(5), 377–402.

Atkinson, D. R., Morten, G., & Sue, D. W. (1993). *Counseling American minorities: A cross-cultural perspective* (4th ed). Dubuque, IA: Brown & Benchmark.

Bishop, M. (2005, *April–June*). Quality of life and psychosocial adaptation to chronic illness and acquired disability: A conceptual and theoretical synthesis. *Journal of Rehabilitation*. Retrieved May 1, 2008, from findarticles.com/p/articles/mi_m0825/is_2_71/ai_n13820423.

Cross, W. E. (1971). The Negro-to black conversion experience: Towards a psychology of black liberation. *Black World, 20*, 13–27.

Elliott, T. R. (1994). A place for theory in the study of psychological adjustment among persons with neuromuscular disorders: A reply to Livneh and Antonak. *Journal of Social Behavior and Personality, 9*, 231–236.

Gallardo, M. E., & Gibson, J. (2005). *Culturally diverse individuals with disabilities: Meeting therapeutic needs.* Framingham, MA; Microtraining and Multicultural Development. Retrieved from www.emicrotraining.com.

Gibson, J. (2006). Disability and clinical competency: An introduction. *California Psychologist, 39*, 6–10.

Gibson, J. (2008). Clinical competency and culturally diverse clients with disabilities: The case of Linda. In M. E. Gallardo & B. McNeill (Eds.), *The clinical casebook of multicultural psychology: Implementation of culturally proficient treatment strategies.* Mahwah, NJ: Erlbaum.

Helms, J. E. (1990). *Training manual for diagnosing racial identity in social interactions.* To accompany *Black and White racial identity: Theory, research, and practice.* Topeka, KS: Content Communications.

Johnson-Greene, D. (2006). Ethics of testing and assessment of persons with disabilities: Moving towards disability-related competence. *Rehabilitation Psychology News, 33*(3), 12–13.

Kreuter, M. (2000). Spinal cord injury and partner relationships. *Nature, 38*(2), 2–6. Retrieved April 29, 2007, from www.nature.com/sc/journal/v38/n1/abs/3100933a.html.

Kübler-Ross, E. (2005). *On grief and grieving: Finding the meaning of grief through the five stages of loss.* New York: Simon & Schuster.

Leeds Metropolitan University. (2005). *Defining disability—medical model.* Retrieved September 7, 2006, from www.lmu.ac.uk/metoffice/stuserv/disability/modelsmedical.htm.

Leigh, I., Powers, L., Vash, C., & Nettles, R. (2004). Survey of psychological services to clients with disabilities. *Rehabilitation Psychology, 49*(1), 49–54.

Livneh, H., & Antonak, R. F. (1997). *Psychosocial adaptation to chronic illness and disability.* Gaithersburg, MD: Aspen.

Taliaferro, G. (2005). Evidence-based practices and disability. *Division 22 newsletter, 32*(4).

U.S. Department of Health and Human Services. (1999). *Mental health: A report of the Surgeon General.* Rockville, MD: U.S. Department of Health and Human Services, Substance Abuse and Mental Health Services Administration, Center for Mental Health Services, National Institutes of Health, National Institute of Mental Health.

Vash, C. L., & Crewe, N. M. (2003). *Psychology of disability* (2nd ed). New York: Springer.

Waldrop, J., & Stern, S. M. (2003). Disability status: Census 2000 brief. March. Retrieved on February 1, 2008, from www.census.gov/prod/2003pubs/c2kbr-17.pdf.

Williams, M., & Upadhyay, W. S. (2003). To be or not to be disabled. In M. E. Banks & E. Kaschak (Eds.), *Women with visible and invisible disabilities: Multiple intersections, multiple issues, multiple therapies* (pp. 145–154). New York: Haworth.

Wren, C. G. (1962). The culturally encapsulated counselors. *Harvard Educational Review, 32*, 444–449.

Wright, S. J., & Kirby, A. (1999). Deconstructing conceptualizations of "adjustment" to chronic illness: A proposed integrative framework. *Journal of Health Psychology*, 259–272.

CHAPTER 10

Disabilities and Employment in the United States, Kenya, and the Philippines: A Race and Class Perspective

Elaine A. Burke and Patricia Denise Lopez

There has been very little attention paid to the needs of People of Color with disabilities. According to the U.S. Census Bureau (2007), People of Color in the United States currently number 100.7 million, one third of the nation's population—a significant proportion of the U.S. population. Latinos and Asian Americans are the fastest growing groups, with 3.4 percent and 3.2 percent increases, respectively, from July 2005 to July 2006. The percentage of African Americans grew by 1.3 percent, while non-Latino/a European Americans showed very little growth (0.3 percent) during the same period. Recent immigration statistics (U.S. Department of Homeland Security, 2007) has further indicated that the percentage of immigrants from Asia, Mexico, Central and South America, and Africa has increased dramatically from the 1950s to 2006. With respect to disabilities, People of Color also have a disproportionately higher number of disabilities and a larger percentage of them are in low-income brackets (Waldrop & Stern, 2003).

The field of multicultural psychology has described the negative impact of oppression on minority individuals, particularly People of Color. Oppression can lead to identity confusion (while attempting to conform to the dominant culture), and this oppression can become internalized, resulting in a decreased self-worth. Some of the potential effects are alcoholism, violence, and suicide. There may be an increase in crime and delinquency and the maintenance of an environment that limits individuals' opportunities for advancement.

David and Okazaki (2006) believe that the negative impact of racial oppression and historical trauma is very similar to the effects of colonization. Internalized oppression is common among many colonized individuals and people from previously colonized countries and can lead to similar beliefs and behaviors. Therefore, there may be commonalities between People of Color in the United States and individuals from previously colonized countries.

The interactions among race, poverty, employment, and disability are complex, with the relationships among many of these constructs being bidirectional and circular. To more fully understand this situation, it is beneficial to explore related areas in more detail. This chapter summarizes the situation of People of Color with disabilities, including a focus on factors affection their employment. We highlight the impact of social class. Finally, we consider the issues of race and class from a more global perspective by exploring how they may apply to less economically developed,[1] formerly colonized countries, using our experience with Kenya and the Philippines as examples.

PEOPLE OF COLOR IN THE UNITED STATES AND DISABILITY

Disability rates tend to be higher among ethnic minorities (Banks & Ackerman, 2006). Data from the 2006 American Community Survey showed that 22 percent of Native Americans and 18 percent of African Americans who were of working age reported a disability compared to 13 percent of European Americans and 6 percent of Asian Americans (Rehabilitation Research and Training Center on Disability Demographics and Statistics, 2007). In 2008, Adams, Lucas, and Barnes (using data from the 2006 National Health Interview Survey) reported that African Americans were significantly less likely than European Americans and Asian Americans to be in excellent health, and they were also more likely to be unable to work due to health reasons. The poverty rates of African American, Native American, and Latino families with members with a disability (25 percent, 26 percent, and 23 percent, respectively) were much higher than poverty rates of their European American and Asian American counterparts, at 8 percent and 12 percent, respectively (Wang, 2005).

Most Asian Americans and Pacific Islander groups seem to have lower levels of disability and have better socioeconomic profiles (Smart & Smart, 1997). However, this finding is not true of the more recent Asian immigrants such as the Hmong, Laotians, Vietnamese, and Cambodians, many of whom were refugees and who tend to be poorer and less educated than other Asian Americans who have been living in the United States for many generations, such as Japanese Americans or Chinese Americans.

Disability and Employment

Among People with Disabilities who are employed full-time, both African Americans and Latinos with disabilities are significantly underrepresented (Bradsher, 1996; Leung, 1993). Trupin, Sebesta, and Yelin (1997) found that disability accentuates the impact of race and ethnicity on employment rates (particularly among men). Reaves (2000) stated that when African American men seek employment, generally they must either find an African American employer, a company with affirmative action hiring practices, or a company that is desperately seeking employees. Even today, employer discrimination, prejudice, and reluctance to hire pose major barriers to the employment of People with Disabilities (National Council on Disability, 2007). People of Color who are disabled face double discrimination in the workplace, even triple discrimination when they are women (Banks & Marshall, 2004).

In addition to the overt and subtle (aversive) racism encountered by many People of Color seeking employment (Dovidio, Gaertner, Kawakami, & Hodson, 2002), there has been a decrease in the amount of blue-collar jobs, a relocation of industries to suburban areas, and a shift to positions that necessitate more specialized training for beginning-level positions (Johnson, 2000). In combination, these factors have impacted the ability of young, urban, People of Color to obtain employment. Instead, their employment opportunities have been limited to low or minimum wage positions that, despite long hours, provide little income.

Factors Contributing to Disability and Employment among People of Color

Thompson-Hoffman and Storck (1991) reported that there are several variables that are consistently correlated to work disability over time and across various survey sources: age, race, income, education, labor force participation, and marital status. Poor prenatal care, poor nutrition, low access to health care, greater risks for physical injuries due to the type of occupations and living conditions, lower education, and lack of health care knowledge all contribute to the higher disability rates among People of Color (Asbury, Walker, Maholmes, Rackley, & White, 1992). According to Smart and Smart (1997), there are five societal conditions that contribute to the disproportionately higher rates of disabilities among racial/ethnic minorities:

1. low income and poverty;
2. employment in dangerous jobs;
3. lack of health insurance;
4. low educational attainment; and
5. faulty testing and diagnostic conditions.

It appears that one of the most important factors contributing to disability rates is poverty. Poverty is often defined in terms of monetary wealth. Some individuals have a sudden change in socioeconomic status (SES) due to the loss of employment. Others live in chronic poverty. There is strong evidence that ethnic minorities, particularly Latinos and African Americans, are overrepresented in the lower socioeconomic classes and they comprise a larger proportion of the working poor (U.S. Bureau of Labor Statistics, 2007a; Webster & Bishaw, 2007). More African American and Latino children live in poverty and are more likely to be chronically poor than European American children (Brooks-Gunn, Duncan, & Maritato, 1997).

Albeda and Tilly (1997) found that the people most likely to be poor tend to live in cities and also do not finish high school or pursue higher education.

McNeil (1993) reported a strong association between years of schooling completed and the likelihood of having a disability. African Americans, Latinos, and Native Americans are less likely to graduate from high school than European Americans (National Center for Education Statistics, 2008). Suzuki and Valencia (1997) reported that African Americans, Latinos, and Native Americans are more likely to be diagnosed with a learning disability or mental retardation. Such diagnoses may well lead to separation from mainstream education, resulting in unequal opportunities in the future. Children from schools in high-poverty areas might be considered less competitive for employment. People of Color might also be less able to leave a high-poverty area due to segregation and discrimination.

Employment in physically dangerous jobs is a major condition related to the higher occurrence of disability among racial/ethnic minorities (Banks & Marshall, 2004). Data from the 2000 U.S. Census show that while European Americans and Asian Americans are dominant in management, professional, and related occupations; African Americans and Latinos are overrepresented in production, transportation, and material moving occupations. Latinos are also prominent in farming, fishing, and forestry jobs (Fronczek & Johnson, 2003). Moreover, members of racial minority groups tend to be in construction and extraction jobs as well as service occupations like building and grounds cleaning and maintenance, protective service and security work, and food preparation and serving (U.S. Bureau of Labor Statistics, 2007b).

Foreign-born workers, the majority of whom are Latinos (50 percent) and Asians (22 percent), are also more likely than their U.S.-born counterparts to be employed in similar occupations (U.S. Bureau of Labor Statistics, 2007c). More physically demanding and higher risk jobs make members of ethnic minority groups more vulnerable to higher disability rates than European Americans (Meadows, 1999). Pritchard (2004) chronicled the working conditions of migrant Mexican American workers and noted that the accidental death rate of migrant farm workers was four times the national average. People of Color and immigrants might have difficulty finding alternative forms of employment due to lower levels of education and acculturation (particularly proficiency with the English language).

People of Color in the United States are much less likely to have health insurance than European Americans (Smedley, Stith, & Nelson, 2003). A disproportionate number of cultural minority populations, particularly Latino Americans, are among the working poor (and perhaps cannot afford insurance) or are not offered or provided insurance by their employers. Latino Americans are overrepresented in either service-oriented or blue-collar positions that generally do not provide employer-based insurance. Lack of insurance is an important factor in health care, and people without insurance may postpone or not seek medical treatment, which could potentially lead to chronic health problems.

To summarize, People of Color in the United States have higher rates of disability, which might be related to issues of low income, low educational attainment, being inadequately diagnosed, and not having health insurance. When they have disabilities, their chances of obtaining and retaining employment are more severely impacted. Many of them work in jobs which are physically demanding and dangerous (due to limited options) and having a physical disability would effectively eliminate their opportunities to work in these positions. They also experience increased employer prejudice and discrimination as racial stereotypes interact with beliefs about People with Disability. People of Color from other countries might face similar experiences. The issues of disability and employment might be particularly profound among individuals in less industrialized countries where there is high poverty, high unemployment, little knowledge about disability, and minimal governmental support for disabled individuals.

GLOBAL PERSPECTIVE ON HEALTH AND DISABILITY

It is estimated that there are half a billion People with Disabilities worldwide, and the global population of People with Disabilities is expected to increase (Priestley, 2001). About 80 percent of the disabled population live in less economically developed countries. However, most of the research and academic literature is from the more economically developed countries in Western Europe and North America, which comprise the numerical minority of People with Disabilities in the world. Importantly, it is the perspective from this *Western minority* that currently creates the worldview about disability (Priestley, 2001).

In both less industrialized countries and more industrialized countries, there are barriers that exist for people who are disabled. However in less industrialized countries, People with Disabilities have to compete with the mainstream population over very scarce resources. While People with Disabilities in more industrialized countries are perceived to be seeking independent living, people in less industrialized countries are trying to survive (Stone, 2001).

Poverty appears to be a recurring theme in various reports on disability in less industrialized countries. Nagata (2007) discussed the vicious cycle of poverty and disability in less economically developed countries. Nagata believes that poverty leads to malnutrition and disease, which in turn lead to impairment and disability, which then contribute to poorer levels of human development and productivity within the community. Due to inadequate funding, there is very little medical care and rehabilitation provided. Very little is done in the way of prevention and early intervention, which again increases the incidence of impairment and disability.

In less industrialized countries, SES might be even more important in regard to disability than in the United States. Ghai (2001), who lives in India, describes from her own experience how disability might differentially affect her (as she has access to a computer and a hand-driven car) as compared to other People with Disabilities who are not as privileged as she is. She indicated that People with Disabilities in less economically developed countries are particularly affected by class. People with adequate means can procure assistants and devices that allow the functional impact of their disabilities to be relatively minimized (Charlton, 1998), and they might be able to work and be more of an active part of society. Being employed has a number of advantages, as it allows the person to cover the additional costs of having an impairment, which can include obtaining access to services and information. Being employed also helps reduce the negative stereotypes that are associated with not working and receiving governmental assistance (in some countries).

The next section discusses issues of disability, employment, and class in two less industrialized and formerly colonized countries with which we have experience: Kenya and the Philippines. Academic research on disability in these countries, as in most less economically developed countries, is extremely limited. However, relevant information is available through reports from government agencies, international organizations, conferences, and the media.

Disability in Kenya

One of the areas of the world which has a large number of less economically developed countries is Africa. The continent has been plagued with a history of colonization and slavery, in addition to ongoing problems of poverty, disease, violence (in some situations massive genocide), and unstable governments. Its history of colonization has strongly contributed to some of the current problems. Africa is a continent that was colonized by various countries in Europe and the enormous impact of this colonization continues to this day. According to Adi and Sherwood (2003), during colonization, Europe gained its wealth through slavery and the work of the Indigenous people. The colonized people were controlled, they were treated as objects, and their culture was destroyed. Majiet (1998), who is South African, believes that Africa has difficulties due to colonialism, exploitation, Europeans' sense of "racial superiority," and apartheid. He thinks that it has been a continent where there has been a disregard for human rights. Although it is not resolved, he believes that the global issue in the 20th century was about race and in the 21st century, it is about poverty. He recommends considering how issues related to disability fit into issues of poverty.

Kenya, located in East Africa, was colonized by Great Britain and gained independence in 1963.[2] According to a report called State of Disabled Peoples Rights in Kenya (African Union of the Blind [AUB], 2007), approximately 75 percent of the work force in Kenya is engaged in agriculture, mainly to provide for the population's own subsistence. There is a high dropout rate from school, and the HIV/AIDS pandemic has also had a significant impact. Unemployment is approximately 40 percent, and 50 percent of the population lives in the slums. Between half a million to a million people live in Kibera, the second largest slum in Africa (second to Soweto, South Africa).

The AUB report estimated that there are approximately 3 million People with Disabilities in Kenya. Fifty-six percent of Kenya's population lives below the poverty line, which impacts the living conditions of people who are disabled within the country. The government has signed the International Convention on the Rights of Persons with Disabilities, but has not yet ratified it. The Kenyan government has also enacted the Persons with Disabilities Act (PDA) of 2003, which was developed to oversee the welfare of People with Disabilities. Although the Kenyan constitution prevents discrimination on the basis of tribe, race, and color, it does not specifically preclude discrimination based on disability and when there have been cases of discrimination based on disability, the antidiscrimination laws have not been enacted.

Kenya does not have a system in which People with Disabilities are given monetary assistance; however, there are programs to assist with their rehabilitation and there is an integration policy in which Children with Disabilities are placed in the general school system. Seventy-four percent of People with Disabilities who were interviewed for the AUB report indicated that they were restricted from making decisions about their lives; 86 percent reported being discriminated against by individuals without disabilities (including their own families), and 80 percent thought that they had been segregated, isolated, and not given adequate support due to their disabilities. Fifty-four percent have been given nicknames based on their disabilities. Seventy-two percent thought that there was abuse and discrimination in a number of contexts.

The AUB report noted that in Kenyan society, there is considerable discrimination toward People with Disabilities in which they are seen as useless, burdens, and even cursed. Even their own families discriminate against them; in some cases, families of Individuals with Disabilities have hidden them or locked them in the house and have not taken them to school or to hospitals. Some parents believe that disability is a curse and that it is hereditary (can be passed from parent to child). Family members might also make negative remarks about Individuals with Disabilities and even deny their right to inherit property and land, thus increasing their likelihood to experience poverty. People with Disabilities have many stories to tell about their abuse by the general public, including police officers and government officials.

About 30 percent of the disabled population surveyed in the AUB report faced discrimination in the workplace. Their performance is considered to be less competent than others. Many people without disabilities do not want People with Disabilities to work near them. Individuals with Disabilities have also been maltreated by their bosses and when they submitted complaints, they were usually ignored and were given even worse treatment by their bosses. Managers often think that People with Disabilities cannot perform work tasks or that they will be unsafe in the work environment and therefore they will not hire them. Many People with Disabilities either sell small items on the street or beg.

The disabled population in Kenya also has problems with transportation to places of employment and accessibility at the workplace. Participants in the AUB study described difficulty with public transportation in which drivers would not wait for them. There are problems with mobility in many places of employment, and elevators are seldom available. They have difficulty accessing government resources. In Kenya, there is corruption in which bribes are expected for performance of government services. People without adequate financial resources are unable to pay such bribes. People with Disabilities who are poor have also found it difficult to obtain the capital to start their own businesses.

Often the ability to obtain a job depends on personal relationship and financial ability (sometimes a bribe is required). People with Disabilities, who are often poor and isolated from others, do not have the means to obtain a position. Even in very poor families, they are considered a burden as they might be seen as being unable to contribute to family duties or tasks. Status in Kenya is based on economic power, and if a Person with a Disability has money, he or she would most likely be protected and his or her rights would not be violated. However, most People with Disabilities have limited economic resources and they suffer considerable discrimination and denial of human rights. Thus, in Kenya, class adds considerably to the impact of a disability on an individual.

While the dominant population in Kenya appears to have negative attitudes toward People with Disabilities, who also face considerable discrimination in the workplace, one of the most traditional tribes, the Maasai, appear to have different perceptions. In terms of monetary wealth, the Maasai might be considered to be one of the poorest populations. The Maasai tend to be herders who are nomadic, although they might be sedentary for some time.

The Maasai culture recognizes a variety of impairments and attitudes toward these individuals are not based primarily on the impairment. According to Talle (1995), the Maasai classify people who are disabled according to functional competence. People who look different from the typical person are only considered to be disabled if it limits them functionally. The impairment is described specifically, and there is not a word for disability. The Maasai believe that disease is due to social or divine relationships, and deviating from moral conduct or rules can lead to problems like diseases that cannot be cured. When a child is born with a disability, the disability might be attributed to misfortune brought about by difficult living circumstances or sin due to the reputation of ancestors. The child is not blamed for this.

Disability and disease can also be caused by a curse or sorcery from other people. When a disease develops, people will seek either traditional or modern methods to cure it. If it does not improve, it might become a disability. Children who are born ill or with an irregular appearance are treated the same way as other children. They are not given special care, they are not favored, and they are not treated poorly. They can have children and if not married, they can live in their home of origin and bear children. They participate in all of the activities in the community that they are able to and are not hidden or ostracized.

A report from the Kenya National Commission on Human Rights (KNCHR, 2007) indicated that to increase the opportunities for employment and alleviate the poverty for disabled people, they need to have access to education. They found that legislation does not adequately address the needs of Children with Disabilities and only a small percentage attends school. Schools are underresourced, teachers have inadequate training, there is no specific curriculum for Children with Disabilities, and there is inadequate inspection of schools to determine if they meet the needs of Children with Disabilities. The authors of the report believed that the problem in educating People with Disabilities is within society (and not with the individual) and that education is a right. The KNCHR stated that "Governments are obligated to make education available, accessible, acceptable and adaptable for all children" (p. 13) and that People with Disabilities should be given vocational training since it is the "bridge" between education and employment. However, one of the difficulties in providing what the children need is the expense, especially as 50 percent of the Kenyan population lives below the poverty line.

Disability in the Philippines

Approximately two-thirds of the world's 600 million People with Disabilities live in the Asia-Pacific region (South Asia Human Rights Documentation Centre, 2003). Many of these People with Disabilities live in poverty, and less than 10 percent of the young People with Disabilities attend school. The employment rates of People with Disabilities appear to vary widely among the Asia-Pacific countries.

The Philippines is a group of islands located in the Pacific Ocean east of Southeast Asia and is populated by multiple ethnic groups, primarily Christian Malays (92 percent), Muslim Malays (4 percent), and Chinese (2 percent). It was colonized by other countries (notably Spain for over 300 years, then the United States for nearly 50 years). In Philippines society, there is a big gap between rich and poor, with very few families controlling the majority of land, industrial assets, and business interests. There is a growing middle class of skilled and semi-skilled workers. However, most Filipinos/as still live in relative poverty, residing in rural areas as well as "urban slums." According to the Asian Development Bank (ADB, 2000), approximately 34 percent of the population is considered to be living below the national poverty level.

The exact number of Filipinos/as with disabilities is not known (Fermin, 2003a). It could range from one million (one 1 percent of the population, as reported by the National Statistics Office, 2005) to eight million (using the World Health Organization estimate that roughly 10 percent of the population of less industrialized countries have disabilities). These differences are due to varying definitions of disability, instrument sensitivity, and data collection issues (Fermin, 2003a; United Nations Economic and Social Commission for Asia and the Pacific [UNESCAP], 2005).

Like many other collective societies in Asia and the Pacific Islands, Filipinos/as make caring for a family member with a disability a priority in terms of time, effort, and finances. Typically they do not readily access service providers regarding a disability in the family. For many Filipinos/as, lack of knowledge, lack of money, shame, and embarrassment contribute to their preference to keep the disability contained within the family. Filipinos/as would initially seek the help of knowledgeable individuals through some social or family connection, and only when this does not work do they go out of their immediate circle to seek professional help (de Torres, 2002).

The general attitude among Filipinos/as is that Individuals with Disabilities should not and need not live apart from their families (Oka, 1988). Outside factors, such as the lack of accessible transportation and buildings, lack of quality education to suit their needs, limited employment opportunities, limited medical services, and the general attitudes of the community and prospective employers, also limit opportunities for independence for Filipinos/as with Disabilities.

There are very few schools in the Philippines that accept Children with Disabilities due to the lack of facilities and appropriately trained teachers (Asia-Pacific Development Center on Disability, 2002). These schools also lack adapted materials and have limited accessibility. The few schools that offer superior curriculum, teachers, and accessibility tend to be private schools that only the middle- and upper-class families can afford. The government supports a number of vocational and rehabilitation centers for training People with Disabilities, but many of the facilities are old and the equipment is either obsolete or dysfunctional.

Based on the 2000 Philippine census (National Statistics Office, 2005), 57 percent of Filipinos/as with Disabilities are gainfully employed (they either have a job or a business). Approximately 30 percent of the Filipinos/as with disability who are gainfully employed are farmers, forestry workers, or fishermen. A little over 10 percent of Individuals with Disabilities are laborers and unskilled workers. These jobs are typically low-paying.

Similar to the situation in other less industrialized countries, most Filipinos/as with Disabilities live in poverty. The exceptions are those at the top of the socioeconomic ladder, whose families have more of an ability to pay for basic needs, health services, rehabilitation, education, and training. To a large extent, the experience of disability in the Philippines depends on the person's social class. Among the majority (poorer, lower SES classes), the challenge is survival. Among the minority upper classes, the challenge is achieving greater independence and becoming contributing members of society.

The Philippines have made great strides toward promoting the rights of People with Disabilities in the past 15 years, starting with its Magna Carta for Disabled Persons, patterned after the Americans with Disabilities Act. The period 2003–2013 was declared the Philippine Decade for Persons with Disabilities. The National Antipoverty Action Agenda was also launched in 2000, and its programs specifically include disabled persons among the 10 groups vulnerable to poverty (ADB, 2000).

Nevertheless, a lot of work remains to be done regarding issues related to disability, poverty, and employment. Job choices for Filipinos/as with Disabilities continue to be limited and the pay relatively low (e.g., hearing-impaired persons work in fast-food chains, and blind persons work as massage therapists or musicians). Sheltered employment (mostly contractual work in manufacturing or handicrafts) is offered by the government as a means of providing work for People with Disabilities who cannot compete in the open market. However, sheltered employment is not necessarily ideal due to the low wages, poor conditions, and segregated work settings (Favis, 2002). Many People with Disabilities earn their living in the streets by begging or vending. A number of them have even chosen to continue with demeaning jobs (like being carnival attractions due to their appearance being markedly unusual) because the extremely low wages at sheltered workshops are not enough to provide for their basic survival (Favis, 2001).

The high levels of unemployment and underemployment in the Philippines pose significant barriers to People with Disabilities in finding suitable employment in the open market. Negative perceptions about People with Disabilities pose another obstacle. Despite government incentives and an antidiscrimination law, employers still tend to be reluctant to hire People with Disabilities and do not want to invest in making their workplaces more accessible. One observer (Kono, 2002) commented that she had not heard of any firm applying to receive government incentives for employing People with Disabilities, most likely due to the paperwork and bureaucracy it entailed. Overall, although there is disability legislation in the Philippines, there is a need for stronger enforcement and implementation (Ilagan, 2006; UNESCAP, 2005).

Nongovernmental organizations (NGOs) and civic organizations play a major role in advancing the rights and welfare of People with Disabilities in the Philippines. These organizations provide services such as job fairs and information and computer technologies for the education and employment of People with Disabilities (Fermin, 2003b). The government coordinates these activities and provides limited financial and technical assistance.

Self-employment represents one of the more promising programs for People with Disabilities in the Philippines, in light of the country's scarce resources, high unemployment, and high underemployment. NGOs and cooperatives (funded partially by international agencies) provide training, business consultation, grants, and loans to income-generation projects for People with Disabilities, particularly women and Indigenous people. Access to capital (micro-credit) is critical.

Community-based rehabilitation, in which volunteers reach out to People with Disabilities in their neighborhoods, appears to be another successful initiative in the Philippines. With the help of community members and NGOs, People with Disabilities receive assessments, early intervention, medical and nutritional guidance, some special education training, access to small loans, employment with local families and business enterprises, and assistance in developing small income-generating projects (Harris, 1997; Ilagan, 1998; Inciong, 1998). While the government provides some assistance, the bulk of the work takes place at the grassroots level.

SUMMARY AND CONCLUSIONS

In the United States, as well as in Kenya and the Philippines, there are commonalities among People with Disabilities as a result of their disability, race, and class. People with Disabilities are less likely than their counterparts without disabilities to find employment, or when they do, the work they find is limited and typically pays less. Class issues, particularly poverty, magnify the difficulties they encounter. Generally, poverty

1. increases people's likelihood of obtaining a disability,
2. decreases their ability to deal effectively with their disabilities (much less advance their lives), and
3. limits their access to health services, education, and employment opportunities.

The less economically developed the country, the more these issues are highlighted. Yet poverty generally has a more significant impact on People with Disabilities from non-European backgrounds in many nations.

The more economically developed the country, the more resources in general are available to People with Disabilities. These resources would include better testing and diagnosis, access to health care, academic resources and programs, and governmental funding such as social security, disability, and welfare benefits. The poor and People with Disabilities in more economically developed countries tend to have a greater access to resources than their counterparts in less economically developed nations. Even People with Disabilities from the upper classes in less economically developed countries might not have the same access and institutional benefits with comparable services as their counterparts in more economically developed countries. In more economically developed countries, the issues of People with Disabilities tend to be centered on accessibility and equality. In less economically developed countries, the issue is survival.

Some areas that could be targeted to improve the situation worldwide would be to focus on health, education, and employability. In the area of health, prenatal care along with early detection, diagnosis, and intervention for health concerns are extremely important. The World Health Organization (2008) advocates that governments develop programs for early diagnosis, followed by assessment and treatment, to prevent or reduce disabling conditions. Minimal health care for less affluent people is critical. Even today, many people in less industrialized regions such as Africa die from illnesses and infections that are no longer considered problems in more industrialized countries. Minimal health care reduces the incidence and severity of disability. Moreover, less technologically advanced countries such as the Philippines and Kenya tend to have less precise means of classifying disabilities (e.g., neurological scans, measures of specific learning disabilities). There is a need for better diagnosis to identify certain types of disabilities and provide appropriate remediation and intervention programs. Otherwise health and learning development could be disrupted.

Generally, less economically developed countries face the challenge of improving the quality and accuracy of disability data. Without reliable information, it is difficult to fully understand the scope of disability issues, build adequate support for funding and programs, and track progress. To compound this, disability issues often receive comparatively less attention in less economically developed nations that have to struggle with a multitude of other issues, such as high unemployment and underemployment, political instability, armed conflicts, natural disasters, and general health concerns.

In the area of education, early detection and intervention for learning disabilities represent a key first step. There should also be accommodations for disabilities, both physical and cognitive, to meet students' educational needs. Strengths of People with Disabilities could be identified early, and their skills in these areas could be developed.

In the area of employability, employers should be encouraged to hire and accommodate People with Disabilities. Stereotypes and other myths can be reduced by providing clear information about skills and attitudes of People with Disabilities. There is some encouraging evidence in the United States as well as other countries indicating that employers who have hired People with Disabilities have found that they produce higher quality work and are more motivated and loyal than many individuals without disabilities. Employers should be encouraged to create work environments where there is more acceptance of disability among employees, and those who do should be recognized so that more organizations will follow suit. Governments should be able to offer incentives to employers who hire People with Disabilities with minimal bureaucracy (Kono, 2002).

Another option that is particularly useful for less industrialized countries is self-employment, where micro-financing for small businesses can be obtained from the government or other sources. In addition, community-based rehabilitation and support programs should be supported. When communities are involved in assisting their Members with Disabilities, there tends to be greater involvement and commitment. This collaboration also helps reduce the burden on the government as the sole provider of funding and services.

Indeed, one interesting way to think about addressing the issues of disability and employment is to address the central issue of poverty. Community efforts can be focused on raising the general socioeconomic level of the community by involving People with and without Disabilities working together on various levels. Much can be learned from the example of traditional groups such as the Maasai, who do not classify individuals as disabled but instead recognize their ability to provide various services based on their functionality. Among the Maasai, People with Disabilities are not stigmatized but made to feel like contributing members of the community. This perspective of community and collaboration can go a long way toward enhancing the plights of poor people with and without disabilities and allows many segments of the population to work together for a common good.

NOTES

1. There are a number of terms that have been used to describe less affluent countries, including "developing," "poor," and "Third World." However a term like "developing" could be viewed as inaccurate or inappropriate because some countries have actually experienced prolonged periods of economic decline; meanwhile terms such as "poor" and "Third World" could be viewed as uncomplimentary and derogatory, especially as many of these countries have abundant natural resources as well as rich cultural and spiritual traditions, though colonization may have had a decimating impact on these societies and continues to exert contemporary ramifications. In this chapter, these countries will be referred to as "less economically developed" or "less industrialized" in an attempt to use more objective terminology consistent with that used by international economic agencies, such as the International Monetary Fund.

2. See also "Disability in Kenya: A Situational Analysis," Chapter 20 in volume 3.

REFERENCES

Adams, P. F., Lucas, J. W., & Barnes, P. M. (2008). *Summary health statistics for the U.S. population: National Health Interview Survey 2006*. National Center for Health Statistics. *Vital Health Statistics, 10*(236).

Adi, H., & Sherwood, M. (2003). *Pan-African history: Political figures from Africa and the Diaspora since 1787*. New York: Routledge.

African Union of the Blind. (2007). *State of Disabled Peoples rights in Kenya.* Retrieved November 26, 2007, from www.yorku.ca/drpi/files/KenyaReport07.pdf.

Albeda, R., & Tilly, C. (1997). *Glass ceilings and bottomless pits: Women's work, women's poverty.* Boston: South End Press.

Asbury, C. A., Walker, S., Maholmes, V., Rackley, R., & White, S. (1992). *Disability prevalence and demographic association among race/ethnic minority pops in the United States: Implications for the 21st century.* Washington, DC: Howard University Research and Training Center for Access to Rehabilitation and Economic Opportunity.

Asian Development Bank. (2000, November). *Technical assistance for identifying disability issues related to poverty Reduction.* TAR:OTH 33529. Retrieved December 12, 2007, from www.adb.org/Documents/TARS/REG/tar_oth33529.pdf.

Asia-Pacific Development Center on Disability. (2002). *Country profile. The Republic of the Philippines.* Retrieved December 12, 2007, from www.apcdproject/org/countryprofile/Philippines/situation.html.

Banks, M. E., & Ackerman, R. J. (2006). Health disparities: Focus on disability. In K. J. Hagglund & A. W. Heinemann (Eds.), *Handbook of applied disability and rehabilitation research* (pp. 45–70). New York: Springer.

Banks, M. E., & Marshall, C. (2004). Beyond the "triple-whammy": Social class as a factor in discrimination against Persons with Disabilities. In J. L. Chin (Ed.), *The psychology of prejudice and discrimination: Combating prejudice and all forms of discrimination. Volume 4: Disability, religion, physique, and other traits* (pp. 95–110). Westport, CT: Praeger.

Bradsher, J. E. (1996). Disability among racial and ethnic groups. *Disability Statistics Abstract, 10,* 1–4. Disability Statistics Rehabilitation Research and Training Center. Retrieved December 1, 2007, from dsc.ucsf.edu/view_pdf.php?pdf_id=8.

Brooks-Gunn, J., Duncan, G. J., & Maritato, N. (1997). Poor families, poor outcomes: The well-being of children and youth. In G. J. Duncan & J. Brooks-Gunn (Eds.), *Consequences of growing up poor* (pp. 1–17), New York: Sage.

Charlton, J. I. (1998). *Nothing about us without us: Disability oppression and empowerment.* Berkeley: University of California Press.

David, E. J. R., & Okazaki, S. (2006). Colonial mentality: A review and recommendation for Filipino American psychology. *Cultural Diversity & Ethnic Minority Psychology, 12*(1), 1–16.

de Torres, S. (2002). *Understanding persons of Philippine origin: A primer for rehabilitation service providers.* Center for International Rehabilitation Research Information & Exchange. Retrieved February 14, 2008, from cirrie.buffalo.edu/monographs/philippines.html.

Dovidio, J. F., Gaertner, S. E., Kawakami, K., & Hodson, G. (2002). Why can't we just get along? Interpersonal biases and interracial distrust. *Cultural Diversity and Ethnic Minority Psychology, 8,* 88–102.

Favis, M. (2001, July–August). Freak shows: Demeaning depictions or empowering employment. *Disability World, 9.* Retrieved December 12, 2007, from www.disabilityworld.org/09-10_02/arts/freakshow.shtml.

Favis, M. (2002, June–August). The Philippines: Life in the sheltered workshops. *Disability World, 14.* Retrieved December 12, 2007, from www.disabiityworld.org/06-08_02/employment/Philippines.html.

Fermin, C. (2003a, September). *The Philippine disability data situation.* Paper presented at the Workshop on Improving Disability Data for Policy Use, Bangkok Thailand. Retrieved December 12, 2007, from www.worldenable.net/escapstats/paperphilippines2.htm.

Fermin, C. (2003b, June). *Country paper: The Philippines.* Paper presented at the Expert Group Meeting and Seminar on an International Convention to Protect and Promote the Rights and Dignity of Persons with Disabilities, Bangkok, Thailand. Retrieved December 17, 2007, from www.worldenable.net/bangkok2003/paperphilippines.htm.

Fronczek, P., & Johnson, P. (2003). Occupations: 2000. *Census 2000 Brief.* U.S. Bureau of the Census. Retrieved February 14, 2008, from www.census.gov/prod/2003pubs/c2kbr-25.pdf.

Ghai, A. (2001). Marginalisation and disability: Experiences from the third world. In M Priestley (Ed.), *Disability and the life course: Global perspectives* (pp. 26–37). Cambridge: Cambridge University Press.

Harris, C. (1997). From disability to opportunity: Self-employment and the disabled in developing countries. *International Development Research Centre Reports, 21*(4). Retrieved December 12, 2007, from archive.idrc.ca/books/reports/v214/disable.html.

Ilagan, V. M. (1998). Development of small enterprises for women with disabilities in the Philippines: The KAMPI experience. *Asia & Pacific Journal on Disability, 1*(3). Retrieved December 12, 2007, from www.dinf.ne.jp/doc/english/asia/resource/z00ap/003/z00ap00306.htm.

Ilagan, V. M. (2006, August). *A disabled people's organization perspective—DPI Philippines.* Proceedings from the National Council on Disability Practical discussion on implementation in the U.S. and other countries. Retrieved December 17, 2007, from www.ncd.gov/newsroom/publications/2006/side_event.htm.

Inciong, T. G. (1998). *Partnership for effective early intervention strategy.* Proceedings from the 7th International Portage Conference, Hiroshima, Japan. Retrieved December 17, 2007, from www.portageproject.org/7th_conf/sA_phil.htm.

Johnson, W. (2000). Work preparation and labor market experiences among urban, poor nonresident fathers. In S. Danziger & A. Lin (Eds.), *Coping with poverty: The social contexts of work and family in the African-American community.* Ann Arbor: University of Michigan Press.

Kenya National Commission on Human Rights. (2007). *Objects of pity or individuals with rights: The right to education for Children with Disabilities.* Retrieved November 26, 3007, from www.knchr.org/dmdocuments/Occassional_Paper.pdf.

Kono, A. (2002). A glimpse of the employment status of Ppersons with Disabilities in the Philippines from a Cebuano perspective. *Asia & Pacific Journal on Disability, 5*(1). Retrieved December 12, 2007, from www.dinf.ne.jp/doc/english/asia/resource/z00ap/vol5no1/glimpse.htm.

Leung, P. (1993). Minorities with disabilities and the Americans with Disabilities Act: A promise yet to be fulfilled. *Journal of Rehabilitation Administration, 17*(2), 92–98.

Majiet, S. (1998, August). *Human rights from Disabled Peoples' perspective in Africa.* Paper presented at the Seminar on Human Rights for Persons with Disabilities from a North and South Perspective, Stockholm, Sweden.

McNeil, J. M. (1993). *Americans with disabilities: 1991–92* (Current Population Reports P70-33). Washington, DC: U.S. Bureau of the Census.

Meadows, M. (1999). *The problem of accessing health care.* Office of Minority Health Resource Center. U.S. Department of Health and Human Services. Retrieved February 14, 2008, from www.omhrc.gov/assets/pdf/checked/The%20Problem%20of%20Accessing%20Health%20Care.pdf.

Nagata, K. K. (2007). Perspectives on disability, poverty and development in the Asian Region. *Asia Pacific Disability Rehabilitation Journal, 18*(1), 3–19.

National Center for Education Statistics. (2008). *Digest of education statistics: 2007.* Retrieved April 28, 2008, from nces.ed.gov/programs/digest/d07/tables/dt07_012.asp?referrer=list.

National Council on Disability. (2007). *Empowerment for Americans with disabilities: Breaking barriers to careers and full employment.* Retrieved October 11, 2007, from www.ncd.gov/newsroom/publications/2007/NCDEmployment_20071001.htm.

National Statistics Office. (2005). *Persons with disability comprised 1.23 percent of the total population. A special release based on the results of Census 2000.* Retrieved December 12, 2007, from www.census.gov.ph/data/sectordata/sr05150tx.html.

Oka, Y. (1988). Self-reliance in interdependent communities: Independent living of disabled persons in the Asia-Pacific region. Independent Living Institute. Retrieved February 14, 2008, from www.independentliving.org/docs4/oka.html.

Priestley, M. (2001). Introduction: The global context of disability. In M. Priestley (Ed.), *Disability and the life course: Global perspectives* (pp. 3–14). Cambridge: Cambridge University Press.

Pritchard, J. (2004). Mexican-worker deaths are rising sharply in U.S. *Deseret News.* Retrieved April 28, 2008, from deseretnews.com/dn/view/0,1249,595048917,00.html.

Reaves, A. (2000). Black male employment and self-sufficiency. In S. Danziger & A. Lin (Eds.), *Coping with poverty: The social contexts of neighborhood, work and family in the African-American community.* Ann Arbor: University of Michigan Press.

Rehabilitation Research and Training Center on Disability Demographics and Statistics. (2007). *2006 disability status report.* Ithaca, NY: Cornell University.

Smart, J. F., & Smart, D. W. (1997). The racial/ethnic demography of disability. *Journal of Rehabilitation, 63*(4), 9–15.

South Asia Human Rights Documentation Centre. (2003, May 29). Rights of the disabled: Towards a new UN Convention. *Human Rights Features.* Retrieved December 17, 2007, from www.hrdc.net/sahrdc/hrfeatures/HRF77.htm.

Smedley, B. D., Stith, A. Y., & Nelson, A. R. (Eds.). (2003). *Unequal treatment: Confronting racial and ethnic disparities in health care.* Washington, DC: National Academies Press.

Stone, E. (2001). A complicated struggle: Disability, survival and social change in the majority world. In M. Priestley (Ed.). *Disability and the life course: Global perspectives* (pp. 50–66). Cambridge: Cambridge University Press.

Suzuki, L., & Valencia, R. (1997). Race-ethnicity and measured intelligence: Educational implications. *American Psychologist, 52,* 1103–1114.

Talle, A. (1995). A child is a child: Disability and equality among the Kenya Maasai. In B. Ingstad & S. Whyte (Eds.), *Disability and culture* (pp. 56–72). Berkeley: University of California Press.

Thompson-Hoffman, S., & Storck, I. F. (Eds.) (1991). Disability in the United States, New York: Springer.

Trupin, L., Sebesta, D., & Yelin, E. (1997). Racial disparity in employment among Persons with Disabilities 1990–1994. *American Public Health Association Meetings.* Indianapolis, IN.

United Nations Economic and Social Commission for Asia and the Pacific (UNESCAP). (2005). *Disability at a glance: A profile of 28 countries and regions in Asia and the Pacific.* Retrieved December 17, 2007, from www.census.gov/prod/2003pubs/c2kbr-17.pdf.

U.S. Bureau of Labor Statistics. (2007a). A profile of the working poor, 2005. Retrieved April 28, 2008, from www.bls.gov/cps/cpswp2005.pdf.

U.S. Bureau of Labor Statistics. (2007b). Household data annual averages 11: Employed persons by detailed occupation, sex, race, and Hispanic or Latino ethnicity. Retrieved April 28, 2008, from www.bls.gov/cps/cpsaat11.pdf.

U.S. Bureau of Labor Statistics. (2007c). Foreign-born workers: Labor force characteristics in 2007. Retrieved April 28, 2008, from ww.bls.gov/news.release/pdf/forbrn.pdf.

U.S. Census Bureau. (2007). Minority population tops 100 million. Retrieved April 24, 2008, from www.census.gov/Press-Resease/www/releases/archives/population/010048.html.

U.S. Department of Homeland Security. (2007). *Yearbook of immigration statistics: 2006*. Washington, DC: U.S. Department of Homeland Security, Office of Immigration Statistics.

Waldrop, J., & Stern, S. M. (2003). *Disability status: 2000. Census 2000 brief*. Retrieved February 14, 2008, from www.census.gov/prod/2003pubs/c2kbr-17.pdf.

Wang, Q. (2005). Disability and American families: 2000. *Census 2000 Special Reports*. Washington, DC: U.S. Department of Commerce, Bureau of the Census.

Webster, B. H. Jr., & Bishaw, A. (2007). *Income, earnings, and poverty data from the 2006 American Community Survey*. U.S. Census Bureau, American Community Survey Reports, ACS-08, Washington, DC: U.S. Government Printing Office.

World Health Organization. (2008). Medical care and rehabilitation. Retrieved April 28, 2008, from www.who.int/disabilities/care/en.

CHAPTER 11

Youth with Intellectual Disabilities in Foster Care: Examining Accompanying Risks and Service Outcomes

Crystal L. Cederna, Melissa Palguta, Jacqueline Remondet Wall, and Steven M. Koch

In the United States, between 30 and 40 percent of youth placed in foster care receive special education services (National Collaboration on Workforce and Disability, 2007; Zetlin & Weinberg, 2004). In addition, 20 percent of youth placed in foster care settings are noted to have intellectual challenges, such as those associated with developmental disabilities and mental retardation (Child Welfare League of America, 2007). Along a similar vein, African American youth are overrepresented in children placed in out-of-home settings and in those youth receiving special education services for intellectual disabilities (Harry & Klingner, 2006; Hill, 2006, 2007). However, little is published about youth with intellectual disabilities in foster care, and even less is offered about youth with intellectual disabilities in foster care who are African American (Ebersole & Kapp, 2007). In this chapter, we summarize the literature on youth with intellectual disabilities and other frequently related risk factors in foster care. Specifically, we provide a programmatic case study to present the relationship between risk factors and outcomes that compares youth with test scores suggesting intellectual challenges to those of average ability. We focus on issues investigated in our study and highlight those identified in research literature—including African American ethnicity and gender—that are associated with greater frequency of foster care placement and poor outcomes. We conclude with recommendations for program development to facilitate success for youth in the foster care system. We suggest ways of incorporating the family into care, utilizing the family's natural strengths, and providing care associated with positive outcomes.

PLACEMENT IN FOSTER CARE

In the United States, foster care is defined as "24-hour substitute care" provided outside a child's home. Foster care placements occur when children are found to be at risk in their own homes, most often due to child abuse and neglect (Harden, 2004; Twigg, 2006). Although definitions vary from state to state, the Child Abuse Prevention and Treatment Act (CAPTA) (Public Law 93-247, 1974) and the Keeping Children and Families Safe Act of 2003 (Public Law 108-36) provide minimum standards for defining abuse and neglect. Further illustrated by the U.S. Department of Health and Human Services (DHHS), abuse and neglect is characterized as "any recent act or failure to act on the part of a parent or caretaker which results in death, serious physical or emotional harm, sexual abuse or exploitation; or an act or failure to act which presents an imminent risk of serious harm" (U.S. DHHS, 2006, 2007).

During the U.S. federal fiscal year 2005, the most recent year for which complete data are readily available, approximately 317,000 youth were placed in foster care. At the end of the year, a total of 513,000 youth were in foster care (U.S. DHHS, 2006). Once foster care is deemed appropriate, youth become the responsibility of the government and are placed in the care of other nonparental adults. The most frequently established goal of foster care placement is the provision of temporary support for children until they can be returned safely to their parents without further risk of harm. If returning home safely is judged not to be possible, parental rights may be terminated and children may be adopted. However, children may remain in foster care until they reach the age of majority and become emancipated.

Foster care often involves placement with relatives (i.e., kinship care) or another family (i.e., nonkinship care). However, it can also include placement in an alternative residential setting. These settings range from small, "homelike" facilities (e.g., group homes) to those that are more institutional (e.g., residential care centers) in nature. Some foster care placements are more specifically termed "therapeutic foster care," to indicate that additional services, such as behavior management or therapy, are provided to meet the child's individualized needs. Even though placement type (e.g., residential care verses foster home care) has been associated with different levels of behavior problems in youth, those in care often demonstrate a range of behavioral and mental health needs (Curtis, Alexander, & Lunghofer, 2001). All types of placement will be referred to as foster care in this chapter, unless the type of placement is salient to the discussion of placement risks or service outcomes.

DISABILITY AND FOSTER CARE

Estimates suggest that one third to one half of youth in foster care placement have a disabling condition (Hanley, 2002; United Cerebral Palsy and Children's Rights, 2006). Specific conditions identified in foster care include cognitive and academic challenges (e.g., intellectual disability), emotional and behavior problems (e.g., psychiatric concerns), and physical health concerns (e.g., special medical needs) (Romney, Litrownik, Newton, & Lau, 2006). For example, the U.S. DHHS (2006) report identified that risk factors for foster care placement included known disability (close to 8 percent of the sample), behavior problems (3.2 percent), and "emotional disturbance" (1.9 percent). The rates of disability are likely to be underrepresented because youth may not undergo a comprehensive assessment during intake processes when entering care.

Maltreatment of youth is the primary factor in foster care placement and children with disabilities who have been maltreated are at significant risk of placement. In one study conducted within the public school system, a 31 percent prevalence rate was identified for maltreatment in youth with a disability verses a 9 percent prevalence rate for youth who were not identified as disabled (Sullivan & Knutson, 2000). The rates for maltreatment were 3.4 times higher for youth with a disability. This increased risk for abuse and neglect has also been found by other researchers (Horner-Johnson & Drum, 2006). Although there are controversies within the field as to why this is the case (e.g., does the greater level of care commonly associated with disability lead to the greater incidence of abuse, or is being born into a family with inherent risks more associated with the presence of a disability), it is evident that youth with intellectual disabilities are at greater risk for placement and are likely to remain in care for longer than youth without disabilities.

PROGRAMMATIC CASE STUDY

The Indiana Association of Residential Child Care Agencies, an organization of residential care agencies, was founded in 1944. As member agencies expanded the array of services they provided to children and families, such as foster care, home-based and outpatient services, the organization changed its name to IARCCA, an Association of Child and Family Services (IARCCA). Both IARCCA and its current membership of 112 agencies have maintained a focus on providing quality care for the children and families they serve. For the past decade, this focus has included a systematic monitoring of programmatic outcomes. IARCCA began to study treatment outcomes for the children and families served by its member agencies in 1998 through the IARCCA Outcome Measures Project (hereafter referred to as the Project). The Project is more fully described in another publication (Wall et al., 2005).

To better understand outcomes for youth placed into care, studies have been performed using data from the Project, examining risk factors identified at program entry and how these risks relate to outcomes (Jackson-Walker, Wall, & Minnich, 2003; Koch & Wall, 2005; Wall & Minnich, 2004). Factors including gender, age, ethnicity, length of stay, and referral source have been investigated and found to be associated with the outcomes of youth in foster care placement. For example, youth with histories of prior physical or sexual abuse have been noted to be at greater risk for being discharged into a more restrictive placement than their foster home. Although these initial studies examined multiple factors, they did not examine the presence of intellectual disability as a risk.

In a more recent examination, primarily examining intellectual status and outcomes on data from the Project (Koch, Cederna, & Wall, 2007), youth with average or near-average intelligence, as measured through the administration of standardized intellectual assessments (i.e., IQ scores above 85) were compared to youth with test scores suggesting the presence of an intellectual disability (IQ scores of 70 or lower). The proportions of risk factors presented by youth with intellectual disability were compared to the proportions of risks presented by youth with average intellectual abilities. In addition, the outcomes obtained by these two different groups of youth were examined for disparities. Analyses were conducted using a sample of youth placed into and discharged from foster care programs (including foster care and residential treatment) between 2003 and 2005. Only youth for whom intellectual testing was provided were included for these analyses, resulting in a total sample size of 576, with separation into groups as follows: average intelligence (IQ over 85), n = 446, and intellectual disability (IQ 70 or below), n = 130. Youth were classified into these groups solely based on the results of standardized intellectual testing (i.e., in the absence of information related to adaptive functioning or any formal diagnosis of intellectual disability).

To identify if youth with an intellectual disability were placed into care with more significant risk factors, demographic, child-specific, parent-specific, and trauma-related factors were examined. Youth classified with an intellectual disability were found to be somewhat younger than those with average intelligence test scores, more likely to be female, and less likely to be European American. Youth with intellectual challenges were more likely to have been recipients of special education than youth whose test scores suggested normal intellectual functioning. They were also more likely to have been in fewer out-of-home placements than youth with average intelligence. Youth with IQ test scores in the intellectual disability range were also more likely than youth with average test scores to have been sexually abused or neglected. Last, youth with intellectual disability were less likely to come from homes where a parent was noted to abuse substances than were youth who came from homes where their parents were not known to abuse substances. No proportional differences were seen in the other risk factors investigated.

To examine outcomes between youth with test scores suggesting average abilities and those with intellectual disability for disparity, various outcomes at discharge and six months postdischarge follow-up were examined. There were no statistically significant differences at discharge for clinical functioning of the child or the family, length of stay in the program, rates of successful placement outcomes, education, or employment. In addition, there were no significant differences six months after discharge for rates of education, court involvement, or education when African American and European American youth were compared. The only statistically significant difference was identified between educational outcomes at six-month follow-up for these two groups of youth. Youth with lower IQ test scores were more likely to experience negative educational outcomes at the six-month follow-up than those whose obtained IQ scores were in the average range.

When the sample was separated by intellectual disability, gender, and ethnicity, few statistically significant differences were noted. Although this may in part be due to sampling or the methods of assessment (e.g., follow-up at six months might not reflect long-term changes) or analysis, these findings may also reflect that foster care placement yields benefits to youth who enter with multiple risk factors. Specifically, the lack of differences may be reflective of the type of care that was provided to these youth, a variable that was not assessed in the program evaluation project.

In sum, results from this investigation suggest that although youth enter into care with substantive differences, there were limited differences in outcomes both immediately following discharge and at follow-up six months later. Although further investigation of these relationships is warranted, these analyses may represent the value of identifying and providing appropriate supports and treatment for children with an intellectual disability and accompanying risk factors that have been shown to impact foster care placement and outcomes.

Intellectual Disability in Foster Care

Although variations in diagnostic terminology exist, there is general acknowledgment that intellectually disabling conditions include two fundamental criteria:

1. significant deficits in intellectual functioning and
2. significant deficits in adaptive skills (American Association on Mental Retardation, 2002; American Psychiatric Association [APA], 2000; World Health Organization [WHO], 2001, 2003).

In addition, two of the most frequently relied on classification systems for identifying intellectual disability, the *International Classification of Diseases and Related Health Problems* (ICD-10; WHO, 2003) and *Diagnostic and Statistical Manual of Mental Disorders* (DSM-IV-TR; APA, 2000), utilize terms that denote the severity of intellectual, and in most cases, adaptive impairment associated with intellectual disability. This becomes particularly important given the difference in clinical and functional needs of children with varying severities of intellectual disability (Batshaw & Shapiro, 2002). Moreover, investigations consistently demonstrate that the severity of intellectual disability is associated with differential outcomes in foster care (Batshaw & Shapiro, 2002; Felce, Lowe, & Jones, 2002), an important consideration to make when planning treatment goals and evaluating outcomes.

Findings in the literature are mixed concerning the potential impact of intellectual disability on foster care placement and outcomes. Although there is general agreement that the presence of intellectual disability is related to risk factors for placement in foster care, there are disagreements about the impact of intellectual disability on treatment effectiveness. In a review of treatment outcomes for individuals with an intellectual disability in foster care, Heller (2002) suggested that outcomes were influenced by the severity of intellectual limitations associated with intellectual disability. Specifically, she found that the higher the intellectual functioning, the more favorable the outcomes were in the domains of adaptive behavior, self-determination, community participation, and use of social networks.

Other researchers have also examined factors related to placement outcomes for youth with intellectual disabilities. Romney and colleagues (2006) investigated whether the presence of emotional/behavioral, physical, cognitive, or communicative disabilities as identified by the caregiver were predictive of placement status two years later. Romney and associates found that children with a cognitive disability (identified as the presence of mental retardation or developmental delay) were less likely to be reunified with their family of origin than those without a cognitive disability. Instead, children with cognitive disabilities were over four times more likely to remain in non-kinship foster care and over five and a half times more likely to be adopted. Thus, disability, and in particular cognitive disability, were both related to a lower probability of a child's reunification with their family of origin.

DISABILITY AND OTHER RISK FACTORS

Studies have demonstrated several risk factors associated with foster care placement and poor outcomes, including characteristics of the child him- or herself, parental problems, and environmental factors (Harden, 2004; Twigg, 2006). When an intellectual disability is paired with these risk factors, the strength of associations to placement and treatment outcomes increase significantly (e.g., Beadle-Brown et al., 2000; Becker, Jordan & Larson, 2007; Emerson, Robertson, & Wood, 2005; Hanley, 2002).

Child-Related Risk Factors

Although youth with an intellectual disability and mild to moderate behavioral or emotional difficulties have been shown to succeed in less restrictive placements (e.g., kinship care versus secure residential facilities), Laan, Loots, Janssen, and Stolk (2001) found that youth with more severe behavioral difficulties in addition to an intellectual disability (e.g., significant personality or psychiatric problems) do less well in similar placements and are particularly prone to poor outcomes. In addition, older youth, those with additional physical and/or mental impairments, and those exhibiting problematic behaviors are less likely to be successfully reunified with their family of origin or adopted following foster care placement. For example, Becker et al. (2007) found that children who were older or had mental impairments were likely to stay in foster care longer than younger and nondisabled children.

Studies have consistently found that minority youth, particularly African American youth, are overrepresented in foster care (U.S. DHHS, 2006; Wall & Koch, 2007), child welfare and juvenile justice systems, independent of the crimes committed or problems displayed by the child (e.g., Crane & Ellis, 2004; Green, 2003; Hill, 2006; Hines, Lemon, Wyatt, & Merdinger, 2004; Wall & Koch, 2007). In addition to disproportionate placement in foster care, studies have found disparities in the services received and in treatment outcomes on the basis of ethnicity, with minority groups being underserved (e.g., Becker et al., 2007; Crane & Ellis, 2004; Green, 2003). Hines and colleagues (2004), for example, found that minority families received fewer services and had poorer outcomes in the child welfare system than European American families. African American children were also less likely to leave foster care due to reunification with family or adoption and more likely to enter the juvenile justice system following foster care (Anderson, 2003). In sum, European American children appear more likely to receive appropriate treatment and counseling (Lu et al., 2004), reunify with family or relatives (Harris & Courtney, 2003; Schuck, 2005), or be permanently adopted if family reunification is not possible (Hill, 2006) when compared to African American children.

The proportion of suspected child maltreatment cases reported is also significantly higher for African American families than for European American families (Schuck, 2005). Despite the ethnic disproportionality in cases reported, Schuck (2005) found that the number of substantiated cases of abuse was significantly less for African American children than for European American children. Even so, it has been noted that African American children are removed from their homes with greater frequency, incarcerated more frequently for delinquent behavior (Crane & Ellis, 2004; Hines et al., 2004), and more frequently labeled as mentally or educationally retarded (cited in Hill, 2006; Salend, Garrick-Duhaney, & Montgomery, 2002).

Given the risk of less favorable outcomes associated with both ethnicity and intellectual disability, it seems plausible that in combination, these two risk factors may increase the likelihood of poor outcomes for children. This hypothesis has gained some support in the literature. Becker et al. (2007) demonstrated that when coupled with the presence of an intellectual disability, being an ethnic minority group member decreased the likelihood of successfully leaving foster care.

Studies suggest there are inequities in treatment and outcomes based on gender, but that both genders experience disadvantage of some kind (Laan et al., 2001). Thus, although it has been noted that girls more frequently enter foster care with higher levels of preplacement risk (Smith, 2004) including sexual abuse (Leve & Chamberlin, 2007), there is limited evidence that gender is an independent risk factor for foster care placement. Even so, Hornick, Philips, and Kerr (1988) concluded that females were more likely than males to be placed in foster care and less likely to receive appropriate services. When considered in conjunction with the presence of intellectual disability, Avery (1999) found that boys were more likely than girls to experience delays in permanent adoptive placement. Given the disparities and lack of studies investigating the impact of gender and intellectual disability on placement and outcomes of foster care, more extensive research on the topic is needed.

Family and Community Factors

Youth placed in foster care are more likely to come from homes where parents have difficulties, such as a history of substance abuse, psychiatric diagnoses, or incarceration (Berger, 2004; Hayward & Depanfilis, 2007; Schuck, 2005). Becker et al. (2007) found that parental substance abuse can place a child at risk of experiencing less favorable outcomes. More specifically, Hines et al. (2004) estimated that one to two thirds of substantiated child maltreatment reports involve parents who abuse substances. Additionally, youth in foster care are more likely to come from a single-parent household and from lower socioeconomic communities where poverty, crime, violence, and substandard living conditions are more common.

Most of the factors that predispose youth to placement in foster care are found more often in families with low socioeconomic status (SES), including higher rates of parental and youth incarceration, lower overall rates of parental educational achievement, higher rates of mental illness, and more limited access to necessary treatment (Becker et al., 2007; Cahn, 2002; Green, 2003; Hines et al., 2004). Green (2002) also noted a correlation between low SES and single-parent households and suggested the combination of being in a single-parent household with low SES could increase the risk of decreased availability of supervision, increased exposure to negative peer pressure, and increased crime rates in the child's neighborhood. Furthermore, Hanley (2002) noted that young children's health and development are compromised by poverty, parenting difficulties, abuse and neglect, prenatal exposure to illicit drugs or alcohol, and exposure to toxic substances. Hanley also explains that young children's health and development are compromised by poverty and associated factors, thereby increasing the likelihood of disability, foster care placement, and associated outcomes.

Family structure impacts foster care placement and outcomes in varying ways. Llewelln, McConnell, Thompson, and Whybrow (2005) conducted interviews 12 to 18 months apart, with 81 parents of children with disabilities who also had other dependent family members. Parents reported difficulty balancing the demands of caring for their child with a disability and maintaining other family responsibilities. They also found that parents were more likely to consider out-of-home placement when the imbalance between these two demands increased, when other family responsibilities increased and there was difficulty integrating the child with the disability into daily life activities. In sum, having a child with a disability, particularly when there are other dependent family members, can impact a family's ability to care for children and increase the likelihood of foster care placement.

Once placed in foster care, structure of the family providing care has been associated with differential outcomes of youth. In one study, children in nonkinship foster care were more likely to exhibit clinically significant behavioral and emotional difficulties than those in kinship care (Keller et al., 2001). When children in kinship foster care were compared with children in the general population, no differences in behavioral and emotional outcomes were present. Together, these findings suggest that the placement of youth with nonfamily members is a risk factor for significant behavioral and emotional difficulties, while placement with other family members produces a level of risk no greater than living in an intact home. Given that the presence of an intellectual disability can enhance outcomes related to other risk factors, this finding warrants efforts to place youth with family members when possible.

Exposure to violence has been associated with foster care placement and negative outcomes. Owen, Thompson, and Kaslow (2006) conducted a study on the effect of domestic violence on children. Their results showed that children whose mothers had experienced violence had significantly higher rates of emotional and behavioral problems on standardized scales assessing these difficulties. In addition, exposure to violence in one's neighborhood, also linked to low SES, has been noted to correlate with higher rates of delinquency and youth incarceration. Preski and Shelton (2001) found that there were significant risks associated with witnessing violence in the community, as youth who had seen violent behaviors were more likely to be placed in a more restrictive juvenile detention facility than those who had not seen violence.

Protective and Favorable Outcome-Promoting Factors

Although there are many factors that can place a child at risk, research has also indicated several family, community, and treatment factors that serve a protective function and/or promote favorable service outcomes. Among these, family and community support are frequently related to improved child outcomes such as better community integration (Ping-Ying, Sing-Fai Tam, & Wai-Kwong Man, 2006), an increased likelihood of the birth family being able to keep and appropriately care for their child (Llewelln et al., 2005), and/or an increased likelihood of attaining successful permanent placement (Avery, 1999; Laan et al., 2001). When the treatment goal is reunification, including the family in the child's care has shown some promise in increasing success rates (Sunseri, 2004; Wulczyn, 2004).

Similar to its favorable effect on reunification, the level of family involvement during foster care placement has been shown to directly relate to the level of positive outcomes following foster care; thus, the greater a family's involvement in activities such as parent preparation programs (Avery, 1999), skill building, instruction in parenting skills (Laan et al., 2001), and intensive family therapy, the more positive the treatment outcomes (Ping-Ying et al., 2006). Additionally, when youth in foster care receive regular visits from their family, reunification is generally more stable. For example, when compared to youth with limited family interactions during foster care placement, youth receiving regular family visits engaged in fewer behaviors after discharge that warranted a return to foster care (Landsman, Groza, Tyler, & Malone, 2001).

When family members with known risk factors for poor outcomes are identified early and these factors are addressed in care, outcomes have also been shown to improve. For example, factors including parental substance use, parent mental health problems, poor housing, and single-parent families have been associated with lower rates of stable placement and higher rates of re-entry into the foster care system (Green, 2002; Hayward & DePanfilis, 2007). In addition, since parent behaviors are the foundation on which reunification decisions are made, ensuring parents understand treatment requirements including safety issues in the home, compliance with scheduled visitations, and following through with referrals for treatment have been shown to have a positive impact on reunification.

Strength-based approaches to treatment have also been shown to relate to positive outcomes. For example, identification and utilization of social supports held by the family has been associated with higher rates of successful reunification (Romney et al., 2006). Whether or not reunification is the identified permanency goal, providing services that address a child's specific needs is critical to improving well-being (Bass, Shields, & Behrman, 2004; Ogden & Hagen, 2006). To do so, child-related difficulties present at the onset of care must be identified and matched with services that when provided can capitalize on the strengths of the youth and meet their individual needs. It is therefore important that children receive evaluations of health—including developmental and emotional/mental health—from the onset of service (Bass et al., 2004). Particular services that have been noted to demonstrate benefit across individualized circumstances include caregiver/family education about the child's abilities (Laan et al., 2001; Llewelln, et al., 2005), financial support (Green, 2002), and the provision of services that build on the youth and family successes rather than limitations (Bass et al., 2004).

Most of the risk factors mentioned have been shown to independently relate to placement in foster care and/or negative outcomes for youth with intellectual disabilities. Children rarely present with only one risk factor. Rather, most children present with a variety of child, family, and/or environment related factors. Similarly, children can have a variety of protective factors available to improve outcomes including family and community involvement, strength-based treatments, parental education, and appropriate intervention. Thus, accurate evaluation of each child at the onset of care is necessary to identify his or her unique strengths and areas of need and construct an individualized plan of care accordingly.

CONCLUSIONS AND FUTURE DIRECTIONS OF CARE

Foster care placement determinations, the provision of adequate services, and treatment outcomes for children with intellectual disability are negatively impacted even further when paired with other risk factors both specific to youth (e.g., emotional and behavioral difficulties, gender, ethnicity) and external to them (e.g., parent problems, poverty, family structure, violence, and crime). Findings of the programmatic case study highlight the importance of identifying specific services most beneficial to each youth with an intellectual disability and other risk factors to improve treatment outcomes and minimize negative outcomes for youth following foster care.

Awareness and utilization of child protective factors should also be a focus of future treatment. Increased family involvement, early identification of risk factors, and the use of strength-based approaches have all shown to relate to positive outcomes. Targeted interventions can be developed within foster care to meet goals for reunification and increase the likelihood of success. Providing training and education targeted at improving parenting skills and understanding the unique needs of a child with an intellectual disability may aid in this goal, as well as in assisting caregivers living with additional substantial stresses. Increased community, familial, child, and educational supports so children can stay in the home (least restrictive environment) as much as possible are associated with positive outcomes (Merrick, Merrick, & Kandel, 2006).

Other researchers have supported offering both training and respite to caregivers and treatment staff as ways to enhance their ability to offer substitute care (Chadwick, Beechman, Piroth, Bernard, & Taylor, 2002; McGill, Papachristoforou, & Cooper, 2006). Similarly, having caregivers and staff who understand the diversity of values, family structures, and languages and who provide culturally competent care in an evidence based manner is critical when intervening with persons and to provide effective interventions (APA, 2003; Farber & Maharaj, 2005). This can be accomplished by offering opportunities for enhanced diversity in the organization, as well as organizational interventions that educate staff on the relationship between the organization and individuals they serve (McPhatter & Ganaway, 2003; Nybell & Gray, 2004).

Reports discussing program outcomes have identified many factors that appear related to positive outcomes for youth entering foster care when intellectual disabilities are evident. These include early identification and development of education based on individual strengths that accommodate weaknesses, with extra supports used as needed (Romney et al., 2006). Some writers support the use of smaller group or family style residences (Lee, 2008) and integrated mental health service (Hall, Parkes, Samuels, & Hassiotis, 2006), while others (Heller, 2002) report that use of home-like architectural features and assistive technology, as well as organizational policies that promote individualization and person-centered planning, are associated with successful outcomes. A final suggestion of recruiting foster parents specifically for caring for youth with disabilities, and training parents to advocate on the behalf of their children, resolve issues and seek needed services has also been noted (Farber & Maharaj, 2005; United Cerebral Palsy and Children's Rights, 2006). The goal of all of these interventions is to provide the best quality of care to children and their families.

REFERENCES

American Association on Mental Retardation. (2002). *Mental retardation: Definition, classification, and systems of supports* (10th ed.). Washington, DC: Author.

American Psychiatric Association, (2000). *Diagnostic and statistical manual of mental disorders* (4th ed., text revision). Washington, DC: Author.

American Psychological Association. (2003). APA guidelines on multicultural education, training, research, practice, and organizational change for psychologists. *American Psychologist, 58*, 377–402.

Anderson, C. L. (2003, September). *African American children in the Indiana Child Welfare System: Identifying areas of overrepresentation and disproportionality.* Paper presented at the meeting of the Indiana Black Legislative Caucus Annual Symposium, Indianapolis, IN.

Avery, R. J. (1999). Identifying obstacles to adoption in New York state's out-of-home care system. *Child Welfare, 78*, 653–671.

Bass, S., Shields, M. K., & Behrman, R. E. (2004). Children, families, and foster care: Analysis and recommendations. *Children, Families and Foster Care, 14*(1). Retrieved January 9, 2008, from www.futureofchildren.org/usr_doc/analysis&recommendations.pdf.

Batshaw, M. L., & Shapiro, B. K. (2002). Mental retardation. In M. L. Batshaw (Ed.), *Children with disabilities* (5th ed.) (pp. 287–306). Baltimore: Brookes.

Beadle-Brown, J., Murphy, G., Wing, L., Gould, J., Shah, A., & Holmes, N. (2000). Changes in skills for people with intellectual disability: A follow-up of the Camberwell cohort. *Journal of Intellectual Disability Research, 44,* 12–24.

Becker, M. A., Jordan, N., & Larsen, R. (2007). Predictors of successful permanency planning and length of stay in foster care: The role of race, diagnosis and place of residence. *Children and Youth Services Review, 29,* 1102–1113.

Berger, L. M. (2004). Income, family structure, and child maltreatment risk. *Children and Youth Services Review, 26,* 725–748.

Cahn, N. (2002). Race, poverty, history, adoption, and child abuse: Connections. *Law & Society Review, 36,* 461–488.

Chadwick, O., Beechman, J., Piroth, N., Bernard, S., & Taylor, E. (2002). Respite care for children with severe intellectual disability and their families: Who needs it? Who receives it? *Child and Adolescent Mental Health, 7,* 66–72.

Child Welfare League of America. (2007). *Children of color in the child welfare system.* Retrieved June 27, 2007, from www.cwla.org/programs/culture/disproportionatestatement.pdf.

Crane, K. D., & Ellis, R. A. (2004). Benevolent intervention or oppression perpetuated: minority overrepresentation in children's services. *Journal of Human Behavior in the Social Environment, 9,* 19–38.

Curtis, P. A., Alexander, G., & Lunghofer, L. A. (2001). A literature review comparing the outcomes of residential group care and therapeutic foster care. *Child and Adolescent Social Work Journal, 18,* 377–392.

Ebersole, J. L., & Kapp, S. A. (2007). Stemming the tide of overrepresentation: Ensuring accurate certification of African American students in programs for the mentally retarded. *School Social Work Journal, 31,* 1–16.

Emerson, E., Robertson, J., & Wood, J. (2005). Emotional and behavioral needs of children and adolescents with intellectual disabilities in an urban conurbation. *Journal of Intellectual Disability Research, 49,* 16–24.

Farber, M. L., & Maharaj, R. (2005). Empowering high-risk families of children with disabilities. *Research on Social Work Practice, 15,* 501–515.

Felce, D., Lowe, K., & Jones, E. (2002). Association between the provision characteristics and operation of supported housing services and resident outcomes. *Journal of Applied Research in Intellectual Disabilities, 15,* 404–418.

Green, M. Y. (2002). Minorities as majority: Disproportionality in child welfare and juvenile justice. *Children's Voice, 11,* 8–13.

Green, M. Y. (2003). Balancing the scales; targeting disproportionality in child welfare and juvenile justice. *Children's Voice, 12*(1), 6–10.

Hall, I., Parkes, C., Samuels, S., & Hassiotis, A. (2006). Working across boundaries: Clinical outcomes for an integrated mental health service for people with intellectual disabilities. *Journal of Intellectual Disability Research, 50,* 598–607.

Hanley, B. (2002). Intersection of the fields of child welfare and developmental disabilities. *Mental Retardation, 40,* 413–415.

Harden, B. J. (2004). Safety and stability for foster children: A developmental perspective. *Children, Families and Foster Care, 14*(1). Retrieved January 9, 2008, from www.futureofchildren.org/usr_doc/3-harden.pdf.

Harris, M. S., & Courtney, M. E. (2003). The interaction of race, ethnicity, and family structure with respect to the timing of family reunification. *Children and Youth Services Review, 25,* 409–429.

Harry, B., & Klingner, J. K. (2006). *Why are so many minority students in special education? Understanding race and disability in the schools.* New York: Teachers College Press.

Hayward, R. A., & DePanfilis, D. (2007). Foster children with an incarcerated parent: Predictors of reunification. *Children and Youth Services Review, 29*, 1320–1334.

Heller, T. (2002). Residential settings and outcomes for individuals with intellectual disabilities. *Current Opinion in Psychiatry, 15*, 503–508.

Hill, R. B. (2006). *Synthesis of research on disproportionality in child welfare: An update.* Washington, DC: Center for the Study of Social Policy.

Hill, R. B. (2007). *An analysis of racial/ethnic disproportionality and disparity at the national, state and county levels.* Casey-CSPP Alliance for Racial Equity in child welfare. Retrieved January 4, 2008, from www.cspp.org/major_intitatives/racialEquity.html.

Hines, A. M., Lemon, K., Wyatt, P., & Merdinger, J. (2004). Factors related to the disproportionate involvement of children of color in the child welfare system: A review and emerging themes. *Children and Youth Services Review, 26*, 507–527.

Horner-Johnson, W., & Drum, C. E. (2006). Prevalence of maltreatment of people with intellectual disabilities: A review of recently published research. *Mental Retardation and Developmental Disabilities Research Reviews, 12*, 57–69.

Hornick, J. P., Phillips, D. M., & Kerr, N. (1988). Gender differences in behavioral problems of foster children: Implications for special foster care. Presented at Second North American Conference on Treatment Foster Care, Calgary, AB.

Jackson-Walker, S., Wall, J. R., & Minnich, H. M. (2003). *IARCCA Outcome project special report: An analysis of outcome measures for children in residential care, transitional living, and foster care.* Indianapolis, IN: IARCCA.

Keller, T. E., Wetherbee, K., Le Prohn, N. S., Payne, V., Sim, K., & Lamont, E. R. (2001). Competencies and problem behaviors of children in family foster care: Variations by kinship placement status and race. *Children and Youth Services Review, 23*, 915–940.

Koch, S. M., Cederna, C. L., & Wall, J. R. (2007, November). *Risk factors for youth with intellectual disabilities in foster care in Indiana.* Poster session presented at the Annual Conference of the Association of University Centers on Disability, Washington, DC.

Koch, S. M., & Wall, J. R. (2005). *IARCCA outcome project special report 2005: An analysis of variables related to intake and discharge in residential care, foster care, transitional living, home-based day treatment, shelter care and crisis stabilization programs.* Indianapolis, IN: IARCCA.

Laan, N. M. A., Loots, G. M. P., Janssen, C. G. C., & Stolk, J. (2001). Foster care for children with mental retardation and challenging behavior: A follow-up study. *British Journal of Developmental Disabilities, 47*, 3–13.

Landsman, M. J., Groza, V., Tyler, M., & Malone, K. (2001). Outcomes of family-centered residential treatment. *Child Welfare Journal, 80*, 351–379.

Lee, B. (2008). Comparing outcomes for youth in treatment foster care and family-style group care. *Children and Youth Services Review, 30*(7), 746–757.

Leve, L. D., & Chamberlin, P. (2007). A randomized evaluation of multidimensional treatment foster care: Effects on school attendance and homework completion in juvenile justice girls. *Research on Social Work Practice, 17*, 657–663.

Llewelln, G., McConnell, D., Thompson, K., & Whybrow, S. (2005). Out-of-home placement of school-age children with disabilities and high support needs. *Journal of Applied Research in Intellectual Disabilities, 18*, 1–6.

Lu, Y., E., Landsverk, J., Ellis-MacLeod, E., Newton, R., Ganger, W., & Johnson, I. (2004). Race, ethnicity, and case outcomes in child protective services. *Children and Youth Services Review, 26*, 447–461.

McGill, P., Papachristoforou, E., & Cooper, V. (2006). Support for family carers of children and young people with developmental disabilities and challenging behaviour. *Child: Care, Health, and Development, 32,* 159–165.

McPhatter, A. R., & Ganaway, T. L. (2003). Beyond the rhetoric: Strategies for implementing culturally effective practice with children, families, and communities. *Child Welfare Journal, 82,* 103–124.

Merrick, J., Merrick, E., & Kandel, I. (2006). Children with intellectual disability in residential care centers. Trends in Israel 1999–2004. *International Journal of Adolescent Medicine and Health, 18,* 653–657.

National Collaboration on Workforce and Disability. (2007). *Negotiating the curves toward employment: A guide about youth involved in the foster care system.* Retrieved June 27, 2007, from www.ncwd-youth.info/intersection.

Nybell, S. M., & Gray, S. S. (2004). Race, place, space: Meanings of cultural competence in three social service agencies. *Social Work, 49,* 17–26.

Ogden, T., & Hagen, K. A. (2006) Multisystemic treatment of serious behaviour problems in youth: Sustainability of effectiveness two years after intake. *Child and Adolescent Mental Health, 11*(3), 142–149.

Owen, A. E., Thompson, M. P., & Kaslow, N. J. (2006). The mediating role of parenting stress in the relation between intimate partner violence and child adjustment. *Journal of Family Psychology, 20,* 505–513.

Ping-Ying Li, E., Sing-Fai Tam, A., & Wai-Kwong Man, D. (2006). Exploring the self-concepts of persons with intellectual disabilities. *Journal of Intellectual Disabilities 10,* 19–34.

Preski, S., & Shelton, D. (2001). The role of contextual, child and parent factors in predicting criminal outcomes in adolescence. *Issues in Mental Health Nursing, 22,* 197–205.

Romney, S. C., Litrownik, A. J., Newton, R. R., & Lau, A. (2006). The relationship between child disability and living arrangement in child welfare. *Child Welfare, 85,* 965–984.

Salend, S., Garrick-Duhaney, L., & Montgomery, W. (2002). A comprehensive approach to identifying and addressing issues of disproportionate representation. *Remedial and Special Education, 21*(5), 289–299.

Schuck, A. M. (2005). Explaining Black-White disparity in maltreatment: Poverty, female-headed families, and urbanization. *Journal of Marriage and Family, 67,* 543–551.

Smith, D. K. (2004). Risk, reinforcement, retention in treatment and reoffending for boys and girls in multidimensional treatment foster care. *Journal of Emotional and Behavioral Disorders, 12,* 38–48.

Sullivan, P. M., & Knutson, J. K. (2000). Maltreatment and disabilities: A population based epidemiological study. *Child Abuse and Neglect, 24,* 1257–1273.

Sunseri, P. (2004). Family functioning and residential treatment outcomes. *Residential Treatment for Children & Youth, 22,* 33–53.

Twigg, R. C. (2006). *Withstanding the test of time: What we know about treatment foster care: A monograph on treatment foster care.* Hackensack, NJ: Foster Family-Based Treatment Association.

United Cerebral Palsy and Children's Rights. (2006, May 1). *Forgotten children: A case for action for children and youth with disabilities in foster care.* Retrieved December 21, 2007, from www.ucp.org/uploads/ForgottenChildrenFINAL.pdf.

U.S. Department of Health and Human Services, Administration for Children and Families, Administration on Children, Youth and Families, Children's Bureau. (2006). *AFCARS report: Preliminary FY 2005 estimates as of September 2006.* Retrieved January 2, 2008, from www.acf.hhs.gov/programs/cb/stats_research/afcars/tar/report13.htm.

U.S. Department of Health and Human Services, Administration for Children and Families, Administration on Children, Youth and Families, Children's Bureau. (2007). *Definitions of child abuse and neglect: State statutes series.* Retrieved August 28, 2008, from www.childwelfare.gov/systemwide/laws_policies/statutes/define.cfm.

Wall, J. R., Busch, M., Koch, S. M., Alexander, G., Minnich, H., & Jackson-Walker, S. (2005). Accountability in child welfare services: Developing a statewide outcome evaluation program. *Psychological Services, 2*, 39–53.

Wall, J. R., & Koch, S. M. (2007, April). *Special report brief: Racial disproportionality and disparity for youth in out-of-home care* (vol. 1, no. 2). Indianapolis, IN: IARCCA.

Wall, J. R., & Minnich, H. M. (2004). *IARCCA outcome project special report II: An analysis of variables related to outcome at discharge and follow-up in residential care, transitional living, foster care, and home-based programs.* Indianapolis, IN: IARCCA.

World Health Organization. (2001). *International classification of functioning, disability and health.* Geneva: Author.

World Health Organization. (2003). *International classification of diseases and related health problems*, 10th revision. Geneva: Author.

Wulczyn, F. (2004). Family reunification. *Children, Families and Foster Care, 14*(1). Retrieved January 9, 2008, from www.futureofchildren.org/usr_doc/6-wulczyn.pdf.

Zetlin, A. G., & Weinberg. L. A. (2004). Understanding the plight of foster youth and improving their educational opportunities. *Child Abuse & Neglect, 28*, 917–923.

CHAPTER 12

Mental Disorder, Disability, and Society

David Pilgrim and Anne Rogers

Disability theory provides the basis for a new direction of analysis from which to understand the societal barriers faced by people with mental health problems in Western countries. Disability theory, drawing as it does on a social approach to disability, has the power to reorient analysis from a focus on the individual to the wider mechanisms and processes of social oppression, discrimination, and exclusion. Disability theory also has the capacity to illuminate the various social and economic restrictions and sources of disadvantage encountered by people with a diagnosis of mental illness. Although disability theorists have been criticised for adopting an oversocialized perspective, it does provide a corrective to the overly individualized perspective by situating problems in the social context and referring explicitly to processes of social invalidation.

This perspective is important for all forms of disability, but in the case of mental health, another dynamic comes into play about the *extent* of social invalidation associated with people who, according to themselves or others, are mentally disordered. As Fabrega and Manning (1972) pointed out more than 25 years ago, "mental illness" is more stigmatizing than other conditions because it is not possible to disassociate the disability from the self or person. The very notion of "mentally disordered," which is applied as a general term to cover those with a diagnosis of mental illness, personality disorder, or substance misuse, has the dubious implication that there is a readily definable fixed or stable notion of mental order. In this chapter, we examine the extent to which social forces determine mental health problems. Second, we consider lay and professional reactions to psychological difference.

EPISTEMOLOGICAL STARTING POINTS

In reviewing the nature of mental health problems, different views are scattered across communities of interest (i.e., professionals, patients and their significant others, politicians, researchers). Three views are addressed here. The first is *medical naturalism* (also referred to as psychiatric positivism), which is reflected in orthodox psychiatric theory and practice and was championed at the end of the 19th century by Emil Kraepelin. This assumes that mental disorders are separate naturally occurring, fixed phenomena (like gasses or type of metal) and are embodied in the individual who has "schizophrenia" or "depression." This reflects an epistemic fallacy (i.e., that the world simply is what its investigators believe it to be at a moment in time) and is typical of naive realism in medicine and other uncritical expressions of natural science when applied to human science.

The second view is *social constructionism* (i.e., where subject precedes object—the inverse of the first view). The work of Szasz (1961) was noted in this regard, though as we discuss later, his arguments may paradoxically legitimate one type of disability but not other forms.

The third view, and the one we have taken in this chapter, is that there is a reality of distress and madness that can be studied, but we must proceed cautiously and skeptically at each step. This position of *critical realism* (e.g., Pilgrim & Bentall, 1998) suggests that knowledge about mental disorder is socially negotiated, thus supporting the arguments about context-specific social constructions, but also acknowledging there are stable features that can be examined. For example, we know that conditioned fear (i.e., anxiety states) is reportable not only in all societies but even across mammalian species. Similarly, misery can be invoked experimentally in animals (i.e., learned helplessness), but human beings attribute particular *meanings* to these states, meanings that are biographically unique and socially and historically situated. As for madness, it is readily recognized by social actors. However, the social value or disvalue that is attached to madness can vary. For example, on one hand, there is a relationship between depression and creativity and mania and industrious success and, on the other hand, a complete social discrediting of those with a diagnosis of schizophrenia.

SOCIAL FORCES AS DETERMINANTS OF MENTAL HEALTH PROBLEMS

We use the notion of "social forces" here in a broad and inclusive way, which is consistent with a critical realist view of world. This approach insists that causes and meanings need to be understood together, rather than one or the other being privileged or discounted. We hope that our position avoids the opposition set up at times between naïve realists and radical constructivists (Rogers & Pilgrim, 2005). The former are naive about meanings and judgments that are inherently social. The latter insist that "everything is socially constructed," thus displacing material reality as the dominant research focus and replacing it with the concept of ideas in action (discourses).

The largest obstacle to our understanding of the social model in mental health research is biological reductionism—the strong tradition within orthodox psychiatry to reduce all mental health problems to brain diseases. In this sense, both physical and psychological disabilities are accounted for by the medical, rather than social model of disability. In the case of physical disability, the body is the testing ground for social order (the ability of the impaired person's body to sense, communicate, and move in a way that befits a given role in society). Generally, this type of social judgment is not the initial consideration in relation to mental health problems. Instead, rule infractions (rather than role failure) are the first pressing concern in mental illness—the way people conduct themselves. Although clinicians may emphasize the presence or absence of mental disorder as a clinical government, it is the way people speak and act in context that determines a diagnosis (or formulation) of mental abnormality. Moreover, formally codified attributions of mental illness are usually preceded by lay attributions by the prospective patient or their significant others. Because mentally disordered patients are judged by themselves or others as being impaired in their ability to function, the social definitions of impairment and the social forces that impact on mental illness are both important.

Economic Deprivation

Disadvantages typically associated with poverty, such as poor education, low pay or unemployment, poor neighborhoods, and poor living conditions, aggravate both physical and mental health (Fryers, Melzer, & Jenkins, 2000; Rogers & Pilgrim, 2003). Class position predicts both morbidity in its broadest sense and longevity in its specific sense. Not only do the poor consistently die younger, this pattern of early death is amplified in poor people who also have a psychiatric diagnosis (Knapp, 2001).

Labor market effects are reliant on the presence or absence of government-provided income maintenance and on the circumstances in which a person becomes unemployed. In most developed countries, unemployed people obtain welfare payments. These payments ensure that poverty is relative, not absolute, and that resources are available to sustain food and shelter. In many developing countries, this safety net is absent. For example, Patel (2001) noted that in India during the 1990s, bonded low-paid farmers lost everything when a monsoon destroyed their crops. They were thrown into absolute poverty, and suicide levels dramatically increased.

Some forms of unemployment may actually be linked to improvements in psychological well-being (for example, a good retirement package, inheriting wealth, or winning the lottery). Thus, although the absence of paid work is not inherently bad for mental health, the context of that unemployment is important to consider. The worst mental health is found not in unemployed people, but in those on low pay and with poor task control or on short-term contracts. This situation is sometimes called "inadequate employment" or "underemployment" (Dooley, Prause, & Ham-Rowbottom, 2000). The best mental health accrues from high wages, good task control, and permanent employment. Thus, unemployment may affect morale but work, especially poorly paid work, brings with it peculiar stressors, as well as low status and inadequate earnings. Low paid work leads to poverty in the domestic arena and, during work time, brings with it tedious and unfulfilling tasks.

In the case of becoming unemployed, however, its effects can be compounded by multiple losses (Fryer, 1995). Identity for many is bound up with work roles; unemployment results in a loss of identity. Daily meanings are bound up with the routines of work, so unemployment can represent a loss of daily structure. For some, being unemployed is a source of shame. For those whose income level drops significantly, there is the direct impact of financial stress.

Economic cycles create advantages and disadvantages to individuals. For example, one generation of young people might encounter a period of growth and can access the labor market readily. The next generation may be less fortunate. Those in insecure employment will be buffered from its effects during times of full employment, but in more economically depressed times, they will be very vulnerable (Kasl, Rodrigues, & Lasch, 1998).

Ecological Effects

Environmental factors begin to affect current and future mental health status from the womb onward. For example, substances that cross the placenta can influence neurological development, which in turn can have a behavioral impact after birth. With regard to loss, abuse, and neglect, these contextual factors impinge on the developing child. The etiology of mental disorders remains controversial (Read, Agar, Argyle, & Aderhold, 2003; Whitfield, Dube, Felitti, & Anda, 2005), but environmentalists have argued that consistent benign child-rearing is at the center of positive adult mental health. In contrast, abuse, particularly sexual abuse, in childhood is highly correlated with contact with mental health services (Pilgrim, Rogers, & Bentall, in press).

It has been known since the 1930s that psychiatric diagnosis is geographically distributed (Faris & Dunham, 1939). These early Chicago studies demonstrated that not only were poorer people more likely to have a psychiatric diagnosis, illness appeared more frequently in poorer areas. However, the ecological fallacy highlights that that not all people in poorer areas are poor, and not all are prone to mental health problems. Thus, ecological effects are evident, but where a person lives is not the only determinant of his or her mental health status.

Urban life generally is more "psychonoxious" than rural life (Paykel, Abbott, Jenkins, Brugha, & Meltzer, 2000), not withstanding our knowledge about pockets of rural poverty. This effect is due to more social disorganization and environmental stressors (crime, vandalism, noise, litter, and motor traffic) in urban areas. In areas of concentrated poverty, the impact at the individual level is profound and negative. Not surprisingly, in these neighborhoods, there are raised levels of depression, anxiety, and substance misuse (Aneschensel & Succoff, 1996).

Apart from the direct exposure to the external ambient hazards of stress in these local contexts, people are less likely to have regular supportive social networks, particularly if there is a high turnover of residence (Sampson, 1988). Some particularly deteriorated localities contain higher rates of presentation of depressive symptomology (Ross, 2000) *in all social groups*, including those with higher levels of economic capital. Similarly, aggregate neighborhood income predicts levels of diagnosis of schizophrenia and substance misuse (Goldsmith, Holzer, & Manderscheid, 1998).

Some localities provide more "opportunity structures" than others as a result of the cultural and environmental possibilities for stress-free or health-giving public behavior. For example, two neighborhoods may be grossly equivalent in terms of income, but one may have safer streets and more spacious green park areas for safe exercise than the other. Generally, more affluent neighborhoods provide more opportunity structures than poorer ones (Ellaway & Mcintyre,1998), emphasizing the fact that social position can be defined as either an individual or a neighborhood characteristic.

Race, Ethnicity, Gender, and Age

In the British context, two groups of ex-colonized people (i.e., those with historical origins in Ireland or the West Indies) have higher rates of psychiatric diagnosis than other groups (Rogers & Pilgrim, 2005). The fact that the Irish are typically white suggests that ethnic minority status may be more important to consider than racial background. The epidemiological data on those from the Indian subcontinent is more ambiguous in that not all studies show higher rates of diagnoses.

In the postcolonial context, a complicating factor is the type of migration involved, which could be either forced on or desired by the migrant. These different conditions could determine whether migration is experienced with hope or in a state of trauma and loss, thus influencing mental health status.

Although much has been researched and written about gender and mental health, its relationship to detrimental outcomes remains unclear (Rogers & Pilgrim, 2005). Although more women than men are recorded as having mental health problems, this may be due to the fact that women present more often to primary care settings and because they live longer than men (and so have a higher prevalence of both dementia and depression in old age). In contrast, men are overrepresented in coercive mental health services (e.g., forensic services). Women are more likely to be diagnosed with panic disorder and depression than men, whereas men are more likely to be diagnosed with substance abuse and personality disorder (especially antisocial personality disorder). Thus, if diagnoses are examined, then any overall differences in the incidence of mental health problems between genders disappear.

Across the life span, mental health problems are unevenly distributed. Young children and very elderly people are most at risk, creating a U-shaped distribution. This suggests that the notion of a middle-aged crisis is a myth. Indeed, some studies have suggested that people in their fifties and sixties enjoy the best mental health (Rogers & Pilgrim, 2003). Yet the investment in service resources tends to be concentrated in the working years age group (services for older people, children, and adolescents receive less investment in the United Kingdom). This financial pattern gives us a hint that mental health services may be more about social regulation for socioeconomic efficiency than an equitable response to need.

SOCIAL FORCES AS DETERMINANTS OF JUDGMENTS ABOUT PSYCHOLOGICAL DIFFERENCE

The foregoing section has explored what we know to date about the social causes of mental illness. It has emphasized predictable differences in society based on structural divisions of class, race, gender, and age, with the first of these having the greatest salience. However, we caution against naive realism. It would be possible to concede the causal role of social factors, but still operate within a naive realist view of the world. Put simply, we could think of social factors being part of a biopsychosocial mix of etiological factors to explain the existence of mental disorder but stop thinking socially from that point onward. We argue instead that although social factors are demonstrably causal of mental disorders, it is a value judgment as to why mental disorders are deemed to be problematic. These value judgments reflect inherently social processes. In other words, mental disorders are not self-evident, naturally occurring phenomena that are global and transhistorical. Instead, our position is that they reflect forms of deviance from or defiance of moral order and socioeconomic efficiency.

Although no society has been indifferent to those who are distressed or act in an unintelligible way, how these differences have been valued has varied over time and place. For example, in antiquity, Socrates considered madness and sanity to have equal value. Psychological distress, as a social problem, has only emerged relatively recently in developed countries following the return of "shell-shocked" combatants returning from the World War I. Depression and anxiety states were framed as forms of disability, and government policies emerged to deal with problems that were stress-related (Stone, 1985). Prior to that in the 19th century, the sole medical discourse was about madness and the assumption that it was a genetically determined brain disease (even though records of asylum admissions would frequently refer to social or family triggers for lunacy). Similarly, drug abuse and recurring personality problems that became medicalized in the middle of the 20th century were previously framed as forms of fecklessness and immorality.

If we examine the current mixture of psychosocial problems that are subsumed under the broad rubric of mental disorder, we find a typology consisting of:

1. Those who act in idiosyncratic unintelligible ways that arouse anxiety and perplexity in others;
2. Those who are miserable and know that they are miserable;
3. Those who in the past would have been seen as weak, antisocial, dysfunctional, and feckless (a range of views exist within this group about whether they have a psychological problem).

The first cluster would receive diagnoses of schizophrenia or bipolar disorder. The second would be described as suffering from the common mental disorders of anxiety and depression. The third group would include those with diagnoses of substance misuse and personality disorders. Each group in its own way reflects a social frame for value judgments.

In the case of the first group, a fundamental meta-rule of intelligibility in modern societies has been violated. This point was at the center of well-known deviancy theories developed in the 1960s (e.g., Goffman, 1961). Adult citizens are expected to act in ways that others understand. If a person breaks a rule and then cannot or will not offer a persuasive account of that rule transgression, then the ascription of serious mental illness eventually occurs. Moreover, once a person is labeled in this way, most or all of his or her conduct thereafter is accounted for in the eyes of others by the presence of illness. This same argument applies to those in the third group.

With regard to the second group, deviancy theorists would label this as a transgression of emotional rules, which can be ascribed to the self as well as by others. According to this view, we all learn from early childhood that there is a subjective state of "good enough" mental health (happiness, optimism, contentment, love of life, self-confidence, and confidence in others). We can contrast this against a wide range of feelings, some of which fail the positive test of psychological well-being. To use the phrase of Thoits (1986), we learn when we are breaking "feeling rules."

What has changed over the past century in Western societies is that the three groups, which represent different styles of rule infraction, have been associated with different levels of governmental interest. So-called mental health policy has been characterized by a twin track approach. On the one hand, there has been a tendency to construct a *legal* apparatus to ensure the proper (i.e., lawful) social control of those in group 1 and some of those in group 3. On the other hand, the government's obligation to respond to self-defined distress has been expressed through *general health policy* (delivered in primary health care settings).

MENTAL HEALTH AND CITIZENSHIP: THE CONTRADICTORY IMPERATIVES OF COERCION AND RECOVERY

Although the social model of disability is applicable in the mental health field, a special dynamic of invalidation needs to be considered.

- First, people express *particular* fears and prejudices, which can be either unique attributions about those with mental health problems or exaggerated forms of stigmatization that are present for all disabled groups.
- Second, it is commonplace for governments in developed societies to install unique forms of legislation that define the conditions under which some people with a diagnosis of mental disorder are lawfully controlled.
- Third, powers created by that unique legislation are usually delegated to health and social care professionals. Each of these issues will now be considered.

Concern, Prejudice, and Stigma in the Public Domain

Those who are sane by common consent have traditionally been concerned with three interweaving political demands. The first demand is that those who arouse fear or perplexity in others should, in some way or another, be dealt with by agents of the government. In this sense, all psychiatric crises are social crises because they are triggered by a judgment in the public arena that something has to be done. The second demand is that those agents of the government should act fairly and reasonably, combining social control and a duty of care (i.e., legal paternalism or *parens patrie*). The third demand is that those who are truly sane should not be dealt with as if they are in the wrong category. For example, public concern about "wrongful detention" dominated the voting discourse at the turn of the 20th century around mental health legislation reform (Bean, 1980). The main public concern related to the unfair detention of the sane but not to the rights of the insane.

By the mid-20th century, ethical concerns were being expressed about the use of the coercive detention and treatment of Soviet dissidents. Ironically, these claims were made by Western psychiatrists who were happy to detain their own "truly insane" patients at home (Bloch & Reddaway, 1978). Thus, the tendency to treat psychiatric patients as being undeserving of citizenship (until proven otherwise) has a long history and is reflected in the political economy of disability. Once a person has been deemed to have lost his or her reason, then citizenship can be removed legitimately until a case is made to reverse the decision. It was only later that century when the demand for duty of care (irrespective of the legitimacy of one's detention) was also expressed by the public. Today, the general public tends to demand that mentally disordered people should, when necessary, be removed from society. At least in many Western countries, such as the United Kingdom, there is a general belief that removal should be achieved in a caring manner with restorative intent.

Studies of decision making about mentally disordered conduct suggest that agents of the government (health and criminal justice personnel) do not roam society searching for patients to diagnose and treat. On the contrary, the decision making has usually already been made in the public domain. For example, police officers who remove patients from public spaces to a place of safety for psychiatric assessment typically do so at the request of the public. Similarly, families vary in their tolerance of psychological deviance before they call health professionals to validate the decisions that have already been made about the identified patient (Coulter, 1973).

Prejudice and stigma about those who are acting unintelligibly is not new and can be traced back to antiquity (Rosen, 1968). To act in an unintelligible way is to break an implicit social contract in most complex societies. Role-rule compliance is expected, and a transgression of this meta-rule demands explanations or excuses from the rule breaker. If these are not forthcoming, then the deviant individual is deemed to automatically warrant social rejection. What has varied over time and place, though, are norms about the threshold and outcome of that social rejection. For example, some societies detain more patients than others. Some societies have treated those detainees well, whereas others have treated them brutally. The worst-case scenario was the systematic elimination of patients under the Nazi regime (Meyer, 1988). The powers of professionals to act within that range from benign paternalism to murder and persecution are ultimately derived from and legitimated by public norms and expectations.

Politicians: Their Moral and Socioeconomic Priorities

In light of the foregoing discussion of public prejudice and decision making, politicians are sensitive to public demands in liberal democracies. However, in societies where this type of responsiveness to public demand is not a main driver of political decision making (i.e., authoritarian regimes of both left and right), psychological difference provokes the need to impose coercive control. In other words, the government apparatus has a vested interest in controlling psychological deviance for more than one reason. On the one hand, politicians reflect, shape and respond to a *moral order*. The role-rule failures committed by people with mental illness are likely to stimulate and legitimate a mandate for political repression to preserve the status quo. On the other hand, those who are unable or unwilling to follow rules and fulfill role expectations represent a potential burden to economic efficiency. Thus, both the moral and socioeconomic order are concerns for politicians.

The response of politicians in liberal democracies is twin-track. The first track provides a legal framework to define when and if mentally disordered people should be coercively controlled. Confusingly and euphemistically, this is usually called "mental *health* legislation." Indeed, the political discourse about mental health is mainly limited to discussions or analyses of legislative frameworks of this type. The other track relates to the equally confusing notion of "mental *health* services." The latter is a relatively new term. Previously, these services were called psychiatric services (reflecting their medical dominance). Before that, there were not services at all but "mental hospitals" and, even earlier, "asylums." Mental health services offer places of protected treatment and restoration (psychiatric therapy and rehabilitation). They are about doing good and ensuring access to help; services are not (knowingly or primarily) about social control on behalf of others.

However, in what sense are these services about mental health? Instead, they are overwhelmingly about the containment and or treatment of mental illness. In what sense are they services? Only in the sense that they have more than one client. Thus, the notion of consumer or customer, which is applied more frequently now, is problematic. Although some services may serve the interest of some people who have accessed them on a genuinely voluntary basis, they also serve many third-party interests, such as relatives, strangers in the street and the court system. For many psychiatric patients, professional interventions are imposed rather than requested.

Therapeutic Social Control: Role Conflict and Strain in Mental Health Professionals

The interaction of public and government interests in defining and responding to mental disorder leaves their servants ("mental health professionals"') in an ambiguous role. The ambiguity, involving a mixture of therapeutic intent and a paternalistic willingness to remove liberty and intervene without consent, has provoked much professional debate. At one extreme, the libertarian psychiatrists (such as Szasz) provide an early constructivist critique of mental illness, suggesting that mental illness is a myth because minds can only be sick in a metaphorical sense. Szasz also insisted that coercion should have no part in helping those with "problems of living." When this happens in the modern therapeutic state, psychiatric staff act like witch finders, not healers.

The professional orthodoxy within psychiatry has ignored these unpalatable accusations and favored the idea that mental disability is a primary and natural pathology (not a secondary and constructed product) and that it ipso facto *requires* paternalism. From this idea stems the doctor's right to treat, which is privileged over the patient's right to liberty. Indeed, during the 20th century, psychiatric leaders consistently lobbied to ensure their right to treat.

A contradiction can be noted in the recent rhetorical shift toward a recovery model in psychiatric services and in the assumption that the disabling impact of stigma is purely a matter of public ignorance. Many psychiatrists and mental health professionals see themselves as part of the solution, not part of the problem. Patients are encouraged to seek help early (implying dire consequences further down the line if they "fail to engage with services"). They are encouraged to define recovery by compliance with treatment rather than by their access to everyday experiences of citizenship. There is an assumption that noncompliance with medication is an irrational act rather than one based on the patient's knowledge and informed decision making.

Thus, on the one hand, patients are encouraged to be collaborators in their treatment plans and informed consent is prioritized, but on the other hand, professionals reserve the right to treat on a compulsory basis and to ensure patient compliance. This paradox triggers dilemmas in the relationship between professionals and patients about balancing risk taking and risk minimization, with the continual threat of accusations from third parties that a patient poses a "risk to self or others," something that the third parties believe should be prevented by mental health professionals.

Health professionals are Janus-faced. Potentially, they could be advocates and collaborators, advancing the individual and collective rights of patients in localities to enjoy fuller citizenship. However, at the same time they are often restricted by their constructs of difference, which focus on reified diagnostic categories. They also, consciously or unconsciously, use conservative decision making. If they are charged with a duty of care, which is reinforced by the powers (and thus responsibilities) arising from mental health law, then they will not be blamed for coercively controlling the low-risk patient. However, they will be blamed if they take a risk that results in an incident of harm to self or others. This conservative decision making will work against the rights of patients to be free in favor of risk avoidance.

THE RELATIONSHIP BETWEEN PRIMARY AND SECONDARY DEVIANCE

In the light of the discussion of social determinants of mental health problems and followed by a consideration of the social context of judgments about the value of psychological difference, a tension can be considered by those interested in applying disability theory to mental disorder. For example, it could appear that social determinists have it both ways. On the one hand, it can be reasonably argued from the evidence that social causes (e.g., the social origins of depression) are sound enough. Oppressive social forces and material deprivation make a significant contribution to the generation of human misery. On the other hand, those emphasizing destigmatization and social valorization would seek tolerance of misery and even its positive valuation.

This contradiction revolves around values. Is misery simply an example of psychological difference that is unfairly stigmatized and socially excluded by those around the identified patient? Or is misery an indication of a failure of our common humanity? This tension is even more evident when we consider those who seem to break the social rule of intelligibility. Putting aside arguments about the validity of diagnoses, such as schizophrenia, when some people speak in ways others do not understand (i.e., thought disordered or delusional) or report sensory experiences not seen or heard by others (i.e., hallucinations), under which form of social arrangement might these forms of conduct be valued rather than devalued? In a Western context, where rationality governs daily activity in the home, street, and workplace and holds us all to account in our moment-to-moment activity, the meta-rule of immediate social intelligibility dominates.

Those who are unable or unwilling to comply with this meta-rule are immediately vulnerable to social rejection. Counterexamples can certainly be found, but these are largely in preindustrial or traditional societies (e.g., the ability to have visions or hallucinate could have positive connotations about extraordinary spiritual powers and insights). The ancient philosophers were ambivalent about the value of madness. For Socrates positive aspects of mad rapture included prophesying (a "manic art"), mystical initiations and rituals, poetic inspiration, and the madness of lovers (Screech, 1985). At the same time, Rosen (1968) noted that in ancient Greece and Rome madness was associated stereotypically, as today, with aimless wandering and violence. Thus, we cannot simply argue that the current ubiquitous rejection of madness is a postindustrial phenomenon, but this ambiguity is a useful point of reflection about the immutable pathologization of severe mental disorder.

Within the broad medical discourse of mental disorder, we can identify distinct groups using social criteria. In particular, a distinction is obvious between those who are fully aware of their rule infractions or their inability to fulfill role expectations (e.g., depressed or agoraphobic patients) and those who lack insight. The latter, which could be applied to acutely psychotic patients, has different implications to the former.

Those without insight are better understood in terms of direct social distrust and rejection (i.e., they act in a way that others find, frightening, threatening, or offensive). By contrast, those who are frightened or sad may be inoffensive to others (i.e., they often elicit sympathy and compassion). They knowingly break feeling rules, and their distress is evident to themselves not just others (Thoits, 1986).

Thus, the notion of mental distress does not do justice to the full panoply of mental disorder. It is a linguistic substitute or preferred euphemism for medical labeling, but it is just as limited in its capacity to comprehend the complexity of mental disorder. As we have shown, it is not always the patient's distress that drives the social transaction, it is often the emotional reactions of others (i.e., pity, fear, disgust, and exasperation). This mixed emotional reaction explains why our commonsense reactions to psychological difference become enshrined in social policy as an admixture of paternalism, compassion and controlling rejection, with mental health services being given the responsibility of juggling all these impulses.

The more a society is rule-bound, the more there will be coercive control of psychological difference. But no society (old or new, liberal or authoritarian) is completely indifferent to rule infractions and role failure. These violations tend to bring with them a set of moral and political prescriptions, even if they vary across time and space. Coercion is not unusual in mental health services, whereas it is very rarely applied to people with physical impairments. This coercive nature limits the capacity of services to respond to the demands of citizenship that are articulated by the disability movement. Whereas barriers to person-centeredness and citizenship operate in relation to all people with a disability, the disproportionate lawful use of coercion creates a qualitative shift in the field of mental health.

Similarities and Differences between Physical and Psychological Disability

Given the arguments we have made in this chapter, we can ask whether disability theory (which has been derived strongly from the consideration of physical disability) can be applied to mental deviance. One challenge relates to whether all disabling processes apply equally to the range of conditions that fall within the ambit of health care organizations.

Some constructivists limit their critique to mental illness. For example, an early, and for some notorious, example came from the dissident psychoanalyst Szasz and his declaration about the myth of mental illness (Szasz, 1961). What he proposed was to legitimate the idea that physical illness was not socially negotiated but ontologically stable across time and place. However, the neat boundary that Szasz (1961) aspired to retain between true and mythological pathology was not readily available. One response from political science to this disputed boundary was to frame *all* illness as deviance (Sedgwick, 1982). A different response was from biomedicine: namely, hoped-for reductionism, under which all mental illnesses were assumed to be brain diseases (Baker & Menken, 2001; Guze, 1989).

The logical difficulty of isolating psychiatric labels for particular critical scrutiny is questioned by inflammatory conditions, such as rheumatoid arthritis, psoriasis, irritable bowel syndrome, and asthma. Similar to mental disorders, they appear to run in families. However, they do not follow precise genetic patterns. Also, like mental disorders, they have weak etiological specificity and poor treatment specificity. Analgesics, steroids, immunosuppressants, and even chemotherapies, developed for cancer, can be applied across a range of inflammatory conditions.

The overlap of features between physical and mental disorders, which cannot be denied, coexists with a unified cultural discourse in both the public and professional arenas that there really is some sort of fundamental distinction between mental and physical deviance. When a diagnosis of a functional mental disorder (e.g., major mental illnesses or personality disorders) is made, it is determined completely on a patient's words or actions. This situation can even hold true for the diagnosis of organic mental illnesses, such as dementia. In contrast, it is rare for physical disorders to be diagnosed on grounds of symptoms alone.

Thus, although an overlap of epistemic features can be demonstrated between mental and physical illness, mental illness has become separate for most of us most of the time for a number of reasons.

- We tend to think of physical injuries, diseases, and ailments *happening* to us, whereas we *are* mentally ill. Mental illness implicates the whole self, which, as a consequence, becomes discreditable (Fabrega & Manning, 1972). However, to temper this distinction, we can note that occasionally this negative socioethical attribution has also been a feature of physical conditions, such as sexually transmitted diseases, tuberculosis, and cancer. Many forms of physical illness have been associated with shame and moral failure.
- The body is *potentially* explicable in physical terms, whereas human conduct can *only* be understood meaningfully via interpretive methods. Hermeneutics not biomedical science is implied (Ingleby, 1980).
- Coercion is commonly applied to those deemed to be suffering from mental disorders, but is rare for those with physical diagnoses. Mentally ill patients are deemed to lack cognitive capacity about their actions far more often than physically ill patients. In the latter case, mental capacity loss is either very temporary (e.g., concussed patient or a hypoglycemic diabetic) or is the result of serious brain trauma. The bulk of physically ill people, even when terminally ill, are deemed to retain their cognitive capacity, whereas people with psychiatric illness are usually considered to have lost their reason.
- At the turn of the 20th century, when institutional care was being eroded, a pecking order of citizenship could be seen in the disabled population. By the mid-20th century, the great bulk of physically disabled people were not in residential care, whereas those with mental health problems and learning disabilities were still overwhelmingly warehoused in institutions. Mental disability was therefore dealt with differently. This othering of people with mental disorders is also discernible generally in society. Stigma is attached to many forms of physical disability, but only epilepsy seems to evoke the same degree of fear, prejudice, and social rejections as mental disorder. These socioaffective responses are a ready platform to justify coercive containment and treatment.

These similarities and differences suggest that on the one hand, hard-and-fast distinctions between physical and psychological difference in society are difficult to construct. On the other hand, they are regularly distinguished, by both professionals and the public, particularly in societies that maintain and reproduce forms of fundamental Cartesian dualism. Probably the strongest distinction relates to the narrow preoccupation in the field of mental disorder with symptoms. Symptoms of mental illness tend to reflect incapacity in relation to role failure and rule infraction, whereas bodily signs of physical conditions are carried across all social settings.

For example, untreated Type I diabetic patients, with their extinct pancreatic cells, will simply die wherever they are. By contrast, people who hallucinate might be discounted as schizophrenics or valued as mystics depending on their social context. Thus, the sick role exists to signal and excuse role failure for those with both physical or psychological problems. However, a psychiatric diagnosis signals a much wider inability to be trusted to follow the rules when operating within a social framework of rationality or moral order. It is only when that moral order values the nonrational that the patient is permitted a socially valued position. Interestingly, nonrational thinking and behavior has its place in artistic and spiritual arenas, so the less a society values these aspects, the more dismissive it will be of psychological deviance.

CONCLUSION

This chapter examined mental disorder in the wider context of the relationship of disability to society to reorient analysis from a focus on the individual to the wider mechanisms and processes of social oppression, discrimination, and exclusion. We have adopted a form of weak rather than strong constructivism throughout, in line with a critical realist approach. The advantage of this approach is that allows us to accept evidence about the social determination of mental disorder, while giving due weight to the shifting and variegated value positions of communities of interest. Communities of interest include professionals, patients, and their significant others, all of whom are embedded within cultural norms about the tolerance or value applied to psychological difference in society.

Those norms vary across time and space—a fact that tempers any naive realist approach to the topic, as is found in the universalism of psychiatric positivism or medical naturalism. To give an illustrative example of this distinction, schizophrenia is a dubious social construction, but some people do hear voices that their fellows do not hear. The critical question then relates to the social value that is ascribed to voice-hearing in particular times, places, or cultures. Similarly, fear and sadness are universal and transhistorical phenomena (found in all mammals, not just humans) but the meanings and social value placed on them vary across time and place.

We also raised some questions in this chapter about the extent to which physical and mental health problems can be conceptually and socially conflated. Though socialized ourselves in Cartesian dualism, we tried to reflect on the dilemmas this creates for social science. At this stage of reflection we can identify similarities, ambiguities, and some persuasive distinctions. In other words, the two types of deviance have much in common, but there is a residual sense that mental disorder *is* different. This difference cannot be simply explained away by the conventions of lazy dualistic thought.

Several grounds were offered to support this conclusion, but the strongest relates to the overreliance on public and professional labeling of what incipient patients say and do rather than on any demonstrable deviation from anatomical or physiological norms. This preoccupation with rule infraction (rather than the focus on impaired roles that is usually associated with physical disability) leads to a shift in focus in dealing with mental disorder. Thus, the socioaffective dimensions to mental disorder are important to understand.

People with mental health problems are viewed as not complying with rules, in a variety of ways and to various degrees. In turn, this view produces a range of affective responses from nonpatients, including fear, loathing, perplexity, and exasperation. In turn, these strong emotional drivers create a social distance between the deviant and the nondeviant actors. In this field of othering we find the rationales or rationalizations for stigma, social exclusion, and therapeutic social control. In the case of mental disorder, this is disproportionately coercive and violates the norms of natural justice. With the exception of laws against terrorism, there are very few examples in liberal democracies where lawful detention without trial can be applied to the prospective rather than past conduct of adults. Mental health legislation is one of those examples.

REFERENCES

Aneschensel, C. S., & Succoff, S. (1996). The neighbourhood context of mental health. *Journal of Health and Social Behaviour, 37*, 293–311.

Baker, M., & Menken, M. (2001). Time to abandon mental illness. *British Medical Journal, 322*, 937.

Bean, P. (1980). *Compulsory admissions to mental hospitals.* London: Wiley.

Bloch, S., & Reddaway, P. (1978). *Russia's Political Hospitals.* Futura Publications Ltd, London.

Coulter, J. (1973). Approaches to . Insanity. New York: Wiley.

Dooley, D., Prause, J., & Ham-Rowbottom, K. A. (2000). Underemployment and depression: Longitudinal relationships. *Journal of Health and Social Behaviour, 41*, 421–436.

Fabrega, H., & Manning, P. K. (1972). Disease, illness and deviant careers. In R. A. Scott & J. D. Douglas (Eds.), *Theoretical perspectives on deviance.* New York: Basic Books.

Faris, R. E., & Dunham, W. H. (1939). *Mental disorders in urban areas: An ecological study of schizophrenia and other psychoses.* Chicago: University of Chicago Press.

Fryer, D. (1995). Labour market disadvantage, deprivation and mental health. *Psychologist, 8*(6), 265–272.

Fryers, T., Melzer, D., & Jenkins, R. (2001). *Mental health inequalities report 1: A systematic literature review.* Cambridge: Cambridge University, Department of Public Health and Primary Care.

Goffman, E. (1961). *Asylums: Essays on the social situation of mental patients and other inmates.* New York: Anchor Books.

Goldsmith, H. F., Holzer, C. E., & Manderscheid, R.W. (1998). Neighbourhood characteristics and mental illness. *Evaluation and Program Planning, 21*, 211–225.

Guze, S. (1989). Biological psychiatry: Is there any other kind? *Psychological Medicine, 19*, 315–323.

Ingleby, D. (Ed). (1980). *Critical psychiatry.* Harmondsworth: Penguin.

Kasl, S. V., Rodrigues, E. & Lasch, K. E. (1998). The impact of unemployment on health and well being. In B. P. Dohrenwend (Ed.), *Adversity, stress and psychopathology.* Oxford: Oxford University Press.

Knapp, M. (2001). The costs of mental disorder. In G. Thornicroft & G. Szmuckler (Eds.), *Textbook of community psychiatry*. Oxford: Oxford University Press.

Meyer, J.E. (1988). The fate of the mentally ill in Germany during the Third Reich. *Psychological Medicine, 18*: 575–81.

Patel, V. (2001). Poverty, inequality and mental health in developing countries. In D. Leon & G. Walt (Eds.), *Poverty, inequality and health*. Oxford: Oxford University Press.

Paykel, E. S., Abbott, R., Jenkins, R., Brugha, T. S., & Meltzer, H. (2000). Urban-rural mental health differences in Great Britain: Findings from the National Morbidity Survey. *Psychological Medicine, 30*(2), 269–280.

Rosenberg, M., & Pearlin, L. (1978). Social class and self esteem among children and adults. *American Journal of Sociology, 84*(1), 53–77.

Pilgrim, D., & Bentall, R. P. (1998). The medicalisation of misery: A critical realist analysis of the concept of depression. *Journal of Mental Health, 8*(3), 261–274.

Pilgrim, D., Rogers, A., & Bentall, R. (In press). The centrality of personal relationships in the creation and amelioration of mental health problems: The current interdisciplinary case. *Health*.

Read, J., Agar, K., Argyle, N., & Aderhold, V. (2003). Sexual and physical abuse during childhood and adulthood as predictors of hallucinations, delusions and thought disorder. *Psychology and Psychotherapy: Research, Theory and Practice, 76*, 11–22.

Rogers, A., & Pilgrim, D. (2003). *Mental health and inequality*. London: Palgrave.

Rogers, A., & Pilgrim, D. (2005). *A sociology of mental health and illness* (3rd ed.). Maidenhead: Open University Press.

Rosen, G. (1968). *Public Health and Mental Health: Converging Trends and Emerging Issues in Madness in Society*: Chapters in the historical sociology of mental illness. London: Routledge & Kegan Paul.

Ross, C. (2000). Neighbourhood disadvantage and adult depression. *Journal of Health and Social Behaviour, 41*, 177–187.

Sampson, R. J. (1988). Local friendship ties and community attachment. *American Sociological Review, 53*, 766–779.

Screech, M. A. (1985). Good madness in Christendom. In W. F. Bynum, R. Porter, & M. Shepherd (Eds.), *The anatomy of madness: Essays in the history of psychiatry*, vol. I. London: Tavistock.

Sedgwick, P. (1982). *Psychopolitics*. London: Pluto Press.

Stone, M. (1985). Shellshock and the psychologists. In W. F. Bynum, R. Porter, & M. Shepherd (Eds.), *The anatomy of madness*. London: Tavistock.

Szasz, T. S. (1961). The use of naming and the origin of the myth of mental illness. *American Psychologist, 16*, 59–65.

Thoits, P. (1986). Multiple identities: Examining gender and marital status differences in distress. *American Sociological Review, 51*, 259–272.

Whitfield, C., Dube, S., Felitti, V., & Anda, R. (2005). Adverse childhood experiences and hallucinations. *Child Abuse and Neglect, 29*, 797–781.

CHAPTER 13

Parental Perspectives on Disability: The Story of Sam, Anna, and Marcus

Heather Douglas and Sally Borbasi

Sam and Anna named their last child Marcus. A few days after Anna and Marcus left the hospital and went home, Sam went back to work, and the older children returned to school. Anna noticed Marcus was fussy, was not easy to feed, or didn't sleep well day or night. She became very tired but tried to keep the household running smoothly. She was very irritable, but hoped the situation would settle down soon. Marcus reacted badly to the first childhood inoculation and cried for three days. Anna phoned the immunization center for advice and was told to give him acetaminophen. One month later, Sam was asked to relocate and work in a different city for a few months. Anna felt she could not cope alone and opted for the whole family to move.

After being in the new city for a few months, Anna became concerned. Marcus was making no attempt to roll or crawl. He was still a fussy feeder, did not seem to respond to speech, and reacted badly when placed on carpet or grass. He cried a lot, and quickly became over stimulated and agitated when in unfamiliar surroundings. It was not easy to go out with him in busy or noisy environments or if there was any delay involved. Shopping was difficult. Sam cared for the children on weekends while Anna did essential shopping or visited the hairdresser, but it was impossible for her to get to services, such as the dentist, unless they opened on weekends.

Anna took Marcus to the local children's service when the family returned to their home town. The service was busy; there was a long queue to see the nurse. Marcus became very agitated and screamed a great deal, so Anna wandered the building with him until it was her turn. The nurse weighed Marcus. He was very underweight. Anna wanted to ask about Marcus' slow physical development but the nurse said the 10 minute appointment was finished.

She suggested Anna come back again the next week to discuss how to introduce new foods. Anna asked if she could make an appointment, or phone instead, but was told the service operated only as a drop-in. The waiting with Marcus had been difficult and embarrassing. Anna did not return.

Marcus was behind on all developmental milestones. At three years he had limited speech, was not toilet trained, and although walking, his gait was unsteady so he often fell and injured himself. He needed constant supervision. He did not play like other children, his attention span was short, and he was impulsive and fearless. He did unpredictable and bizarre things, such as climbing furniture and jumping, hitting other children, lunging onto a busy road, or trying to get out of a vehicle traveling at full speed. Anna was terrified she would lose Marcus in shopping centers and tied him to her so he could not escape. At home she always locked the doors and windows securely. Marcus did not sleep through the night. Anna got up to ensure his safety. To get as much sleep as possible, Anna went to bed as soon as the children did, but Sam usually stayed up late, so she and Sam were not together much.

Sam complained about Anna's sleeping habits and the lack of sex. He was concerned about the situation at home, and considered his primary responsibility was to provide for his family. To survive, the family needed his income. He could provide for his family by concentrating on his work. This was the most important thing he could do. He prioritized his work over family issues. Sam could do no more to help at home than he was already, but he could supply a secure future for them by building his career. He did not discuss this situation with Anna because there were no other options. Sam left Anna to care for the children. He did not get involved with Marcus. Sam saw Anna was very involved and knew she would tell him if there was something he needed to do. He concentrated on his job prospects. He wanted to succeed and make a career. He started to work long hours, usually coming home after the children were in bed. He was promoted, but the job had some tensions. He did not talk much to Anna as she always seemed tired.

Anna continually felt irritable, stressed, and anxious. She often shouted at the children, but usually at home when no one was around. There seemed to be no relief from constantly attending to family problems. One of the children was hitting and biting other children at preschool. Although concerned, Anna did not know what to do. The oldest child often wet the bed at night and seemed very unhappy at school. Anna made an appointment with a social worker, was referred to a psychologist, and implemented rewards programs, but the bed wetting continued. In frustration, Sam threatened to beat the child if the bed wetting did not stop. Anna intervened. She stayed alert at all times to protect the children. It became her job to get up at night; after all, she wasn't working. Anna would have liked to return to work, but could not find suitable care for Marcus. He was too demanding and was not offered a child care place. None of Anna's friends agreed to care for him, and with no family living nearby, the only option was to become a full-time mother. It was easier to stay at home. Anna's life contracted. Money was tight with only one income. Sam and Anna's social life declined. There was never an escape. There was no money for a holiday. The family was fragile.

Anna continued to seek support services. She took Marcus to a variety of health practitioners who examined him, took a history of his condition, and then referred her elsewhere. The appointments and tests were expensive, but she felt obliged to go to provide the best possible future for Marcus. One helping agency told Anna they must talk to Sam before they might offer a service. Sam attended the interview and indicated he was aware of the issues with Marcus' behavior. The service asked Anna to implement a home program. This was more work. Anna asked if Marcus could attend the early intervention program at the agency instead, but was told he was too old. Nor did Marcus qualify for the special school. She looked for other services but found the criteria always excluded Marcus: he did not have the appropriate condition, his behavior was too difficult to fit in with other children, he was the wrong age or capability level, not at the appropriate intelligence level, the service did not cover the area where they lived, and so on. Anna really wanted services to help Marcus. She complained to regional directors of education, disability, and health services. She wrote to relevant ministers. She received polite letters outlining the present policies, but no offer of services. Anna was unsure what else she could do. She felt she should be able to cope—after all, she had been a competent professional woman before having the children.

Anna observed that services were more attentive when Sam was present. They tended to talk to Sam, negotiate any change or commitment, and then discuss ongoing program implementation or future appointments with Anna. As a committed feminist and previously successful career professional, Anna found it rather strange that the mainly female staff in support agencies privileged Sam as the family decision maker while expecting Anna to deliver the traditional caring role. Sam did not notice this tendency, but did not dispute it when Anna mentioned it. Subsequently, he accompanied Anna if there a serious issue was to be discussed.

Sam was puzzled about the issues at home. His relationship with Anna had been good before the children arrived, but now there seemed to be lots of tension. He was not really sure why Anna seemed so stressed. He tried to talk to her, but she seemed to avoid conversations about their relationship. He knew he could not fix the family problems himself, so instead he preferred to focus on aspects of his life where he could be useful. He did not search for help. The helping agencies did not contact him. Sam had other concerns. On top of the problems at home, he had missed out on work promotions. He wondered if his career had come to a halt. He looked for a second job. He seemed distracted. He did solitary things at home. Sam devoted himself to the garden. He took up fishing. He rejected Anna's suggestion he might be depressed. He was emphatic he did not need assistance or medication. He had no need to discuss his private concerns in public domains, and would not have been comfortable probing personal parts of his life with strangers. His private life was not for public consumption. He might reveal his concerns to a trusted friend, in private, preferably during a quiet time alone while they were fishing. This person must be someone special. It must be a person Sam had confidence in. It would certainly be a man; Sam didn't want to talk to a woman about his personal issues. It would be someone who would offer useful advice but not be judgmental or reveal his secrets. Otherwise there was no advantage in exposing himself. It might be an older relative or someone who had been in similar circumstances. Sam had no such friend or relative. He remained silent. For several years, Sam and Anna's relationship was loving but brittle.

Marcus did small tasks for this mother and helped his father with jobs. He played with his siblings. Sam took him fishing. Home and family was a safe haven for Marcus, but otherwise he seemed lonely, friendless, and isolated. Children were reluctant to play with him after school. He was never invited to birthday parties. Every Sunday night he cried at the thought of returning to school the next day. Sam was distressed. He contacted the school to discuss the issue, but was assured that everything was fine. When possible, Anna attended school functions to observe Marcus interacting with other children. He often reacted badly to teasing and seemed to be an easy target. The school refused to increase supervision and instead suggested Marcus would benefit from an anger management program. Anna searched for a more accommodating school where he would be free of bullying.

The new school was much better for Marcus. Although he was still teased, the school responded to Anna's request to manage the situation. Marcus could contact a staff member at any time to clarify issues or if he needed support. This made a lot of difference. Marcus still had no friends, but he no longer seemed unhappy at school. Anna got a part-time job. For the first time, the family was able to go out to dinner to celebrate a birthday. Sam bought a computer. The children were delighted they now could exchange computer games with school friends. To celebrate their wedding anniversary, Anna organized a weekend away with no children—their first in many years since the children were born. The older children could be left alone, but Marcus needed to be somewhere safe. This was difficult: no family lived nearby and Marcus had no close friends. The family took a beach holiday instead. Sam and Anna's relationship improved a little. They started a social life. Sometimes they went out in the evenings without Marcus. Finally, Sam was promoted. He felt more positive. Life seemed better. Anna started a full-time job with increased responsibilities. She found it very rewarding and the increased family income was very welcome, but finding time for Marcus was difficult. She often had to negotiate time off work to take Marcus for assessments or attend the school to discuss behavioral issues.

Marcus was in trouble—an official warning from the police. It might have been much worse if they had not been considerate of his disability. This was serious. Sam convened a family meeting and instructed Marcus to apologize to each family member. Marcus was crying. The family was distressed. Sam had tears in his eyes. The family had a big hug. The problem was never mentioned again. Later Sam explained male discipline to Anna:

> Boys understand pain. They can cope. Even if it is really painful at the time, boys prefer to get it over and done with than to have it dragging on. They prefer immediate action, even direct physical punishment. It might be painful, but there are no long term repercussions. Fathers understand because that's what happened to them. They have done a lot of this stuff themselves. This is a father's way of providing discipline. It might seem hard at the time, but it's

over and done with now. Boys prefer that to a long drawn-out punishment, or emotional blackmail.

To have more time for Marcus, Anna gave up her full-time job. Marcus bumped through the middle years of school. He was elected to school leadership roles. He delighted in the extra attention and status and seemed to perform well. By the mid-teen years he no longer seemed unhappy. He was attracted to girls. He joined a drama group and a dance group and took up singing and public speaking. He was an excellent entertainer. He expressed a desire to establish a theater career. Sam was concerned. He worried about how Marcus could earn an adequate living in the precarious cultural industry when he still had trouble negotiating routine daily activities. Being able to eat and pay the rent was extremely important. Marcus would have to find a suitable job that paid a decent income to support himself. He was cheery and kind, but not worldly. He was generous by nature and had no concept of the value of money. He had already been robbed. He was easily persuaded, and sometimes his judgment was poor. He was not wary of Internet scams and con artists. He had trouble making appropriate decisions. He had trouble identifying potentially dangerous situations. Although he now reliably attended to his personal hygiene, he often neglected to do routine tasks even if requested to do so. He still did not do ordinary social things, such as return phone calls or attend to his responsibilities at home. He did not attend to deadlines. He never thought to ask for assistance. His negotiations skills were minimal. He either had no friends or made friends with people who tended to lead him astray.

Sam suggested Marcus would be better off in more regular employment rather than working in the theater. He suggested Marcus could look where work was more abundant. He suggested some possible jobs, but did not continue when Marcus clearly was not interested. Anna took over this role. She spent many hours discussing future options with Marcus. She made suggestions about courses he could do when school was finished, and what kinds of jobs they might lead to. She taught him how to read a map and find his way around new places. She coached his budgeting and banking habits. She encouraged him to learn to drive, took him shopping, and advised him on the relative value of different kinds of goods. She taught him to cook and do the laundry. He became proficient in most household tasks. He took responsibility for mowing the lawn and barbecue cooking.

Marcus completed school and started applying for jobs. Sam coached him on how to approach potential employers and answer the kinds of interview questions they were likely to ask. A school friend persuaded Marcus into a sales job. After one week he was asked to leave. His fast food job lasted a little longer. Anna suggested this was not the best type of work for someone with his skills and abilities. Marcus did not get another job for several months. Although content living at home, he seemed unsure what he wanted to do with his life or what kind of work he could do successfully. To encourage him to become more alert to life dangers, Anna organized for Marcus to live with another family for a period. This was expensive for the family, but it might help Marcus learn how to make decisions. The host family was kind and considerate and provided minimal supervision. He had to look after himself and organize his travel. Anna organized two different ways for Marcus to reach the family at any time when he might be distressed. She drilled him in how and when to contact them if anything went wrong, and reminded him always to have his phone with him. Marcus went camping with a group. He lost his phone and half his gear. He traveled alone to sightsee in another city for a week. Potentially this was very hazardous. Sam and Anna worried a lot but resisted contacting Marcus. He returned apparently without catastrophe—at least he shared no problems with his parents. Maybe Marcus talked to his siblings? Sam and Anna respected his privacy and did not ask.

Gradually Marcus' siblings left home. He continued to live with his parents while completing postschool study. He grew a beard. Sometimes he went out at night and didn't return. Sam offered advice on how to mix drinks at parties. He discussed dating and how to approach girls, talked about the need for safe sex. Anna showed him where to buy condoms. Sam discussed how to be a man and masculine social customs, such as how to greet older women and when to wear a suit and tie. He showed Marcus how to change a tap washer and how to maintain a car. Sam and Anna left for a week's holiday. They returned to find Marcus had been very ill but had not gone to the doctor, contacted his siblings, or sought help from neighbors. He was ill for several months. Marcus organized more solitary trips. These seemed successful, or at least without serious mishaps. He organized a visit to another country alone. Sam and Anna prepared him for a month to ensure he understood potential dangers and coping strategies. Anna helped him pack, Sam gave him extra money. After a week, Marcus sent a text message he was in hospital, then another that he had lost his credit card. Sam wanted more details. Anna phoned Marcus to discuss strategies. Marcus did not make contact again for several weeks. Anna worried constantly about potential dangers and possible problems. It was a difficult balance to let Marcus take risks and learn to manage his life while trying to help him stay out of trouble. To become fully independent, Marcus must be respected as a competent person. Sam worried much less. It was normal for boys to take risks. He trusted Marcus. Eventually he would learn how to manage. Marcus would grow up and become a respectable citizen. He left Marcus to get on with his life.

Sam was offered another new job. It required a move to another new town. What about Marcus? Sam worried about the future for his son. Was he ready to live away from home successfully? Did he still need supervision? The caring role had ceased for the other children, but they might have to care for Marcus forever. Would Marcus ever leave home? Unless he did, Sam and Anna would have to maintain a carer's role and close contact with Marcus for the rest of their lives. Their role was not difficult, but there was no break, ever. They loved their son, but the constant vigilance was wearing. Sam and Anna wanted some time together with no children before they were too old to enjoy life.

THE IMPACT OF DISABILITY ON PARENTS

This case of Anna, Sam, and Marcus shows how disability influences the daily life of all family members. Disability affects the health and well-being of both parents (Dyson, 1997; Heller, Hsieh, & Rowitz, 1997; Raina et al., 2005), but mothers and fathers are affected in different ways (Krauss, 1993). Particularly when children are young, families with a disabled child have a higher degree of stress than families without a disabled child (Hadadian, 1994), and this impacts not only the immediate family but grandparents and wider family structures (Findler & Taubman, 2003; Roach, Orsmond, & Barratt, 1999). Parental stress is critical to the future of the children and the family, so it is important to understand how and why parents respond differently.

Most research focuses on mothers, so the impact of disability on mothers is much better recognized than the consequences for fathers (Hornby, 1995). Mothers may *express* more emotion than fathers, but both parents report a similar level of stress (Dyson, 1997; Pruchno & Patrick, 1999; Saloviita, Italinna, & Leinonen, 2003). Mothers may be more exposed than fathers to the strains of providing direct everyday child care and to the responsibilities of managing economic hardship in the family (Ross & VanWilligen, 1996). However, fathers experience different kinds of stress, often associated with attachment to their children, their children's behavior and temperament, social acceptance of the child, and concerns about the future (Hadadian, 1994; Saloviita, Italinna, & Leinonen, 2003). Like mothers, fathers plan for the future of their children—they love their children as much as mothers, but they interact with them differently (Bruce, Schultz, & Smyrnios, 1996; Ricci & Hodapp, 2003; Russell & Russell, 1994). There are several reasons fathers and mothers respond differently when they have a child with a disability. Mothers and fathers bring equal but different contributions to the life of a child with a disability. They use different coping strategies and different social expectations are placed on them. Further, helping services treat them differently.

DIFFERENT COPING STRATEGIES

Following the birth of a child, men find their fathering role rewarding but also challenging (St John, Cameron, & McVeigh, 2005). Fathers tend to gradually and steadily adjust to their changed situation, whereas mothers report patterns of continuous sorrow and periodic crises (Katz, 2002). Mothers usually are more involved in delivering daily care, whereas fathers tend to focus more on matters external to the family (Pelchat, Lefebvre, & Perreault, 2003). The extent of daily support is important for mothers, whereas fathers are more sensitive to the external environment (Krauss, 1993). Research has shown that mothers cope by adjusting to their circumstances and looking inward to their home—family becomes their entire life. In contrast, fathers tend not to separate from the world—instead, they focus on their external world (Pelchat et al., 2003).

Research has also shown that fathers worry more than mothers about the long-term implications of their child's disability. For instance, in a study exploring the transition of people with a disability from institutional care to community-based housing, Borbasi, Bottroff, Hunt, and Williams (2005) found fathers expressed equal concern for their child's well-being as mothers.

They reported a sense of "always being worried" about the child even though these children were well into adulthood. One father whose profoundly disabled adult daughter was recently placed into care expressed relief he no longer worried "what's going to happen to her if we die." Whereas mothers tended to focus on the emotional aspects of their child's life trajectory (i.e., the need for comfort and dignity), fathers raised more practical concerns. Many fathers went to great lengths to modify their homes to enable their child to come home at weekends. One father described how he modified a $1,200 special boot for his son so that it no longer caused pressure sores. "One night at 10 o'clock I said 'we'll make something.' We went to the shed got a bit of plywood and I shaped it to his lower foot and up his calf and his mother padded it" (Borbasi et al., 2005).

When asked about the community house his daughter now lived in, another father stated he believed she was better off, but he had noticed several drawbacks in the house that included cupboards and mirrors that were too high, a risk for those that were bed-bound if there was a fire, and significantly inefficient use of electricity. He had a number of practical solutions but stated that no one was interested in his opinions or suggestions. "People like me [and my wife] with years and years of experience with a family member being disabled . . . nobody takes any notice of us. . . . We're not listened to, nobody cares about us and what we think, what hardships we've gone through."

Several studies have identified differences in the impact of disability on fathers. A child's disability had a significant effect on the fathers' sense of competence and self-esteem, which then affected marital satisfaction (Katz, 2002). Fathers helped by playing with the child, providing discipline, and deciding on services (Simmerman, Blacher, & Baker, 2001). The fathers' involvement with the child improved the mothers' sense of well-being. Although fathers were equally committed as mothers to the welfare of their family, activities beyond their home, such as their work, were important to their personal well-being (Ellis et al., 2002). Success at work was important. Increasing external activities, such as employment, reduced the father's stress, and a higher family income was related to higher marital satisfaction, but it tended to increase their isolation from spouses (Willoughby & Glidden, 1995). Hence, increasing working hours for fathers may reduce the intimacy between the parents and result in less marital satisfaction. Indeed, fathers who have a child with a disability are more inclined to leave the family than fathers without a child with a disability (Hornby, 1995). Marital breakdown creates a double disadvantage for families by reducing the physical, financial, and emotional support two people can provide.

Both parents reported a need for support, but they sought support in different ways. Mothers are visible. They openly talk to others about their situation and use positive coping strategies more frequently than fathers (Laws, 1998; McLinden, 1990). Mothers seek interpersonal contact to reduce their isolation and access support from a variety of sources (Katz, 2002; Pelchat et al., 2003). Mothers are comfortable seeking support and assistance from family members, friends, and helping agencies. They ask for help, and doing so is not seen as a sign of incompetence or failure.

Like mothers, fathers feel emotions about their child and their situation but display their emotions less often and less publicly (Lillie, 1993). Men value their relationships as much as women, but rely on a different communication style that does not always enable them to discuss their personal problems. For instance, fathers have been found to be less likely to request help, and thus less likely to find support for their needs (Pelchat et al., 2003). They are raised to be strong and conceal their emotions, which may account for fathers' needs being overlooked by helping agencies.

Sam preferred not to discuss his feelings. He preferred to use cognitive approaches to problem solving, mull over issues alone, and muddle through by himself, assuming he should be able to manage, and presuming he would manage if he could just find the right solution. Asking for help may have implied he was incompetent, that he could not cope. In general, fathers were less inclined to acknowledge difficulties publicly, even if they find the situation problematic (Rodrigue, Morgan, & Geffken, 1992). Instead, they concentrate on tasks and achieving outcomes (Laws, 1998; Skene, 1998). This approach may appear adaptive (i.e., attending to problems and seeking solutions), but there may be no solutions to the issues and concerns of having a child with a disability.

DIFFERENT SOCIAL EXPECTATIONS FOR MOTHERS AND FATHER

Mothering is a social institution, and mothers are expected to become absorbed in their children. This societal role is nonnegotiable; it is not discretionary. Mothers are recognized as an essential part of a child's life (Skene, 1998). The mothering role and the child's future are intertwined, and if mothers fail to commit to their children, they will be socially ostracized. When a mother has a child with a disability, additional roles are added to the usual tasks of family care (Crowe, VanLeit, Berghmans, & Mann, 1997), and these additional demands have an impact. Often mothers are expected to contribute to the child's therapy. They may have additional health tasks to attend to beyond the usual care children require. On the basis of the social requirements of motherhood, mothers must become absorbed in providing all the care their child with a disability requires. There is often little choice for mothers as the child must be cared for, and society expects this nurturing work to be provided by mothers. Society may offer sympathy and agencies may provide support, but mothers must adjust their lives and wholly commit to their children.

Research has found that mothers are more prepared than fathers to strive to achieve high standards of care for their children with disabilities (Pelchat et al., 2003). Mothers are expected to assume control, take charge of the child's situation, and assume responsibility (Crowe, VanLeit, & Berghmans, 2000). They get to know their child better than anyone else. They make decisions about the child and organize the family. A mother of a child with a disability learns to focus on their child, but inadvertently the mother's role may not leave much role for fathers (Pelchat et al., 2003). Mothers are expected to take primary responsibility for the household and children, and fathers are often considered peripheral (Skene, 1998).

Nevertheless, fathers are significant and play an important role in modern families (Laws, 1998). Fathers are as aware of problems and issues with their children and experience grief to the same extent as mothers, but they experience the family situation differently, which influences their actions (Pelchat, Lefebvre, & Levert, 2007). Indeed, a father's role is often cast as being separate from his children (Lillie, 1993). Fathers as well as mothers require emotional and practical support to maintain the family, particularly when a child has a disability, but the circumstances and contributions of fathers is less recognized than for mothers (Lillie, 1993; Nicholson & Rempel, 2004).

Although fathers may wish to be engaged in the daily care of their children, many traditions and customs constrain their opportunities to do so. Fathers are expected to maintain full-time jobs and have the main responsibility for providing financially for their family. Having a child with a disability affects the decisions both parents make about employment (Einam & Cuskelly, 2002). Indeed, mothers of children with disabilities often struggle to adjust to the change in their family role and also have to reassess their expectations of employment. In modern societies, mothers have an expectation of continuing paid employment (Lupton & Schmied, 2002). Paid employment offers considerable personal benefits to mothers, including opportunities for self-fulfillment and increased self-esteem. However, mothers of children with disabilities have been found to have much lower employment levels than mothers with dependent children who do not have disabilities (Shearn & Todd, 2000). Shearn and Todd (2000) found the ability to work was influenced by many factors, not the least of which is the societal demand to care for a child with needs. It was more difficult for these mothers to access suitable child care or to find work that fitted their family responsibilities. Mothers who worked full-time became stressed by the dual demands of work and home. They found employment difficult. Conversely, those who decided not to work had little relief from their care responsibilities, which increased their sense of isolation and feelings of low self-worth. Either way they felt they had failed as mothers (Shearn & Todd, 2000). Another study (Einam & Cuskelly, 2002) found that mothers tended to work fewer hours, but those who worked had better psychological health.

Although some fathers reduce the time they are in paid employment to be able to contribute to caring responsibilities, most felt the need to work longer hours to provide a higher income for the family and enable the family to better meet its requirements created by the disability. Especially when children were young, fathers who increased their hours of work reported fewer needs for support than those who did not increase their work (Ellis et al., 2002). Fathers found personal satisfaction and fulfillment in their work environments, but their decision to work longer hours affected the emotional health of the family (Einam & Cuskelly, 2002).

Both directly and indirectly, fathers make meaningful emotional contributions to the family (Skene, 1998). Children become stronger emotionally when fathers are involved in their direct care (McKeering & Pakenham, 2000). Mothers provided better emotional care for their children when fathers provided emotional support to mothers (Hadadian, 1994). In the current social structures, however, fathers are less involved in providing daily care for the family than mothers (Skene, 1998).

DIFFERENT RESPONSES OF HELPING AGENCIES

The approach of helping agencies determines the different ways mothers and fathers respond to having a child with a disability. Services need to consider how they interact with and discuss disability-related issues with parents. In Sam and Anna's case, the father was taken more seriously than the mother when he attended an agency interview. Mothers are present at these meetings more often than fathers, but anecdotal evidence seems to suggest that if fathers do attend, agency staff interpret the issue as being more significant.

Couples always commence their disability journey as a result of contact with a health service of some kind. Health agencies provide the first diagnosis, either at birth in the hospital, or later through medical services. Health services tend to focus on fixing health problems, but often a disability does not manifest as a major health problem. Not all children with a disability are sick. For instance, if a child has autism or learning disabilities, they may not come to the attention of health professionals and will be unlikely to be prescribed medication or medical interventions. Disability is a lifestyle issue, not necessarily a health issue. In general, health services concentrate on providing diagnostic services based on scientific evidence. Health services excel in assessment and diagnosis. Health services offer solutions to illness, cures, and normative outcomes. However, there is no cure for disability, and there may be no conventionally normal lifestyle that results from intervention by a health service. Disability is not a disease, but a socially constructed circumstance.

Over time, families engage with helping agencies beyond the health system. Helping agencies provide a wide variety of support services that vary depending on the particular disability and the family's situation. However, there are patterns in the relationships formed between helping agencies and parents of children with disabilities that differ from those found in the health system. Anna discovered there was a tendency for busy helping professionals to interact with and focus on the mother when agencies relate to couples with a child with a disability. They give paperwork to the mother, not the father. They ask her to complete details of the child and the disability. They direct questions to the mother about the child's history and the family's current situation. Helping agencies acknowledge the family care work of mothers and assume that mothers will be responsible primarily for caring for the child. They expect mothers to become the expert caregiver, which puts the father at risk of being isolated from the family unit (Katz, 2002).

This presumption is evident in all agencies, including medical specialists, screening services, support services, schools, and government agencies. Helping agencies acknowledge the father, but they tend to be mother-oriented (Skene, 1998). They expect to talk to the mother. Throughout the child's life, agencies continue to contact mothers to discuss problems or issues concerning the child, presuming mothers will be the first point of contact for all issues. The father is contacted only if the mother is unavailable, or if there is a very serious problem where both parents need to be interviewed.

Fathers observe and absorb this practice. They learn that the child with a disability is "mother territory." Fathers, even those with a professional background and highly responsible positions, quickly understand that in the Western health care system agency contact is skewed toward mothers.

To complicate this situation, most contact between helping agencies and the family takes place during business hours, when fathers are usually at work. A father may take time off work to attend the first few interviews about the child, but over time he prioritizes his work commitments to provide for the family's material needs (Laws, 1998; Skene, 1998). Thus, even if they wish to be involved with their child's treatment, fathers tend not to engage with helping agencies. After several years, fathers withdraw and leave the domain of helping agencies to mothers. Fathers concentrate on attending to other matters where their input is valued more highly, such as paid work. Confining service contact to office hours is therefore an exclusionary practice that limits the engagement fathers can have in their child's life. Children with disabilities need both parents to be involved with their daily activities and their future. Although helping agencies may not intend to exclude fathers, the practical arrangements tend to prevent fathers from becoming involved in the systematic care of their child.

Perhaps because fathers are less visible, few helping agencies adequately acknowledge them, but focus more on the needs of the mother and the child. Few agencies offer services or information to fathers or support them in their role (Hadadian, 1994). Agencies seldom contact fathers directly, and in return, fathers may be wary of health professionals or have difficulty relating to them (Pelchat et al., 2007). Fathers do not tend to ask for services, and in the absence of requests for assistance, services suppose that fathers not need help. For a father to remain actively involved in the daily life of his disabled child, helping agencies need to acknowledge the child has two parents and design their service arrangements accordingly (Lillie, 1993). Research has acknowledged that helping both parents will help the child in the long term (Einam & Cuskelly, 2002).

DIFFERENT BUT EQUAL CONTRIBUTIONS

Fathers provide masculine role models for their children and expose their children to male interests and experiences. Fathers offer alternative views on the world around them and provide manly experiences for their children (Ross & VanWilligen, 1996). They have a traditional role of playing with their children and also of dispensing discipline. Fathers are concerned to maintain some semblance of normality within the family, and this includes expectations of acceptable behavior (Pelchat et al., 2007). Fathers have high expectations of their children, especially sons. Fathers dispense discipline differently from mothers (Burbach, Fox, & Nicholson, 2004). Fathers can distance themselves when hard decisions need to be made; they can be detached from their emotions. Fathers may appear to have more head and less heart, but this does not mean they are heartless. They care for their family as much as mothers, but they display their attachment and commitment in a different way. They are concerned about different things and do the same things differently. Their contribution is different but no less important (Laws, 1998; Skene, 1998).

Fathers can take their child into masculine territory and demonstrate ways of behaving that are unfamiliar to mothers. Unless the child is given supportive space in which to try out new behaviors, their lives will be cramped. Yet offering a learning space involves great risks. Accidents may happen and the child may be harmed physically or emotionally. Mothers offer emotional and practical support to enable the child to grow into a mature adult. They want to maintain regular contact to know their child is safe. Fathers are more comfortable with risks. Fathers assess the risk of each situation with detachment, information, rationality, and logic.

A LIFELONG FAMILY COMMITMENT

A child with a disability is not a short-term event but a lifelong commitment, often without a break. The family involvement may never stop. Even when the disabling condition might seem relatively minor, such as Marcus' Asperger's syndrome, there are observable long-term impacts for families. Portway (2006) found parents continued to express concern about the exclusion and discrimination their children experienced as young adults. Asperger's syndrome remained an observable condition. As young adults, they still did not "quite fit in" with mainstream society and its expectations. Parents found there was no end to the need to watch over their offspring to ensure their well-being. They continued to provide for their child's emotional needs, companionship, and needs for shelter, physical security, and money. Few services offered support for families once the children were adults. Parents struggled alone to provide the best they could for their children.

A family may wear out before the child is able to live independently or support themselves, if indeed they are ever capable of doing so. Parents may need to place their child in a group home or some other type of community residence. Parents express regret they cannot care for their child at home themselves, but as parents age, the task of caring for their grown child becomes physically impossible. It is not certain if the need for constant vigilance affects fathers differently from mothers, but fathers certainly are affected very significantly by the need to be constantly alert and on guard to support and protect their children. In Borbasi et al.'s study (2005), fathers in particular spoke of the need for vigilance in making sure their disabled child was cared for adequately. One father said, "we have to come [to visit the institution] so often—so we can keep watch." Later he said, "people say have a holiday, go away. . . . But, how can we?" Parents spoke of the need to advocate constantly on behalf of their child to receive services and then make sure the services that were provided were adequate—this they called "a continual pushing or fighting for things," which was draining and affected their health and well-being. One father rationalized this by saying, "he's our son and we are his only voice." Having two parents in the struggle for recognition of a child's needs, however, considerably eased the burden. One father summed up his thoughts on having a disabled child by saying, "you see this is a marathon we're in, it's not a sprint it's a marathon."

Clearly the need for continual concern does not go away even when the child with a disability is grown. A range of social barriers and negative attitudes continue to exclude adults with disabilities from full participation in society. As a result, the parenting role has no end. The need for constant vigilance is exhausting. The consequences for families, however, of continuing to provide care for their adult children with disabilities, are not well researched.

CONCLUSION

When a family has a child with a disability parents are plunged into an emotional maelstrom and often feel their dream of a "perfect child" has been shattered (Pelchat et al., 2007). Disability stays with a family for life: it is a lifelong commitment. It affects opportunities and plans for the future. Having a child with a disability is challenging. Life is complicated. Problems are compounded rather than being isolated to one child or confined to a single health incident. Disability is demanding. It affects family structures. It redefines every aspect of family life for both parents. In the context of disability the experiences of mothers are well recognized, but the perspectives of fathers are not well documented. The case of Sam and Anna, along with the research outlined here, indicates clearly that fathers are significant in all families; in particular, they play a very important role in families with a child with a disability. They provide income to support the family. They offer emotional support for mothers who provide most of the daily care for the child. Fathers provide male role models and experiences for their children. They dispense discipline differently from mothers, and have different expectations of their children (Laws, 1998; Skene, 1998). Fathers offer their children a masculine set of life experiences and understandings that are different from mothers (Laws, 1998).

Fathers experience disability in their family differently from mothers. The stress on fathers extends beyond the home to other spheres of their lives. It affects how fathers feel about themselves and may subsequently flow on to effect their working life. Services need to support the whole family unit, siblings, grandparents, and especially fathers. They need to be proactive in contacting fathers. Disability is demanding on family time and emotional energy. It may destabilize or jeopardize the marital dynamic. All parents express a desire to be involved in the care of their child, yet this is not always easily accepted by helping agencies. It would be beneficial if the gate-keeping role of mothers and the excluding present structures of helping agencies could be reassessed to allow fathers to become more involved. Men, like women, need to be given the opportunity to raise concerns through relevant and accessible services. Services need to attend to all family members. Provision for the identification and ongoing support of all family members by staff would assist this process. It is more difficult for fathers than mothers to engage closely with their children, but their contribution to family life needs to be recognized and appreciated. Fathers, and families in general, need to be endorsed and celebrated as a vital part of the life of a child with a disability.

REFERENCES

Borbasi, S., Bottroff, V., Hunt, I., & Williams, R. (2005). *Developing a best practice quality of life service delivery model for people with disabilities requiring high levels of support. Final report of qualitative data.* Adelaide: Flinders University Disability Research and Education Group.

Bruce, E. J., Schultz, C. L., & Smyrnios, K. X. (1996). A longitudinal study of the grief of mothers and fathers of children with intellectual disability. *British Journal of Medical Psychology, 69,* 33–45.

Burbach, A. D., Fox, R. A., & Nicholson, B. C. (2004). Challenging behaviors in young children: The father's role. *Journal of Genetic Psychology, 165*(2), 169–183.

Crowe, T. K., VanLeit, B., & Berghmans, K. K. (2000). Mothers' perceptions of child care assistance: The impact of a child's disability. *American Journal of Occupational Therapy, 54*(1), 52–58.

Crowe, T. K., VanLeit, B., Berghmans, K. K., & Mann, P. (1997). Role perceptions of mothers with young children: The impact of a child's disability. *American Journal of Occupational Therapy, 51*(8), 651–661.

Dyson, L. L. (1997). Fathers and mothers of school-age children with developmental disabilities: Parental stress, family functioning, and social support. *American Journal on Mental Retardation, 102*(3), 267–279.

Einam, M., & Cuskelly, M. (2002). Paid employment of mothers and fathers of an adult child with multiple disabilities. *Journal of Intellectual Disability Research, 46,* 158–167.

Ellis, J. T., Luiselli, J. K., Amirault, D., Byrne, S., O'Malley-Cannon, B., Taras, M., et al. (2002). Families of children with developmental disabilities: Assessment and comparison of self-reported needs in relation to situational variables. *Journal of Developmental and Physical Disabilities, 14*(2), 191–202.

Findler, L., & Taubman, O. (2003). Social workers' perceptions and practice regarding grandparents in families of children with a developmental disability. *Families in Society—The Journal of Contemporary Human Services, 84*(1), 86–94.

Hadadian, A. (1994). Stress and social support in fathers and mothers of young children with and without disabilities. *Early Education and Development, 5*(3), 226–235.

Heller, T., Hsieh, K., & Rowitz, L. (1997). Maternal and paternal caregiving of persons with mental retardation across the lifespan. *Family Relations, 46*(4), 407–415.

Hornby, G. (1995). Effects on fathers of children with Down syndrome. *Journal of Child and Family Studies, 4*(2), 239–255.

Katz, S. (2002). Gender differences in adapting to a child's chronic illness: A caUSl model. *Journal of Pediatric Nursing, 17*(4), 257–269.

Krauss, M. W. (1993). Child-related and parenting stress—similarities and differences between mothers and fathers of children with disabilities. *American Journal on Mental Retardation, 97*(4), 393–404.

Laws, T. (1998). Men's contribution to health care within the family. In T. Laws (Ed.), *Promoting men's health—an essential book for nurses.* Melbourne: Ausmed.

Lillie, T. (1993). A harder thing than triumph—roles of fathers of children with disabilities. *Mental Retardation, 31*(6), 438–443.

Lupton, D., & Schmied, V. (2002). "The right way of doing it all": First-time Australian mothers' decisions about paid employment. *Women's Studies International Forum, 25*(1), 97–107.

McKeering, H., & Pakenham, K. I. (2000). Gender and generativity issues in parenting: Do fathers benefit more than mothers from involvement in child care activities? *Sex Roles, 43*(7–8), 459–480.

McLinden, S. E. (1990). Mothers' and fathers' reports of the effects of a young child with special needs on the family. *Journal of Early Intervention, 14*(3), 249–259.

Nicholson, J. M., & Rempel, L. A. (2004). Australian and New Zealand birth cohort studies: Breadth, quality and contributions. *Journal of Paediatrics and Child Health, 40*(3), 87–95.

Pelchat, D., Lefebvre, H., & Levert, M.-J. (2007). Gender differences and similarities in the experience of parenting a child with a health problem: Current state of knowledge. *Journal of Child Health Care, 11*(2), 112–131.

Pelchat, D., Lefebvre, H., & Perreault, M. (2003). Differences and similarities between mothers' and fathers' experiences of parenting a child with a disability. *Journal of Child Health Care, 7*(4), 231–247.

Portway, S. M. (2006). *Living with Asperger's syndrome—the phenomenon of "not quite fitting in."* PhD diss., City University, London.

Pruchno, R., & Patrick, J. H. (1999). Mothers and fathers of adults with chronic disabilities—caregiving appraisals and well-being. *Research on Aging, 21*(5), 682–713.

Raina, P., O'Donnell, M., Rosenbaum, P., Brehaut, J., Walter, S. D., Russell, D., et al. (2005). The health and well-being of caregivers of children with cerebral palsy. *Pediatrics, 115*(6), E626–E636.

Ricci, L. A., & Hodapp, R. M. (2003). Fathers of children with Down's syndrome versus other types of intellectual disability: Perceptions, stress and involvement. *Journal of Intellectual Disability Research, 47*, 273–284.

Roach, M. A., Orsmond, G. I., & Barratt, M. S. (1999). Mothers and fathers of children with Down syndrome: Parental stress and involvement in childcare. *American Journal on Mental Retardation, 104*(5), 422–436.

Rodrigue, J. R., Morgan, S. B., & Geffken, G. R. (1992). Psychosocial adaptation of fathers of children with autism, Down syndrome, and normal development. *Journal of Autism and Developmental Disorders, 22*(2), 249–263.

Ross, C. E., & VanWilligen, M. (1996). Gender, parenthood, and anger. *Journal of Marriage and the Family, 58*(3), 572–584.

Russell, A., & Russell, G. (1994). Coparenting early school-age children—an examination of mother father interdependence within families. *Developmental Psychology, 30*(5), 757–770.

Saloviita, T., Italinna, M., & Leinonen, E. (2003). Explaining the parental stress of fathers and mothers caring for a child with intellectual disability: A double ABCX model. *Journal of Intellectual Disability Research, 47*, 300–312.

Shearn, J., & Todd, S. (2000). Maternal employment and family responsibilities: The perspectives of mothers of children with intellectual disabilities. *Journal of Applied Research in Intellectual Disabilities, 13*(3), 109–131.

Simmerman, S., Blacher, J., & Baker, B. L. (2001). Fathers' and mothers' perceptions of father involvement in families with young children with a disability. *Journal of Intellectual & Developmental Disability, 26*(4), 325–338.

Skene, C. (1998). Healthy fatherhood. In T. Laws (Ed.), *Promoting men's health—an essential book for nurses.* Melbourne: Ausmed.

St John, W., Cameron, C., & McVeigh, C. (2005). Meeting the challenge of new fatherhood during the early weeks. *Journal of Obstetric Gynecologic and Neonatal Nursing, 34*(2), 180–189.

Willoughby, J. C., & Glidden, L. M. (1995). Fathers helping out—shared child-care and marital satisfaction of parents of children with disabilities. *American Journal on Mental Retardation, 99*(4), 399–406.

CHAPTER 14

Bullying of Children with Developmental Disabilites: An Ecolocial Approach to Program Development

Rocky Liesman

Bullying has been linked to highly publicized school shootings; increased rates of depression, anxiety, and low self-esteem among victims and bullies (Hawker & Boulton, 2000; Heinrichs, 2003); and an increased chance of being involved in criminal behavior into adulthood for those who bully (Nansel, Overpeck, Pilla, Ruan, Simons-Morton, & Scheidt; Olweus, 1993). This combination of devastating consequences for bullies and their victims has contributed to the growing awareness of bullying among researchers and mainstream American culture over the past two decades.

Researchers have also focused on groups of children who are particularly at risk for becoming the victims of bullying (Mishna, 2004). One of the more researched at-risk groups in the bullying literature has been students with developmental disabilities (Dawkins, 1996; Knox & Conti-Ramsden, 2003; Little, 2002; Martlew & Hodson, 1991; Norwich & Kelly, 2004; O'Moore & Hillery, 1989; Sabornie, 1994; Savage, 2005; Sweeting & West, 2001; Whitney, Smith, & Thompson, 1994). Despite the relatively large number of studies, there is still a dearth of methodologically sound research regarding the bullying of children with disabilities.

This chapter examines the bullying literature for children with developmental disabilities and then presents some research that has highlighted the difficulties associated with developing programs for this population. Finally, I introduce the knowledge, immersion, natural observation, data collection, and development (KINDD) model, as a proposed approach to bullying research and program development among students with developmental disabilities.

BULLYING OF CHILDREN WITH DEVELOPMENTAL DISABILITIES

In the United States, developmental disability is defined by federal law (Public Law 98-527) as:

> severe, chronic disability of a person that (a) is attributable to a mental or physical impairment or a combination of mental and physical impairments, (b) is manifested before age 22, (c) is likely to continue indefinitely, and (d) results in substantial functional limitations in three or more of the following areas of major life activities: self-care, receptive and expressive language, learning, mobility, self-direction, capacity for independent living, and economic self-sufficiency. (Petersilia, 2001, p. 2)

Individuals with mental retardation, autism, cerebral palsy, epilepsy, and severe learning disabilities are considered to have developmental disabilities.

The United States remains years behind European researchers in the study of bullying in general, as their European counterparts have been studying bullying since the late 1970s (Smith & Brain, 2000). The bullying research conducted over the past two decades on children with developmental disorders has also primarily taken place in countries such as Ireland, England, and Scandinavia. Researchers in the United States initially focused their attention on the attitudes of teachers and students without disabilities toward students with disabilities in response to new mainstreaming policies (Kavale, 2002; Nougaret, Scruggs, & Mastropieri, 2005). These early studies did not focus on the incidence or effects of bullying for the victim and relatively ignored the occurrence and consequences of bullying of children with developmental disabilities.

Only 10 studies (one conducted in the United States) have explored bullying of children with developmental disabilities. These studies have included a wide range of disability categories, multiple methods of assessment (peer, self-, and parent reports, teacher questionnaires, and researcher observations) and children from a variety of settings (i.e., special education schools, mainstream classrooms, language-based programs, and special education classes). Disability categories included in these studies were learning disabilities (Knox & Conti-Ramsden, 2004; Martlew & Hodson, 1991; Norwich & Kelly, 2004), Asperger's syndrome (Little, 2002), physical disabilities (Dawkins 1996; Llewellyn, 1995), and other speech-related disabilities (Hugh-Jones & Smith, 1999; Savage, 2005). Despite these differences, all studies found that children with disabilities were two to three times more likely to be the victims of bullying than their nondisabled peers. Researchers also found that the bullying experienced by these children was more chronic in nature (O'Moore & Hillary, 1989; Sweeting & West, 2001) and was most often directly related to their disability (Norwich & Kelly, 2004; Sweeting & West, 2001; Whitney et al., 1994).

Several studies found that children with developmental disabilities were more likely to be involved in bullying behavior as both victims and perpetrators than their peers without disabilities (Kaukiainen et al., 2002; Whitney et al., 1994). However, children with disabilities were more at risk of becoming provocative victims than are children without disabilities. "Provocative victim" is a term first introduced by Olweus (1978) to describe those children whose impulsive, emotionally reactive, and socially inappropriate behavior combined with uncontrolled aggressive behavior often provokes bullying behavior from others. Because many children with disabilities have a lack of social skills, information-processing deficits, impulsivity, and hyperactivity, the likelihood that they will become provocative victims is increased.

This research has increased the awareness and understanding of involvement in bullying by children with developmental disabilities, both as victims and as perpetrators. However, several limitations are present in these studies that serve to prevent generalizability across studies. Limitations present in these studies included lack of a consistent, clear definition of bullying (Doren, Bullis, & Benz, 1996; Little, 2002; Martlew & Hodson, 1991; Norwich & Kelly, 2004; O'Moore & Hillary 1989; Sweeting & West, 2001), low numbers of children with developmental disabilities (Martlew & Hodson, 1991; Savage, 2005), absence of a control group (Dawkins, 1996; Little, 2002; Norwich & Kelly, 2004; Savage, 2005), and unclear distinctions between disability categories and amount of time spent in regular education classrooms (Dawkins, 1996; Doren et al., 1996; Knox & Conti-Ramsden, 2004; Martlew & Hodson, 1991; O'Moore & Hilary, 1989). The limitations in these studies not only restrict their generalizability but also contribute to the relative absence of bullying research and program development in this area during the early part of the 21st century.

In one of the most significant and comprehensive studies on the bullying of children with disabilities, Whitney et al. (1994) improved on many of the bullying studies conducted with this population through inclusion of a control group, multiple sources of assessment, detailed definition of bullying, and a qualitative approach to understanding bullying in this population. They were also the first researchers to examine the effects of a bullying prevention program, developed for students without disabilities, on students with disabilities. They found that two-thirds of the 93 "special needs" children included in their study complained about being bullied. Most important, they found eight months after the implementation of a bullying prevention program developed for children without disabilities, the special needs children reported significantly fewer experiences with being bullied than their peers without disabilities and also an increase in their numbers of friends.

Teachers included in that study were interviewed after the completion of the bullying prevention program and reported that the success of such a program would increase if it were adapted to the specific needs of students with disabilities. However, Whitney et al. (1994) did not provide suggestions regarding possible provisions to the prevention program, nor did they gain the students', teachers', or parents' perspectives in terms of possible program elements specifically tailored to the needs of students with disabilities. Despite the demonstrated effectiveness of their bullying prevention program on students with developmental disabilities and the expressed belief that modifications to these programs would improve their effectiveness among children with disabilities, researchers have yet to develop a program that is tailored specifically to the prevention of bullying among children with developmental disabilities.

PILOT STUDY

This section examines the feasibility and effectiveness of using an ecological, qualitative design for the study of bullying among children with developmental disabilities. Quantitative data were collected from three groups of participants (parents, teachers, students) regarding the forms, location, and incidence of bullying committed against children with developmental disabilities. However, weaknesses inherent in the design (i.e., absence of a control group, difficulty comparing responses between groups due to the use of nonempirically supported surveys, convenience sampling, etc.) and implementation (i.e., low response rate, incomplete data, etc.) of this study made quantitative interpretations difficult and generalization of results impossible.

This pilot study discussed in this chapter expanded on the method used in Whitney et al. (1994) by not only surveying teachers' desire for a bullying prevention program developed specifically for children with developmental disabilities but also assessing the expressed needs of both the students with disabilities themselves and their parents. This study was the first to use a phenomenological, needs-based research approach for the study of bullying among this population. The phenomenological research design allowed me to gain a complete understanding of a phenomenon (i.e., bullying among children with disabilities) by studying a small group of participants who are deeply affected by the phenomenon (Creswell, 2003). Using a phenomenological approach, I was able identify school-specific resources and components that would be helpful in the development of a bullying prevention program specifically for children with developmental disabilities.

The conclusions drawn in this chapter are based on data collected from teachers, parents, and students with disabilities from one middle school that had a large number of students with disabilities and a long history of mainstreaming students with developmental disabilities. Regular teachers, special education teachers, students with disabilities, and parents participated in the study.

Ten teachers were nominated by the school to participate, but only seven responded, two of whom identified themselves as primarily special education teachers. The number of years each teacher reported working with children with special education ranged from 1 to 16 or more years. All seven of the teachers, two males and five females, were European American.

Of 65 families identified by the school, five parents (three males and two females) participated in the study and agreed for their children to participate. Three of the five parents were unaware of their child's specific diagnosis, but each was aware of the child's need for special education. The remaining two parents stated their children had been diagnosed with a combination of attention deficit-hyperactivity disorder (ADHD) and a learning disability.

The students were five male junior high students between the ages of 11 and 14 years (two were African American and three were European American). All five were eligible for special education services and, thus, had an individualized education plan (IEP) developed by school staff. Three of the students were considered to be high functioning, as evidenced by demonstrated level of expressive and comprehension abilities. The remaining two students appeared to have severe impairments and remained quiet throughout the entire data-collection process. Thus, the data in this chapter represent the views of the three vocal students.

Methods of Data Collection

I used several measures to gather information from the participants. First, I developed a needs survey to identify both the necessity for and essential components of a bullying prevention program as expressed by the students, parents, and teachers. Questions were generated from themes identified in the literature and were then reviewed for relevance and readability by a prominent researcher in the field of bullying research among children with developmental disabilities (R. R. Heinrichs, personal communication, August 18, 2006). The student version of the survey focused mainly on their current knowledge of bullying, evaluation of past bullying prevention programs (if any), desire for such a program, possible interventions, and their belief in the possible effectiveness of such a program if implemented. The parent and teacher versions of the survey also contained questions about the individual and school resources needed to successfully implement such a program.

In addition to the needs survey, I also used the Modified Inventory of Wrongful Activities (Heinrichs, 2003) and the Colorado School Climate Survey (Garrity, Jens, Porter, Sager, & Short-Camilli, 1994). The Modified Inventory of Wrongful Activities (Heinrichs, 2003) is a self-report questionnaire used to measure the incidence of multiple forms of bullying behavior (i.e., hitting, teasing, social exclusion, etc.). The inventory was modified from Brown's (n.d.) Inventory of Wrongful Activities to specifically address the needs of children with Asperger's syndrome by stating questions concisely and providing concrete examples to aid in understanding.

The modified version contains 53 items, each of which contributes to 1 of 10 categories. It provided qualitative information regarding the forms of bullying experienced, typical location of bullying, the students' responses to being bullied, as well as individuals from whom they are most likely to seek help.

The Colorado School Climate Survey (Garrity et al., 1994) is a paper-and-pencil self-report questionnaire developed to measure parents' views of the safety of their child's school environment as measured by ratings of the frequency of bullying, number of "safe" locations within the school, and the overall "climate" provided by their child's school.

The survey was used as a source of quantitative and qualitative information regarding the incidence of bullying as viewed by the parents of children with developmental disabilities and parents' perception of the safety of the school environment.

Data Collection

The data-collection process with the student group included the completion of surveys using a group format, in an attempt to decrease the stigma associated with bullying and to facilitate conversation among the participants.

The questions were presented orally to allow students with severe reading or cognitive deficits to better comprehend the questions and also to provide an opportunity for clarification. Although the group format was valuable in allowing me to see the interactions and interpersonal dynamics of the group members, it became clear that this was not an effective or efficient means of collecting specific and meaningful data. More meaningful information might have been gathered through one-on-one interviewing, allowing for more individualized accommodations and ensuring that all voices were heard. Nevertheless, the main themes and observations that emerged from each group (students, parents, and teachers) are presented in the next sections.

STUDENTS' DISCUSSIONS ABOUT BULLYING

Provocative Behavior

The three most active students displayed a range of behaviors that were often disruptive, aggressive, hyperactive, and inattentive during the data-collection phase. The oldest member of the group (eighth grade) demonstrated significant distractibility and hyperactivity throughout most of the focus group. He spent the majority of the group time exchanging insults (i.e., "You idiot.") and, at times, threatening comments (i.e., "I could take you.") with the seventh-grade group member. He appeared to have been the group member most deeply affected by bullying. He was observed during several points in the group to become quiet and visibly embarrassed when endorsing several of the bullying-related items.

Just as the aggressive behavior of the three boys might have been labeled as provocative, the silence of two of the students could have contributed to their vulnerability to bullying. Specifically, their inability to communicate clearly and effectively would make the identification of bullying difficult and protections against bullying nonexistent. Thus, the nature of provocative behavior was unclear.

Definition of Bullying

When asked to define bullying, each of the three boys identified behaviors such as punching, giving wedgies, pushing against lockers, and pinching as indicators of bullying behavior. One of the boys described bullying as a fight between two students, while another seemed to vaguely understand that bullying, unlike fighting, involves a power differential. Overall, the boys identified only physical forms of bullying and were relatively unaware of the multiple forms of bullying behavior.

Experiences of Bullying

The three boys differed in terms of the location of bullying they had experienced. One boy indicated that bullying had occurred both between and during classes. The other two boys identified after school and lunch as times when they were vulnerable to negative comments and actions by others.

All three of the boys endorsed having "mean things" done to them at least once each week. Responses then varied, with one boy stating that people were "mean" to him at school "more than once a day," and another boy stating that he was bullied "several times a week."

The three boys all indicated that they had been victims of physical bullying. They reported having been hit, pinched, kicked, tripped, bitten, or spat on within the last school year. Two of the three boys also indicated that someone had stolen from them within the last school year, and one boy endorsed having had his clothes torn and things broken by another student.

The three boys also reported having experienced relational or psychological bullying. Items endorsed by at least one of the three boys included having bad things said about a family member; being scared or threatened into doing things they would either get in trouble for doing or that they did not want to do; being left out of group activities; being afraid to talk in class or to make mistakes for fear of teasing; having difficulty learning in school because of feeling scared, angry, sad, or upset about the way they were treated by others; and having been laughed at by other students.

All six items relating to teasing due to physical, racial, or educational differences were endorsed by at least one of the students. The three boys all indicated that classmates had insulted them over the last school year because they were in a different class or program. The African American student also endorsed being insulted because of his race.

Four of the seven items representing experiences of sexual harassment or assault were endorsed by at least one of the three boys, and three of the seven items were endorsed by at least two of the three boys. All three of the boys endorsed having been grabbed, pinched, or kicked in a private body area. Two of the three boys admitted to having had sexual rumors spread about them and sexual insults written about them on walls, desks, or somewhere else.

Responses of Others to Bullying

All three of the boys endorsed feeling that teachers did not like them as much as they liked other students. They also endorsed being hurt or angry (once a week or more) about a teacher's actions or words. Two of the three boys also reported wishing their teachers would stop someone who was bullying them.

The three boys reported that they did nothing if they witnessed bullying. Two of the three boys stated their typical response to being bullied was to act mean back, with one boy stating that he simply told bullies to stop. Despite their stated high rates of mistreatment by others, two of the three boys indicated they never told anyone about the incidents, and one boy indicated telling others only some of the time. Although they appeared unwilling to tell others about their experiences, all three reported that telling an adult at the school helped. Two of the three boys stated that telling a parent also helped, whereas one of the boys reported that it made things worse. All three of the boys reported that teachers did very little when they saw students bullying others.

All three of the boys identified the school vice principal and parents as adults to whom they would go for help if someone was being mean to them. One of the boys said he would also go to the school psychologist for help. None of the boys endorsed the school counselor, teachers or resource teachers, the principal, or a police officer as individuals they would go to for help.

When asked if they thought parents or teachers were aware of the problems they experienced with being teased, hit, or threatened, two of the boys stated their parents were aware, and one said he had never told his parents. All three of the boys stated that teachers were unaware of the problem; interestingly one boy even stated, "Sometimes teachers are the ones who bully."

The three boys stated that no one at school or home had provided them with information on bullying (i.e., what do when you experience bullying, how to prevent bullying, etc.). The boys also seemed confused about the presence of a bullying prevention program at their school. Two of the boys referred to "anger management classes," which appeared to be a type of disciplinary system for dealing with aggressive children. The boys thought this program was helpful, despite the fact that none of the boys had ever been to the program nor could explain its purpose.

Future Bullying Resources

In regard to the perceived usefulness of a bullying prevention program, two of the three boys stated that such a program would not be useful because "Some people don't what to change, because they were raised around violence." The other boy indicated that such a program would be helpful for him. When asked what they would include in a bullying prevention program, each of the boys agreed they would benefit from a designated individual to whom all students would report incidents of bullying, extra police officers, and additional security cameras.

PARENTS' THOUGHTS ABOUT BULLYING

Frequency of Physical and Relational Bullying

All of the parents confirmed their child had experienced physical bullying of some form (i.e., hit, kicked, punched, etc.), but the frequency varied. One parent indicated that bullying only happened once to his or her child and another parent endorsed "five or more times per week." Two of the parents endorsed that their child had also experienced several forms of relational and psychological bullying (i.e., name calling, being threatened, left out of activities, etc.). Again, frequency ranged from "one time per week" to "five or more times per week." Overall, results suggested that the parents were aware of at least one incident of physical bullying experienced by the child. Parents, like the students, were more aware of physical bullying than the more subtle forms of bullying behavior (i.e., teasing, leaving out of games, name-calling, etc.).

All of the parents indicated that a single individual committed the incident(s) against their child, and in all four cases the identified perpetrator was a boy. Parents identified a wide range of locations in which bullying occurred, but reported the classroom as the typical location of bullying behavior. Hallways and lunchroom, bathroom and locker room, and going to and from school were listed as additional locations of bullying. All of the parents stated that their child had informed them after the incident(s).

Safety of Child's Environment

Despite all of the parents indicating their child had experienced at least one incident of physical bullying at school, the parents rated the classroom, playground, hallways, and lunchroom as safe.

Possible Informants

When asked whom their child could tell if they were being bullied, parents suggested that persons of power and authority need to be available (i.e., police, principal, teachers, and counselors). One parent responded that she could tell no one about her child's experiences with bullying despite his being bullied more than once a week. Like the students, the parents seemed to believe that others, specifically authority figures, were "unaware" of their experiences with bullying, suggesting a lack of faith and trust.

Beliefs about Bullying Programs

Like the students, parents were unaware of the existence of a schoolwide bullying prevention program and were unable to answer questions regarding its quality or how it could be improved. Three of the parents expressed their desire for a bullying prevention program developed specifically for children with disabilities, whereas the remaining two left this question blank. When asked what elements parents would include if they could create such a program, responses varied greatly in terms of depth and specificity. One parent identified the need for such a program to include parents through regular meetings with parents and calling parents when school personnel identified incidents of bullying. The remaining responses included vague suggestions aimed at both children and teachers (i.e., "Children need to get along with one another," "Teachers need to be nicer to parents," etc.).

Parents were asked to identify the resources they and their child's school would need to successfully implement such a program. Responses varied, with one parent indicating her desire for someone whose job was "guiding children with disabilities on a daily basis." Similarly, another parent wanted "Someone for my child to talk to every time bullying occurs." One parent simply listed "concern from the child's school" as a necessary component of such a program. Another parent stated that "kids, teachers, staff, and parents would all need to work together."

In terms of who they would include in such a program, parents seemed to understand that the successful implementation of such a program would need to include a wide range of individuals, or as one parent expressed, "everybody." This list included parents, teachers, principles, counselors, police offers, and psychologists, each of whom would be dedicated to the prevention of bullying.

Parents saw their role in the prevention of bullying as being a model and a moral compass (i.e., "Inform my child about what is right and wrong," "Informing my children to accept differences between children.").

Limitations

The most prominent limitation of the parent group was a low response rate. Only 15 of the 34 contacted parents were willing to both participate and have their children participate in the study. All 15 of the parents seemed open and willing to discuss their child's experiences with bullying, as well as express their concerns regarding the safety of their child's environment. Unfortunately, the expressed passion and willingness verbalized when contacting the parents via telephone did not generalize to the successful completion of a significant number of surveys. Specifically, only 5 out of the 15 participants returned the required information for themselves and for the child.

Second, those surveys that were returned had additional problems, including unanswered questions and incomplete answers, and one parent did not complete an entire survey. Review of the open-ended questionnaires suggested some of the parents had limited reading and writing abilities, as several frequently misspelled words, had difficulty creating complete sentences, and on several occasions misunderstood the questions being asked. For example, one parent responded to the question, "Who do you feel you can tell if your child is being bullied?" with "They look sad, crying, and scared."

Retrospectively, based on the low response rate and suggested lower education level of many of the parents, more accurate and complete information could have been obtained by completing the surveys in person or via telephone. These methods may have controlled for possible difficulties in reading and writing, thus allowing parents to truly have their voices heard.

Despite these limitations, useful information was provided by the parents, highlighting the need for schools to engage parents in future. Indeed, the lack of parental voice leads to an incomplete understanding of bullying and, worse yet, splinters any effective and systemwide approach to bullying.

TEACHERS

Researcher Observations

I made two separate trips to a special education classroom at the participating school to collect the completed consent forms and surveys. During both trips, I was allowed to sit in the classroom during a class period. These two trips resulted in a total of one hour of unexpected classroom observation. As a result, it became obvious that it was necessary to include natural observations in future studies of bullying. Specifically, natural observations can provide invaluable information regarding the workload of special education teachers, the behaviors of students with developmental disabilities, and the context within which both teachers and students with disabilities exist. Additionally, natural observations can better inform program development.

Teacher Views on Bullying

Teachers were asked similar questions to those asked of the students and parents, including:

1. incidence, location, and type of bullying;
2. presence, effectiveness, and possible improvements of current bully-prevention program;
3. desire for a bully prevention program, necessary elements, desired resources;
4. teachers' role in bully prevention; and
5. additional comments.

The following sections outline their responses to these questions.

Incidence, Location, and Type of Bullying

All seven of the participating teachers indicated that bullying was a problem for children with developmental disabilities at the middle school. Relational bullying (i.e., calling names, teasing, excluding from games, etc.) received the most endorsements—it was checked by six of the seven teachers. Teachers showed greater awareness of multiple forms of bullying behavior (i.e., physical, relational, psychological) than did participating parents and students. Five of the seven teachers also endorsed both physical (i.e., hitting, kicking, pushing, etc.) and psychological (i.e., threatening to hurt the child) bullying as forms of bullying experienced by children with developmental disabilities.

The hallway was listed by five of the seven teachers as the location in which bullying behavior most frequently occurs. Classrooms, bus, and cafeteria were also listed as locations in which bullying behavior occurs. One teacher stated that children with disabilities experienced bullying in "all areas." The classroom was listed by all three sets of informants (students, teachers, and parents) as a location in which bullying frequently occurred.

Bullying Prevention Program

As was true of both parents and students, the participating teachers varied in their awareness of a schoolwide bullying prevention program. Four of the seven teachers were unsure whether their school had a bullying prevention program in place. The remaining three teachers described the positive behavior system (PBS) as the school's current bullying prevention program. Of the three teachers listing PBS, however, only one stated that the program was helpful for children with developmental disabilities. The remaining teachers stated that whatever was currently in place was not working for these children. Reasons for the perceived ineffectiveness of the school's current stance on bullying varied and included the cognitive deficits of children with disabilities, carelessness on the part of administration, inability of programs to address the environment in which the children live, and lack of information provided to both teachers and students.

Participating teachers stated that the current programs could be improved by:

1. educating the students about their rights, appropriate responses, and correct steps to take when experiencing bullying;
2. teaching the children respect; and
3. decreasing stigma of snitching.

To implement these improvements, teachers identified a need for the following resources: time, money, materials (i.e., workbooks and videos), workshops on bullying, district support, and motivation. One teacher expressed a need for "a nonbroken school system that is not focused solely on test scores." This teacher's response reflected a level of dissatisfaction and powerlessness expressed by several others regarding the school's current policy (or lack thereof) and its exclusion of teachers in the decision-making process.

Future Bullying Prevention Programs

Six of the seven teachers stated that a bullying prevention program developed specifically for children with developmental disabilities was necessary. One responded, "Yes, students (with disabilities) may not understand that what is happening to them is a form of bullying, that it shouldn't be happening, and what they can do to stop it." These six teachers also provided a detailed and varied list of elements they would include if they were to create such a program. Responses included making it a schoolwide program, inclusion of parents, addressing students' rights and proper reactions, specific individual to whom students could report incidents of bullying, conflict management training, use of mediation, training, bullying resources, and surveys. One added that resources such as videos, role-plays, and puppet shows should be used to address the cognitive deficits present in many of these children. Last, teachers provided an extensive list of resources needed for the successful implementation of such a program. The most frequent responses included:

1. professional training (i.e., workshops),
2. money,
3. materials (i.e., lesson plans, books, videos, Web sites, etc.), and
4. community/parent support.

Teachers' Role in Bullying Prevention

The most frequent response from teachers regarding their role in bullying prevention was to step in when they saw students being bullied by other students or "referee." Additional roles included serving as a role model of appropriate behavior and serving as a resource for children who are being bullied in school. One teacher expressed her role as a resource for other teachers regarding what types of behaviors to look for and how to respond to incidents of bullying. Despite their depth of views about bullying, teachers varied widely in terms of their understanding of the dynamics involved in bullying behavior and in its prevention. The majority of responses came from two special education teachers who had received outside training in both recognizing and intervening with the various forms of bullying behavior. Thus, it would seem that education of teachers is a critical component in future programs.

LESSONS FOR DEVELOPING BULLYING PROGRAMS

The results presented here only begin to scratch the surface of understanding the dynamics involved in the bullying of children with developmental disabilities. The process of completing this research provided me with a first-hand perspective on the lived experience of all involved in the creation and enabling of bullying. Consequently, it highlighted the complexity of the problem as well as the challenge presented to those involved in the development of an effective bullying prevention program for children with disabilities. Due to a relative absence of methodologically sound research on bullying behavior among children with disabilities, little is known about the lived experiences of all who are impacted by its presence.

Through my use of a phenomenological approach, the ecological nature of bullying became clear and the need for a whole-school approach to bullying prevention was evident. Each group (students, parents, and teachers) of participants was aware of the severity and frequency of bullying among this population, and each expressed a sense of helplessness in addressing the problem alone. The students were burdened by behavioral and social deficits resulting from their disabilities, which served to increase their chances of victimization, decrease their believability as victims, increase their chances of becoming involved in bullying behavior, and decrease their trust in the school system and in their own sense of self-efficacy for preventing bullying in the future.

Participating parents also expressed a sense of burden, as they felt excluded from their child's education. However, their apparent lower level of education and decreased cognitive abilities, likely decreases their chances of expressing these needs to a large school system. Last, teachers expressed a sense of burden based on a perceived lack of support, follow through, and resources on the part of administration for appropriately dealing with bullying behavior among their students. Overall, these results are suggestive of a system that is burdened with limited resources and support, which ultimately increases the vulnerability of students with disabilities for future victimization. However, both parents and teachers expressed a strong desire to be involved in the prevention of bullying among this population and understand it will take a community effort.

THE KINDD MODEL

KINDD stands for knowledge, immersion, natural observation, data collection, and development. I developed KINDD as a proposed method of developing a school-specific bullying prevention program. The KINDD model was designed for use by both researchers and clinicians (e.g., psychologists, counselors) working in or with local school districts. The model is based on the strengths and limitations of existing methods discovered through a pilot study as well as the identified gaps in bullying literature. The model provides both researchers and clinicians with a more reliable and ecologically valid method of data collection, program development, and program evaluation.

Sobsey's (1994) integrated ecological model of abuse serves as the foundation for each step of the KINDD model. It focuses on the role of context and environment in the abuse of individuals with disabilities. Sobsey's (1994) model includes three major contexts: *relationships, environments,* and *cultural.* The relationship aspect of the model refers to the characteristics of both potential victims and offenders that make them more prone to receive or perpetrate abuse. The environment aspect highlights the role of different environments in facilitating or inhibiting the abuse of disabled individuals. Last, the cultural aspect stresses the importance of understanding the role of cultural beliefs and value systems in creating a climate that is conducive to the abuse of disabled individuals. The KINDD model emphasizes the importance of data collection at each point to ensure the ecological validity of a bullying prevention program.

Knowledge

Developing a school-specific bullying prevention program must be based on detailed information about the community within which the school exists. As Pepler, Smith, and Rigby (2004) noted, "Efforts to extend an understanding of bullying and strategies to address bullying problems into the broader community may enhance the potential for change" (p. 312). Thus, the information gathered must include an understanding of all aspects of the community context for the school including its history, basic values, demographics, and socioeconomic status. Researchers and clinicians can gather this information by simply speaking to parents and teachers about the history of the school and its surrounding community. To gather this knowledge, it is essential to talk to teachers, parents, and interested community members who make up the school community.

Immersion

Program developers must immerse themselves in the school environment, as suggested by Sobsey (1994). They should attempt to become a part of the environment that helped create and maintain bullying while simultaneously maintaining an objective and unbiased perspective. Teachers, parents, and students must be comfortable with the program developer's presence and knowledgeable about her or his mission. This step should occur before any formal data collection begins. This step involves meeting with school personnel from all levels in the hierarchy and includes making oneself available to parents by having group meetings. More important, it is necessary to be present at educational planning meetings and parent–teacher conferences where interactions can be had with parents on an individual basis. This step is crucial for increasing the response rate, openness, and trust of parents, teachers, and students during the process of data collection. In addition, this step allows the researcher to truly hear, respect, and speak to the challenges that teachers, parents, and students face in addressing the problem of bullying. Last, the simple step of immersing oneself in the environment not only increases trust and legitimacy of the researcher but adds a richness to the data gathered that is missing when the researcher remains a distant, uninvolved observer to the process.

Natural Observation

Program developers should spend the greatest amount of their time observing children as they interact naturally in the classroom, hallways, cafeteria, at recess, and so forth. Natural observation corresponds to the relationship component of Sobsey's (1994) model, requiring program developers to become direct observers of the interplay of power and inequality in the bullying experiences of children with developmental disabilities. For natural observation to be successful, researchers must be clear about how to define bullying behavior and how the bullying of children with disabilities will look different from that experienced by children without disabilities.

Particular attention must be paid to the provocative victim. The provocative victim is more likely to provoke their attacker through irritating, aggressive, and socially inappropriate behavior (Olweus, 1978; Schwartz, Proctor, & Chien, 2001). Intervention for such a child may need to be different from that used for the nonprovocative victim. During the natural observation phase, researchers are more concerned with the quantitative nature of bullying (i.e., number of incidences observed, types witnessed, teachers responses, etc.). Natural observation provides a more accurate view of those children who are at risk for victimization and are currently experiencing bullying. Further, natural observation provides a clearer view of the role teachers and parents play in creating an environment that either fosters or inhibits bullying behavior.

Data Collection

The data-collection phase is concerned with qualitative data from the identified participants through individual interviews, focus groups, surveys, and questionnaires. This phase should be based on a phenomenological approach where the voices of students, parents, and teachers are used to develop an understanding of the phenomenon of bullying and how to prevent its occurrence. This includes perceptions about where victims feel the least safe, who should be included in such a program, and what resources would be needed to implement such a program.

Focus groups and surveys with teachers and parents will help inform the necessary components of a bullying prevention program as well as resources needed to successfully implement such a program. Mishna (2004) noted the importance of parental and teacher involvement in bullying prevention because it is highly correlated with program success and successful implementation. The inclusion of multiple data points increases the credibility of qualitative research by providing a triangulated view and allowing program developers to compare and contrast multiple perspectives, leading to a more accurate view of bullying and its prevention (Llewellyn, 1995). These data also provide a strong baseline against which to assess program effectiveness.

Development

The final phase of the KINDD model is the development stage. The program developer integrates all information gained about the community, from immersing him- or herself into the school environment, observing children and teachers in their natural environment, and gathering detailed information from several data points.

By following the phases of the KINDD model, the program developers can create a comprehensive and ecologically valid bullying prevention program. Since the development of the Olweus Bully Prevention Program (Olweus, 1993), the first comprehensive whole-school intervention program to be implemented and evaluated, there has been a call for the further development of ecologically valid whole-school bullying prevention programs (Smith, Schneider, Smith, & Ananiadou, 2004). Programs such as the Peaceful Schools Project (Twemlow et al., 2001), Bully Busters (Newman, Horne, & Bartolomucci, 2000), and Bully Proofing Your School (Garrity et al., 1994) are just a few of the frequently cited programs (Orpinas & Horne, 2006). Smith et al. (2004) in their meta-analysis of effectiveness studies for whole-school bullying prevention programs, found the majority of these studies were methodologically flawed (i.e., no control groups, limited adherence to protocol). As a result, the findings were too inconsistent to conclude that the approach is successful.

Over a decade ago, Galloway (1994) wrote that a successful whole-school approach must

1. create a climate in which students view any form of bullying behavior as unacceptable and thus look to teachers for support when it occurs;
2. explore children's views on bullying through both whole class discussion and individual or small group interviews;
3. understand and respond accordingly to the motivation, self-concept, and resulting self-esteem of both bullies and victims;
4. consider how current method of teaching and organizing (i.e., full-inclusion, part-time, etc.) students with special needs might contribute to their experiences with bullying;
5. include parents as potentially powerful sources of support both in detecting and in dealing with bullying; and
6. evaluate the effectiveness of the program.

Many of these components are missing in several of the most frequently applied whole-school bullying prevention programs, which may account for their inconsistent effectiveness.

Each school district provides its own unique set of strengths and weaknesses, and the effectiveness of whole-school bullying prevention programs will likely increase when such programs are developed with these strengths and weaknesses in mind. With the movement toward "off-the-shelf" programs, districts run the risk of ignoring the individual needs of each district.

Despite the emergence of whole-school bullying prevention programs, none have gone the lengths suggested by the KINDD model in terms of program development. Further, none of these programs speak to the unique needs of children with developmental disabilities. The KINDD model is a method of program development that can be responsive to each individual school and its students with disabilities.

The effective prevention of bullying of children with developmental disabilities is complicated by the physical, behavioral, social, and cognitive deficits present in many of these children, making interventions for this population difficult and labor-intensive. The KINDD model involves extensive use of valuable resources in the form of time, money, and administrative motivation. However, the complications in developing interventions for this population highlight the importance of a participatory and ethnographic approach to program development. The burdens of the KINDD model might outweigh its benefits in some contexts. Yet research and experience shows that current interventions are not addressing the complexity of bullying, particularly when students with developmental disabilities are involved. Therefore, despite the burdens associated with the KINDD model, it ensures the ecological validity of a program, and empowers a disempowered community by providing its members (i.e., parents, students, and teachers) with a voice in the creation of such program. So, in the words of neuropsychologist Dr. Jeffery Allen (personal communication, June 28, 2007), "Let the burden begin."

REFERENCES

Creswell, J. W. (2003). *Research design*. Thousand Oaks, CA: Sage.

Dawkins, J. L. (1996). Bullying, physical disability and the pediatric patient. *Developmental Medicine & Child Neurology, 38*, 603–612.

Doren, B., Bullis, M., & Benz, M. R. (1996). Predictors of victimization experiences of adolescents with disabilities in transition. *Exceptional Children, 63*, 7–18.

Galloway, D. (1994, Spring). *Bullying: The importance of a whole school approach*. Paper presented at the launch of Durham London Educational Association.

Garrity, C., Jens, K., Porter, W., Sager, N., & Short-Camilli, C. (1994). *Bully-proofing your elementary school: Working with victims and bullies.* Longmont, CO: Sopris West.

Hawker, D. S. J., & Boulton, M. J. (2000). Twenty years' research on peer victimization and psychosocial maladjustment: A meta-analytic review of cross-sectional studies. *Journal of Child Psychology and Psychiatry, 41*, 441–455.

Heinrichs, R. R. (2003). *Perfect targets: Asperger's syndrome and bullying: Practical solutions for surviving the social* world. Shawnee Mission, KS: Autism Asperger's Publication.

Hugh-Jones, S., & Smith, P. K. (1999). Self-reports of short- and long-term effects of bullying on children who stammer. *British Journal of Educational Psychology, 69*, 141–158.

Kaukiainen, A., Salmivalli, C., Lagerspetz, K., Tamminen, M., Vauras, M., & Maki, H., (2002). Learning difficulties, social intelligence and self-concept: Connections to bully-victim problems. *Scandinavian Journal of Psychology, 43,* 269–278.

Kavale, K. A. (2002). Mainstreaming to full inclusion: From orthogenesis to pathogenesis of an idea. *International Journal of Disability, Development and Education, 49,* 201–214.

Knox, E., & Conti-Ramsden, G. (2003). Bullying risks of 11-year-old children with specific language impairment (SLI): Does school placement matter? *International Journal of Language & Communication Disorders, 38,* 1.

Little, L. (2002). Middle-class mothers' perceptions of peer and sibling victimization among children with Asperger's syndrome and nonverbal learning disorders. *Issues in Comprehensive Pediatric Nursing, 25,* 43–57.

Llewellyn, A. (1995). The abuse of children with physical disabilities in mainstream schooling. *Developmental Medicine & Child Neurology, 37,* 740–743.

Martlew, M., & Hodson, J. (1991). Children with mild learning difficulties in an integrated and in a special school: Comparisons of behavior, teasing and teachers' attitudes. *British Journal of Educational Psychology, 61,* 355–369.

Mishna, F. (2004). A qualitative study of bullying from multiple perspectives. *Children and Schools, 26*(4), 234–247.

Nansel, T. R., Overpeck, M., Pilla, R. S., Ruan, W. J., Simons-Morton, B., & Scheidt, P. (2001). Bullying behaviors among US youth: Prevalence and associations with psychosocial adjustment. *Journal of the American Medical Association, 285,* 2094–2100.

Newman, D. A., Horne, A. M., & Bartolomucci, C. L. (2000). *Bully busters: A teacher's manual for helping bullies, victims, and bystanders.* Champaign, IL: Research Press.

Norwich, B., & Kelly, N. (2004). Pupils' views on inclusion: Moderate learning difficulties and bullying in mainstream and special schools. *British Educational Research Journal, 30*(1), 43–65.

Nougaret, A. A., Scruggs, T. E., & Mastropieri, M. A. (2005) Does teacher education produce better special education teachers? *Exceptional Children, 71,* 217–229.

Olweus, D. (1978). *Aggression in the schools: Bullies and whipping boys.* Oxford: Hemisphere.

Olweus, D. (1993). *Victimization by peers: Antecedents and long-term outcomes.* Hillsdale, NJ: Erlbaum.

O'Moore, A. M., & Hillary, B. (1989). Bullying in Dublin schools. *Irish Journal of Psychology, 10,* 426–441.

Orpinas, P., & Horne, A. M. (2006). *Theoretical perspectives on bullying and aggression.* Washington, DC: American Psychological Association.

Pepler, D., Smith, P. K., & Rigby, K. (2004). Looking back and looking forward: Implications for making interventions work effectively. In P. K. Smith, D. Pepler, & K. Rigby (Eds.), *Bullying in schools: How successful can interventions be?* (pp. 307–324). Cambridge: Cambridge University Press.

Petersilia, J. R. (2001). Crime victims with developmental disabilities: A review essay. *Criminal Justice and Behavior, 26,* 655–694.

Sabornie, E. J. (1994). Social-affective characteristics in early adolescents identified as learning disabled and nondisabled. *Learning Disability Quarterly, 17,* 268–279.

Savage, R. (2005). Friendship and bullying patterns in children attending a language base in a mainstream school. *Educational Psychology in Practice, 21,* 23–36.

Schwartz, D., Proctor, L. J., & Chien, D. H. (2001). *The aggressive victim of bullying: Emotional and behavioral dysregulation as a pathway to victimization by peers.* New York: Guilford.

Smith, J. D., Schneider, B. H., Smith, P. K., & Ananiadou, K. (2004). The effectiveness of whole-school anti-bullying programs: A synthesis of evaluation research. *School Psychology Review, 33*, 547–560.

Smith, P. K., & Brain, P. (2000). Bullying in schools: Lessons from two decades of research. *Aggressive Behavior, 26*, 1–9.

Sobsey, R. (1994). *Violence and abuse in the lives of people with disabilities: The end of silent acceptance?* Baltimore, MD: Brookes.

Sweeting, H., & West, P. (2001). Being different: Correlates of the experience of teasing and bullying at age 11. *Research Papers in Education: Policy & Practice, 16*, 225–246.

Twemlow, S. W., Fonagy, P., Sacco, F. C., Gies, M. L., Evans, R., & Ewbank, R. (2001). Creating a peaceful school learning environment: A controlled study of an elementary school intervention to reduce violence. *American Journal of Psychiatry, 158*, 808–810.

Whitney, I., Smith, P. K., & Thompson, D. (1994). Bullying and children with special educational needs. In P. K. Smith & S. Sharp (Eds.), *School bullying: Insights and perspectives* (pp. 213–240). London: Routledge.

CHAPTER 15

Mosaic Reflections of American Muslims on Disability: Challenges and Solutions

Mobin Tawakkul, Isra Bhatty, and Mohammed Yousuf

The* American Muslim community is ethnically diverse and consists of an estimated two to six million adherents. As in any other community, American Muslims must address the challenges of accommodating the needs of the disabled. This chapter features three experiential narratives that highlight the breadth of emotion and context of living with disability in the American Muslim community. The first narrative touches on Mr. Tawakkul's challenges to participate in community-based activities as a person who is deaf. In the second narrative, Ms. Bhatty describes her childhood encounter with accessibility challenges at the mosque. The third narrative discusses Mr. Yousuf's struggles to adapt as a new immigrant to community life with a physical disability. These unique reflections will underscore the community resources and perseverance shared by the authors in overcoming challenges. Finally, the chapter offers solutions for the American Muslim population when attempting to address disability issues. All resolutions are derived from personal successes by the authors, the Islamic code of ethics, and the experiences of other successful American communities.

Like the greater American society, the Muslim community in the United States is ethnically diverse, with members ranging from Indigenous African American, European American, and Native American converts to immigrants from Africa, the Middle East, and Asia. Muslims are adherents of the religion of Islam, a word that means submission to the will of God. They are followers

---

* *Disclaimer:* The opinions or views expressed in this narrative are those of the authors only and do not reflect the position or views of the organizations that they are part of.

of the Abrahamaic tradition, which features the core values of compassion, tolerance, respect, equality, and love of one omnipresent and merciful God. Muslims have had an extensive but often overlooked history in the United States.

Muslims from West Africa and Spain reached America long before Columbus (Quick, 1996). Moreover, there were an estimated 2.25 to 3 million African slaves on arrival in the Americas who were Muslims (Diou, 1998). The institutional and community life of Muslims in America, however, did not take shape until the 1960s and 1970s, after the birth of African American Muslim movements of the 1930s and the massive waves of immigration of Muslims from Africa, Asia, and the Middle East following the passage of the Immigration Act of 1965.

The population of American Muslims today ranges from the 2007 Pew National Study figure of a conservative 2.35 million to a 2004 demographics study of around 6 million (Ba-Yunus & Kone, 2004; Pew Research Center, 2007). American Muslims have greatly assimilated into society, where the majority is middle-class (Pew Research Center, 2007). They participate and contribute to American public life in a wide variety of ways, as professional athletes, actors, rap artists, doctors, engineers, teachers, and public servants. Approximately 65 percent of American Muslims are foreign-born and 35 percent are native-born. African American Muslims constitute 20 percent of the American Muslim population (Pew Research Center, 2007).

CHALLENGES OF A DEAF PARTICIPANT AT AMERICAN MUSLIM COMMUNITY EVENTS

From the perspective of a deaf Muslim, Mr. Tawakkul discusses various challenges for deaf people in Muslim communities and religious gatherings. He offers suggestions for easing the integration of deaf Muslims into the greater community, in the form of technical resources, supporting organizations, and research.

Struggles

A couple of years ago, I attended a weekly congregational prayer on a serene, bright Friday afternoon at a local mosque. This mosque was comprised of a diverse set of American Muslims, both Indigenous and immigrants, coming from a wide range of backgrounds—from inhabitants of the shores of Atlantic and the Bay of Bengal to the urban metropolitan districts of the United States. Due to the hustle and bustle of noon rush-hour traffic, I arrived during the middle of this congregational prayer and sat at the back end of the mosque, on top of Persian carpets with intricately repeated geometric mosaics. In loud, audible monotones detected by my cochlear implant's signals, the imam was speaking through the microphone while moving his face right and left to attract the audience's attention on matters of importance related to life and spirituality.

Unfortunately, due to the distance between my peripheral vision and the imam's mouth as well as the bright lights emanating from the ceiling where a crystal chandelier was placed above the pulpit, it was an arduous task for me to read his lips. Further complicating my present situation was my desire to block out the occasional tinnitus (ringing or hissing in the ears; National Institute for Deafness and Other Communication Disorders, 2002) caused by several surgeries to both of my ears in my preteen years. These ear surgeries have resulted in profound sensorineural hearing loss, meaning the absence of function in inner ear parts, such as the cochlea (American Speech-Language-Hearing Association, 2008). Thus, the hearing aids that I had worn since the age of five were of no benefit to me.

Through informed consent with my family, teachers, and the medical community, I underwent cochlear implant surgery at the age of 15. I still rely on lip reading and speech recognition of sounds into actual words via the cochlear implant. The implant's success can vary on certain circumstances, such as the speaker's accent, the speed at which he or she is speaking, and background noises. Thus, according to my understanding, the cochlear implant is not a cure for deafness but an avenue to afford the hearing impaired the ability to hear certain sounds via electrical impulses that stimulate the remaining auditory neurons in the inner ear.

The degree of speech and recognition skills of the cochlear implant depends on several factors such as the user's background, medical history, and degree of deafness. Research has shown that deaf children who get cochlear implants early in their life (as young as the age of two) tend to do better in terms of speech recognition and language skills (Kileny, Zwolan, & Ashbaugh, 2001). A thought was brought to my mind while trying to read the imam's lips: to participate in the lecture, I needed a laptop or notepad on which a volunteer could type or write notes for me. In the oral deaf program, I had usually depended on such services in my mainstreamed classes.

Because I felt left out of the lecture, I eventually turned my head down to daydream at the intricate Persian carpet's mosaic tilings until I was patted on my shoulder by an African American deaf individual who asked via sign language if I used sign language. I gave a smile and shook this brother's hand and said the Muslim greeting, "Salaam," and responded, "Very few" in simple sign language. I am still learning American sign language (ASL) and converse mostly via the alphabet signs. We were both experiencing the same hardship because there was a lack of interpreting services available to deaf and the hard of hearing Muslims at this community gathering.

Interpreting services (e.g., sign language, a notepad/laptop note taker, or a professional stenographer) are currently lacking in American Muslim community events. There have been numerous instances in which I would have loved to have participated in popular weekend events but could not do so fully due to the lack of such interpreting services. There were instances in which I was left out during cultural plays, *nasheed* (Islamic song) concerts, inspirational lectures (both live and Webcast), the hilarious dialogues of our comedians, or educational workshops for enrichment of life skills. For members of the deaf American Muslim community who are left out of these types of events, there can be a sense of isolation or, at worst, depression.

The lack of accommodations to meet the needs of the deaf American Muslim community as well as the greater disabled Muslim community in their activities and events is analogous to a situation which arose at the time of Prophet Muhammad and is described in the first few verses of Surah (chapter) "Abasa" of the Qu'ran (Ali, 2001). A blind companion, Abdullah Ibn Umm Maktum, was thirsty for knowledge so he asked the Prophet a question related to Islamic law. The Prophet frowned and turned away from Maktum because his primary attention at that time was devoted toward trying to speak to the elite tribal leaders on matters pertaining to Islam. God reproached and later forgave the Prophet for not including everyone wishing to learn about matters of spiritual significance. The American Muslim community can learn from this lesson of inclusion and unity in diversity, two of Islam's core ideals. It is important for us to make every effort to include the deaf and other members of our community with disabilities.

Solutions

Fortunately, through the wide range of available services provided by the greater American society for the deaf and hard of hearing community, there are several solutions for the American Muslim community to use when accommodating deaf members of their congregations in community activities.

1. The American Muslim community should become educated on the Americans with Disabilities Act (ADA), which was passed in 1990. The ADA protects individuals with disabilities from discrimination in employment, public accommodations, transportation, and communication. While the law has increased awareness about access issues for the disabled, attitudes of acceptance and inclusiveness have not been universal. For this attitude change to be realized and for real change to occur, proactive efforts via education and empowerment must happen through motivated individuals and communities.

2. The American Muslim community should employ individuals who work with and assist the deaf and hard-of-hearing community. There should be more culturally competent interpreters who are proficient in sign language, individuals who can type efficient notes via laptop, or professional stenographers who use the mechanism referred to as Communication Access Realtime Translation (CART). With this device, spoken word is translated into English text using a stenograph machine and a laptop.

According to the U.S. Department of Labor's Bureau of Labor Statistics, the employment of interpreters and translators is projected to increase 24 percent over the 2006–2016 decade, much faster than the average for all occupations (U.S. Department of Labor, 2007). Pending legislation called the Training for Realtime Writers Act of 2007 from the U.S. Senate (S. 675) and House floor (H.R. 1687) proposes to authorize $100 million in grants over five years to recruit and train realtime writers and captionists (National Court Reporters Association, 2007). There are an estimated 28 million Americans who are deaf and hard of hearing who would benefit with such interpreting services ranging from sign language to CART options (National Institute for Deafness and Other Communication Disorders, 2007).

While growing up in the United States as a deaf Muslim, I was supported by a wide support network of professionals who graciously worked with me and my parents through the strenuous process of overcoming obstacles and succeeding in society. I soon learned that there were myriad professionals who helped the deaf community: speech therapists, audiologists, devoted special education teachers, school administrators, otolaryngologists, personal assistants in college who were hired to take notes via laptop for me, as well as professional CART reporters. The Muslim community should encourage its youth to consider such professions for employment opportunities. In doing so, the entire community can become more educated and empowered on how to meet the needs of the deaf—both American Muslims and those in the greater society.

3. American Muslim institutions should invest in making accessible technology available for the public. These technological solutions range from providing accessible Web-based solutions that are captioned or providing captioning on large plasma displays during community-wide conventions, theatrical plays, and musical concerts. I once joined a convention where I was able to fully participate with the assistance of a CART reporter.

I also participated in a live hip-hop concert showcasing captioning on the plasma flat-screen TV during the University of Michigan's Martin Luther King Jr. festivities in 2008. Captioning would not only assist the deaf and hard-of-hearing community, it would also assist the audience who use English as a second language (ESL) as well as youth and the functionally illiterate who desire to improve their reading skills. In fact, the use of closed-captioned TV programs has been shown to improve ESL students' English vocabulary and reading comprehension skills (Neuman & Koskinen, 1992). It is also well known that captioning results in better comprehension as visual stimuli for the deaf and hard of hearing (Lewis & Jackson, 2001). My parents, whose primary language is Urdu, always watch television with closed captioning. As a result, in their e-mails to me, I have noticed that their English proficiency skills have increased.

Fortunately, there are several resources available on the Web that the community can utilize when looking for captioning on the web or live events, including but not limited to the following:

- National Center for Accessible Media (NCAM): NCAM does research and development to make rich media content resources and technology accessible to individuals with disabilities. Instructions to add captions to Web-based videos or making Web sites more user friendly are available electronically (National Center for Accessible Media, 2007).
- ProjectReadOn: ProjectReadOn allows deaf and hard-of-hearing Web visitors as well as potential institutions to install captions to their Web-based videos for free through providers of captioning content (ProjectReadOn, 2008).
- Described and Captioned Media Program (DCMP): DCMP provides captioned resources to support and improve the academic achievement of students who are blind, visually impaired, deaf, hard of hearing, or deaf-blind (Described and Captioned Media Program, 2008). The American Muslim institutions who wish to have their videos and documentaries with captions to share their heritage with the greater public, especially the individuals with disabilities, can utilize DCMP's services.

- National Court Reporters Association (NCRA): NCRA is a U.S. professional organization that serves court reporters and captioning professionals. American Muslim organizations and communities looking for captioning services for their events or multimedia content can look for local captionists and CART reporters through NCRA's directory of professional services locator (National Court Reporters Association, 2008).

Future legislative mandates may be made to ensure Web and other telecommunications high-content media be accessible via captions for the deaf and hard-of-hearing community. For instance, recent draft legislation in the U.S. House of Representatives titled 21st Century Communications and Video Accessibility Act for People with Disabilities may require the telephone and video programming industries to consider the concerns expressed by the deaf as well as the greater disabled community so they can be allowed to fully participate in society (Markey, 2007). Such mandates, if fully reached, may require the American Muslim community as well as the greater society to adjust to these legislative realities to ensure that high-tech digital content is made accessible to individuals with disabilities.

4. Event planners should be more proactive in soliciting requests for any special accommodations via e-mail, Web site, and other widespread public relations announcements. Every American Muslim organization and community centers should have a contact person to coordinate special accommodations so that individuals with disabilities can wholly participate in their publicized events. Such a contact person should be well versed in searching for potential contacts and accessible solutions such as a sign language interpreter, a laptop note taker, or a CART reporter. This contact person can serve as a mediator between the deaf members of their community and the event speakers and planners on how to meet the needs of the individuals so that full participation of community activities can be achieved.

I have experienced several frustrating incidents where I have tried to reach the appropriate individual to meet my needs for a particular community event but did not know which individual(s) I should contact. There was one event in which the organizers of a community-wide event did not even answer my request to bring my laptop so that a volunteer could type notes for me. At that event, as a last resort, I asked a college friend of mine to graciously provide me with notes; he did so by scribbling as quickly as he could on a notepad. My friend admitted that his notes were not written to the best of his ability because the speakers were speaking too quickly. I also realized that the notes did not fully capture the content of the speech, which was to be expected because he was not experienced in this skill.

5. The American Muslim organizations and community members should practice outreach and collaboration with national, regional, and local organizations that work with the deaf and hard-of-hearing community. Such experiences would allow American Muslims to understand and become empowered on how to meet the needs of deaf Muslims. Organizations such as the National Association for the Deaf (NAD) or the local independent centers for individuals with disabilities can assist American Muslim community centers and organizations with a consortium of great resources and

services pertaining to assisting the deaf and hard-of-hearing members of their community.

FROM STIGMA AND SEPARATION TO ACCESSIBILITY AND ACCOMMODATION: REFLECTIONS ON DISABILITY IN THE CHICAGOLAND MUSLIM COMMUNITY

Here, Ms. Bhatty shares her experiences dealing with issues of accommodation and awareness in the American Muslim community. As a sibling of a child with disability, she relays an account of some of these challenges and offers lessons and advice for the community today.

Introduction

Few Muslims are talking about disability in the United States. Thirteen years ago, there were certainly fewer. I can say as much with assurance, because 13 years ago, I—along with most of my immediate community—had no idea that the world of *disability* existed, or at the very least, paid little attention to it.

The northern Chicagoland Muslim community as I was growing up in the 1990s was both bustling and diverse. It had no shortage of variety when it came to race, ethnicity, and social class, but was undeniably deficient when it came to knowledge or interest regarding disability. This stagnant social situation was shaken from its stupor when my younger brother entered the scene, illuminating the realities of Muslims with wheelchairs, mosques and community centers without ramps or elevators, and the gaping informational and support vacuum that surrounded affected families.

I can attribute the ignorance and apathy of my community on the issue of disability to a number of factors: the general absence of individuals with disabilities in community settings, a pervasive stigma associated with certain social issues such as disability, and—as both a cause and effect of the first two factors—an overall lack of accommodation for individuals with disabilities. As my brother grew older, these problems came into increasingly clearer focus, as did their solutions.

Presence

One of my most vivid memories of growing up in the northern suburbs of Chicago during the 1990s was selling chocolates to raise funds to build one of the largest mosques and community centers on the north side. The fundraising and organizing were successful, and the building we acquired became the first of its kind—not just a mosque but also a full-time school, Sunday school, and community center. I attended the Sunday school, and my parents were very closely involved with the school's administration, serving as upper-level administrators and teachers. In my first five years of attending the school, I had never seen a single individual with a disability in the school, at congregational prayers, or at the community events. When my brother was born in 1995, he became the first obviously disabled child to frequent the school. And everyone took notice.

There was no real name for the disability my brother had, which I think made it harder for people to understand his condition. The straightforward story was simply that he had limited motor and speech skills because of some complications at birth. In any case, the relevant fact to most of the public was that he used a wheelchair to move about, and such visible disability was enough to change the landscape of the school's setting.

In my remaining five years as a student at the Sunday school, plus my two years as a teacher, I witnessed the slow and steady emergence of other individuals with disabilities and their families. My brother remained the only child in a wheelchair, but there were other children who now added faces and personalities to the nebulous concept of disability—children with physical disabilities who used splints, walkers, and crutches, as well as others with mental and developmental disabilities.

The seemingly sudden surge of individuals with disabilities made me think—what was the reason for their increase in presence? I doubted that all of a sudden the pool of individuals with disabilities had suddenly ballooned since 1995. The more likely story was either that families affected by disability were encouraged by the presence of other similarly situated families—like some sort of informal support group—or that individuals with disabilities had always been present in the community and I had simply not taken any notice. I cannot say with certainty which of these hypotheses is true, but the lesson for me has involved elements of both. I realized quickly from the demographic changes that disability was a reality of whatever community we lived in, no matter how intimate. To the extent that affected families felt somehow excluded from the community and wished not to attend the school or its events, such a feeling of exclusion needed to be rectified.

Knowledge

I do not recall any sort of calculation or a deliberate decision-making process that took place when my family entered the school for the first time with my younger brother. Or the first time we brought him there in his new wheelchair. Yet as an awkward youth on the brink of her teenage years, I felt some sort of hesitance or, dare I say, embarrassment at the time. It seems, in hindsight, that my discomfort resulted in part from the fact that I did not really know how to greet the reality of disability. No one around me—neither my family nor my community—had any more knowledge or experience in the matter than I did, so there was a prevailing cloud of ignorance shrouding the issue and contributing to my discomfort.

In a way, as a child, I did not know how to feel, or how I *should* feel, about having a sibling with a disability because I did not know how to feel about disability as a concept. Was it something natural—simply a normal fact of life? Did God create some people able-bodied and others disabled? I felt some determination within me to believe that was the case, but could not overcome the unease I felt when in the presence of others. Why was it the case that I could accept the normalcy of disability in my own home and when one-on-one with my brother, but not when others were looking?

The answer had something to do with general ignorance about disability, but also with the s-word: *stigma*. Stigma, I learned, combined ignorance with psychological discomfort. Stigma surrounded issues that people did not know much about but that disturbed them when they thought about them—issues like disability. Because of stigma, I, too, felt uneasy escorting my brother at school and at various community events. Somehow, his presence was penetrating a bubble of blissful ignorance, forcing people to think about subjects they would rather not face. Each time his wheelchair would enter the school building, the bubble would break, the stigma would unwillingly surface, and what was formerly taboo became at once a stark and present reality. All the latent questions people were previously thinking came into light: was disability "normal," how did Islam treat disability, how should *we* treat someone with a disability? The surfacing of stigma created my discomfort.

But the stigma about disability did not just exist because people were ignorant or disturbed by reality. There was a deeper story at play, which I noticed much later in retrospect. The fact that the issues that were commonly stigmatized in my childhood community were pervasive social problems—such as delinquency, substance abuse, mental illness, or environmental destruction—demonstrated an unwillingness to address these issues and a deemphasis on critical engagement with society. Disability, unfortunately, fell into the category of issues that were neglected, no matter their importance, because the community as a whole failed to emphasize or value them.

Accommodation

Of course, both the problem of the absence of individuals with disabilities from the school scene as well as the problem of general ignorance and stigma surrounding disability, were exacerbated by, perpetuated by, and even themselves causal factors of the lack of accessibility, facilities, and accommodations. While the former two problems were more complex and difficult to discern, this latter problem was readily recognizable from day one. At the moment my family first brought my brother to Sunday school in his wheelchair, we were greeted by the gaping nonexistence of ramps and elevators. Sure, this deficiency was due to the fact that there were none in the original structure—before the Muslim community had purchased it—but it was also clear that adding such amenities was not at the top of the community's priority list. Indeed, I had only noticed the deficit myself on the day I actually needed to make use of them.

The lack of accommodation was not particular to the Sunday School my family frequented. Nearly every mosque or Muslim community center that I went to had accessibility problems, whether in the form of a lack of elevators, ramps, or lifts, or accommodation issues, such as classroom aides and technology for children with disabilities or teachers trained in special education. Despite my frustration with these realities, I could not fully blame the Muslim community, which had worked so hard to acquire buildings. Buildings that were affordable were often only small, two-story houses or older school buildings that only had stairs. Still, to the extent that accommodations were affordable but merely neglected, such as the frequently out of order elevator that never seemed to get fixed, the community *was* to blame.

Perhaps inaccessibility was the reason I had never before seen individuals with disabilities in the school or mosque. Maybe these individuals and families had noticed the lack of accommodations, and so decided not to attend. Or maybe they took the lack of structural accommodation as symbolic of a more pervasive lack of acceptance of individuals with disabilities within the facility. Of course, such a lack of acceptance stemmed from the lack of knowledge about disability, which was certainly perpetuated by the absence of individuals with disabilities. There was a cycle of deficiency in presence, knowledge, and accommodation. I knew such a cycle would never end until someone was determined to break it.

Lessons

Since the moment my brother introduced disability to my northern Chicagoland Muslim community, and the cycle of inadequacy was finally halted, there has been a distinct shift in the attitudes of the community, the demographics of the school, and the physical structure of the facility. These changes have largely been mirrored across the Muslim community of Chicago and throughout the nation. The presence of individuals with disabilities has increased, the knowledge and understanding of disability has been enhanced, and the level of accommodation and accessibility has risen.

The Muslim community in northern Chicagoland has undertaken a number of mosque and school expansion projects, and, happily, the finished structures have been physically accessible. It is my hope that the breaking of the cycle of inadequacy brings about a new cycle of positive change—that the newly constructed accommodations encourage other individuals with disabilities to join community events and attend the school, and that this increasing presence enhances our awareness of disability and the needs of impacted families.

In my years of experiencing the elimination of both physical barriers and barriers to acknowledging and understanding disability, I learned two major lessons. Hopefully, these lessons will foster the same positive changes experienced by the Muslim community in northern Chicagoland in other, similarly situated communities.

Lesson 1: Tackle the Ignorance

Much of the problem that confronts activists working on disability rights issues is the sheer ignorance about disability that pervades communities. This issue must be addressed to pave the way for further change, whether in the form of increased accessibility or for raising awareness for its own sake.

To raise awareness in communities, individuals with disabilities, their families, or others who have first or secondhand experience with disability must be present in the community. There is no better way to illuminate a highly taboo and underrecognized issue than to add faces, personalities, and life stories to the issue. The value of having knowledgeable individuals available to answer questions about disability that will undoubtedly arise or to merely show that disability is a normal fact of life cannot be underestimated.

As demonstrated by my brother's story, the presence of individuals with disabilities in the community can help break the incessant cycle of deficiency that surrounds issues of disability. I saw firsthand how a lack of accommodation and ignorance perpetuated a lack of presence among individuals with disabilities, which in turn contributed to a lack of awareness and, as a result, cemented the lack of accommodation. The cycle must break somehow, and having a critical mass of individuals with disabilities or others willing to speak out and make known the reality of disability can help break it.

The onus of this lesson, therefore, falls squarely on individuals with disabilities, their families, and the people who know how to break the cycle and raise awareness. We have this responsibility and must act on it for the benefit of our communities.

Lesson 2: Build Support

The second lesson I learned from my brother's story is to build support in the community, which means both support in the form of structures (i.e., accommodation) and support in a moral and psychological sense that is geared toward affected individuals and families.

The need and benefit of having structurally accessible facilities is obvious. To the extent that building wheelchair ramps, elevators, and lifts is financially feasible, every effort must be made to ensure their realization. For more financially restricted communities, such features should be emphasized and prioritized as a use of future funds.

A less straightforward form of support that is no less necessary is moral and psychological support for individuals with disabilities and their families. It is extremely difficult, as I have experienced, for affected families to be engaged and to participate in their communities. In a way, such actions make these families feel vulnerable, so creating support groups for affected individuals and families would be very beneficial. These groups let their members know that they are not alone and that they have support, and inform them of the various sorts of help and options they have.

For most Muslim communities, the creation of support groups is the next step toward true accessibility and accommodation. Such groups can begin small, in the form of mingling rooms at large-scale events such as the Islamic Society of North America Convention or even locally at various mosque-centered events. The critical task in creating these groups are to make sure that they are advertised well, especially in places that families with disabilities frequent, such as certain hospitals, therapy centers, and other support centers in the community. Of course, word of mouth is a powerful advertising tool in itself. In creating support groups, the community will not only offer much-needed support to individuals with disabilities and their families within community settings, such as mosques or education centers, but will also increase awareness about disability in the community itself.

FROM AN IMMIGRANT'S PERSPECTIVE: INCLUSION OF INDIVIDUALS WITH DISABILITIES IN THE MUSLIM COMMUNITY

In the final narrative in this chapter, Mr. Yousuf narrates his story of coming to the United States as a college student. He contrasts his American experience with his experience in India as a youth disabled by a childhood battle with polio, sharing his reflections on the numerous challenges he has faced.

A New Beginning

August 26, 1990. It might not be a special day for most; however, it was a great day for me when the Air India flight landed at the Kennedy airport in New York. Unfazed at the challenges that remained ahead of me in adjusting to a new lifestyle without the support of my family and friends, I was willing to give it try and a chance, to make it worthwhile in pursuit of a new destination, a new dream, and a new lifestyle—to become successful in leading a meaningful, independent yet fulfilling life.

Yes, I had left behind all the dear ones, but the barriers and the attitudes of people toward individuals with disabilities in India seemed more difficult to handle than the pain of living without the dear ones. I missed the connecting flight to Detroit that night and was allowed to stay in a hotel. Although I was lonely there, looking out of the window, I could see the bright, full moon shinning its glory and calm on a city bustling with activities. I felt different looking at the same moon that I used to see in India, where there were challenges . . . many challenges.

Life in India

At the age of two and a half, I came down with a high fever, and over the course of few days, I became so weak that I was not able to walk. My worried parents took me to the doctor, who failed to recognize that I had polio. By the time I was diagnosed, the disease had done its damage, leaving me unable to walk. Polio made it impossible for me to walk without leg braces and crutches. For years my family coped with the indifferent attitude of family and friends and kept me at home, assuming that an education was not in the realms for me. At the age of 12, I started attending school at the encouragement of my grandmother, and I did well enough to skip fourth grade and advanced through the grade levels.

When I graduated with a degree in electronics and communication engineering, I thought that my challenges would be over. Even though there were so-called provisions to hire individuals with disabilities in India, none of the corporations and the private companies came anywhere close to adhering to those guidelines. Much to my disappointment, an engineering degree did not result in a career in engineering nor in an independent life. I went from pillar to post asking for suitable employment. But it was not there. People felt that I would not be able to perform the duties of an engineer because I had a disability. The feeling among the employers then was that I should pursue menial skills, such as becoming a telephone operator or a clerk.

The disappointment was actually a blessing in disguise since it forced me to explore opportunities outside of India. I came across a school catalog from the United States that talked about special handicap places for vehicle parking. That caught my attention and a little bit of research convinced me that it would be most meaningful to try and land in the United States to seek a career based on abilities. I fulfilled the requirements and applied to a couple of universities in the United States. I was issued a student visa and was allowed to study at a masters program in electrical/computer engineering. I was accepted by two universities, the University of Arkansas and Wayne State University in Detroit. I chose the latter. I waited anxiously to see what the future would hold for me.

Life in the United States

When I reached Detroit, I could not find a place to live on campus. The only residence that was available was about couple of blocks away from the university. In that old red-brick, six-story building lived a couple of people from the same town that I had come from—Hyderabad. They were all very willing to help and made me feel welcomed and comfortable. To this day we are all good friends and have become a part of each other's families. I lived with two other roommates who, to my surprise, were very caring and sensitive to my needs. I learned how to cook, and we all took turns cooking meals for each other. On my insistence, they would allow me to do some home chores where and when possible.

It all seemed easy until the first big snow hit the ground. I remember one of my roommates jumping up in excitement, looking at the bright white landscape outside. While they were just excited to see the snow, inside I was afraid and frightened as I did not know how I would cope with the snow's effect on my mobility. I knew walking with leg braces and crutches would not be fun or easy as mounds of snow accumulated. As the days went by, I learned how to walk in snow and on slippery surfaces. I knew walking out every day that it would only take a little accident for me to slip and fall down. I used to count my blessings every day and would go out on simple faith. I did fall a couple of times on campus, but thankfully I was not injured.

A couple of weeks into my education, I was able to get an on-campus job. I made US$4.75 per hour working as a student assistant at a library. Twenty hours of work, two classes, the walk to the campus, and the chores at the apartment were enough to keep me busy. But I was happy that I was able to do things on my own. I could see that I was one step closer to getting my goal.

I was soon able to obtain a manual wheelchair, but it was not much help as the apartment and building that I was staying in was not wheelchair-accessible. There was a set of stairs to get into the building, but the elevator that took me to the sixth floor was out of service most of the time. I used to walk up the six flights of stairs sometimes. Little did I know that even the Americans with Disabilities Act, which was passed in 1990, would not enforce compliance due to the old age of the building.

The campus was about a 20-minute walk for me, and to make things worse, one of my classes was almost at the far end of the university campus, necessitating a 45-minute walk. I walked that distance every week during the fall semester, navigating a set of stairs that led to my classroom as the campus building lacked an elevator, and sometimes the slippery sidewalks that were not shoveled did not make it any easier. I still remember those cold wintery nights when the temperature and chill factor used to dip below zero; it was difficult to find many people even walking. I braved the weather; Almighty God gave me the spirit to get somewhere and kept me going.

By the end of the first semester, things started to change for the better. I was able to get a housing unit on campus and was awarded a housing allowance by the engineering college. A Muslim community center was able to get me a scooter. I became a member of the President's Committee on People with Disabilities at Wayne State University in 1991. Little did I know that this would become my passion—to work for the betterment of individuals with disabilities within and outside of the United States.

I received my master's degree in computer engineering in 1992. Soon after, I bought a used car and was able to obtain a driver's license. I was ecstatic to be able to drive a vehicle fitted with hand controls for the first time. I felt great pleasure to be independent, to be able to go wherever and whenever I wanted. I joined Chrysler Corporation as a product engineer and got married to a caring and understanding woman from India, Humera. We now live in Michigan with our three lovely children.

Throughout the years, I volunteered on several initiatives. I soon realized that although there were a number of nongovernmental organizations working on different relief and social development alternatives for India, Pakistan, Palestine, Somalia, and so on, no other group or organization in the United States was working to specifically address the needs of individuals with disabilities in India. So I founded the HelpHandicap Foundation in May 2001 with the help of few other friends. The HelpHandicap Foundation is a nonprofit organization that seeks to better the lives of individuals with disabilities in India (HelpHandicap Foundation, 2008). It has helped over a thousand people with various disabilities pursue education, receive equipment assistance, and start self-employment in different parts of India.

I have also associated myself with a number of community-related projects for the betterment of individuals with disabilities in the American Muslim community and in mainstream America. However, it seems that not much has changed within the American Muslim community since 1990 when it comes to attitude, acceptance, and sensitivity toward individuals with various disabilities.

Seeing some parents and individuals with disabilities struggle in our community reminds me of my childhood, when even a casual walk with braces and crutches across my neighborhood was an arduous task as it invariably invited curious onlookers and noisy name callers. I realized that the name calling had to do with how I looked and walked. I did not have an issue with that. However, I started to feel different emotionally since I was treated differently because of the way that I looked physically. As a result, I turned away from the world around me and mostly confined my life to myself.

While polio is currently virtually nonexistent in the United States, other impairments like autism and mental impairments in particular are a cause of worry to thousands today. Our community seems to be particularly lacking due to a serious level of deficient awareness about available resources and how to cope and live with a disability.

More and more, children with disabilities and their parents are living a life of despair and isolation. Parents may prefer to stay at home with their children with disabilities rather than participate in social events and gatherings. The burden is mostly shouldered by the mothers, while the fathers go out to earn a living and be at social events within the community without the child. Imagine the psychological impact on these parents. The trend is alarming and is causing huge psychological damage to the family, the individuals with disabilities, and the society at large.

There is a certain degree of social stigma attached to a physical disability and that in turn adversely influences inclusion in the community, thus leaving individuals with disabilities feeling isolated and unwelcome. This might be the reason some families are reluctant to disclose that their child has a disability. This might be the reason they do not want to take the child to a social event because people offer an abundance of sympathy and bombard them with embarrassing personal questions in public. We do not seem to understand that it was not their choice to have a disability; if they had a choice, they would prefer a life without a disability. However, just because they have a disability does not mean that their disability should become the topic of the evening. This is a subtle and inadvertent form of maltreatment.

Reflections

Parents need not feel insecure about having a child with a disability or be apprehensive about exposing her or him to the mainstream; the sooner they do so, the better it will be for them and the child. In society, some children often tease and mock a child with a disability in an unabashed manner. The impact of this teasing can be minimized if the children become educated and empowered about disability-related issues as they become older, so that these children may eventually come around and learn to live and deal with children with disabilities in much the same way as the siblings, friends, and peers of children with disabilities.

Although the ADA, disability advocacy groups, and independent living centers have helped increase awareness and community inclusion for individuals with disabilities in the United States, my American friends with disabilities point out that they had to deal with a lack of sensitivity and awareness in the past. The progress we now see today in the United States is the result of many years of concentrated effort from various individuals and groups. A similar effort needs to take place in the American Muslim community now. The change has to come from all sides—parents, individuals with disabilities, and the broader society as well.

GENERAL CONCLUSIONS

The American Muslim community is at a unique stage in its development. Recognizing and utilizing its diversity, the community has begun thinking critically and seriously about issues of social justice. On the issue of disability, however, the community has a long way to go. Based on our experiences, we suggest that the American Muslim community incorporate the following four recommendations in their future institutional and social development plans.

Increase Awareness about Disability

The Muslim community as a whole should make an effort to increase awareness about disability on all levels, beginning with their leadership. Imams, educators, and religious leaders should use various forums, including Friday sermons and Sunday School classes, to discuss disability and the community's responsibilities towards individuals with disabilities. Families and individuals with experience in disability issues should also take the initiative to educate their leaders and peers, pushing the latter to disseminate the information to others. Although leaders may be educated one on one, we can also set up general education classes. Such classes should make sure to extend their education services to children and youth.

Build Internal Support Systems

Muslims with disabilities and their families suffer from public stigma and informal segregation. The community, with the help of affected families, should create support systems for Muslim individuals and family members. These support systems should serve as networks of individuals with shared experiences that can rely on each other for moral support, guidance and counsel, expertise, and resources. Such systems have been a cornerstone in various social service settings and are much needed in American Muslim circles to provide support for individuals with disabilities and their families.

Think about Accessibility as Minimum Requirements

Just as various American disability provisions, including the ADA, use the concept of minimum requirements when making facilities accessible, the American Muslim community should develop its own minimum requirements for its various mosques, schools, and community centers. Architecturally and design-wise, these requirements may involve, at the very least, ramps and elevators. In terms of resources, mosques and learning centers should require that certain religious materials (e.g. the Qu'ran and major texts) be provided in alternative forms for the visually impaired. Similarly, Friday sermons and major lectures should be accompanied by interpreters or electronic caption services for the hearing impaired. The community, including individuals with disabilities, should decide collectively on what minimum requirements should be in place.

Move toward Thinking about Universal Design

American Muslims should also move toward thinking about universal design in their facilities. Universal design minimizes the stigma associated with disability by using barrier-free technology and design. Some examples of universal design include wide hallways and doorways, ramps, and volume and speed controls on audio output devices. Moving toward this system of design would send a message of inclusion to all individuals with disabilities and their families.

By following recommendations such as these, the American Muslim community can demonstrate in its dealings with and attitude toward individuals with disabilities the same broadmindedness and humanity that has historically characterized Islam's view on disability.

REFERENCES

Ali, A .Y. (2001). *The meaning of the Holy Qur'an*. Beltsville, MD: Amana.

American Speech-Language-Hearing Association. (2008). *Type, degree, and configuration of hearing loss*. Retrieved May 31, 2008, from www.asha.org/public/hearing/disorders/types.htm.

Ba-Yunus, I., & Kone, K. (2004). The mosque and the American public square. In Z. H. Bukhari, S. Nyang, M. Ahmad, & J. L. Esposito (Eds.), *Muslims' place in the American public sphere: Hopes, fears, and aspirations*. Walnut Creek, CA: Altamira.

Described and Captioned Media Program. (2008). *Described and Captioned Media Program home page*. Retrieved February 13, 2008, from www.dcmp.org.

Diou, S. A. (1998). *Servants of Allah: African Muslims enslaved in the Americas*. New York: New York University Press.

HelpHandicap Foundation. (2008). HelpHandicap Foundation home page. Retrieved February 17, 2008, from www.helphandicap.org.

Kileny, P. R., Zwolan, T. A., & Ashbaugh, C. (2001). The influence of age at implantation on performance with a cochlear implant in children. *Otology and Neurotology, 22*(1), 42–46.

Lewis, M. J., & Jackson, D. W. (2001). Television literacy: Comprehension of program content using closed captions for the deaf. *Journal of Deaf Studies and Deaf Education, 6*(1), 43–53.

Markey, E. (2007). 21st Century Communications and Video Accessibility Act for People with Disabilities draft bill. Retrieved February 13, 2008, from markey.house.gov/docs/telecomm/draft_of_telecom_legislation.pdf.

National Center for Accessible Media. (2007). NCAM rich media accessibility. Retrieved February 13, 2008, from ncam.wgbh.org/richmedia.

National Court Reporters Association. (2007). Federal initiatives: The Training for Realtime Writers Act will help meet the demand for closed captioning and provide new opportunities for court reporters. Retrieved February 12, 2008, from ncraonline.org/PubPolicyAdvoc/fed_init.

National Court Reporters Association. (2008). National Court Reporters Association home page. Retrieved February 13, 2008, from www.ncraonline.org.

National Institute for Deafness and Other Communication Disorders. (2002). The noise in your ears: Facts about tinnitus. Retrieved May 31, 2008, from www.nidcd.nih.gov/health/hearing/noiseinear.asp.

National Institute for Deafness and Other Communication Disorders. (2007). Statistics about hearing disorders, ear infections, and deafness. Retrieved February 13, 2008, from www.nidcd.nih.gov/health/statistics/hearing.asp.

Neuman, S. B., & Koskinen, P. (1992). Captioned television as comprehensible input: Effects of incidental word learning from context for language minority students. *Reading Research Quarterly, 27*(1), 95–106.

Pew Research Center. (2007). *Muslim Americans: Middle class and mostly mainstream*. Washington, DC: Pew Research Center for the People and Press.

ProjectReadOn. (2008). About ProjectReadOn. Retrieved February 13, 2008, from www.projectreadon.com/index.php?pg=about.

Quick, A. H. (1996). *Muslims in the Americas and the Caribbean from before Columbus*. London: Ta-Ha.

U.S. Department of Labor. (2007). Interpreters and translators. Retrieved February 13, 2008, from www.bls.gov/oco/ocos175.htm.

CHAPTER 16

Voices of People with Disabilities (PWD) in Vietnam

David N. Morrissey

While serving in grassroots disability organizations and self-help clubs in Vietnam for three months in 2006 as part of my graduate fieldwork, I surveyed people with disabilities in that country. Working with a Vietnamese translator and community advisory committee, I designed a set of questions that encouraged people to provide genuine and personal narratives about their experiences. Personal narratives and storytelling provide access to the experiences of groups who lack or are denied power to make their voices heard (Booth, 1996). My questions contained categorical demographic questions, such as gender, age, and types of disabilities. I then asked five attitude or narrative-eliciting questions with open-field answer spaces. These questions pertained to misunderstandings among peers about disabilities, interactions with disability service organizations, unmet needs, memorable experiences as a person with disability in school, and hopes and dreams for people with disabilities in Vietnam.

Sixty-two people were surveyed in Vietnamese, and their responses were translated into English. Those responses are presented in this chapter. I have supplemented the voices of people with disabilities with my own journal entries, recorded during this time on the ground in Vietnam. The narratives presented in the chapter give voice to Vietnamese people with disabilities and their communities, and reflect real situations for people with disabilities around the world, in both industrialized and developing nations, and convey universal hopes. People with disabilities in Vietnam today are expressing their truths to change policy and raise awareness of their potential to work, to study, and to succeed.

DISPATCHES FROM VIETNAM

Toward completion of the master's of public service degree at the University of Arkansas, Clinton School of Public Service, I spent 11 weeks in Vietnam serving grassroots disability organizations and surveying people with disabilities to fulfill the international fieldwork requirement of the program. With a background in community-based disability and health-related organizations, I developed a project vision with Peacework Development Fund to go to Vietnam under their auspices. I was hosted locally by their partner organization, the Hop Tac Tre YMCA of Vietnam, and a project advisory committee.

This advisory group was comprised of independent researchers and disability advocates with extensive working history in the promotion of social awareness of people with disabilities and whose members have been engaged in both social work practicum training programs at National Vietnam University of Social Sciences and Humanities, Ho Chi Minh City, and with nongovernmental organization (NGO) projects in Vietnam and abroad. The committee provided me with documents and networking linkages and facilitated logistical considerations for me and my assistant-translator. My emersion was defined by life in a guest house in a nontourist area of Ho Chi Minh City, formerly Saigon, and my time was spent in site visits to various service organizations and self-help clubs, teaching grant-writing workshops, assisting grassroots organizations in grant application development, assisting disability educators in curriculum development, consulting in a visioning meeting of university students with disabilities, and participating in various disability forums.

In addition to these activities, I surveyed 62 Vietnamese people with disabilities and conducted approximately 20 interviews with Vietnamese and international NGO staff persons, disability activists and consultants, and one government official working in disability services coordination. I reviewed recent Vietnamese government and international reports.

Finally, I engaged in extensive journaling during the three months in Vietnam. The injection of my own observations into this chapter is intended to provide local color and a first-person account of my observations of the lives of people with disabilities in Vietnam. My observations also convey my experiences as a person with a disability in Vietnam.

From my journals, I selected excerpts to send by e-mail to friends and family; I also posted entries to an online blog, along with photographs and video clips. Loved ones back in the United States and in other countries were able to reply with encouragement and interest in the posted details of my work, creating a global community of instant communication not delayed by courier mail nor constrained by expensive telephone calls. Voice-over-Internet Protocol telephone and video conferencing software turned my laptop computer into an international communication station. I was fortunate that the guest house where I lived had high-speed Internet to make this technology feasible, though the service was sporadic. When on the road in Vietnam, Internet cafés were readily available for plugging in and dispatching news of my experience. Within my first 48 hours on the ground, I had posted the following notes online:

> I have arrived in Ho Chi Minh City and I am exhilarated, yet exhausted by a long journey through five airports and four long flights. The scene outside the

Ho Chi Minh City airport was crowded and noisy, with hordes of people in the stifling heat and sun, women mostly, pushed up tight to the barriers, calling out, holding signs with names, reacting with wails when a long-gone relative emerges from the airport and is seen. The barricaded path through the middle of this mob leads to the taxi stand with drivers offering rides, where I identified my liaison by the sign she held with my name and I waved at her and she back. We got into a taxi and left the airport and into the famed streets of Saigon, teeming with motorbikes and bicycles mostly and only a few cars, the women frequently in mouth coverings like surgeons to keep out the dust and exhaust but sewn of flowery prints, along with wide-brimmed hats or traditional cone hats and no one wearing a helmet. Streets curve and circle and merge with streets and the uncontrolled traffic merges awkwardly, dangerously, accented by honking horns in all styles. To be suddenly in this traffic, weaving through Saigon with its mix of old and shiny new structures was thrilling.

Although my time in Vietnam would be temporary, my status as someone disabled by mobility impairment is not. My identity as an adult with spina bifida has provided me a guiding inspiration for my career work, but in my work abroad it provided recurring contextual awareness for me as a foreigner and traveler. Another excerpt from that first journal entry written on arrival illustrates this:

In anticipation of the long journey, I had arranged for transport between gates at every airport. Each time, a sky cap was waiting on the gangway from the plane with a wheelchair. I am so glad I did arrange for that, as Dallas, Los Angeles, and Hong Kong all involved great distances between gates. It really would have been exhausting to walk those airports on foot with a carry-on pack on my back. At some point I realized, perhaps while being pushed in a wheelchair, that my journey to find the disabled of Vietnam is allowing me to experience disability myself in a new way.

BACKGROUND: THE BOY AND THE MOTORCYCLE

The Socialist Republic of Vietnam is a communist state in Southeast Asia. The country's geopolitical history since the mid-19th century has been defined by nearly a century of French colonial rule, an ensuing war for independence from 1945 to 1954, Japanese occupation during World War II, division into North and South by the Geneva Conventions, and war with the United States for reunification from 1954 to 1975. Today it is a country of approximately 84 million people with a poverty rate just under 20 percent and is categorized as a low-income nation by the World Bank. Although the tumult of the 20th century delayed development in infrastructure, health care, and education, the 1986 *Doi Moi* (Renovation) free-market reforms placed the country in a position of increasing economic growth. By 2006, it was regarded as one of the best-performing developing economies in the world (World Bank, 2007).

Disability rates in Vietnam are only estimates due to a variety of challenges to surveying. The conditions that define disability in Vietnam is a challenging task, and thus accurate estimates of disability prevalence are elusive. Discrepancies stem from inconsistent definition of disabilities and imprecise groupings, inadequate staff training in collection procedures, and insufficient analysis. This inconsistency, openly acknowledged by both the Vietnamese government and international organizations, has led to a variety of estimates. Data discrepancies exist between various governmental ministries and NGOs' surveys; geographic data-collection programs have also varied among provinces. The quality of reported data varies widely.

However, it is believed that disability in its most inclusive definition is highly prevalent in Vietnam, that children comprise a high proportion of the disabled population, and that service deliverers do not have the capacity to fully address need. A 1999 meta-analysis of existing reports on disability in Vietnam acknowledged the reporting issues and determined that although the range of estimates for the overall prevalence of disabilities in Vietnam ranged from 2 to 10 percent, it was most likely 5 to 7 percent (Kane, 1999). This remained the case seven years later in a 2006 report on disability to the 11th Meeting of the National Assembly of the Socialist Republic of Vietnam. Here, the Social Affairs Committee also acknowledged the challenge of the lack of measurement standards, but concluded that approximately 6.34 percent of the population, or 5.3 million people, had a disability (National Assembly of the Socialist Republic of Vietnam, 2006).

Prevalence estimates for each specific type of disability also vary widely from one source to another; national survey estimates and community-based rehabilitation data indicate that motor disabilities make up more than one third of disabilities. The 2006 parliamentary report provided a slightly smaller number of 29.4 percent mobility impaired, with the overall breakdown for types distributed as 29.4 percent mobility impairment, 13.8 percent vision impairment, 23 percent mental impairment, and 20 percent multiple impairments (National Assembly of the Socialist Republic of Vietnam, 2006).

Despite the lack of a uniform framework for defining disability in Vietnam, it was my observation among Vietnamese professionals, as well among people with disabilities themselves, that the "four major impairments" framework remains dominant: mobility, hearing and speech, vision, and mental disabilities. I decided to employ the four major impairments framework in my surveys, with the addition of a fifth category ("other"), providing the opportunity for respondents to further explain their self-identified disability. One Vietnamese activist with disability told me that Vietnamese culture tends to define disability by observable impairment, resulting in misunderstandings about the legitimately disabling effects of some hidden conditions, such as persons with mental impairments being regarded as deviant.

The prevalence of acquired disabling conditions is profound in Vietnam due to the high incidence of construction site and traffic accidents as part of the nation's economic boom. According to Handicap International, which operates a number of therapeutic and prevention programs for people with spinal cord injuries, these injuries are frequent and increasing in Vietnam due to a lack of safety conditions on building yards and on the road network. "The recent improvement of the socio-economic conditions in Vietnam (more particularly in the large cities) has significantly increased the number of motor vehicles and particularly the number of motorcycles which comprise approximately 80% of the traffic" (Handicap International, 2004, p. 64).

During my time in Vietnam, over the course of a summer, I watched from my bedroom window as five-story homes grew like mushrooms around me, growing vertically almost overnight, and accomplished by the labor of everyday Vietnamese men, women and teenagers, all without helmets. One would see a professional crew involved only in the most specialized and heavy building activities, such as setting the steel I-beam inner cores of buildings. The flooring, roofing, tiling, finishing were predominantly accomplished by regular folks, families, and friends, it seemed to me.

The traffic in the cities of Vietnam is famous for its density of motorcycles and motorbikes, frequently overburdened in transporting multiple passengers, groceries, construction equipment, and even panes of glass. Internet Web sites now feature video clips of this traffic to amaze foreigners with its recklessness. Today, NGOs are engaged to try and mitigate the risk of injury by providing helmets for children. The following excerpt from my field journal was written a few weeks into my time in Vietnam. It concerned the traffic and was written on the weekend of my first venture onto a motorbike.

> Most transportation in Vietnam is motorbike or bicycle and the streets are filled with them both, rode by whole families on single units, pregnant women, babes in arms, children wedged between parents, man doubling up with construction materials such as panes of glass between them, all in a motorized chaos mixed with pedestrians. Traffic lane markings and control lights are really just a suggestion. Cars are very rare, except for taxis, which I am using mainly, but tonight I was to ride and felt it was time. A volunteer showed up to get me and I hopped on and held his shoulders and off we went through the enclave and then we were out on the streets of Saigon, my first time out in it not in a taxi.
>
> Now I was truly among the masses of Vietnamese on the Volkswagen of Vietnam: the *xe om* (motorcycle). I was nervous at first, holding on tight to his shoulders and he could tell, asking me what I thought of the traffic, and then more directly, "Does the traffic make you nervous?" I relaxed my grip a bit. Sitting at stoplights with dozens of people on mopeds and motorcycles, whole families on single units, pregnant women, babes in arms, children wedged between parents, it all seems normal, not so daring, and almost safe. Young girls on the backs of bikes don't hold on at all and even ride side-saddle. They flip through their purses or look in their shopping bags. As we got onto progressively busier streets, into the major roundabouts, down the big thoroughfares of District 1, I did begin to enjoy it. He was a fine driver, though he did take a cell phone call once mid-ride.
>
> As the evening progressed and we journeyed from the restaurant to a dark café and finally to home again, I became very comfortable with the ride, abandoned his shoulders for the handle behind me, which was actually much more comfortable, and was able to look around as we rode and enjoy the ride through this famed city, participating in the mode of transport which takes lives, causes disability, and inspires awe upon first sight. I felt a sense of accomplishment when I was returned home for having accepted the motorbike challenge and survived the ride. The traffic of Saigon was not so bad, it now seemed to me.
>
> The next morning I watched as a child ran out into the street and was hit by a motorcycle just a few feet from where I sat on the curb. I cried out. He spun like a top, running into the side of the moving bike and bouncing back, whipped around in a spin, then falling out flat upon the pavement. I jumped up. His mother came running into the street from the pharmacy where she had

been and where it seems he had come running out. I backed away. The biker came to a stop and yelled to them. It was a bright Sunday morning and the neighborhood was busy. People came to doorways, the video game lady and my landlords and neighbors, though none intervened. I couldn't look at the boy laid out and his mother kneeling over him and so I looked away for a moment to walk up the curb and onto the stoop of our guest house, also to just get out of the way. The house folk could see the shocked look on my face. I turned back to look and the woman was picking the boy up. He was conscious and perhaps in shock and she picked him up though he was a big boy, maybe even seven years old, and carried him hurriedly down the quiet cross street and into a nearby home. He didn't begin to wail until they were nearly there.

I had been reading these last couple of days a UNICEF report on Children with Disabilities in Vietnam. Traffic in this city alone is estimated to take five lives each day. Government and NGO efforts are now engaged in awareness campaigns and getting helmets to children. I have already been amazed at the independence of children here in the enclave, walking and playing in the streets with the countless bicycles and motorbikes dodging them. There are no sidewalks in Ho Chi Minh City and no yards, only a few parks and schoolyards. When we returned later that Sunday afternoon from the university in Thu Duc, we inquired with the video game lady downstairs if she knew any more about the boy and she indicated that no ambulance had come to the house, so he must be okay. If no injury is apparent, a poor family will forgo a trip to hospital, but who knows if there is damage: a chipped vertebrae or whiplash or closed head trauma may not immediately present itself to the family's eyes. I will hope for the best for him. Maybe I needed to see this accident for myself. I had seen it up close and heard. The impact and the boy's subsequent spinning are etched in my mind. I was terribly upset in the moments after witnessing the accident and was tempted to run to my flat and hide, not to go on about with the day, fearful of the effect of this event on my psyche here, on my dreams tonight, but fortunately my advisory team had soon arrived after the mother and boy disappeared into the home and we were suddenly in a taxi ourselves bound for our meeting at the university. Those first few moments in the taxi I was shaking, staring out bitterly at the traffic of Saigon.

STRANGE QUESTIONS

People with disabilities traditionally and universally lack or are denied power to make their voices heard and, in Vietnam, this has been true. Only in contemporary Vietnam, where a grassroots disability movement is in nascent stages, are these voices beginning to find the clout and social influence that can be derived from authentic expression. The authentic voices of the people with disabilities in Vietnam are now expressing their truths to change policy and raise awareness of their potential to work, study, and succeed. My surveys would allow me to compare stories, identify common experiences of systems and society, and synthesize the stories into this shared story of a group people.

I structured my questions in such a way as to invite subjective interpretation by each respondent and allow them to answer in a way they found suitable to their understanding of the question. The questions were designed to merely open up topics of conversation. To invite narratives, the questions prompted for recollections of experiences and allowed the respondent to freely structure their response (Riessman, 1993).

I relied on my contacts within the organized disability movement, particularly the grassroots self-help clubs, to identify people to be surveyed. This resulted in most respondents being participants in these self-help clubs or recipients of these programs. The vocabulary and described values therefore may be characteristic of individuals who are acquainted with disability issues. For example, the use of the acronym PWD (Person with Disability) is popular among disability activists, and this was used frequently in responses. In another example, many of the people surveyed from a particular self-help club employed the phrase "inferiority complex" in reference to something they had overcome or which they hoped PWDs across Vietnam would one day overcome. One respondent explained that the club's sponsor had taught her to overcome her inferiority complex.

Respondents were found in large cities and middle-sized towns, but none were collected in small towns or rural settings due to the limitations on time and travel for the author. However, a few people referred to having been born in a rural or small town environment and then moving to a larger town or city in search of employment, education, or rehabilitation services. The following description from my journal about engaging a group of participants from a grant-writing workshop in completing my questions in a written survey was an important point of learning for me:

> Today was the Grant Writing Workshop and it was a great success! We had 25 students, which filled the room. The space was not air conditioned as I had been told it would be, but that was okay; it was hot, but a breeze rolled through the open doors and it was not unbearable. The students had a diversity of disabilities: at least four were blind, several were crutch users, several had walking impairments without assistive devices, one young woman was missing a hand. The able-bodied still identified themselves as being with self-help disabilities organizations. . . . At break time, we distributed the surveys for the students to complete for me. Several were perplexed by the questions, so we told them that these were "experimental" questions devised to allow them to answer in any way they chose and that if they could not answer any questions, this was alright, they could skip those. Upon preliminary review of the responses, only a few were returned with incomplete sections.

The final survey instrument was titled "The Voices of Persons with Disabilities (PWD) in Vietnam" and was made available in both English and Vietnamese versions. The first questions were intended to collect categorical demographic information about the respondents and therefore were structured by limited response fields or choices.

1. Please tell us your age and your gender.
2. Are you a person with disabilities? If Yes, for how long? Please circle your disabilities (mobility, mental, visual, hearing, or other). Please circle the cause of your disabilities (birth effect, traffic accident, labor accident, accident at home, war effect, or other).

3. What is the highest level of education you have achieved? (never attended school, home schooling, or other).
4. Please describe your occupation.

The remaining questions all provided large blank areas for narrative answers.

5. Can you describe a misunderstanding others frequently have about your abilities?
6. Can you describe the needs you might have related to your disability that no organization has been able to help you with enough or even at all?
7. Can you describe memorable experiences you have had when you searched for or contacted organizations to assist you with a need you had related to your disability?
8. Can you describe memorable experiences from when you were in school related to your disability?
9. What are your hopes and dreams for PWDs in Vietnam?

The questions were distributed to leaders of self-help clubs and other disability activists to redistribute and return to the researcher. Answers were received in Vietnamese and the research team collaborated on translation into English. The translator and I discussed translation choices extensively to honor the particular meaning conveyed in Vietnamese and also to construct logical phrasing for the English translations.

DEMOGRAPHIC RESULTS: PEOPLE WITH DISABILITIES

Sixty-two completed surveys were collected. Twelve respondents completed the survey with assistance from volunteers due to visual impairments. The respondents ranged in age from 13 to 66 years old. The average age was 27.6 years old, and the median age was 24 years old. Thirty respondents were female (48 percent) and 32 were male, (52 percent). Two thirds of respondents identified as having mobility impairments (64 percent, 40 respondents) and just under one third identified visual impairment (29 percent, 18 respondents). Another 2 percent identified mental impairments, and none identified hearing or speech impairments. Only 5 percent failed to identify their disability (see Table 16.1). The overrepresentation of mobility and visual impairments was related to the particular self-help clubs where recruitment occurred.

In terms of the cause of their disabilities, 12 respondents (19 percent) indicated the presence of birth effects (e.g., Agent Orange, lack of vitamin A, petechial fever, poisonous chemicals from father, retinal detachment; see Table 16.2). One participant was born with a missing hand or arm (the respondent used the Vietnamese word that is imprecise and represents both hand and arm). Traffic accidents (6 percent), labor accidents (5 percent), and war (5 percent) accounted for 10 of the respondents (see Table 16.3).

More than half of the respondents (55 percent) chose "other" as the cause of their disability. In providing further explanation of these other causes of disability, most respondents wrote "polio." Only 10 percent of respondents declined to attribute a cause for their disability. The remaining causes included scarlet fever (two people), disease (two people) and fever, tuberculosis of the meninges, corneal disease, optic nerve paralysis, health condition resulting in paralysis, and sunlight (one person each) (see Table 16.4).

Table 16.1 Self-Identified Types of Disabilities Derived from Survey Instrument Criteria Based on the Four Major Impairments

Impairment Classification	Response Count	Percent of Total Reponses
Mobility impairment	40	64
Visual impairment	18	29
Mental impairment	1	2
Hearing or speech impairment	0	0
Other	0	0
No response	3	5
Total	62	100

Table 16.2 Explanations for the Choice of Birth Effect as to the Cause of Disability. of 12 Respondents Who Chose Birth Effect, 6 Opted to Explain Further

Explanation for Disability Cause: Birth Effect	Response Count
Agent Orange	1
Lack of vitamin A	1
Born missing left hand/arm (respondent employed a Vietnamese word that is imprecise and represents both hand and arm synonymously)	1
Petechial fever	1
Poisonous chemicals from father	1
Retina fell off	1
Total	6

Table 16.3 Cause of Disability as Guided by Survey Instrument Criteria

Cause of Disability	Response Count	Percent of Total Responses
Birth effect	12	19
Labor	3	5
Traffic	4	6
War effect	3	5
Other (See Table 16.4 for further explanations)	34	55
No response	6	10
Total	62	100

Table 16.4 Explanations for the Choice of Other as to the Cause of Disability.

Explanation for Disability Cause: Other	Response Count
Polio	24
Scarlet fever	2
Disease	2
Fever	1
Tuberculosis of the meninges	1
Corneal disease	1
Optic nerve paralysis	1
Health condition resulting in paralysis	1
Sunlight	1
Total	34

QUALITATIVE RESULTS: EMERGING THEMES

The content of the responses allowed me to group the personal stories thematically. Although these themes were often elicited by different questions, the stories emerged with considerable cohesion and corroboration. Stories are presented in the following order, followed by a discussion of any unique survey responses:

1. Raising issues of employment (emerging from multiple questions)
2. Raising issues of education (emerging from multiple questions)
3. Other unmet needs (from question 6)
4. Memories of school time (from question 8)
5. Hopes and dreams for PWDs in Vietnam (from question 9).

1. Raising Issues of Employment

The need for stable and appropriate employment opportunities was the single greatest concern expressed by survey respondents. Employment issues were raised in answers to the three questions, "Can you describe a misunderstanding others frequently have about your abilities?" "Can you describe the needs you might have related to your disability that no organization has been able to help you with enough or even at all?" and "Can you describe memorable experiences you have had when you searched for or contacted organizations to assist you with a need you had related to your disability?"

Respondents wrote about need for gainful employment, accommodation in the workplace, and social acceptance for pursuing employment. "People don't believe in my working ability," wrote a 26-year-old male, mobility impaired from polio. Other responses raising issues of employment included the following.

> [I was] looking for a job after graduation but most of the companies don't accept PWDs. (24-year-old male, mobility impaired from polio)

> I really need a job to have a stable salary and really wish to have jobs I can work at home in order to be comfortable for my moving and daily life. (42-year-old male, mobility impaired from labor accident)
>
> I need jobs that are appropriate to my health, such as always having to sit on a wheelchair. After two hours of working I must rest for five minutes. In the workplace there should be toilets that wheelchairs can access. (42-year-old male, mobility impaired from labor accident)
>
> I wish there are certain places that help me have a stable job in the future so I can take care of myself. (23-year-old female, mobility impaired from polio)
>
> In 1995, I went to a joint-venture sewing company to ask to work there. They thought I wasn't a PWD at first so they accepted. But when I worked with the machine, they realized I have a disability so they refused. (29-year-old female, mobility impaired by polio)
>
> Employers ask for nice appearance from applicants. Can PWD fit that requirement? (25-year-old female, mobility impaired from polio)

In the responses to the question about hopes and dreams for PWDs in Vietnam, employment was also the most common thread. Out of 62 responses to this question, 24 included a reference to employment, with seven of those qualifying the hope even further with the expression "stable job." Many respondents also framed their hope for jobs as not just for their personal benefit but for all PWDs in society.

2. Raising Issues of Education

Although a question in the survey asked specifically for memories related to educational experiences, many respondents utilized earlier questions to raise issues relating to education. Three questions (about others' misunderstandings, unmet needs, and memorable experiences when searching for organizational assistance) elicited issues about participation in educational opportunities. These responses echoed many of the barriers experienced in employment. Responses included:

> When I asked to go to school, I was refused. They say, the blind cannot do anything, so you cannot study. (19-year-old female with visual impairment from birth)
>
> I felt sad because I was refused to take English class. (23-year-old female with visual impairment from scarlet fever)
>
> People often feel suspicious about my education. They assume I will not be able to do anything after graduation. (24-year-old male with mobility impairment from polio)
>
> Studying materials for the blind my university does not have. (27-year-old male with visual impairment from disease)
>
> I'm not accepted to go to school. In sighted school, I didn't see well. In blind school, I see very well. So, both schools don't accept me. (13-year-old male, ethnic minority, with visual impairment from birth)
>
> I need elevators in the companies or universities where I study at. There's very few universities have elevators, the most of them don't. I'm taking evening classes in a university where I have to climb the stairs to the third or fifth floor everyday. (24-year-old female, mobility impaired from birth)

3. Other Unmet Needs

The question "Can you describe the needs you might have related to your disability that no organization has been able to help you with enough or even at all?" yielded a variety of concerns in addition to employment and education. Comments included public accessibility, funding for grassroots activities, and advancement of medical services and treatments. The highlights included:

> I asked the Student Communist Party to help my disabled association but they refused. (24-year-old male, mobility impairment from polio)
>
> We wish the society to change their thinking which is not yet right for PWDs such as their learning ability, working capacity, and social activities, in order for PWDs to integrate into the community. (61-year-old male, visual impairment from war)
>
> [I searched for] an eyes operation that Vietnam is not able to do. (24-year-old male, visual and verbal impairments, attributed to "disease")
>
> Be able to have health checks, be guided how to limit side effects or complications because of disabilities. For example, how to treat spinal twisting for people who are mobility impaired. (24-year-old male, mobility impairment from polio)
>
> I wish PWDs have priority in medical checks and treatment because we the PWDs can't wait in line right now. When I went to Tu Du Maternal hospital to check for my infertility, they didn't give priority for women with disability. I waited from mornings to the afternoons but there wasn't my turn yet. I couldn't be patient enough to wait for the hospital's "favor" so I said goodbye to the hospital after three times waiting there. (42-year-old female, mobility impairment from polio)
>
> My need is to be integrated in the community and wish to have equality with people without disabilities. (24-year-old female with mobility impairment from birth)

4. Memories of School Time

When asked to recount memorable experiences related to their disability from when they were in school, answers ranged from appreciative to critical, from both inclusive to special educational settings, and for both childhood and adult education. Positive memories of being assisted or encouraged by peers and faculty in both mainstream and special educational settings were prevalent, such as, "When I was in school, my friends helped me, cared for me, and accompanied me so I could overcome three years in high school" and "I have sympathies from my teachers, as well as from friends, and have encouragement from school and it is a memory I can't forget." Other appreciative comments included:

> I often fall down on the ground and my friends usually help me to stand up. (24-year-old male with mobility impairment from polio)
>
> When I integrated with other PWDs, I realized that when your friends are weaker than you, you can help them by moving the wheelchairs for them or passing the rice to them. (27-year-old female with mobility impairment from polio)

I have lots of friends who are not disabled. They don't discriminate. We play with each other impartially and they always listen to my ideas. This makes me feel very confident and sometimes I forget I am a PWD. (28-year-old female with mobility impairment from polio)

Since I was born, I haven't taken part in any school for PWDs because my home town is very poor and has no resources to open a sheltered school. When I came to Ho Chi Minh City, there are friends who led me to join the disabled youth club. Here, I can make friends, study, and join other activities. My memorable experience is in the club many teachers usually hold cultural and musical exchange with other PWDs. The smiling faces are the things I remember most. (24-year-old female with mobility impairment from birth; cited Agent Orange as cause of her disability)

In 1999, from a newspaper I learned there was a vocational training program for PWDs. Upon arriving, I was really surprised when I was welcomed cordially and was guided whole-heartedly to take A-level applied computer class. Nowadays, from the help of that center, I have computer certification as a technician which serves in the job I am doing. (29-year-old female with mobility impairment from polio)

Memories of the awkward uniqueness of being a PWD in a mainstream school were recurring in the responses and are captured in the following statement by a 19-year-old with a visual impairment: "In school, I have to sit really close to the board to see and write, so my friends devour me with their eyes." Other narratives included:

In schools and university, I had to stay in class at gym time and military training time. I was very lonely and upset. When it was raining and slippery during my teenage years, I remember falling down on the ground among the crowd. I also had to hold the back of my friend's bike to walk during my university time, I was very nervous and shy because of everybody's eyes around me. When I became a teacher, one day I walked from the teachers' room to the school yard to salute the flag. I stepped on a wire and fell down in front of other teachers and all of the students. The bread in my bag spilled out as well. I was very shy in front of my colleagues and the students. (48-year-old female with mobility impairment from polio)

I started to have inclusive education. My teacher held my hand and walked me into the room and everybody teased me because they thought I was getting special care, not realizing I was blind. (22-year-old female with visual impairment, cause not stated)

When I was six I went to school and I was teased by other friends and they call each other to come and see me and they watched me and they asked each other why I only had one arm and I cried and I ran home crying. (24-year-old female with mobility impairment from birth)

Memories of having to self-advocate for systems change or accommodation included:

My university has nine floors but when I was in the first year, I realized that elevators were just for teachers and staff. I talked with my dean and principal about this and after that we the students with disabilities were allowed to use the elevators. (28-year-old female with mobility impairment from polio)

I passed the entrance exam to Hanoi Teacher Training University in 1971, but because I had an eye problem, I wasn't allowed to study there. Me and two other individuals had to have the help of the chairperson of MOET [Ministry of Education and Training] and then we were allowed to study there. (61-year-old male with visual impairment from war effect)

When I was in 11th grade, I happened to hear news from the radio saying that PWDs could have free tuition fees according to how serious their disability was. However, when I asked my school about this, they said it didn't exist. I was very surprised and wrote a letter to the radio station to ask about that and then the Educational and Training office reprimanded the principal of my school and then I didn't have to pay the tuition fee. (24-year-old female with mobility impairment from birth)

5. Hopes and Dreams for PWDs in Vietnam

The final survey question, "What are your hopes and dreams for PWDs in Vietnam?" included recurring calls for stable employment (24 people), educational opportunities (13 people), social inclusion (17 people), and happiness (13 people). Other responses included the hope for benefactors (17 people) and concern from society (13 people) (see Table 16.5). Example comments made by respondents were:

> Every person with disability has a stable life and job and happiness to all of them. (24-year-old male, mobility impairment from polio)
>
> Integrate more and more in society. More and more PWDs are able to go to school and have stable jobs. (42-year-old male, visually impairment from labor accident 13 years ago)
>
> I dream and hope that PWDs in Vietnam get what is good for them and always love their lives and live more pleasantly. (23-year-old female, mobility impairment from polio)
>
> I hope everybody around the world help us and are concerned for us and people in Vietnam have to give all conditions to us so we can overcome difficulties in life. (19-year-old male, visually impairment from sunlight)
>
> I have a wish and that is the benefactors and government always concerned with PWDs more and more so that they have a job to work and to feed themselves. I wish companies and organizations help PWDs. And my bigger wish is PWDs, let's try to overcome. (23-year-old female, mobility impairment from traffic accident 3 years ago)

Table 16.5 Most Prevalent Response Themes in Answer to the Question, "What Are Your Hopes and Dreams for PWDs in Vietnam?"

Hopes and Dreams	Response Count
Jobs	24
Concern from society	17
Integration in community life	17
Education opportunities	13
Happiness	13
Benefactors	11

> The biggest dream of mine is to have appropriate concern from the community and society; have job, as well as the minimum facilities that are appropriate to each specific physical condition. For example, can go to working place by wheel chair, go to toilet, and participate in sport activities in each province. (42-year-old male, mobility impairment from labor accident 10 years ago)
>
> Every PWD wishes to have care from the society so that they can have opportunities to have appropriate jobs, stable life, and integrate in their community. (61-year-old male, mobility impairment from war effect 39 years ago)
>
> I wish to have lots of supporting means and service for PWD in our country, i.e., equipment on busses so that wheelchairs can access. (28-year-old female, mobility impairment from polio)
>
> I hope PWDs in the Vietnam get over their difficulties, don't feel shy in front of others, have stable life, and are always happy. (34-year-old female, mobility impairment from polio)

Although the open survey queries yielded trends and common concerns, as shown in the previous sections, the goal of the survey was not to quantify opinions so much as to record authentic voices, and thus unique responses elicited from various questions must be presented as well. These responses did not appear as frequently across the respondents, but reflected an important aspect of the experiences of PWD.

> People look at me with strange eyes when I am moving on my handshake wheelchair because they think I am a lottery seller.[1] (23-year-old female with mobility impairment from polio)
>
> People define PWDs by a different eye, the eye that is scared of the PWDs. (21-year-old female with mobility impairment)
>
> We once practiced singing and there was a teacher coming to our homes to help us practice. Day after day we were just sitting when practicing. As the performance date neared, the teacher asked me to stand up and perform. He thought I have healthy arms. He told me, "You must reach out your hand and perform." That day, I asked him, "You've been practicing with us all of these days but you don't even know that I am PWD!" He shrugged his shoulders and said, "Sorry."' (23-year-old female with mobility impairment from traffic accident)
>
> When I joined the social security club,[2] which is now the disabled club where I live, when people saw me they thought I couldn't do anything without one hand, but I did the laundry, and people wanted to do it for me because everybody tries to outdo each other, but I could do it myself and they were really surprised. (24-year-old female with mobility impairment from birth)
>
> A misunderstanding between my close friend's mother and me. He is just a close friend, but his mother thought we were together, so she came up to me and spoke frankly with me to not block his future. I was very sad because she saw me as her child but not as her son's girlfriend. (22-year-old female with mobility impairment from polio)
>
> In my high school, I had to study in a school that was 3 km from my house. Sometimes I had to walk. I wished to have a hand-shake wheelchair, but I did not know where to ask for one and my family was very poor and in my hometown PWDs were so disadvantaged that they didn't have any place that offered standard crutches. We had to buy them from other places or use patchy crutches to help ourselves. (22-year-old female with mobility impairment from polio)

THE JOURNEY TO THE MEKONG

The experience of being a Vietnamese with disability is no different from being a PWD in any other country, developed or developing. When asked, the person with a disability wants to work; learn; be meaningfully engaged in their community; have respect, autonomy, and equality; and be understood. They also express a hope for the realization of things only imagined: treatments and services and attitudinal shifts, not only for their own individual experience but for the experience of others, their peers, and those who will come after them, and for their society at large. There is a desire to have an acknowledged identity, both personal and global, from the girl wanting to be regarded for her abilities at the sewing machine to the boy looking to the international community to bring treatments currently unavailable in his country. By sharing our stories, PWD increase the understanding others have about our circumstances and possibly inspire them to act, not only to respond to the call of another person but to positively impact the world they share with PWDs in a way that will continue beyond them.

I close this chapter with another selection from my journal, written late in the fieldwork experience, concerning my journey out of Ho Chi Minh City and down into the Mekong River delta and the small city of Can Tho. This is a beautiful region. Can Tho has a much slower pace than that of the megacities of Ho Chi Minh and Hanoi. Set beside the Mekong River with all of its floating commercial activity, its misty, tropical atmosphere instantly won my heart. For the PWDs with whom I met and the self-help work they were doing, I have great affection. I hope this passage captures that affection. Reading it now takes me back to Vietnam, my experiences there, and the voices of in PWDs in Vietnam that are stored fondly in my mind.

> We have arrived in Can Tho after a long van ride. The journey was disappointingly less rural than I had hoped, with the two-lane highway dotted by crowded small towns the entire route. Only on occasion did we see a rice field, women in cone hats bent over working in it, sarcophagi of dead ancestors on concrete slabs rising from the fields on the periphery, small white monuments in the family rice fields. More water and frequent bridges characterize this region, with small canals and streams and large river bodies. Many shirtless men along the trip, either working or lounging in hammocks; one woman who seemed to have dipped into a canal beside the road for a wash or to cool was emerging bare breasted, pulling on a dress.
>
> At the River Mekong we arrived at the boarding docks for the ferry to cross to Can Tho. The place was like a market of desperation, with trash strewn about, people coming up to the cars to sell produce or bottled water or lottery tickets. A man without hands on either arm banged his stumps against my window begging repeatedly. This was a harried experience, with us passengers getting out of the van and walking through the ticket line with many others, bicycles and motorcycles, children. I saw a man slip on his brake on his motorcycle while we were together paused in line for the ferry and his toddler in his lap lurched to the side and banged his head on the iron gate. The mother and other women standing beside were all upset by this and hugged and passed the child among them.
>
> Finally, we boarded the ferry, an iron furnace in the sun all day, emblazoned with Danish-Vietnamese flags and branding, and we climbed to the upper deck

to view the river scene and its opposing shores for the short voyage to Can Tho. We watch the fishermen and vendors boating in fruits and vegetables and passenger ferries unloading these cargos at the docks. It was quite idyllic watching the women in cone hats in their long shallow boats mooring alone with long poles, silhouetted in the morning sun and river mist.

NOTES

I thank everyone engaged with Hop Tac Tre YMCA of Vietnam and those who served on my advisory team: Luu Van Loc, Tran Van Trung, Le Quy Ha, Truong Vu Thuy Loan, Tran Ba Thien, and Grace Mishler. Grace is a licensed social worker and a teacher whose longtime work in Vietnam made so much possible for me. Her connections, insight, and faith brought many wonderful people together and made many unforgettable events develop around me. Her dedication to the people living with disabilities in Vietnam and around the world is boundless, and her resolve to continue working side by side with them is inspirational.

Finally, my gratitude is immense for Le Kim An Nhien. An Nhien served as my research assistant, translator, travel companion, colleague, and friend. We agreed on many things in the daily decision making, scheduling, and translations, and without her, my time in Vietnam may not have been so abundantly fruitful. Her professionalism as a sociologist and sincere concern for others make her an asset to her country.

My experience of being immersed in Vietnam was one of awe and humility, humor and challenge. My most wonderful memories are of the people I am so fortunate to call my friends in Vietnam. The Vietnamese people with disabilities warmly welcomed me and shared their hearts with me, for which I am so grateful and humbled. I am particularly honored to know the disability activists who are working so hard at the grassroots level to make real those hopes and dreams of PWDs in Vietnam.

1. Selling lottery tickets is a common vocation of persons with disabilities in Vietnam. Roaming lottery sellers are frequently seen on city streets using handshake wheelchairs or white canes.

2. This is a reference to a group home environment for PWD. The same respondent answered elsewhere that they now "live and study with other PWDs who have the same problems and since then I feel that my life is useful. Since then, I no longer feel inferiority complex and it changed me so far from a person with inferiority complex to one with courage, who is brave and has a will."

REFERENCES

Booth, T. (1996). "Sounds of silence": Narrative research with inarticulate subjects. In *Disability and Society: Emerging Issues and Insights* (Longman Sociology Series). London: Longman.

Handicap International. (2004). *Vietnam annual report*. Ho Chi Minh City: Author.

Kane, T. (1999). *Disability in Vietnam in 1999: A meta-analysis of the data*. Washington, DC: U.S. Agency for International Development.

National Assembly of the Socialist Republic of Vietnam. (2006). *Social Affairs Committee report on disability*. Ho Chi Minh City.

Riessman, C. K. (1993). *Narrative analysis*. London: Sage.

World Bank. (2007). *Vietnam: Laying the foundation for steady growth* (Country Brief). Washington, DC: Author.

CHAPTER 17

Substance Use Disorders and Disability: An Examination of Co-occurring Disorders in Nigeria

Stephanie L. Lusk and Teresia M. Paul

Research has shown repeatedly that substance use and its associated problems have manifested themselves worldwide, and Nigeria is no exception. According to Odejide (An Overview of Substance Abuse Prevention and Treatment in Nigeria, unpublished paper, n.d.; 1989), problems with substance use disorders have grown continuously within Nigeria, affecting all aspects of its culture. Alcohol, cannabis, and amphetamines were more prominent in Nigeria in the 1960s, whereas in the 1970s and 1980s, drugs such as benzodiazepines and barbiturates were added to the list of most commonly abused drugs. By the 1980s, drug trafficking had come into prominence, and substances such as cocaine, heroin, cannabis, pemoline (used to treat attention deficit-hyperactivity disorder and narcolepsy), ephedrine, and pethidine (a synthetic narcotic drug) were introduced to more individuals in more areas across Nigeria.

The United States is continuing to encounter individuals from a variety of cultures and ethnic groups, and to effectively assist and serve these individuals, it is imperative that one understands their worldview. In understanding their worldview, it is also important to better understand who we are as Americans and what is required to move forward in creating a world that is culturally sensitive and responsive to the needs of others. One trend that has been noted across all nations is the need for culturally responsive mental health services and addiction treatment. However, there is an astounding lack of information on evidence-based treatments and best practices for different cultures, especially for some African countries. Nigeria is one country in particular that has lacked research on mental health, culture, and best practices for providing treatment for mental illness and addiction. However, as this problem continues to grow, so do the number of professionals who are conducting research and providing prevention, intervention, and treatment services.

To learn more about the mental health system and the role of culture in Nigeria, we developed a qualitative research project, from which this chapter is solely based, that focused on the relationship between substance abuse, mental illness, Nigerian culture, and the influence of American stereotypes on substance use. The project involved participation in cultural activities and interviewing numerous mental health professionals, psychiatrists, social workers, and individuals in community agencies across Nigeria. The goal of this research was threefold in that it was to (a) assist in helping us gain a better understanding of Nigerian culture and its unique needs and concerns in relation to substance use disorders and its impact on mental illness, (b) assist in highlighting how important culture is in regard to the provision of appropriate treatment, and (c) assist in establishing best practices that can be used when counseling individuals from this culture. With the growing number of students and individuals immigrating to the United States from Nigeria, this chapter becomes globally relevant.

Individuals who are suffering from mental health and substance abuse disorders do not suffer alone—their families are affected as well. These effects ripple out through the community, the nation, and eventually across the globe. Understanding and developing appropriate services is an important reason for studying culture, and it is also important to understand how culture impacts other issues related to drugs, such as trafficking and the connection to religious and cultural ceremonies. Vesely (2000) noted the presence of major drug trafficking operations in Nigeria and observed that Nigerian women have become major players in the trafficking of illicit drugs. It is important for us to better comprehend the dynamics of the Nigerian culture and its relationship to drugs if we are to provide better services to those affected by drugs and continue to fight the war on drugs.

Designing culturally responsive substance abuse programs requires careful examination of the target population's unique characteristics and cultural heritage (Atkinson & Hackett, 2004). Nigeria is a country that has been overlooked by the world of academia and neglected in terms of substance abuse and mental illness treatment. Although every racial/ethnic minority group is characterized by unique cultural, migratory, social, economic, and political experiences, three themes are prevalent in Nigerian culture: (a) family structure, (b) cultural healing, and (c) spiritual beliefs (Robinson, 2005). These concepts are at the foundation of Nigerian culture and permeate the field of mental health and substance abuse treatment.

A BRIEF LOOK AT NIGERIAN HISTORY

Nigeria has ties to civilization as early as 500 B.C.E., when the Nok people roamed the Earth. Nigeria was an official British colony, but gained its independence in 1960 and became a republic in 1963. After gaining independence, conflict arose between ethnic groups and a civil war erupted throughout the nation from 1967 to 1970. Over 1 million Nigerians are estimated to have died during the civil war, and the effects are still seen today (Falola, 1999).

Although Nigeria has slowly worked toward a democratic government system, military dictators meant that the country saw some of the bloodiest military coups and human rights violations against civilians (Oyeshile, 2004). Elections have been plagued by corruption, greed, tribalism, violence, and oppression. Political leaders have mismanaged the country's lucrative oil resources and catapulted Nigeria into economic turmoil (Ake, 1996; Oyeshile, 2004). Injustice, marginalization, and ethnic conflict have created a structural imbalance in Nigeria's political and governmental system. Fortunately, two international foundations, the African Union (AU) and the New Partnership for Africa's Development (NEPAD) have been established to aid with debt relief, economic aid, employing democracy, and combating political instability (Ake, 1996; Oyeshile, 2004).

Demographics of Nigeria

In 2007, the population is estimated to have reached 128.8 million, which includes over 250 different and unique ethnic groups that speak over 250 different languages. The largest ethnic groups in Nigeria include Hausa (21 percent of the population), Yoruba (20 percent), Ibo (17 percent), and the Fulani (9 percent) and a range of other smaller ethnic groups (33 percent) (Falola, 2001). Each ethnic group has a distinct cultural legacy and heritage that is infused in the broader Nigerian culture.

Although English is the official language of Nigeria, less than half of Nigerians can actually speak it. A mixture of English and local language (pidgin English) is often used to communicate between ethnic groups. Nigerians often become fluent in many languages and dialects, although they will have a "host language" depending on the area in which they live (Falola, 1999, 2001). Language is also tied to religion.

The religions of Nigeria are Islam and Christianity. Individuals residing in the north are primarily Muslim (50 percent), and those residing in the southeast are Christians (40 percent) (Falola, 1999, 2001). The remaining 10 percent of the population follow traditional Nigerian belief systems that differ from state to state. Many Muslims and Christians incorporate these traditional African belief systems and Indigenous traditions into their religious practices. In the northern regions of Nigeria, Muslims have written Shari'a law into the constitution. Shari'a law is a policy with moral guidelines that can be instituted in court proceedings. However, many Nigerians, and particularly Christians disagree with Shari'a law, which has fueled a growing conflict in Nigeria.

Cultural Dynamics

Nigerians will identify first with their ethnicity, followed by their religion, and finally their nationality. This has proven to be a barrier to Nigerian unification and sovereignty. Conflicts based on religion or ethnicity have been at the core of many Nigerian civil wars and riots (Falola, 1999; Oyeshile, 2004).

Nigerians take pride in their culture and heritage, and of utmost importance is the family. The family system in Nigeria is a source of strength and organization, serving as the moral center for individuals and influencing the path an individual takes in life. Family systems are extensive, usually including extended family, and are often a closed system. Families tend to reside together in familial compounds, especially in rural regions of Nigeria. The family is male-dominated, and the male head of household makes all major decisions for members of the family. Respect for elders is taught at a very young age and is also common across ethnic groups. Nigerians have maintained their high level of respect for elders by preserving the closed family system (Falola, 2001). Child-rearing is similar to the concept of "being seen and not heard," and respect for adults is embedded in the moral teachings of children. Depending on religious affiliations, some families may practice polygamy, which creates a larger network of familial relations. Polygamy is common in Nigeria across all religions (Falola, 2001). Before a man can introduce a new wife into the family, he must have permission from his family, including support from his wife or wives. He must also prove he can financially support a new wife. Family is just a small part of Nigerian cultural identity, and it is important to understanding social issues such as mental illness and drug abuse.

MOST COMMONLY ABUSED DRUGS

The drugs most commonly abused in Nigeria today are very similar to those we have seen in the United States. Presently, the most commonly abused substances according to Odejide (1989) are (a) alcohol, (b) tobacco, (c) *igbo* (marijuana, Indian hemp), (d) stimulants/mild stimulants, and (e) hypnosedatives.

Alcohol and Tobacco

Alcohol is the most commonly abused legal drug almost everywhere, including Nigeria. Initially, the production of alcohol in Nigeria was local. Thus, limited quantities were produced, and rates of misuse were low and seldom reported. Drinks such as palm wine (*ogogoro*) and ferments of cereals such as corn (*burukutu*) were a common part of the culture. Palm wine is reportedly used in religious celebrations and ceremonies and for everyday drinking. Children have access to these drinks because they are commonplace in Nigerian society. Most individuals do not view alcohol as a drug, which, when coupled with its easy access, increases the potential for abuse.

Before the Nigerian civil war of 1967–1970, little attention was paid to the drinking problems that were beginning to emerge, particularly in males (Odejide, n.d.; Odejide & Ohaeri, 1989). Males were drinking heavier amounts and developing pathological problems that required hospitalization. Alcohol abuse was crossing ethnic, social, religious, and even gender lines. Even though males still dominated treatment facilities for alcohol abuse and addictions, the rates of women abusing alcohol had increased dramatically (Odejide, 1989).

This rise in alcohol consumption was due to an increase in the number of breweries and industries that produced spirits. There were only 7 breweries in Nigeria in 1977; this number increased to 34 by 1985 (Odejide, 1989). Thirteen more industries that produced distilled liquors or wine were built during this time. The volume of wine and spirits produced increased from 1.0 million hectoliters (1 hectoliter = 26.4 gallons) in 1982 to 5.9 million hectoliters in 1983. Following this increase in production, corresponding increases in consumption, addiction, and treatment were seen. Alcohol-related disorders were seen in women and students. Alcohol-related social pathologies (e.g., lack of parental control, dropping out of school, accidents, criminal offenses, family disruption), health problems (including HIV/AIDS), and financial problems also increased (Odejide, 1989).

The rates of smoking for males and females have also consistently increased over the past years for males and females. In 1990, approximately 15.4 million males and 1.7 million females smoked. These numbers increased to 23.9 million males and 17 million females in 2001 (World Health Organization, 2008). Obot (1990) observed that individuals who were poor and uneducated smoked more than those of higher socioeconomic and education status. Also observed was that these individuals had higher incidences of health problems and were generally unaware of the correlation between smoking and these problems. According to the British American Tobacco Web site (2008), the volume of tobacco produced in Nigeria increased from 1,260 tons in 2001 to 2,230 tons in 2004, and the number of growers increased from 899 to 1896.

Igbo (Cannabis, Indian Hemp, Marijuana)

Igbo was relatively unknown in Nigeria until after World War II (Klein, 1999). This herb was brought back to Nigeria by soldiers returning from war. It spread quickly across the nation and became associated with individuals who were considered to have "loose morals" (Klein, 1999, p. 55). There have been several laws passed in Nigeria that prohibit the use of cannabis, such as the Indian Hemp Decree of 1966 and the Indian Hemp Amendment Act of 1975. However, none of these laws have been effectively enforced. Researchers have hypothesized that the use of cannabis is primarily for self-medication (i.e., to reduce or alleviate the psychiatric symptoms or stress; Green, Drake, Brunette, & Noordsy, 2007). Cannabis is domestically produced and is considered by some to be the biggest danger to Nigeria (Klein, 1999). In 1960, Lambo (as cited in Odejide, 1989) noted a correlation between cannabis use, maladaptive behaviors, and psychiatric disorders.

Stimulants/Mild Stimulants

The abuse of "Superman pills" or stimulants such as amphetamine, methamphetamine, and the prescription drug Ritalin (methylphenidate) is growing in popularity within Nigeria (Odejide, 1989, p. 14). Coffee, tea, and kola nuts are milder stimulants that are also readily available and widely used. Cocaine use was relatively unheard of until the 1980s, when drug trafficking became more prominent in Nigeria. Intravenous use of cocaine has not been widely reported, which has reduced the risk of transmitting bloodborne pathogens, such as HIV/AIDS and hepatitis C (Odejide, n.d.). However, Adelekan (1996; as cited in Odejide, n.d.), found that intravenous injection of these drugs is increasing.

Individuals who have been admitted to psychiatric hospitals for complications related to stimulant use/abuse have been found to suffer from schizophrenia-like psychosis, toxic psychosis, affective psychosis, anxiety states, personality disorders, and "brain-fag syndrome" (Odejide, n.d., p. 10). Brain fag is identified as a culture-bound syndrome by the American Psychiatric Association within the *Diagnostic and Statistical Manual*, fourth edition, text revision (2000). It was initially identified in West Africa and is defined as "a condition experienced by high school or university students in response to the challenges of schooling. Symptoms may include difficulties in concentrating, remembering, and thinking" (p. 900). These students may also experience pain and pressure around the head and neck and blurring of vision.

Hypnosedatives

The most commonly abused sedatives in Nigeria are benzodiazepines, such as Valium (diazepam), and barbiturates. Often, these drugs are prescribed by physicians to patients who are seeking to self-medicate underlying psychiatric conditions (Odejide, n.d.). Women are more likely to abuse drugs in this class, and they generally seek benzodiazepines to relieve anxiety (Odejide, 1989).

THE COMBINATION OF SUBSTANCE ABUSE AND MENTAL ILLNESS

Mental illness is still considered taboo in Nigeria. Most individuals believe such disorders as being caused by evil spirits or as punishment for the wrongdoing of ancestors. As a result, the occurrence of mental illnesses in Nigeria is underestimated. Other reasons for this underestimation of mental illness include lack of appropriate assessment and the inability to classify those who may not meet the full criteria for a disorder (Gureje, Lasebikan, Kola, & Makanjuola, 2006).

It is well known that there is a link between substance use disorders and either a diagnosed mental illness, such as depression, psychotic disorder, or anxiety disorder (Green et al., 2007). Researchers in Nigeria noted that individuals seeking treatment were generally young males with psychotic behaviors. Odejide (1989) noted that these individuals were likely to have "defective personality development" (p. 11) and a history of unstable families and parental deprivation. Both privileged and less privileged socioeconomic backgrounds in Nigeria were equally likely to abuse cannabis (Ihezue, 1988). Odejide (1989) found that males who displayed chronic cannabis use were likely to drop out of school.

The most common disorders observed in Nigeria are drug-induced psychosis, schizophrenia, affective or mood disorders (bipolar I, II, and depression), and organic mental disorders (Abiona, Fatoye, & Okwerekwu, 2006). More often than not, individuals with mental illness seek the help of a religious leader or traditional healer before seeking assistance from a hospital or other therapeutic setting. For example, religious leaders may perform an exorcism or traditional healers may prescribe a herbal remedy. If there is no relief through these resources, treatment may be sought at a psychiatric hospital as a last resort. When the individual finally enters treatment, they have worse symptoms due to delayed treatment. They may also present not only with the psychiatric illnesses, they may also have acquired physical ailments as a result of traditional treatments (personal communication, Dr. Victor Lasebikan, New World Specialist Hospital, Ibadan, Nigeria; June 25, 2007).

USERS AND ABUSERS OF SUBSTANCES

Area Boys

From the foregoing research, individuals, particularly males, in Nigeria have a tendency to begin experimenting with substances very early on. These individuals often find themselves unemployed and addicted to drugs and engaged in a plethora of illegal activities to support their habits. As a result, these men have been dubbed "area boys" by their peers. Because of their mobility, it is difficult to determine their numbers. These young men are more likely to be addicted to drugs that are cheap and readily available, such as alcohol and cannabis (Morakinyo & Odejide, 2003).

The street cost of cannabis is cheaper than the cost of some brands of cigarettes and can be bought from petty traders. Even though these youths abused cannabis, this study showed that they were less likely to use drugs such as hypnosedatives, solvents, cocaine, and heroin. This is thought to be due to the higher cost associated with these drugs. Positively correlated to drug use was the length of time these young men lived on the streets (Morakinyo & Odejide, 2003). It is believed that drug use serves as a coping mechanism for these individuals; it helps them deal with the many adverse situations they may face such as poverty, loss of family ties, unemployment, and so on.

Inmates

The Nigerian Drug Law Enforcement Agency (NDLEA) noted that drug use was spreading at a rapid rate across the country. This organization believed that drug use was leading to activities that promoted the break-up of the family and the civil unrest leading to poor implementation of laws and policies. The creation and leadership of this organization has lead to the arrest of over 3,000 individuals who were involved in drug activities such as trafficking and selling drugs (Klein, 1999). Klein (1999) noted a large portion of individuals are incarcerated because of these drug-related offenses. Harsh penalties have been assigned to these individuals, such as imprisonment for up to 25 years, and General Musa Bamayi, who has served as chairman of NDLEA, even advocated for the death penalty for these individuals (Klein, 1999).

Amdzaranda Fatoye, Oyebanji, Ogunro, and Fatoye (Psychoactive Substance Use and Associated Factors amongst a Sample of Prison Inmates in

Nigeria, unpublished study) found that there were several common sociodemographic factors found among those incarcerated. Found in this study were nine variables strongly associated with current drug use: (a) unemployment, (b) being a sentenced prisoner, (c) previous mental disorder, (d) previous arrest(s) for drug offenses, (e) being charged for a major offense, (f) previous imprisonment, (g) longer duration of imprisonment, (h) being male, and (i) belonging to a higher age group. While all drugs included in this study correlated significantly to these nine variables, some presented extremely strong relationships. Individuals who abused tobacco were more likely to have previous drug arrests. Previous arrest for drugs and committing a major violent crime were acts more likely seen among those who abused alcohol. Cannabis use was associated with high correlations between previous drug arrests, previous imprisonment, and higher age group. Substances most likely used among this population included tobacco, hypnosedatives, alcohol, stimulants, cannabis, morphine, inhalants, cocaine, and heroin. Most notable was that large portions of their sample reported heavy use; 68 percent of tobacco users, 71 percent of cocaine users, 34 percent of alcohol users, 31 percent of stimulant users, and 12 percent of hypnosedatives users.

Commercial Workers

An increase in traffic accidents related to alcohol and other drug consumption have been documented in Nigeria (Abiona, Aboba, & Fatoye, 2006). It is a known fact that individuals under the influence of substances have poor judgment, decreased response time and decision-making abilities, impaired vision, problems with coordination, and slowed reflex skills (Doweiko, 2002). As a result, there is an increased likelihood of traffic accidents for individuals who choose to drive while under the influence. The results of these accidents can possibly lead to disabling physical conditions, economic loss, and even death. Nigeria does not currently have a policy against drinking and driving, even though it is assumed that the majority of traffic accidents are related to alcohol consumption (Abiona, Aloba, & Fatoye, 2006).

Abiona, Aloba, and Fatoye noted that the study participants were more likely to be heavy users (47 percent) and were more likely to use beer (68 percent). Also noted was that the majority of the commercial drivers interviewed during the study reportedly used alcohol as a way to cope with frustration, increase energy, boost morale, to assist in socializing, and to keep alert. These workers expressed frustration related to the increasing prices of gas and parts to repair vehicles, debt, and harassment of policemen and law enforcement agents. To relax, initiate sleep, control temper, and to ward off illness were also listed as reasons for use. The majority of the participants in this study were aware of the relationship between drinking and driving; however, they were not aware of the physical consequences of alcohol addiction, such as cirrhosis of the liver.

Students

Factors leading to student use include peer influence, parental deprivation, study difficulty, poor mental health, low levels of religious participation, gender (males), polygamous family background, lack of parental supervision (Fatoye, 2007), the desire to compete at work or play (Klein, 2001) and examination stress (Abiona et al., 2006). The four leading substances used by students include alcohol, stimulants (coffee and kola nuts), hypnosedatives (diazepam), and tobacco (Fatoye, 2007). These substances are relatively cheap and easily accessible, and more than half of students surveyed in this study were heavy users of cannabis and tobacco. (Odejide, Ohaeri, Adelekan, & Ikuesan, 1987).

Alcohol consumption was found to be more common among students from middle- to upper-class families (Odejide et al., 1987; Pela, 1989). Also noted was that students who are raised in "Westernized" homes were more likely to use alcohol earlier and to continue to use.

PREVENTION EFFORTS

Several organizations such as the NDLEA and the Nigerian Institute on Substance Abuse (NISA) have been created to assist in addressing the growing problems associated with drug use. However, because of the scarcity of available resources, it is difficult for these organizations to function (Klein, 2001). Several laws and policies, such as the Dangerous Drug Act, have been created, but there have still been problems associated with making sure they are enforced because the Nigerian government has not been very strict in enforcing policies, regulating the production of alcohol or its distribution and consumption (Bennet, Campillo, Chandrashekar, & Gureje, 1998). Other strategies have included the training of law enforcement officers and other officials and enlisting their help in reducing supply. Odejide (1989, p. 27) stated that "it is when law enforcement agents are well trained, well equipped, and well remunerated that they will be happy to perform their jobs and be motivated to implement the existing legislations necessary to reduce the supply of these harmful drugs."

According to Odejide (1989), for primary prevention efforts to be successful, there needs to be an implementation of strategies to reduce supply and demand. Because of the great demand for drugs, drug trafficking has grown exponentially since the early 1980s. Nigerian drug cartels pose a serious threat to any prevention efforts that are being put into place. The Blackstone Rangers, a Nigerian gang in Chicago, have set up a training school that teaches its members how to avoid detection, and the Vice Lords, a Nigerian drug cartel, practices shotgunning, which requires multiple carriers to travel on the same flight in an effort to ensure that some of its shipment reaches its destination (Vesely, 2000). Nigerian women have also become major players in the trafficking of illicit drugs where one group smuggled over $26 million worth of heroin from Bangkok, which is a major supplier, throughout Nigeria to Chicago. Because the trafficking of heroin is such a lucrative operation, it is attractive to individuals living in Nigeria where the average minimum wage is $60 a month (personal communication, Dr. Babalola, University Hospital, Ibadan). Not only is trafficking a major source of problems in relation to drug supply and demand, Nigeria is also a major producer of marijuana.

These factors, coupled with the low enforcement of laws and policies against drug use, create a serious quagmire. The best defense against this problem is to significantly decrease the demand.

In reducing the demand for substances, Odijede noted that youths need to engage in activities that help them develop positive personality traits. Along with positive personality traits, these individuals need to have stable home environments, opportunities for gainful employment, high morals and values, and positive social habits. Odejide (1989, p. 27) also stated that there needed to be an increased awareness of the environmental factors that may lead to drug abuse. By doing this, society can be educated as to what is considered a "suitable atmosphere" for the healthy growth of Nigerian youths.

Pela (1989) noted four factors to take into consideration when working to curtail the problems of drugs, including (a) creating new recreational facilities so that students are attracted to and participate in the positive activities held there, (b) enforcing existing drug laws, (c) implementing drug abuse education in primary and secondary school curricula, and (d) encouraging youth to partake in social clubs and organizations.

The Goodworkers Movement International has recently implemented its Prevention Is Better than Cure campaign. This organization currently operates a 10-bed facility in its church, where it uses spiritual counseling in an effort to help individuals overcome addictions. The idea for the prevention program came after realizing it is much more effective to deal with problems relating to drug use and abuse before it ever starts. The prevention program is missionary in style. Pastor Tunji Agboola and members of the church go out into the communities and along the streets of Ibadan and educate individuals about the perils of drug addiction. The next phase of the prevention program will include designing a curriculum that can be used within the school systems.

One of the major problems faced by the Goodworkers Movement International is funding and resources (personal communication, Pastor Tunji Agboola, June 27, 2007). He stated that even thought he feels they have been very successful with their treatment program, they are oftentimes pressed for necessities to run the program effectively. They have been able to print materials that are being distributed throughout the community, but they have only been able to reach a small portion. With more funding and resources, he feels as if they could reach a larger number of individuals and thus further the education of Nigerians about the dangers associated with addiction.

TREATMENT ISSUES

Wang et al. (2007) found that individuals in low-income countries, particularly Nigeria, are less likely to seek treatment when compared to high-resource, high-income countries such as the United States, Spain, and New Zealand. Another problem for individuals who seek treatment in Nigeria is the fact that there are no aftercare services available (personal communication, Dr. O. A. Owoeye, Federal Neuropsychiatric Hospital, Lagos; June 28, 2007). At the psychiatric hospital in Lagos, an eight-week treatment program cost approximately N25,600 or US$200 ($1 is equivalent to approximately 128 naira). Many individuals are turned away because they cannot pay.

Even among individuals who have government jobs, only a few have health insurance. Furthermore, addiction treatment is often not covered by standard health insurance policies.

Untreated addiction and mental illness due to poverty and unavailability of treatment can have global implications as they are not individual or isolated disorders. An old African proverb states, "The ruin of a nation begins in the homes of its people." When one person is affected, the entire family suffers. The family is part of a larger community, which is nestled within the state. This creates problems not only within the state but the country as a whole. The problems within the country eventually manifest themselves worldwide, as can be seen with increases in usage of specific types of drugs, drug trafficking, HIV/AIDS and other bloodborne pathogens, and the need for financial assistance and legal and social services. Within the Lagos hospital, numerous services are provided, including psychotherapy, psychopharmacology, case management, and family counseling. When an individual can afford and completes the required course of treatment, the likelihood of relapse is significant due to the absence of follow-up services. Follow-up care is paramount in treating individuals with addictions. However, because of the lack of funding and resources, these services do not exist.

Cultural Taboos and Traditional Healers

Klein (2001) noted that drugs are predominantly identified as being "instruments of the devil" and "inherently evil" by individuals in Nigeria (p. 117). What made drugs evil was that they could cause an individual to become isolated, cutting contact with family members and friends, which is seen as a serious problem by individuals in Nigeria who strongly value family, tribal, and cultural ties. Other reasons for the inherent evil of drug use according to Klein included easing an individual's guilt over committing crimes and breaking trust. Mental illness is also viewed as the result of evil spirits or as retribution for the sins of ancestors (personal communication, Dr. H. T. Ladapo, Federal Neuropsychiatric Hospital, Lagos; June 28, 2007).

It is strongly believed by many in Nigeria that traditional methods should be the first line of defense when problems such as these arise. These traditional healers assist in alleviating ailments by connecting the individual to the spiritual world through specific ceremonies and concoctions. Because these substances are not regulated, their true medicinal properties are unknown. Individuals often emerge from the ceremonies with physical damage and fragile mental states.

Family members, particularly those in rural areas, assist in engaging traditional methods of healing. They often participate in the ceremonies. Individuals who resist ceremonies are sometimes forced by the family to receive treatment from these sources.

THE INFLUENCE OF AMERICAN CULTURE

American culture has a huge influence on individuals in other countries (personal communication, Dr. H. T. Ladapo, Federal Neuropsychiatric Hospital,

Lagos; June 28, 2007). The United States is viewed as being a world leader in medicine and technology and many other areas both positive and negative. When we asked the individuals we interviewed during our research about their views of Western culture's influence, particularly the United States, the answers received were quite surprising. Each individual interviewed felt as if the American culture, not just its drug culture, has a very profound impact on the trends that are being expressed in Nigeria. America's family system was viewed as lacking in morals and values, which in turn contributed to the current drug problem in Nigeria.

In America, hip-hop music has been associated with the degradation of women, perpetuation of violence, and glamorization of drugs. This culture has been so commercialized by the media that it has infiltrated all aspects of American society. Interestingly, in Nigeria, hip-hop culture and its more negative aspects are seemingly more apparent among younger generations belonging to families from higher socioeconomic statuses. Of all the individuals interviewed for this research project, it was reasoned that this was due to having access to programs such as MTV (Music Television), BET (Black Entertainment Television), and other forms of media. These individuals could afford to travel internationally as well as obtain resources necessary to emulate what had been portrayed by the media.

FUTURE DIRECTIONS AND CONCLUSIONS

Several organizations such as the NDLEA and NISA have been created to assist in addressing the growing problems associated with drug use. Because of the scarcity of available resources, it is difficult for these organizations to function effectively in their fight against its problems (Klein, 2001). Drugs are attractive to individuals for a number of reasons. They help alleviate stress and feelings of depression and other psychological ailments; they allow an individual to feel invincible and work and perform longer hours. Drugs also provide economic relief for individuals who have suffered from poverty. Because of this magnetism, alleviating this problem will take hard work and dedication from everyone in every imaginable arena of society. As an ever growing and changing world, it is our collective duty to assist all individuals in need. As a society, we cannot ignore the plight of those suffering from substance use disorders here or abroad. No one and no place is immune to the effects of substance use and distribution and its numerous devastating effects. What happens in one corner of the world eventually affects other corners. It is important that we work collectively as a global community to understand the affects and appeal of drugs and its subsequent impact on mental health. By doing so, we can develop policies and practices that serve to best benefit us all.

NOTE

This chapter is dedicated to the memory of Dr. Olabisi Odejide, professor of psychiatry at University of Ibadan, College Hospital, Nigeria. Funding for this project was provided by the Center for International Rehabilitation Research and Information Exchange (CIRRIE). Special thanks to Dr. Olabisi Odejide and the psychiatry residents, College Hospital, Ibadan, Nigeria; administrators and faculty, University of Ibadan; Pastor Tunji Agboola and staff, Goodworkers Movement International; Drs. Victor Lasebikan and Kejeem Adebayo, New World Psychiatric Hospital; staff at the Department of Mental Health-Obafemi Awolowo University; Drs. H. T. Ladapo and O. A. Owoeye and Mr. Nwaogu Marcellinus A., Federal NeuroPsychiatric Hospital-Yaba, Lagos.

REFERENCES

Abiona, T. C., Aloba, O. O., & Fatoye, F. O. (2006). Pattern of alcohol consumption among commercial road transport workers in a semi-urban community in south western Nigeria. *East African Medical Journal, 83*, 494–499.

Abiona, T. C., Fatoye, F. O., & Okwerekwu, R. O. (2006). Psychiatric manifestations from mid-adolescence to early adulthood: The experience in a Nigerian teaching hospital. *Nigerian Journal of Psychiatry, 4*, 38–49.

Adelekan, M. L. (1996). *The epidemiology and social context of amphetamine and psychostimulant use in Nigeria.* Paper presented in Geneva, Switzerland at the WHO Program on Substance Abuse Meting on Amphetamines, MDMA, and Other Psychostimulants.

Ake, C. (1996). *Democracy and development in Africa.* Washington, DC: Brookings Institute.

American Psychiatric Association. (2000). *Diagnostic and statistical manual of mental disorders* (4th ed.), text revision. Washington, DC: Author.

Atkinson, D. R., & Hackett, G. (2004). *Counseling diverse populations.* New York: McGraw-Hill.

Bennett, L. A., Campillo, C., Chandrashekar, C. R., & Gureje, O. (1998). Alcoholic beverage consumption in India, Mexico, and Nigeria: A cross-cultural comparison. *Alcohol Health & Research World, 4*, 243–252.

British American Tobacco. (2008). Responsible tobacco production. Retrieved on February 20, 2008, from www.batnigeria.com/oneweb/sites/BAT_58TD2C.nsf/vwPagesWebLive/48256B92007865B480256BD4003F89BC?opendocument&DTC=&SID=.

Doweiko, H. E. (2002). *Concepts of chemical dependency* (6th ed.). Pacific Grove, CA: Thompson Learning.

Falola, T. (1999). *The history of Nigeria.* Westport, CT: Greenwood.

Falola, T. (2001). *Culture and customs of Nigeria.* Westport, CT: Greenwood.

Fatoye, F. O. (2007). Substance use among university undergraduates: A study of patterns and beliefs in Ile-Ife. *Nigerian Postgraduate Medical Journal, 14*, 37–41.

Green, A. I., Drake, R. E., Brunette, M. F., & Noordsy, D. L. (2007). Schizophrenia and co-occurring substance use disorder. *American Journal of Psychiatry, 164*, 402–408.

Gureje, O., Lasebikan, V. O., Kola, L., & Makanjuola, V. A. (2006). Lifetime and 12-month prevalence of mental disorders in the Nigerian survey of mental health and well-being. *British Journal of Psychiatry, 188*, 465–471.

Ihezue, U. H. (1988). Alcohol and drug taking behavior among medical students at a Nigerian university campus: Part 2, sociodemographic factors of etiological significance. *Journal of the National Medical Association, 80*, 191–195.

Klein, A. (1999). Nigeria and the drug war. *Review of African Political Economy, 26*, 51–73.

Klein, A. (2001). "Have a piss, drink *ogogoro*, smoke *igbo*, but don't take *gbana*." Hard and soft drugs in Nigeria: A critical comparison of official policies and view on the street. *Journal of Psychoactive Drugs, 33*, 111–119.

Lambo, T. A. (1960). Medical and social aspects of drug addiction in West Africa with special emphasis on psychiatric aspects. *Bulletin on Narcotics, 17*.

Morakinyo, J., & Odejide, A. O. (2003). A community study of patterns of psychoactive substance use among street children in a local government area of Nigeria. *Drug and Alcohol Dependence, 71*, 109–116.

Obot, I. S. (1990). Substance abuse, health and social welfare in Africa: An analysis of the Nigerian Experience. *Social Science and Medicine, 31*, 699–704.

Odejide, A. O. (1989). *A nation at risk: Alcohol and substance abuse among Nigerian youth*. Inaugural lecture delivered at the University of Ibadan.

Odejide, A. O., & Ohaeri, J. U. (1989). *Drug-related admissions in 28 mental health institutions in Nigeria in 1989*. Study commissioned by the Honorable Minister of Health, Professor Olikoye Ransome-Kiti.

Odejide, A. O., Ohaeri, J. U., Adelekan, M. L., & Ikuesan, B. A. (1987). Drinking behavior and social change among youths in Nigeria: A study of two cities. *Drug and Alcohol Dependence, 20*, 227–233.

Oyeshile, O. A. (2004). Communal values, cultural identity and the challenge of development in contemporary Africa. *The Journal of Social, Political, and Economic Studies, 29*(3), 291–303.

Pela, O. A. (1989). Patterns of adolescent psychoactive substance use and abuse in Benin City, Nigeria. *Adolescence, 24*, 569–574.

Robinson, T. L. (2005). *The convergence of race, ethnicity, and gender*. Upper Saddle River, NJ: Pearson Prentice Hall.

Vesely, M. (2000). Africa: Highway to drug hell? *African Business, 253*, 8–10.

Wang, P., Aguilar-Gaxiola, S., Alonso, J., Angermeyer, M. C., Borges, G., Bromet, E., et al. (2007). Use of mental health services for anxiety, mood, and substance disorders in 17 countries in the WHO world mental health surveys. *Lancet, 370*, 841–850.

World Health Organization. (2008). Retrieved on February 20, 2008, from www.who.int/tobacco/media/en/Nigeria.pdf.

CHAPTER 18

Chasing Your Dreams

Connie Susa

Some years ago, conference planners for the National Association of Developmental Disabilities Councils scheduled a rock-climbing demonstration as a break in the meeting schedule. I watched in awe of the woman who used the widely spaced rocks on the vertical face of the hotel as hand- and footholds to climb straight up several stories to the roof. It was so beyond my capabilities that I could not imagine overcoming any greater challenge.

Then my belief system exploded as each succeeding climber performed even more difficult tasks:

- A man with a double prosthesis rappelled down the wall.
- An able-bodied climber scaled the wall with a man who had cerebral palsy strapped to his back.
- Finally, the audience was invited to round the corner where swooping architectural forms stood in bas relief against another wall of the hotel. I watched in complete astonishment as a man rappelled off the roof, over and around the jutting forms in his wheelchair.

At that moment, I changed. I, who had long advocated for appropriate supports for individuals with disabilities, came to understand in a whole, new way that with *sufficient* supports, almost anything is possible to all of us. With proper planning and assistance, any person can achieve almost any dream.

LEARNING FIRSTHAND

As an example, my husband and I had been seeking full inclusion in a typical, sixth-grade classroom for our son, Mark. Since it would have been the first time that a student with multiple disabilities would be enrolled full-time in a general education setting in our state, we were encountering strong resistance. Having Mark educated in the least restrictive environment with appropriate supports became a strong and insistent longing for us.

One of the administrators in Mark's segregated out-of-district placement told me that she could not recommend an integrated setting because she had never seen it work. She emphasized that her agency could not afford to lose credibility by recommending a situation which might not succeed. So while we had the right to pursue the kind of education that we wanted for Mark, we would have to do so on our own. We were facing a due process hearing where we would have to establish a preponderance of evidence to prevail, and I felt defeated and powerless in light of the agency's refusal to help.

Soon after this conversation, I found myself across the table from another representative of Mark's school at an unrelated meeting. I asked him if we could talk for a few minutes after the meeting ended late in the afternoon. We sat for nearly an hour as I my poured out my vision of who Mark was and who he had the potential to become. As I shared these motherly aspirations, my eyes glistened in the waning light of the day. As I shared my deepest fears of what a future devoid of normal experiences and associations would do to our precious son, my eyes glistened again in a different way. Later, this man broke with his agency and testified before our hearing officer on our behalf. By doing so, he actually sacrificed his career in the segregated school but then moved into the public schools where he gained a statewide reputation as an innovative teacher who consistently engaged his secondary students with disabilities in work and other activities in the community. Now, Mark sometimes reads his college geography textbook into the wee hours, unwilling to stop learning, even though his abilities only warrant an audited class in his area of greatest interest. The sacrifice had become a win-win situation for both the teacher and our son.

ALL FIRED UP

Here follows another example of hope: "Don't follow your dreams; *chase* them," Debbie Sprengel told her son, Kurt. He eventually confided that his dream was to become a firefighter, but when he started high school, he was afraid that he would never graduate or be able to earn a living. He would not even go to the movies with friends because he was afraid he might misread something in the lobby or on screen and be teased.

Then his mom discovered print recognition software as an aid to her son's dyslexia. With the technology, Kurt could highlight a section of text for the computer to read aloud to him. Hearing the words at the same time he scanned them helped him understand and remember. He began to master words and facts that he could not learn in the past.

Kurt was so encouraged by his progress that he confessed to his dad, Jack, a volunteer fire fighter, that he wanted to serve the public in the same tradition.

Kurt called a volunteer fire department to see if they would accept him as a junior fire fighter. They welcomed him, and Kurt worked hard to qualify on the engines and rescue trucks. He said, "By the time I take my EMT [emergency medical technician test], I'll be ready. I feel confident with what I have achieved so far."

Eight years later, he now serves in the 169th military police, helping Iraqis learn to police themselves. He reports that for the first time he truly feels comfortable in his skin because he knows that he is "making a difference." He now hopes to become a police officer when he returns home. Because he chased his dream, Kurt has a fire inside him.

ACCENTUATE THE POSITIVE

The Secret by Rhonda Byrne (2006) maintains that as we focus positive energy on our dreams, they will come to pass. By the same token, when we respond with fear, shame, or other negative emotions, these feelings may erect barriers to these goals. Similarly, the motion picture *The Bucket List* suggests that given the motivation to overcome our stumbling blocks, we may systematically achieve our fondest desires. These examples indicate that the zeitgeist of pursuing aspirations with hope has arrived for the general public. It also holds equally true for people with disabilities and their families. This is not always easy to accomplish, as there are innumerable barriers to positive outcomes for people with disabilities.

For example, parents are often told that they, themselves, are major impediments to their children's successes. When my husband and I were pursuing a typical classroom placement with accommodations for our Mark, his individual education plan included a note that his parents were obviously in denial about the extent of his disabilities and needed a year's worth of counseling to help accept reality. Rather than accept that negative assessment, my husband returned his own note on the rejected IEP that our school district was out of touch with current best practices and could benefit from a year's worth of good in-service.

The misuse of grief theory is a form of labeling that often haunts other families as well. During the 1970s and 1980s it first became popular to apply Kübler-Ross' (1969) seminal work *On Death and Dying* to caregivers of relatives diagnosed with disability. Denial, anger, bargaining, and sadness—all born of "the loss of the dream child"—were seen by the untutored public as pathological responses to the initial diagnosis. However, Kübler-Ross' original work saw them as *natural* responses that directed the grieving person toward eventual acceptance.

It is only when the person who has experienced loss gets stuck in one or more of these stages of grieving that intervention is needed. Our fast-paced society, our school systems, our adult human service agencies are often too impatient to allow grieving relatives of those newly diagnosed to wend their way through the process to regain their equilibrium. They label many family members as having emotional difficulties when they are clearly on the well-worn path to acceptance. One of Elizabeth Barrett Browning's (1992) lesser known sonnets, "Grief," compares the stolid state of emotional paralysis to a marble statue. It ends with the apt description, "Touch it; the marble eyelids are not wet: If it could weep, it could arise and go" (p. 4).

Even worse than the personal labeling of specific parents is the *categorical* labeling of parents as the cause of their children's disability. Mothers were, at one time, identified as emotional "refrigerators" who supposedly created the social isolation of their sons and daughters with autism. While such volleys of shame are still fired against families far too often, progressive practitioners now use person-centered and family-centered procedures such as those advocated by Beth Mount. They actively seek out the strengths, talents, and gifts of family caregivers and their relatives with disabilities and build on them.

Just as shame can stop a dream in its tracks, so can fear. As people with disabilities and their families, we fear many things: the unknown, failure, rejection, loss of safety, and loss of our personally valued roles as nurturers, controllers, or martyrs. How can we project a vision of a full life if there have been no role models to demonstrate it? How can we ask for more if we have never seen the best practices? A limited market of services most often leads to a limited life for a person with a disability. A limited vision of the future yields a frightening outcome of deprivation.

In an examining room at St. Luke's Roosevelt Hospital, where our second son, Frank, and I waited for the results of his six months of chemotherapy, hung a print of a room with a glass door that opened onto a vast expanse of water. If you looked closely, you could even perceive the curve of the Earth, where the horizon of the ocean met the sky. There was no land in the picture, nor even a porch or a step. Nor was there a boat. We commented as we waited for the doctors to enter with the results of Frank's PET scan that to venture beyond that glass doorway was to step either "off the deep end" or into a limitless sea of possibilities. Luckily, when the news finally came, it was those vast possibilities. The chemotherapy had been effective; his lymphoma was gone, and he could resume his normal life. He has returned to his rewarding work and his circle of friends, filled with hope for the future and a zest for every precious moment.

Fear can be an impediment to normalcy. A friend has a daughter with multiple disabilities, like our son. She often commented that she saw our respective children as being very similar. We had both been told that our children would never have language or be able to function outside the segregated day placement, where it would take up to 20 minutes to move and arrange all the wheelchairs in the library for therapeutic story time.

As my husband and I attended conferences, read the professional journals, and visited model programs that all endorsed inclusive education as the logical way to prepare students for adult life in the community, we shared the principles with our friend. We served on our city's Special Education Advisory Committee together, where we debated the pros and cons of age-appropriate content, curriculum modification, team teaching, project-based learning, and other practices that contribute to the successful inclusion of students with disabilities in typical classrooms. We urged her to bring Annie (name changed for confidentiality) back into our home district and into typical classes, but she did not want to invite the ire of the school administrators. She was also afraid that Annie would be ignored in favor of typically functioning students in a regular education classroom.

Now that our children are adults, their lives look very different. Mark is a product of his experiences in a rich language environment with good social role models. He speaks with confidence, having given oral reports before his peers. He follows the news and votes with pride in his citizenship. He works with support at his own entrepreneurial business based on his interests and strengths, and he serves on statewide committees. He holds an office at church and is honored to serve a part-time mission as well. He has competed in road races with a custom-built racing wheelchair and works out either at a local gym or on the stationary bike in his own apartment. None of this is true for Annie or other "developmental twins," that is, age mates with the same kind and level of disability as Mark's, who clung to the traditional, segregated path.

DREAM BIG DREAMS

Goethe wrote, "Dream no small dreams for they have no power to move the hearts of men." Etmanski (2004) agreed in *A Good Life*. His innovative work in creating personal support networks in Canada has won an Ashoka Award for Social Entrepreneurship. He maintains that the secret to crafting life-shaping goals is to ask not what specialized services we may rely on but what constitutes "a good life." In other words, we should not focus on merely accommodating the needs of the individual but should envision those indicators of a meaningful and rewarding experience, whether or not they now exist. We ought not worry during this visioning stage about the individual's readiness; after all, who among us would ever learn to swim if we could not enter the water until we had mastered the skill? Nor should we concern ourselves at the beginning with other barriers as we dream our big dreams for the future. Rather, we should establish the finish line and then work our way toward it.

O'Brien (1989) set the values that guided our son into the abundant life he now enjoys. As I have encouraged literally thousands of individuals with disabilities and their families over the years, this is how I have described the O'Brien's quality indicators:

- *Sharing places*—Maintaining or increasing our presence in the community until we attain genuine membership there; using natural supports, as opposed to traditional human services, wherever possible.
- *Making choices*—Controlling the directions our lives take by expressing our interests and preferences; learning what we need to so that our decisions will be based on sound information.
- *Increasing respect*—Building a positive reputation through valued communication, roles, and associations; standing up for ourselves when the need arises; taking opportunities to contribute in a giving role.
- *Improving skills*—Lifelong learning of things that make a difference; building on interests and other areas of strength; accessing adaptive equipment

and modern technology to solve problems; using skills where they make the most sense.
- *Building relationships*—Increasing the number and quality of our social interactions with others of all abilities and ages; drawing on natural supports in the community, those who demonstrate that they care by committing their time and effort with us and reciprocating with them insofar as possible.

Note that these are not merely segregated activities in community settings. Throughout the country thousands of individuals with disabilities are, as Putnam (2000) stated, *bowling alone*. Driven in an agency van, accompanied by paid staff, and whisked back into a group home to which someone else holds the key, these people are experiencing a shadow of what might be. It is as if they are in Plato's (1974) cave, unaware that beyond their view, the real experience of recreating with friends of their own choosing and returning to their own supported homes are an abundant reality which could be theirs. No, O'Brien's quality indicators are about self-determined lives where friends value the real contributions and choices that people with disabilities make.

MYLES TO GO

One example from real life can illustrate how each of these values builds on the others.

Myles (name changed for confidentiality) insisted from the beginning that he wanted "a good job," one "in the community." He wanted to receive competitive pay and rewards for the overtime and helpful suggestions that he offered at the Arc Center. He wanted less down time than he had in the sheltered workshop that he began attending in the 1970s. There, he had been promised that he could work out in the weight room if there was not enough bench work but was instead given magazines that he could not read or was left to the unwanted advances of a fellow worker. He resented the five percent that the center held out of his skimpy pay to support recreational programs that he rarely participated in.

At one point, he was so frustrated that he stopped attending his day program and secured a job "under the table" doing custodial work. There, he grossed more than 11 times his earnings at the sheltered workshop, but he quit when his income nearly disqualified him from other, needed government benefits. Rather than return to the workshop, he spent nearly 15 years at home, doing very little. He remembers almost nothing about the long days that all seemed the same to him. However, his increasing anger being acted out against people and their possessions prompted his parents to move him into a shed without running water at the back of their property.

Both Myles and his parents recognized that he needed more structure, since the boredom was frustrating him. Reluctantly, he returned to his old day placement. Still, he had specific ideas about other jobs he might try, based on his former experiences. He knew he could box items, stamp things, and run a foot press, and he frequently expressed his desire to leave the workshop.

At one point, his workshop supervisors told him that if he left the Arc Center to work in the community, "everything will stop." They explained that he would lose both his Supplemental Security Income and his Medicaid coverage if he left.

Myles entered the Family Futures Planning Project (a three-year, federally funded project of the Rhode Island Developmental Disabilities Council), and his life began to change. He began attending self-advocacy meetings, where he met other people with developmental disabilities who worked in the community. Myles' planning facilitator arranged a substantial discount for him to enroll at the YMCA, where he began working out three times a week. The exercise gave him pain to begin with, so his friend found a university-based physical therapy clinic where Myles could get free help from graduate students who had professional supervision. He soon became independent by using the exercise equipment and found that he enjoyed shooting baskets after his workouts.

Myles had spent enough time at the YMCA that one night the manager there offered him a job at minimum wage. His friends who had advocated for his paid position knew of the plan in advance and gathered in a darkened office off the gym to give him a surprise party. As Myles adjusted to his new role, his support staff gradually withdrew. Myles found taxis too expensive to take to work and tried the public buses instead. However, he remained very uncomfortable around strangers and was especially sensitive to the smells of a bus. A co-worker offered him a ride to and from work.

Myles began purchasing furniture, one piece at a time, for an apartment where he eventually went to live with a roommate. He had successfully improved in everyone of the five quality indicators.

FIGHTING FOR KATE'S RIGHTS

In 1969, when Kate was four months old, her dad was appointed to a high-level role in the government.[1] They were anticipating a big family celebration on their second Christmas Eve in Washington. That was also the day that a physician of Washington Children's Hospital reported to them on the interdisciplinary workup their team had conducted on Kate. She advised the family to institutionalize Kate because "she will never give you any love."

On the drive home, Kate's mother, Addie, asserted that she simply did not believe all the negative medical opinions about her daughter's future. She slammed her hand against the dashboard as she resolved aloud to create a normal life for Kate. As the family celebrated the holiday that night, Addie's mind was whirling, beginning to formulate the how-tos that have guided their actions for the past 36 years.

Loving Kate was the easy part, but when her dad's term in Washington was complete, the family moved back to Wenham, Massachusetts. Kate was wait-listed for therapy services by the Massachusetts Department of Mental Retardation (DMR) for nine crucial months. On the recommendation of DMR, the parents made the long drive to the Hogan Regional Center. The caretaker used the ring with scores of keys on his belt to show them around.

Addie took in the rows and rows of white metal cribs and the overwhelming stench of the place and determined again that Kate would grow up in her home with her family, the same as any other cherished child.

Another crushing assessment was made at the Developmental Evaluation Clinic at Boston Children's Hospital. Even with Kate's extensive needs identified, it took almost 10 months for the school department to come up with an educational placement. It was a Special Education Consortium, where Kate was transported by taxi to seven different schools with seven different communication systems in as many years. Put-downs came in many forms during those years. For example, Addie discovered that while Kate was strapped into a prone stander, the staff had slipped Pringles canisters over her arms to straighten them. This reflected a total disregard for the unusual bone structure in Kate's elbows and just left her frustrated.

Kate's profound dual hearing loss was not diagnosed until 1983 when the Auditory Evoked Response Test became available. She was 14 years old. Each physical, social, and emotional insult that focused only on Kate's deficits raised Addie's ire again, and each time she used the pent-up energy to find a new solution. Dr. Allen Crocker contributed positively when Addie asked him where she could go for more answers. He suggested they look into TASH, The Association for Persons with Severe Handicaps.

Addie and Brock registered for the TASH national conference in Chicago. There, they found themselves surrounded for the first time by professionals who all shared the same research-based vision of quality lives for individuals with complex physical and cognitive needs. In fact, as far as the couple could tell, they were the only parents among positive-minded professionals. The executive director at the time invited Addie and Brock to begin a parents' committee.

Through that association, they gained useful information and hope. They hired local students from Gordon College as mothers' helpers, so that Addie could be free to make phone calls, study the research, visit families with innovative solutions, and write. Eventually, they co-founded a chapter of TASH. Addie later served two terms on the national board, chairing its Family Committee and presenting at conferences across the country.

In return, the family received support from the organization in their two due process hearings to secure an inclusive educational setting for Kate in high school. The family's medical insurance paid for a physical therapist, who taught Kate to use the stairs safely and got her exercising in a community-based health club. They sought another specialist to teach Kate to swim the length of the pool independently. In a learning team in her high school home economics class, Kate wiped the counters independently and threw away the paper towel with pride. She did vocational exploration in white-collar settings. Success bred success, and for the first time, Kate was embraced among lively friends, who invited her on outings and dropped in to visit. At graduation, Kate received a certificate on stage, while all her classmates cheered.

Following graduation, Kate accepted a job offer from a cable television station. She functioned with the support of a job coach as an office assistant. She attended office parties and appeared in the office yearbook, and the company received the Best Employer Award from the Massachusetts Rehabilitation Commission.

Before Brock died of lung cancer in 1998, the family certified Kate for a federal Home of Your Own Program. Kate and her mom moved to Providence in 2000 to be near Kate's sister, Lee, and her family. Kate's great-great aunt Folly left a trust that allowed them to secure a small brick house, which is staffed around the clock and feeling, according to Addie, "very much like home."

MARK ACTS FOR HIMSELF

With his low muscle tone, my son Mark was still not creeping at two years old. His therapist taught us to sling his torso in a big bath towel to lift him into the all-fours position. This would help him experience the appropriate position for crawling and strengthen his arms and legs. Through many repetitions of the bath towel therapy, Mark eventually began to raise himself up on all fours. He was tenuous and every time he would fall forward, he would lead with his face, hit his face on the floor, pop the tight skin on the bottom of his chin, and need stitches in the emergency room.

Still we all persevered. We sought the advice of his occupational therapist for a toy that would motivate him to move forward. She suggested a particular battery-operated dog that would scoot across the floor when you hit its hat. Mark could not hit the mechanism hard enough to activate it himself. When I would tap the hat, the toy would zoom across the floor too quickly for Mark to track. We needed something that would go on its own and do so slowly enough that it would always stay just out of his reach.

On my way to my friend Sallee's home in the country, I stopped on a dirt road to avoid hitting a turtle was in my path. Sallee examined the animal I had brought to her and pronounced him to be an Eastern box turtle, a creature that closed up his bottom carapace when he withdrew his head. "There is no way for any random motion to hurt it," she assured me. "Perfect," I thought, and quickly learned about the care and feeding of our new pet, Foster. Not only did he meet all our original criteria, he also modeled the reciprocal movement that Mark needed to reproduce in his own arms and legs. By the time Foster was liberated from his outdoor sun bath by a neighborhood child, Mark had learned to creep like any respectable turtle.

From that time forward, Mark wanted to *go*. He would creep to the plastic "map" of a small town on which he drove his matchbox cars. He loved the room in the Children's Museum where the state's highways were grooves on a map that covered the entire floor of one room. We enrolled him in Cub Scouts, where he received advancements and awards with his nondisabled peers. When the second Blue and Gold Banquet was scheduled in the same banquet hall as it had been the year before, Mark bragged that he knew the way to the site in next town. Even though Mark had only been there once, a whole year before, he properly advised every turn and every lane change along the way. We were amazed because we had been told that Mark had significant cognitive limitations. He proved his strengths in visual memory, directionality, and mental mapping repeatedly through the years, and when he finally went into a sixth-grade classroom with typical students, he was thrilled to discover that geography would be part of his regular curriculum.

When Mark needed content for his high school summer program, John suggested that our son learn to use the public buses. Then he taught the school personnel to use them so that they, in turn, could prepare Mark for independent travel. Mark spent two years in our city's new Travel and Tourism vocational program. By the time he turned 20, we arranged for his last semester in high school to include a half-day internship with the Rhode Island Public Transit Authority. His supervisor there expected and received daily memos as Mark spent time in each department, learning everything from bus maintenance standards to the names and roles of dispatchers. He crafted a plan for Mark to prove his abilities by taking a day-long intermodal trip on the public transit system, looping throughout the state.

At first, I balked at the idea of my vulnerable son being out in public, entirely on his own. In spite of what our special education director called "splinter skills," Mark had not outgrown the developmental disability identified before he started in early intervention. His teacher suggested a cell phone as a lifeline. My husband reminded me that it is more often when people are shut away in places that occlude the view of the public that most abuse takes place. Mark's mentor at the bus company reminded me that he needed to complete this culminating activity to graduate from high school.

On the appointed day, having practiced pieces of the trip with supports throughout the spring, Mark set out in his wheelchair for the fixed-route bus stop nearest our home. He phoned twice: once to a dispatcher when he missed a bus and needed to know the time of the next one and a second time to us when his baseball cap fell into a trash can and got melted ice cream on it. He transferred buses at two hubs in our statewide system, took a commuter train back up to the center of our capital city, and relaxed on a paratransit van for the final leg of his trip.

All of us who were planning Mark's transition to adult life rode the crest of that wave all the way to a peer travel training business. Our statewide Developmental Disabilities and Vocational Rehabilitation systems collaborated to help Mark establish Accessing Community Transportation (ACT) and certify him as a state vendor to train job seekers who were unlikely to have their own transportation. After the business incorporated, a dedicated microboard helped Mark make business decisions. He has since branched out into contracting with school districts that want to provide travel training for their transitioning high school students. Board members are also members of Mark's broader personal support network, which is facilitated by one of his former racing partners.

In addition to using grab bars, hearing aids, a fiscal manager, and a wheelchair, Mark also enjoys his own apartment, a diverse group of friends, popular entertainment in community venues, valued roles, and, best on his own list of priorities, several trips out of state each year. He is still seeking Ms. Right, and needs that goal in his life as much as the ones he has already achieved.

As one reviews the stories of these individuals and their family members, we can see that the process of pursuing dreams of normalization is similar in each instance. Each of these people has recognized that achieving the desired vision will be a long process. Their determination is stronger than the voices of all the naysayers. They keep their eyes on the prize even as they live with the discomfort of uncertainty. That ability to let go of control and of those aspects of caregiving that are either unnecessary or that may be shared with others contributes to their success. The positive values of community membership, personal autonomy, contributing to society, using adaptations to compensate for weaknesses, and always fostering reciprocal relationships—all can outweigh the fears that would keep us from worthwhile goals for a good life. They are the five points of a star that is, at the beginning of the journey, far beyond our reach. As we climb over the stumbling blocks we rise gradually higher until we can pluck that star from the darkness and bring its light into our own lives. The climb may be steep and difficult, but if we can overcome our fears of the dizzying heights to look down at where we have come from, the view will be exhilarating, and the prize of more normalized experiences and associations at the summit will be priceless.

NOTE

1. Kate's story is a personal communication to Connie Susa by Adelaide Eich Comegys; used with explicit permission to use personally identifying information.

REFERENCES

Browning, E. B. (1992). *Sonnets from the Portuguese and other poems.* New York: Dover Thrift.

Byrne, R. (2006). *The secret.* New York: Atria Books.

Etmanski, A. (2004). *A good life for you and your relative with a disability.* Vancouver: Orwell Cove.

Kübler-Ross, E. (1969). *On death and dying.* New York: Macmillan.

O'Brien, J. (1989). *What's worth working for? Leadership for better quality human services.* Paper delivered at Responsive Systems Associates, Lithonia, Georgia.

Plato. (1974). "The cave," in *Republic.* Translation by G. M. A. Grube. Indianapolis: Hackett.

Putnam, R. D. (2000). *Bowling alone: The collapse and revival of an American community.* New York: Simon & Schuster.

Afterword: Reclaiming Globalization for Disability—Further Insights

Why did we need a book entitled *Disability: Insights from across Fields and around the World*? In all other sectors of life, globalization is a force that is bringing significant advantages (and challenges). Global collaboration can provide an opportunity to appreciate both cultural differences and similarities; it can encourage sensitivity to diversity and strength through cohesion. Through global cooperation, we may be able to address the extent to which people with chronic illness and disability and their issues are taken seriously. In his review of globalization, Kunitz (2000) concluded that globalization in the health arena has the "potential, incompletely realized, to create both an audience for the airing of injustices . . . and a means of redress" (p. 1538). However, to collaborate globally, we must first understand and overcome very real differences without losing our cultural distinctiveness. We must learn about each other and appreciate difference as a fundamental starting point in life (see chapter by Gibson). But we must also recognize and respect the impact of historical legacies such as colonialism (see chapters by Campbell, Barlow, & Barlow; Kelly), cultural or religious nuances (see chapters by Al Attiyah & Mian; Gharaibeh; Gotto; Sovani; Manyibe, Mamboleo, Mugoya, & Kampfe; Tawakkul, Bhatty, & Yousef), different degrees of social development (see chapter by Söderström), and geographical challenges (see chapter by Morrissey). We must also acknowledge that inequality is an inherent scar on the world's health and social landscape (Jong-wook, 2003) that profoundly alters the experience of disability. For all these reasons, we needed to explore insights about disability from around the world.

Is it possible for people with disability to reclaim the globalization movement and redirect its energy toward outcomes, such as access for all and the elimination of disparities in health and human services? As Emmerson, McConkey, Noonan Walsh, and Felce (2008) noted, the importance of a global approach to understanding and addressing disability is emerging. Globalization is fundamental to the establishment of the United Nations' Millennium Development Goals (www.un.org/millenniumgoals) and to the work of the World Health Organization around the International Classification of Functioning, Disability and Health (2001). However, the most exciting global initiative in the area of disability is the United Nations Convention on the Rights of Persons with Disabilities, which was launched in December 2006. As we noted in the introduction, the convention has raised important human rights of citizenship for people with disabilities and has proposed a definition of disability that is remarkable. It is a definition that is not based on cause or a threshold of functioning (Leonardi, Bickenbach, Ustun, Kostanjsek, & Chatterji, 1996). Instead, disability is recognized to be an evolving concept that is always contextualized and relational as we have represented in this series.

The chapters contained in this series are testament to the importance of rights-based legislation and the aspirations it can engender in society. In countries without suitable legislation that acknowledges disability, people with disabilities are invisible, their rights are not upheld, and their needs are not met (see chapters by Al Attiyah & Mian; Campbell; Bhatty, Moten, Tawakkul, & Amer; Gotto; Sovani; Spirito-Dalgin, Ergene, Marrone, & Munir). However, the fallibility of legislation is also a common theme across the chapters. Even in countries where legislation has been passed to provide access to buildings, education, or employment, it can remain unenforced or incomplete in its implementation (see chapters by Agorastou, Kalyva, Kaderoglou, & Stefandis; Kuemmel & Kuemmel). Some chapters highlight the unintended consequences of legislation, often created by the fact that legal rights are applied and interpreted inconsistently or are only ascribed to those who fit the "legal" definition of disability or conform to the expectations of that legislation (see chapters by Campbell; Hedlund; Pilgrim & Rogers).

Too often in the industrialized world, we think there is nothing to learn from other places. We perceive those places as being in need of improvement through the adoption of the values that dominate industrialized countries. Through this contemporary form of colonization, we continue to export Western ideology without seeing its negative impact on other countries (see chapter by Lusk & Paul), instead assuming that Western ways are aspired to by all other cultures. This pervasive attitude perpetuates a belief among scholars from "developing" nations that solutions emanating from the United States (or other industrialized countries) are more legitimate than their own localized knowledge.

In this series, we highlight some of the lessons that can be learned through global collaboration. Kendall and Marshall describe the creation of a global community of influence through which the voices of Indigenous women with disability can be magnified. Throughout this series, we have tried to highlight lessons that transcend countries, explore how globalization affects each of us, and identify where we are each located in this global community.

As an extension of this argument, it is equally clear from these volumes that lessons can be learned from minority populations that are marginalized within our nations. Barnett and Barnett; DiCowden; Hickey; and Leisman clearly describe the lessons that health professionals can learn from Indigenous models of health, recognition of spirituality, and multifaith approaches to rehabilitation. Begay, Brown, and Bounds demonstrate the way in which we each see the world through our own cultural lens, cautioning us to be open to the lessons from other cultures. We need to constantly ask ourselves, "what can we learn from other contexts, other countries, other cultures, and even from history?" (see chapter by Tawakkul, Bhatty, & Yousuf for a description of the two-way nature of cross-cultural learning). Have we dealt with disability in better ways in the past? Have we learned from failures of the past, such as that described in the "journey of sanctioned injustice" (see chapter by Kelly)?

So what are some of the common lessons and trends that emerge through these chapters? In dividing the chapters into three volumes, we note the arbitrary nature of the divisions—disability is an entire experience that cannot be easily divided into experiences, contexts, and responses as we have done here. In reality, these three facets interact to create a whole that is far more complex than we can readily represent in words. Our division of chapters could have been based on any number of other themes that emerged as we read them.

A major observation was that several chapters describe the global shift from biomedical constructions of disability to those based in the social world. This complex shift is discussed in many other texts on disability, and only some of the complexities are described in this series. Importantly, several chapters comment on the fact that somewhere between these two extremes is a point where the biological, psychological, social, and cultural experiences come together and contribute to a holistic understanding of disability.

Some chapters focus specifically on definitions of disability that are derived from these frameworks (see Crocker; Gibson; Hedlund; Pilgrim & Rogers). These chapters describe how different definitions and conceptualizations of disability translate into practices and policies that impact on people. Other chapters use social analysis or critical disability discourse analysis to explore the impact of social constructions and language on the way people with disability are experienced and experience themselves. These chapters (see Campbell; Hodgkins & Baility; Pilgrim & Rogers) are important because they challenge the way in which we think about disability and encourage us to extend our minds, rather than unquestioningly conforming to the prevailing pressures.

The shift to a rights-based approach to disability (see chapters by Crocker; Kuemmel & Kuemmel; Morrissey) is another important theme. Although the social model has been a useful tool for shifting responsibility for disability from individuals to societies, some chapters comment on how this model has also denied the very real existence of physical impairment and the impact of that impairment on individuals (see Campbell; Susa; Gover). An important corollary of the rights-based approach is the fact that it moves us one step closer to an approach where difference is expected, accommodated, and celebrated. Approaches based on equality tend to assume that we need to create balance across people by ignoring or rectifying difference (i.e., through welfare systems). By definition, some individuals are seen as unequal, inadequate, and unacceptably different. In contrast, responses based on the principle of universality promote a model where difference is expected, celebrated, and accommodated.

It is obvious from the chapters in this series that the experience, definition, acceptance, and/or rejection of a "disability identity" varies enormously across individuals and depends a great deal on the extent to which it is personally relevant or meaningful, often because it prevents participation in a desired activity (see Susa) or if it is religiously significant (see chapters by Al Attiyah & Mian; Bhatty, Moten, Tawakkul, & Amer; Gharaibeh; Tawakkul, Bhatty, & Yousef). There are also chapters that highlight how culture, or individual choice (see Stager; Yazzie-King) can create or remove disability simply through the way it is viewed. In some cases, this social interpretation of disability alters the experience of the same impairment within a given culture (see chapter by Gotto); in other cases, it simply denies the presence of real difficulties (see chapters by Ackerman & Banks; Catalano & Kendall; Salley), and in yet other cases, it creates stigma and a sense of illegitimacy (see chapters by Campbell; Cederna, Palguta, Wall, & Koch).

The experience of being excluded from society is particularly relevant for people whose disability does not fit the normative views, stereotypes and definitions—for instance, people whose disability differs from what would be expected. For example, Catalano and Kendall describe the isolating experiences of young people who have had a stroke—usually considered to be an elderly person's disability. Kampfe describes the high incidence of preventable hearing disability in elderly people that is often overlooked because it is attributed to simple age-related decline.

Conceptions of disability in society are heavily influenced by discourses in the popular media, the general use of language, and social norms (see chapters by Hodgkins & Baility; Morrissey; Campbell; Sovani). It was not possible to find a consistent language for this series because the words used to describe people with disability represented an entire body of hidden meaning. Chapter authors used various forms of language to refer to people with disability. "People first" language was preferred by many because it addresses people before it acknowledges disability. Other authors preferred to use the language of "Disabled People" to acknowledge the implicit nature of disability and the fact that it is inextricably interwoven into a person's character, in the same way as their gender, ethnicity and personality. Finally, some authors used the abbreviation PWD that is common among advocates. This language positions individuals within a collective identity that is not about deficit, but about having the power to self-advocate for change. In some sectors of the United States, it is customary to capitalize terms that refer to people with disability (i.e., People with Disability). In contrast, to capitalize words in Norwegian (i.e., Deaf) brings with it connotations of stigma (as if they were a special group). The Norwegian deaf community never spells with a capital D first, just an ordinary d to show they are ordinary people (see chapter by Hedlund).

Several chapters demonstrated how people with disability are influenced by languages, discourses, and constructions. Stigma and its impact are common themes across many chapters, often created by local cultural ways of explaining disability as a consequence of one's own actions, a repercussion for one's sins or just bad luck (see Al Attiyah & Mian; Manyibe, Mamboleo, Mugoya, & Kampfe; Sovani). However, stigma is also present in countries with advanced legal and social service frameworks around disability, as demonstrated by Campbell. In negotiating such frameworks, people with disability are required to legally "prove" their disability to receive rights. Further, they must often demonstrate that they have made attempts to mitigate their "loss." They are only deemed worthy of society's assistance if they follow these rules (see also Gibson). McDonald's chapter describes how young people with invisible disability respond to these unreasonable demands by obscuring their disability and "passing" themselves off as nondisabled. Other chapters described the denial of parents when they first confront disability in their child (see Bursnall, Kennedy, Senior, & Violet; Douglas & Borbasi).

The Sovani chapter about people with schizophrenia in India demonstrates a language-based attempt to alter stigma. Other chapters describe ways in which service systems are responding to stigma by developing models based on wellness (see Breen & Saggers); the integration of mind, spirit, and body on a continuum of ability (see DiCowden); and person-centered planning (see Blessing, Golden, & Bruyère). Unfortunately, however, the responses of health professionals are not always helpful—throughout these chapters, there are examples of hostile systems (see Burnett; Bursnall, Kennedy, Senior, & Violet; Douglas & Borbassi; Madrid, Grant, & Rosen), inactive or unresponsive systems (see Leisman; Gibson), ill-informed systems (see Agorastou, Kalyva, Kaderoglou, & Stefanidis; Kuemmel & Kuemmel; Spirito-Dalgin, Ergene, Marrone, & Munir; Tawakkul, Bhatty, & Yousef), and actively harmful systems (see Kendall & Muenchberger).

Confronting an unhelpful system is an exhausting reality in the lives of people with disabilities. Gibson, for instance, describes her relief on the one occasion when she did not need to fight the system for her rights. We have included chapters that demonstrate the helplessness and passivity that individuals sometimes experience when they confront unhelpful systems and the internalized sense of inadequacy that can result. Other chapters describe responses that seek to change systems through self-advocacy (see Koch, Beggs, & Bailey; Susa; Zuver, Dorton, Finks, & Fisher), legal mobilization, and capacity-building (see Campbell). There are stories written by people with disabilities who have become health professionals and proceeded to influence models of practice (see Barlow; Gibson; Pieper). There are also stories of health professionals who have experienced disability leading to a change in their practice (see Kendall; Susa; Morrisey).

The stories about preventable disability are particularly disturbing—violence (see chapter by Ackerman & Banks), war (see Gharaibeh; Manyibe, Mamboleo, Mugoya, & Kampfe), preventable disease (see Morrissey; Sovani; Gharaibeh), accidents caused by unregulated worksites or driving conditions (see Morrissey), deliberate self-harm (see Campbell), and the neglect of an entire cultural group (see Barlow; Gotto). These chapters highlight the excessive level of unnecessary and preventable disease and injury that results in disability. With appropriate health interventions or sufficient protection of innocent citizens, this level of disability could be avoided. Natural disasters feature prominently (see chapters by Campbell; Spirito-Dalgin, Ergene, Marrone, & Munir). Our lack of preparation for such disasters and prevention of subsequent disability is senseless, particularly in areas where disasters are known to occur. However, as Madrid, Grant, and Rosen show in their chapter on the aftermath of Hurricane Katrina in the United States, poorly planned responses to natural disasters that create disability and neglect people with disability during disaster occur in the most unexpected places.

Article 11 of the UN Convention on the Rights of People with Disability extends the right to life and survival to situations of emergencies. Under the convention, countries are required to ensure the protection and safety of persons with disability in situations of risk, including armed conflict, humanitarian emergencies, and natural disasters. Article 16 extends the right to freedom from torture or cruel, inhuman, or degrading treatment and from all forms of exploitation, violence, and abuse. Clearly we have a long way to go in some parts of the world, including the United States, if we are to see these rights upheld in future. Several chapters have identified the important role of health promotion, rehabilitation, and prevention for the future—in the workplace (see chapters by Blessing, Golden, & Bruyère; Buys & Randall), in schools (see Liesman), on the roads (see Morrissey), and within service systems (see DiCowden; Breen & Saggers; Parkinson).

There is a fine line between respecting individuals who already have disability and promoting cure, prevention, and amelioration, which automatically places a particular type of discourse on disability (i.e., as a "harmful" state that should be removed if possible). This dilemma is faced by many people with disability when they are presented with opportunities to "remove" or reduce their disability (see chapters by Campbell; Gibson). It seems that we must seek a society that accepts diversity as a natural part of human existence and responds to that diversity in a way that acknowledges its presence and its right to be expressed at the same time as valuing human health and life, creating environments in which people can flourish and achieve their dreams (see chapter by Susa). How do we walk this fine line? Is the rights-based approach with its universal doctrine able to provide a way forward? Or does a rights-based approach focus attention on the individual—ensuring rights but also implicitly assigning individual responsibility? Might a "collective welfare" approach (see chapter by Hedlund, Landstad, & Svensson) provide an equally promising way forward?

The most common area where universal access rights have been sought is in relation to physical access. Several chapters show that even this simple universal right cannot be easily implemented or enforced (see Gharaibeh). The chapter by the Kuemmel and Kuemmel is a good illustration. These two sisters, one with a disability and one without, describe their travel experiences in parts of Europe and show how access is meaningless unless it is universally applied. They describe how autonomy was jeopardized by their inaccessible environment and noted the impact this had on both sisters. The demands placed on family members when environments are not supportive of autonomy are highlighted in several chapters. For instance, Catalano and Domalewski describe how the daughter of an elderly person loses her important role of daughter and instead becomes a case manager. Pakenham describes the impact on youth who care for a parent with a disability. From the perspective of the youth, this parental reliance reduces their independence and can place unrealistic expectations on them. Ackerman and Banks note that family members who become caregivers do so without adequate training and support.

The role of technology in improving participation in society is highlighted by Söderström in her chapter about the "digital town square." She describes how the internet has provided a new way of interacting for young people with disability. However, she notes that, like any other context or environment, this digital town square can exclude particular people. The Wheaton and Bertini chapter goes on to describe efforts to make technology accessible around the world.

In explaining the lack of access in some countries, Kuemmel and Kuemmel observe that the collective ideals in some countries may mean that people with disability are expected to rely on family, and that family is expected to care for a member with a disability. This interesting interaction between independence and interdependence is one that emerges through several chapters, the most clearly of which is Gotto's chapter about two young Mixe men with disability. In this chapter, Gotto describes how disability is a relational and social phenomenon.

The impact of the context on disability and the important impact of disability on its context is outlined by the chapters on bullying in schools (see Liesman), foster care (see Cederna, Palguta, Wall, & Koch), and families (see Douglas & Borbasi). In contrast, Susa describes the dreams that can be achieved by people with disability when the context is right. This is also demonstrated by Gibson, Gover, and others. Several chapters highlight ways in which we are beginning to respect the personal needs and rights of individuals who have disability. Blessing, Golden, and Bruyère describe the development of person-centered planning and Bell, Henthorne, Hill, Turnball, and Zito describe the process of supporting autonomy. Several chapters outline movements in their countries to make schooling more accessible and appropriate for students with disability (see Agorastou, Kalyva, Kaderoglou, & Stefandis; Spirito-Dalgin, Ergene, Marrone, & Munir) or to build capacity among its citizens with disability (see Campbell; Sovani).

What is the role of these movements in countries or populations where the intersection between poverty, race, and disability delivers a triple disadvantage? Whether in developing countries or in a minority group within the richest countries in the world, people with disability who live in poverty are confronted by an intricate web of effects—they are more likely to be exposed to risks (see chapter by McDonald, Keys, & Balcazar), they are less likely to receive treatment (see Burke & Lopez), and they are less likely to have access to healthy alternatives (see DiCowden). The chapters in this series highlight the vast differences between regions of affluence and those affected by poverty. This issue is articulated more fully by Paul Leung in his preface to the series.

In conclusion, understanding disability issues that impact on people from a global perspective can contribute to the redress of health disparities and reduce marginalization caused by inappropriate services or insensitive practices.

However, as described by Kunitz (2000), "there is no assurance that all countries will benefit equally from the global economy that has emerged since World War II" (p. 1531). Indeed, Kunitz wrote that globalization could be profoundly deleterious to the capacity of some countries to provide for all their citizens, especially people with disability. The chapters in this series have clearly identified the different capacities of countries to meet the needs of their disabled citizens, as well as cultures within countries, and, of course, individuals within cultures and local communities. Thus, although we look to globalization with optimism, we understand and respect the choice of diverse countries, communities, and individuals to make their own decisions.

The chapters have highlighted the fact that not all voices are heard with the same intensity. In our introduction to this series, we lamented the fact that we were unable to represent many populations adequately. Nevertheless, our thinking in preparing these volumes was informed by voices from other places, voices that are not reproduced in these volumes, but does this type of "silent" or "secondary" representation equate to actual participation? It is clear that considerable effort is required to represent voices that are not usually heard. The assumption that globalization can equalize voices is a fallacy. Indeed, several chapters in this series comment on the unequal representation of particular populations and the methods that are being designed to give voice to silenced populations (see chapters by Campbell; Morrissey; and the many other personal narratives throughout the volumes).

The narratives are particularly important to the series because they represent voices of women and men who may not otherwise publish their stories, so we may not otherwise have the opportunity to learn from their experiences. In each volume, we have combined scholarly texts with those written from personal experience, narratives that reflect reality from the perspective of those who are living with disability rather than from those who study disability. We have combined the power of personal narratives with the rigor of academic research to highlight the value of the community voice and place it on the same level as empirical and scholarly theory and professional practice. All perspectives are important. It is only through cross-fertilization that perspectives are enhanced and solutions become apparent.

Indeed, the chapters in this series have identified both strengths and weaknesses in all countries—lessons to be learned in all directions. Throughout, there are strong common global messages that all people with disability seek to be valued, understood, and respected in all areas of their lives. They seek to be accepted as they are, rather than placed into stereotyped categories, judged, and asked to prove themselves. They seek to be connected to other people and to have dreams for the future. Around the world, systems are seeking to be more responsive to the needs of people with disability. Important trends are apparent in this series, including the need for systems to respond from a perspective of health rather than disease or deficit, for professionals to promote autonomy and capacity rather than to deplete natural resources and support systems, for communities to honor the relational and contextual nature of life rather than creating silos and pockets of isolation for people with disability. Given these global trends and demands, it is plausible then that global collaboration might lead to a stronger and unified voice for people with disability. We hope that this series goes some way toward reclaiming the globalization movement for people with disability. Perhaps if we approach the diverse global community with tolerance and respect as core values, then we may see a day when disability is a part of life, just like our gender, our height, our religion, and the color of our skin. That was one of our hopes—only time will tell, but it is an honor to have been a part of the discussion. We hope that this series becomes part of the process of finding a way forward that both respects diversity, yet contributes to the elimination of disparities.

REFERENCES

Emerson, E., McConkey, R., Noonan Walsh, P., & Felce, D. (2008). Editorial: Intellectual disability in a global context. *Journal of Policy and Practice in Intellectual Disabilities, 5*(2), 79–80.

Jong-wook, L. (2003). Global health improvement and WHO: Shaping the future. *Lancet, 362*, 2083–2088.

Kunitz, S. J. (2000). Globalization, states, and the health of indigenous peoples. *American Journal of Public Health, 90*(10), 1531–1539.

Leonardi, M., Bickenbach, J., Ustun, T. B., Kostanjsek, N., & Chatterji, S. (2006). The definition of disability: What is in a name? *Lancet, 368*, 1219–1221.

Index

Aboriginal people. *See* Indigenous model of health; SIPES model of well-being
Accessibility, 254, 306–7; from stigma and separation to accommodation and, 247–49
ADAPT framework, 11–12
African Americans, xvi. *See also* Race and ethnicity
Alcohol use. *See* Nigeria
American Psychological Association (APA), 145
Americans with Disabilities Act of 1990 (ADA), xvi, 22, 31, 242, 251; definitions of disability, xix
Amnesia, posttraumatic, 107
Annan, Kofi, xxi
Antidiscrimination laws: first countries to adopt, 22. *See also specific legislation*
Appraisal, 50
Asperger's syndrome, 213
Association for Persons with Severe Handicaps, The (TASH), 296
Attachment theory, 51–52
Australian Indigenous health, 111–13. *See also* SIPES model of well-being
Autism, experience of parenting a child with, 81, 82–89; changeable child, 86–87; depression, stress, and exhaustion, 92–93; devastation, 90; discovering a diagnosis, 83–84, 93; emotional rollercoaster, 89–94; grief and loss, 91; guilt, 91; having to battle over everything, 84; isolation, 91–92; loss of control, 94; negotiating the hostile system, 84–86, 93–94; never-ending story, 94–96; relationship stress, 87–88; research on, 81–82; searching for answers, 83; sibling stress, 88–89; suboptimal services, 84–86; the system's lack of regard for carers, 84–86
Autonomy, 17; ability to act with, 24; acting for oneself, 297–99; definitions and related terms, 18–20, 23; legislation and, 22–23; professional support and, 23–24; providing opportunities to function with, 24; types of, 21, 28–29. *See also* Supporting (and maintaining) autonomy
Awareness for disability, increasing, 254

Barlow, Lauraine, 113–14, 123, 124
Becker, S., 39–42, 44, 53
Black, A. E., 25

Brain injury: as family affair, 101–2; taking care of someone with a, 100–110
Britain, 53
Browning, Elizabeth Barrett, 291–92
Browning, P., 25
Bullying, 220–21; defining, 224; experiences of, 224–25; frequency of physical and relational, 226–27; incidence, locations, and types of, 229; parents' thoughts about, 226–28; possible informants, 227; provocative behavior and, 220–21, 224; research on, 220–21; responses of others to, 225–26; and safety of child's environment, 226–27; students' discussions about, 224–26; teachers' role in preventing, 230–31; teacher views on, 229–31
Bullying prevention programs, 226, 229–30; beliefs about, 227–28; future, 230; KINDD model, 231–35; lessons for developing, 231; whole-school approach, 234
Bush, George H. W., 31

Canada, 22
Cardol, M., 21
Caregiver roles, 129; case manager *vs.* daughter, 129–36. *See also* Young caregiving
Caregivers, 129–30, 136–37; financial burden, 129–30, 136–37; "surely someone can support me," 135. *See also* Young carers
Carter Center Mental Health Program, ix–x
Case management, 129. *See also under* Caregiver roles
Children: with disabilities, 158, 160. *See also* Young carers
Choice, 19, 22, 32, 293. *See also* Autonomy
Citizenship and mental health: concern, prejudice, and stigma in the public domain, 191–92; contradictory imperatives of coercion and recovery, 191–94 (*see also under* Mental health problems); moral and socioeconomic priorities of politicians, 193; therapeutic social control, 193–94
Civil rights movement, xvi

Classroom: supporting autonomy in, 27–28. *See also* Bullying
Clinical work, disability competency within, 145–49
Cochlear implant, 241
Cognitive autonomy support, 28, 29
Commission on Rehabilitation Counselor Certification (CRCC), 23–24
Communication Access Realtime Translation (CART), 242, 243
Communication technology. *See* Information and communication technology
Community, x
Community health centers, 6
Community support: building, 249. *See also* Support
Computers. *See* Information and communication technology
Control, loss of, 94
Coping resources, 50
Coping strategies, 50
Courtesy stigma, 47
Crisis counseling, 9
Critical realism, 186
Cultural encapsulation, 146

Deaf persons. *See under* Muslim community
Deci, E. L., 25
Decisional autonomy, 21
Decision making, 19
Declaration of Independence, 17, 20
"Declaration of independence," 26
Deficit model, 21
Denial, 90, 93–94
Dependence, 51
Depression. *See under* Autism
Described and Captioned Media Program (DCMP), 243
Developing countries, xvi. *See also* Economically developed countries
Developmental disabilities: defined, 220. *See also* Bullying
Developmental Disabilities and Bill of Rights Act (DD Act), 22, 31
"Digital town square," 65–69
Disability competency within clinical work, 145–49
"Disability identity," 304
Disability identity development model (DIDM), 139, 147–48

INDEX

Disability(ies): barriers to making it unessential, 69–70; causes, 265–66; context and, 307; definitions and meanings, xix, 21, 64, 259–60; life's journey with a, 139–45; opportunities to make it unessential, 67–69; overview, xiii; promoting cure, prevention, and amelioration of, 306
Disability psychology, 145–49
Disability rights perspective: on young caregiving, 41. *See also* Legislation; Rights-based approach to disability
Disability theory, 185, 195
Disabled person(s): goals, 32; opportunities to "remove" or reduce their disability, 306; terminology, 30n.1, 304
Disaster responses: recommendations for better, 10–12; in U.S. over past decade, 8–10, 12
Disasters and mental health, 2–3, 12. *See also* Hurricane Katrina
Discrimination: race, ethnicity, and, xv, xvi
Dreams (of normalization): dreaming big, 293–94; examples of chasing, 289–91, 294–99; focusing positive energy on one's, 291–93
Drug abuse. *See* Nigeria

Economically developed countries, less, 155–56, 161–63, 163n.1, 307. *See also* Developing countries; *specific countries*
Economic deprivation: and mental health problems, 187–88. *See also* Poverty
Education, 267–70. *See also* Bullying; Classroom
Elwan, A., xiv, xvi
Emotional health, 120–21. *See also* Disability psychology
Employment: among disabled People of Color, 153–55; in dangerous jobs, 154; disability and, 152–55, 160–63, 266–67; and mental health, 187–88
Ethnicity. *See* Race and ethnicity
Executional autonomy, 21

Family commitment, lifelong, 213–14
Family ecology model for understanding reactions to parental illness, 50

Family Futures Planning Project, 295
"Family health situation," defined, 56n.1
Family members: how disability effects daily life of, 201–7; "whole family approach" to meeting needs of young carers, 54
Family structure and foster care placement, 176
Family systems-illness model, 51
Fathers. *See* Mothers and fathers
Fear, 292
Federal Emergency Management Agency (FEMA), 2–4, 6, 9
Financial burden and support, 136–37. *See also* Poverty
Foster care, intellectual disability in, 169, 173–74, 177–78; child-related risk factors, 174–75; family and community factors, 175–77; programmatic case study, 171–74; protective and favorable outcome-promoting factors, 177–78; and reunification, 177–78
Foster care placement, 170; disability and, 170–71
Friendships, 105–9. *See also* Social relationships

Galloway, D., 234
Gender differences and gender roles, 189. *See also* Mothers and fathers
Global collaboration, 301–3
Globalization movement in health arena, 301–3, 307–9
Global perspective on health and disability, 155–61, 307–9
Goodworkers Movement International, 284
Gould, M., 30
Grief, 91
Grief theory and stages of grieving, 291–92
Group advocacy, 30
Guilt, 91
Gulf Coast: as region of disadvantage, 4–5. *See also* Hurricane Katrina

Halloran, W. D., 29–30
Hawks, S., 124
Health: definitions, conceptions, and models of, 123 (*see also* SIPES model

Health: definitions (*cont'd*) of well-being). *See also under* SIPES model of well-being
Health professionals, when disability strikes, 99–109; return to work, 109–10
Hearing impairment, 240–45, 296
HelpHandicap Foundation, 252
Ho Chi Minh City, 258–59, 262, 269. *See also* Vietnam
Holistic health, 112. *See also* SIPES model of well-being
Human rights legislation for persons with disabilities, 22–23; first countries to adopt, 22. *See also specific legislation*
Hurricane Katrina, 1–2; case vignettes, 3–4; depleted health services, 5–6; Gulf Coast as region of disadvantage, 4–5; and mental health, 2–4 (*see also* Disasters and mental health); protracted recovery and retraumatization, 7–8; social disconnection, 6–7. *See also* Disaster responses
Hurricane Rita, 2

IARCCA, an Association of Child and Family Services, 171
Ignorance, tackling, 248–49
Inclusion, 22, 290. *See also* Dreams (of normalization)
Independence, 22, 32. *See also* Autonomy; "Declaration of independence"
Indiana Association of Residential Child Care Agencies (IARCCA), 171
Indigenous issues, x, 281, 285. *See also specific cultures*
Indigenous model of health, 112–13. *See also* SIPES model of well-being
Individuals with Disabilities Education Act (IDEA), 22, 27, 29
Information and communication technology (ICT), 61–62, 307; and disability in a Norwegian context, 64–65; and the experience of solitude, 70–73; ICT experiences of disabled youths, 65–76; and the notion of disability, 67–69; and permeability of the real and virtual, 73–77; research on disabled people, social relations, and, 64; research on youth, social relations, and, 62–63

Instant messaging (MSN), 63, 66–68, 72–76
Integration into mainstream society, 22. *See also* Dreams (of normalization)
Intellectual health, 116–17. *See also* Foster care, intellectual disability in
Intensive care unit (ICU), experience of, 102–4, 106
International Classification of Functioning, Disability and Health (ICF), xiii
International Convention on the Rights of Persons with Disabilities (ICRPD), 156. *See also under* United Nations
Internet, 63, 71, 75–76; resources on, 243–44. *See also* Information and communication technology
Islam, 277. *See also* Muslim community
Isolation, 91–92. *See also* Information and communication technology; Solitude of young disabled persons

"Journeys of Healing" (Barlow), 113–14, 123, 124

Kant, Immanuel, 18
Kenya, disability in, 156–59
Kenya National Commission on Human Rights (KNCHR), 158–59
KINDD (knowledge, immersion, natural observation, data collection, and development) model. *See under* Bullying prevention programs
Kübler-Ross, Elisabeth, 291
Kunitz, S. J., 301

Lau-Smith, J., 19
Least restrictive environment (LRE), 27
Legislation: autonomy and, 22–23; human rights, 22–23. *See also specific legislation*
Loneliness. *See* Information and communication technology

Maasai, 158
Marginalization, 146
Marital stress, 87–88. *See also* Mothers and fathers; Parental perspectives on disability
Medicaid, 9–10
Medical naturalism, 186
Medical sociology literature on young caregiving, 41

Mekong River (Vietnam), 272–73
Mental distress, notion of, 195–96
Mental health: ecological effects on, 188–89; of Indigenous people, 117–18. *See also* Citizenship and mental health; Disasters and mental health; Hurricane Katrina
Mental health problems, 198–99; coercive detention and treatment of, 192–94, 196, 197; epistemological perspectives on, 186; primary and secondary deviance, 194–98; race, ethnicity, gender, age, and, 189; social forces as determinants of, 186–89; typology, 190–91. *See also* Psychological difference
Mental health professionals, role conflict and strain in, 193–94
Mental illness, 117, 118, 185, 186, 190, 192; Indigenous taboos regarding, 280; in Nigeria, 276, 280–81; physical illness and, 196–98
Micro-financing, xv
Middle adulthood, 33
Moral order, 193
Mothers and fathers, 87–88, 214–15; different but equal contributions, 212–13; different coping strategies, 207–9; different responses of helping agencies, 211–12; different social expectations for, 203, 209–11. *See also* Parental perspectives on disability
MSN (instant messaging), 63, 66–68, 72–76
Muslim community, American, 239–40, 253; challenges of a deaf participant at community events, 240–45; inclusion of individuals with disabilities in, 249–53; recommendations for, 254–55; reflections on disability in Chicagoland, 245–49

Nagata, K. K., 155
National Center for Accessible Media (NCAM), 243
National Court Reporters Association (NCRA), 244
National Response Plan, 8
New Orleans. *See* Hurricane Katrina
Nigeria, 275, 286; alcohol use, 278–79; combination of substance abuse and mental illness, 276, 280–81; cultural dynamics, 277–78; cultural taboos and traditional healers, 285; demographics, 277; future directions regarding substance use in, 286; history, 276–78; hypnosedative use, 280; igbo (marijuana) use, 279; influence of American culture, 276, 285–86; most commonly abused drugs in, 278–80; stimulant use, 279–80; substance abuse prevention efforts, 283–84; substance abuse treatment issues, 284–85; substance use among "area boys," 281; substance use among commercial workers, 282; substance use among inmates, 281–82; substance use among students, 282–83; tobacco use, 278, 279
Nongovernmental organizations (NGOs), 161, 252, 258
"Normalization," 21. *See also* Dreams (of normalization); Integration into mainstream society
Norway, 63–65; "digital town square" (central meeting place), 65–67. *See also* Information and communication technology

O'Brien, J., 293–94
Older adulthood, 33
Organizational autonomy support, 28

Parent, W. S., 20
Parental disability/illness, impact of, 46; negative, 47–48; positive, 48–49; predictors of, 49. *See also* Young caregiving
Parental perspectives on disability, 214–15; case study, 201–7; a lifelong family commitment, 213–14. *See also* Mothers and fathers
Parentification, 51
Parenting: with a disability, 42–43. *See also* Mothers and fathers; Supporting (and maintaining) autonomy
Paternalism, 194
Paternal model, 21
Pedersen, S., 50
People of Color with disabilities, 151; in United States, 152–55
Perske, Robert, 18

Persons with Disabilities Act of 2003 (PDA), 156
Persons with disabilities (PWDs). *See* Disabled person(s); *specific topics*
Philippines, disability in, 159–61
Positive behavior system (PBS), 229
Posttraumatic amnesia (PTA), 107
Posttraumatic stress disorder (PTSD), 3, 7
Poverty (and disability), xiii–xvi, 155; foster care and, 176; and health, 121; and mental health problems, 187–88; race, ethnicity, and, 153–54, 161–63. *See also* Caregivers, financial burden; Economically developed countries, less
Preventable disability, 305–6
Procedural autonomy support, 28–29
ProjectReadOn, 243
Psychiatry, 192–94
Psychological difference, social forces as determinants of judgments about, 190–92
Psychological disability: similarities and differences between physical and, 196–98. *See also* Mental health problems; Mental illness

Quality indicators, O'Brien's, 293–94

Race and ethnicity, xv–xvi; and mental health problems, 189. *See also under* Poverty
Racial/ethnic minorities, 151–55; reasons for higher rates of disabilities among, 153. *See also* People of Color with disabilities
Racial oppression, 151–52
Redlener, I., 2
Rehabilitation. *See* Brain injury
Rehabilitation Act of 1992, 22, 31
Rehabilitation Counselor Certification, Commission on, 23–24
Relationships, social. *See* Friendships; Social relationships
Resilience, 52
Respect, 293
Revenson, T. A., 50
Rice, B. D., 32
Rights-based approach to disability, 303–4. *See also* Disability rights perspective; Legislation

Risk, dignity of, 18
Risk/resilience framework, 52
Rock-climbing demonstration, 289
Rolland, J. S., 51

Schools. *See* Bullying; Classroom; Education
Self-advocacy, 29–30; group, 30
Self-determination, 18–19, 22, 28, 29; defined, 19. *See also* Autonomy
Self-management, 25. *See also* Autonomy
September 11, 2001 terrorist attacks, 7
Serna, L., 19
Shame, 292
Sharing places, 293
Sibling stress, 88–89
SIPES model of well-being, 111–14, 123, 124; emotional health represented by fourth (ring) finger of left hand, 120–21; intellectual and mental health represented by left index finger, 116–18; physical health represented by middle finger of left hand, 118–20; social health represented by left thumb, 114–16; spiritual health represented by small (fifth) finger of left hand, 121–23
Sisson, Graham, 20
Skills, improving, 293–94
Skype, 67, 68
SMS (text messages), 63, 66
Sobsey, R., 232, 233
Social, intellectual, physical, emotional, and spiritual (SIPES) aspects of health. *See* SIPES model of well-being
Social constructionism/constructivism, 186, 193–94, 196
Social construction of disability, 64–65; shift from biomedical construction to, 303
Social disconnection, 6–7
Social exclusion, 304
Social forces: as determinants of judgments about psychological difference, 190–92; as determinants of mental health problems, 186–89
Social relationships, 294; barrier in establishing, 75–76; opportunity to enhance, 73–75 (*see also* Information and communication technology). *See also* Friendships

Social support. *See* Support
Socioeconomic status (SES): and foster care placement, 176. *See also* Poverty
Solitude of young disabled persons: barrier to escaping, 71–73; experience of, 70–73; ICT as opportunity to escape, 70–71
Spiritual health, 121–23
Stafford Act, 9
Stefanou, C. R., 28
Stigma, 47–48, 191–92, 247, 304–5
Stress and coping theory, 49–50
Stress process models, 49–50
Stroke patient, caregivers of a, 130–32; eighteen months poststroke, 135–36; fourteen months poststroke, 133–34; ten months poststroke, 132–33
Substance use disorders. *See* Nigeria
Support: building community, 249; financial, 136–37; need for, 135; professional, and autonomy, 23–24. *See also under* Young carers
Supporting (and maintaining) autonomy, 25; adult roles and, 32–33; disabilities and, 20–34; features of, 28; as life commitment, 25–26; in postschool environments, 31–32; at preschool age, 26–27; at school age, 27–30; throughout adulthood, 30–33
Support systems, building internal, 254
System, confronting an unhelpful, 84–86, 305. *See also under* Autism; Mothers and fathers
Szasz, Thomas, 186, 193–94, 196

TASH (The Association for Persons with Severe Handicaps), 296
Technology. *See* Information and communication technology
Text messages (SMS), 63, 66
Thayer, T., 32
Trauma, psychological. *See* Posttraumatic stress disorder

Unemployment. *See* Employment
United Kingdom (UK), 53

United Nations (UN), 22–23; Convention on the Rights of Persons with Disabilities, xiii, xxi, 22, 302, 306 (*see also* International Convention on the Rights of Persons with Disabilities)
Universal design of facilities, 254–55

Values, 293–94; building on one another, 294–95
Vietnam, 257, 259–64; definition and prevalence of disabilities in, 259–62; demographics of people with disabilities, 264–66; dispatches from, 258–59; employment issues, 266–67; hopes and dreams for persons with disabilities (PWDs) in, 270–72; journey to Mekong River, 272–73; unmet needs, 268; voices of people with disabilities in, 257, 262–71
Violence, exposure to: and foster care placement, 176–77
"Voices of Persons with Disabilities, The" (survey instrument), 263–64

Walmsley, J., 51
Wehmeyer, M. L., 19

Young caregiving: experience of, 45–46; factors that pull and push children into, 44–45; impact, 43–44, 46–49; nature of, 43–44
Young carer field, research traditions in, 40–41
Young Carer of Parents Inventory (YCOPI), 45–46, 55; factors and themes in, 45–46
Young carers, 40; contextual process models for understanding, 49–51; defined, 39–40; family-level support for, 54; parent-level support for, 54; pathology and risk models for understanding, 51–52; policy and, 52–53; prevalence, 41–42; research on, 55–56; service provision for, 53–55; systemic-level support for, 54–55
Youths, disabled, 65

About the Advisory Board Members

Lesley Chenoweth, BSocWk, MSocWk, Ph.D., is the inaugural Professor of Social Work and Co-Director of the Griffith Abilities Research Program at Griffith University in Australia. She has more than 35 years of experience as a social work and human service practitioner and academic, 20 of these in the disability area. Lesley's research has spanned disability issues, human services and rural communities, welfare reform, recruitment and retention in human service organizations and child welfare, social work practice, disability policy analysis, deinstitutionalization, families, violence and abuse. She is a regular consultant to government and community organizations and has served on numerous boards and committees for disability, legal, and family welfare agencies. Lesley serves on several editorial boards and is a regularly invited speaker in Australia and overseas.

Jean Lau Chin, Ed.D., ABPP, is Professor and Dean of the Derner Institute of Advanced Psychological Studies at Adelphi University in Garden City, New York. Chin is also series editor for the Praeger series Psychology in Race and Ethnicity. Her prior executive management positions include Systemwide Dean, California School of Professional Psychology at Alliant International University; President, CEO Services; Regional Director, Massachusetts Behavioral Health Partnership; Executive Director, South Cove Community Health Center; and Co-Director, Thom Child Guidance Clinic. She is a licensed psychologist with almost 40 years of clinical, educational, and management experience in health and mental health services. Jean has published extensively with 10 books and over 200 presentations in the areas of cultural competence in health, education, and mental health; ethnic minority and Asian American mental health issues; and women's issues, including leadership. Her most recent book is *Women and Leadership: Transforming Visions and Diverse Voices* (Blackwell, 2007) and an upcoming three volume set on Diversity in Mind and in Action (Praeger Press, in press).

Sue Kroeger, Ed.D., is currently Director of Disability Resources at the University of Arizona. Prior to coming to Arizona in 1999, she was Director of Disability Services at the University of Minnesota for 14 years. She manages a staff of 40 full- and part-time employees that, guided by a social construction of disability, provide services to faculty, staff, and students with disabilities, assist the university in meeting its legal obligations, and provide consultation and education on designing inclusive learning and working environments. Sue received her master's degree in rehabilitation counseling at the University of Arizona and her doctorate in human rehabilitative services at the University of Northern Colorado. Prior to coming to higher education, she worked in public and private rehabilitation. In addition to her administrative duties, Sue has presented at numerous conferences, published articles on disability and higher education, and coedited a book titled *Responding to Disability Issues in Student Affairs*. She has been Treasurer and President of the National Association of Higher Education and Disability. She holds adjunct faculty status in the Department of Rehabilitation, where she teaches undergraduate courses in disability studies and advises graduate students. Sue has been principal investigator for numerous federal grants and has consulted nationally and internationally.

Paul Leung, Ph.D., is currently Professor in the Department of Rehabilitation, Social Work and Addictions at the University of North Texas. He has held previous academic and administrative appointments at Deakin University (Melbourne, Australia), the University of Illinois–Urbana, the University of North Carolina at Chapel Hill, and the University of Arizona. Paul's interests have included rehabilitation and disability of persons from diverse racial/ethnic backgrounds and students with disabilities. He is a fellow of the American Psychological Association (APA) and a past president of APA's Division of Rehabilitation Psychology (22), the National Council on Rehabilitation Education and the National Association of Multicultural Rehabilitation Concerns. He is a recipient of APA's Division 22 Lifetime Achievement Award.

Joseph E. Trimble, Ph.D., formerly a Fellow at Harvard University's Radcliffe Institute for Advanced Study, is Professor of Psychology at Western Washington University. He has held numerous offices in the International Association for Cross-Cultural Psychology and the American Psychological Association (APA). Joseph holds Fellow status in three APA divisions. He is past President of the Society for the Psychological Study of Ethnic Minority Issues and a former council member for the Society for the Psychological Study of Social Issues. He has generated over 130 publications on cross-cultural and ethnic topics in psychology, including 17 edited and coauthored books. His recent books include the *Handbook of Ethical Research with Ethnocultural Populations and Communities* and *Counseling across Cultures* (6th ed.).

Joseph has received numerous excellence in teaching and mentoring awards for his work in the field of ethnic and cultural psychology, including the Excellence in Teaching Award and the Paul J. Olscamp Outstanding Faculty Research Award from Western Washington University; APA's Division 45 Lifetime Achievement Award; the Janet E. Helms Award for Mentoring and Scholarship in Professional Psychology at Teachers College, Columbia University; the Washington State Psychological Association Distinguished Psychologist Award for 2002; the Peace and Social Justice Award from APA's Division 48; and the Distinguished Elder Award from the National Multicultural Conference and Summit in 2007.

About the Editors and Contributors

ABOUT THE EDITORS

Martha E. Banks, Ph.D., completed her training in the American Psychological Association (APA)-approved Clinical Psychology Program at the University of Rhode Island, followed by an APA-approved internship at the Des Moines Child Guidance Center. She is an APA fellow and a fellow of the Society for Women in Psychology, with membership for more than two decades. She has over 30 years of professional experience as a clinician, researcher, and professor in psychology. Martha is currently an APA Council Representative and President of the Society for the Psychology of Women, among other roles at APA. Her service to APA was recognized with a presidential citation in 2008. Martha has also been a Professor of Black Studies at The College of Wooster. In 2003, she was the recipient of the Sue Rosenberg Zalk Award for Distinguished Service. Throughout her clinical career, she has been invited to participate as a presenter at conferences and to publish. Her most recent outstanding contribution is the editorship of the book *Women with Visible and Invisible Disabilities: Multiple Intersections, Multiple Issues, Multiple Therapies.* Many of Martha's professional presentations have involved the neuropsychological assessment and treatment of female victims of abuse; these presentations have reflected the coauthorship of and ongoing research involving the Ackerman-Banks Neuropsychological Rehabilitation Battery and the Post-Traumatic Brain Injury Interview and Checklist.

Reva Mariah S. Gover, M.A., or Mariah, the name to which she is commonly known, was born in Sacaton, Arizona. Her mother, Juana Casillas, is from the village of Cowlic in the Sells District of the Tohono O'odham Nation. Her father, George E. Gover, a Skidi-Pawnee, was raised in Pawnee, Oklahoma.

Currently, Mariah, a writer and consultant, resides in Tucson, Arizona. During her two-year tenure working for the Tohono O'odham Community College as their first writing instructor, Mariah was also a member of the Tohono O'odham Nation's Radio Task Force. As an avid writer and perpetual student, Mariah served a total of three years as a student editor for *Red Ink: An American Indian Student Publication* and has had her poetry published in publications such as *Brooklyn Review*, *Cimarron Review*, *Salt Fork Review*, as well as *Sister Nations: A Native American Woman's Anthology*.

Elizabeth Kendall, Ph.D., is Research Professor at the Griffith Institute of Health and Medical Research, Griffith University, and Associate Director of the Centre for National Research on Disability and Rehabilitation, at Griffith University and University of Queensland. She has a B.A. in psychology and special education and postgraduate qualifications in rehabilitation psychology. Elizabeth completed her doctorate in 1997 on adjustment following traumatic brain injury and received the Dean's Commendation for Outstanding Ph.D. Thesis (University of Queensland). She was awarded a Medal for Excellence in Research Supervision in 1999, and all her graduate students have also received commendations for excellence. For the past 20 years, she has maintained both community/clinical practice and a research agenda in the issues faced by people with acquired disabilities or chronic conditions. She has focused on participatory methods for developing innovative service models. Elizabeth has published in over 60 international peer-reviewed journals and books and maintains an active role in the development of non-government organizations that address gaps in service delivery for people with disability or chronic disease.

Catherine A. Marshall, Ph.D., CRC, NCC, is Research Professor in the department of Educational Psychology, Northern Arizona University, and Adjunct Professor, Centre for National Research on Disability and Rehabilitation Medicine, Griffith University, Australia. She has more than 25 juried publications. Recently, her work has focused on cancer as a chronic illness/disability and the impact of the cancer experience on the family. In April 2007, Catherine received a Ruth L. Kirschstein National Research Service Award for Individual Senior Fellowship, funded by the Department of Health and Human Services, National Institutes of Health, National Cancer Institute to support her new work. Catherine is a Senior Scholar with the UA National Center of Excellence in Women's Health. A Fulbright scholar who researched the needs and resources of Indigenous people with disabilities in Oaxaca, Mexico, her research in Oaxaca was also sponsored for six years by the National Institute on Disability and Rehabilitation Research. Catherine was the recipient of a 1997 National Council on Rehabilitation Education Outstanding Researcher of the Year award for research with American Indian families and chronic illness/disability. She is Founder and President of the nonprofit organization Women's International Leadership Institute (WILI; www.wili.org), the purpose of which is to benefit low-income women seeking to improve their educational and economic status. Through WILI, Catherine participated in the coordination of the 2004 international forum Participatory Action Research and Indigenous Ways of Knowing in Oceania and the

United States: Women as Researchers and Partners in Community-Based Disability and Rehabilitation Research.

ABOUT THE CONTRIBUTORS

Dianne Barnett, RN; M. Remote Health Practice; M. Remote Health Management, has been working as a registered nurse since 1972 and currently holds the position of District Director of Nursing with the Mackay Health Service District. Dianne holds qualifications in the areas of community health, midwifery, and child health. Additionally, she has obtained master's degrees in both remote health practice and remote health management through Flinders University of South Australia. Dianne has spent the majority of her career in rural and remote areas of Queensland and Western Australia in the preferred area of indigenous health. Her understanding of the cultural gaps in Western medicine's ability to meet the spiritual and emotional needs of Australian Aboriginal peoples has caused her to develop a more comprehensive and holistic approach to health service delivery.

Leda Barnett, B.A., B.Ed., B.Psych.(Hons)., is an Australian Aboriginal woman; her grandmother was taken from her family as a baby (one of the stolen generation). Her educational qualifications are in arts, education and psychology and she is currently working as a psychologist-intern. Leda has published articles on indigenous ways of knowing and indigenous women with disabilities and has researched chronic disease management in Australian Aboriginal communities. Her experiences in indigenous research have allowed her to explore the meaning of holistic health in Australian Aboriginal culture and its relationship with Western medicine.

Bedarius Bell Jr., M.S., C.R.C., is a Certified Rehabilitation Counselor (CRC) who received his master's of science degree in rehabilitation counseling from Auburn University. He has worked for 10 years as a Vocational Rehabilitation Counselor for the Alabama Department of Rehabilitation Services, serving the deaf and hard-of-hearing populations. Bedarius is the current President of the Alabama Association of Multicultural Rehabilitation Concerns. He is also a doctoral student in Auburn University's Department of Rehabilitation and Special Education.

Isra Bhatty, B.A., is studying for her J.D. at Yale Law School and her MPhil at Oxford University. In 2006, she graduated from the University of Chicago with bachelor's degrees in Economics and Near Eastern Languages & Civilizations. Her research interests are in criminal law, disability law, and comparative Islamic law.

Sally Borbasi, R.N., Ph.D., is Professor of Nursing in the School of Nursing and Midwifery, Griffith University, Brisbane, Australia. She is a long-standing nursing academic and qualitative researcher with a particular interest in phenomenologies. Sally has a background in nursing care of people with a disability as well as acute and critical care nursing. She has conducted studies exploring the quality of life of people with a disability who transition from institutional type care to community settings. Sally is a member of the Griffith Abilities Research Group.

Elaine A. Burke, Psy.D., is Associate Professor at Alliant International University, California School of Professional Psychology, in Los Angeles. She received her degree from the University of Denver, School of Professional Psychology. Her research interests include health and neuropsychology, sex roles and gender, and multiculturalism and internationalism. Elaine has numerous publications/presentations related to her interest areas. She spent a semester in Kenya during her sabbatical. During that time she was teaching, developing a program, and conducting research related to health and gender issues in Kenya.

Samantha Bursnall, B.Beh.Sc. (Hons), Ph.D., is a psychologist within the Department of Child and Family at the Tavistock Centre and an affiliated inner London Child and Adolescent Mental Health Service (CAMHS) that specializes in disability and autism. She has a particular research and clinical interest in the impact of disability and illness on family members and has been involved with a number of published articles and book chapters on the subject both in Australia and the United Kingdom. Samantha's research has focused on young carers, the impact of acquired brain injury on siblings, and parenting a child with autism and learning difficulties.

Tara Catalano, BA (Hons), MHuServ (Hons) has extensive practice and research experience in the area of disability and chronic illness over the past 15 years. Tara began her career in human services working in the community with seniors in her hometown of Staten Island, New York. Following a move to Australia in the mid-1990s, she worked in collaboration with people with intellectual disability and their families for a number of years in the community sector before shifting to the university environment. She has particular interests in the individual and family perspective, the interaction between service users and service providers, self-management of chronic illness and acquired disabilities (e.g., acquired brain injury), peer support interventions, and partnerships between and within the health and community sectors.

Crystal L. Cederna, M.A., is a doctoral student in the School of Psychological Sciences at the University of Indianapolis, where she also received a master's degree in clinical psychology. Her doctoral studies have an emphasis on child and health psychology, and she has aspirations of serving this population through the provision of evaluative and psychotherapeutic services.

Debra Domalewski B.Hum.Serv (Rehab Couns) is a rehabilitation consultant at CRS Australia. Debra was awarded the Human Services Medal for academic excellence and the Rehabilitation Association of Australasia award for the highest achieving graduate in the rehabilitation stream. Debra is currently studying for her Ph.D. at Griffith University. Her research experience has included projects in the field of community rehabilitation, adolescent health issues, international research partnerships, health partnerships, and community rehabilitation curriculum development. Her current research interests are partnerships, rehabilitation, and community development.

Heather Douglas, Dip OT, MSWAP, MBA, Ph.D. Candidate. Heather has a long-standing interest in the exclusionary aspects of disability. After working as an occupational therapist, Heather broadened into community capacity building. Later she developed a research agenda on change processes in social policy and also within organizations. Some of her research considers the exclusion of disadvantaged groups from decision making. She has published in social change processes and management of small organizations such as those that offer services to people with disabilities. Currently, Heather is researching social entrepreneurship as a change process and is a Ph.D. candidate at Griffith University in Brisbane, Australia.

Jennifer Gibson, Ph.D. is on staff as a psychologist at the University of California, Davis. Her research interest is the advancement of mental health care to clients with disabilities. She is a,writer, consultant, and provides disability competency training to mental health professionals nationwide. In 2006, she won the Disability Service Award for distinguished contributions in promoting disability within education from the American College Personnel Association's (ACPA) Standing Committee on Disability.

Roy Grant, M.A., is Director, Applied Research and Policy Analysis, The Children's Health Fund, New York. He has published more than two dozen articles in peer-reviewed journals and book chapters on diverse topics including infant and early childhood development, disaster mental health, and public health policy, with a focus on high-risk and medically underserved populations.

Shelley R. Henthorne is a third-year doctoral student in rehabilitation and special education at Auburn University. She received her undergraduate degree in mild learning behavioral disorders in 2001 and her master's degree in collaborative teacher special education in 2003, both from Auburn University. Shelley is a member of the Council for Exceptional Children and Delta Epsilon Iota Honor Society. Her research interests include transition and parent involvement in education.

Doris Adams Hill is a board-certified behavior analyst and a doctoral candidate in rehabilitation and special education with a focus in autism and behavior disorders at Auburn University. She entered the teaching field after a career as an officer in the U.S. Army. Doris has presented at numerous conferences alone in and in collaboration with other professional educators. She is currently working on her dissertation and several other articles in the field of autism and leadership.

Melissa Kendall Ph.D.; B.Sc. (Psych), Grad. Dip. App. Sci (Prof. Psych), MHumSrv, is Research and Development Officer for the Transitional Rehabilitation Program (Queensland Spinal Cord Injuries Service) and the Acquired

Brain Injury Outreach Service, both state-funded community rehabilitation services for people with spinal cord injury and acquired brain injury, respectively. She is also a doctoral candidate with the School of Human Services, Griffith University. Melissa has an emerging publication record on rehabilitation- and disability-related topics and has research interests in the areas of long-term care needs, friendship, and social support following injury.

Eilis Kennedy, M.B., B.Ch., B.A.O., M.R.C.Psych., is a Consultant in child and adolescent psychiatry at the Tavistock Centre, London. She works in a team offering a specialist psychotherapy service to children with autism and their families. Eilis is particularly interested in the impact of autism on the family system. She is involved in a number of research projects evaluating the effectiveness of psychological treatments in child and adolescent mental health and has published several articles in this area.

Steven M. Koch, Ph.D., H.S.P.P., is an Adjunct Assistant Professor for the Department of Pediatrics, Indiana University School of Medicine. He is a school psychologist on the interdisciplinary team at the Riley Child Development Center, where he assesses children with suspected intellectual and neurodevelopmental disabilities. In 1998, he was given the Friend of Children Award for his work on measuring outcomes for children in foster and residential care.

Rocky Liesman is Clinical Psychology resident with the U.S. Air Force. He received his doctorate training at Wright State University's School of Professional Psychology, where he received the Elizabeth B. Wolf Award for his outstanding enthusiasm, compassion, optimism, collegiality, and contribution to the field of clinical psychology. Rocky completed his doctoral dissertation on the subject of bullying among children with developmental disabilities and has been published in the *National Psychologist.*

Patricia "Denise" Lopez, Ph.D., is Assistant Professor at Alliant International University, Marshall Goldsmith School of Management, in Los Angeles, California. She received a Ph.D. in Organizational Psychology from Columbia University, New York. Her research and consulting interests include organizational behavior, change management, workforce diversity, multiculturalism, and internationalism. Denise is originally from the Philippines and previously taught various courses in organizational behavior and human resource management at the Asian Institute of Management.

Stephanie L. Lusk, Ph.D., C.R.C., is Assistant Professor at the North Carolina Agricultural and Technical State University in Greensboro. She earned her doctorate in rehabilitation and her B.A. in psychology from the University of Arkansas and her master's in rehabilitation counseling from Arkansas State University. Stephanie has prior work experience in career development and placement, transition planning, substance abuse treatment, and teaching addictions studies courses. Her primary areas of research interests include attitudes toward individuals with addictions; treatment and health disparities among substance users; relationships among culture, mental illness, and addiction; and co-occurring disorders among African American women.

Paula A. Madrid, Psy.D., is Associate Research Scientist, Columbia University's Mailman School of Public Health; Director, Psychosocial Preparedness Division, National Center for Disaster Preparedness, Columbia University; and Senior Director, Children's Health Fund's Mental Health Program. Paula's research interests include trauma, PTSD, resilience, psychosocial preparedness, disaster recovery, and increasing community resiliency. She has published articles on establishing mental health services postdisaster and on the impact of trauma and children and those who care for them.

David N. Morrissey, MPS, is the Executive Director of the United States International Council on Disabilities, based in Washington, DC. David was a member of the inaugural class of the Clinton School of Public Service at the University of Arkansas, through which he performed the fieldwork project in Vietnam recorded in this volume, earning his Master of Public Service degree in 2006. David was the 2007 Disability Policy Leadership Fellow with the Association of University Centers on Disabilities and advanced there to manage projects under federal contracts with the Administration on Developmental Disabilities and the National Center on Birth Defects and Developmental Disabilities at the Centers for Disease Control and Prevention. He has presented on the transition to adulthood for youth with disabilities, particularly youth with spina bifida, both nationally and internationally.

Kenneth I. Pakenham B.A., M.A.P. (clinical), Ph.D. is Associate Professor in Clinical and Health Psychology in the School of Psychology at the University of Queensland, Australia. He has published over 70 refereed journal articles on disability, illness, and caregiving. In particular, Ken and his colleagues have pioneered intervention, measurement and theory development research in young caregiving.

Melissa Palguta, B.S., is a doctoral student in the School of Psychological Sciences at the University of Indianapolis. She has a B.S. in psychology from the University of Wisconsin, Madison, and has experience treating and assessing children and adolescents in residential treatment facilities.

Teresia M. Paul is a graduate student at North Carolina Agricultural and Technical State University, pursuing a master's of science degree in rehabilitation counseling with a specialization in behavioral addictions. She received her B.S. in family and community services with a concentration in psychology and ethnic studies from East Carolina University. Teresia is currently a Rehabilitation Services Administration Long-Term Training Scholar. She has research interests in issues concerning culture, addiction, and mental health in the domestic and international arena.

David Pilgrim B.Sc., M.Sc. (Soc), M.Psycol (Clin), Dip.Pscyhother., Ph.D. is Professor of Mental Health Policy at the University of Central Lancashire.

He trained and worked as a clinical psychologist before completing a Ph.D. and going on to research various aspects of mental health services and policy. David has published extensively in these fields.

Anne Rogers SRN, B.A. (Hons), M.Sc. (Econ), Ph.D. is Professor of the Sociology of Health Care in the School of Community Based Medicine at the University of Manchester. She has long-standing research interests in the sociology of mental health and illness and currently leads a program of research on self-management and long-term conditions.

Rachel Rosen is Coordinator for Mental Health and National Programs at the Children's Health Fund. She graduated cum laude from Tufts University with a B.A. in child development and community health. Rachel's interests include psychosocial issues impacting children postdisaster/trauma.

Rob Senior, M.B., B.S., M.Sc., M.R.C.Psych., is Consultant in Child and Adolescent Psychiatry and Senior Research Fellow at University College, London. He is currently Medical Director of the Tavistock and Portman NHS Foundation Trust. A systemic psychotherapist by background, Rob's research and clinical interests are in the intergenerational transmission of psychological distress and disturbance and early intervention to improve outcome.

Sylvia Söderström is Research Fellow at the Norwegian University of Science and Technology in Trondheim, Department of Social Work and Health Science. Her research interests are on disabled children and youth's experiences of inclusion and exclusion in everyday life and on the social construction of disability. Sylvia's Ph.D. project is on disabled youth and the significance of ICT in exclusion and inclusion processes in their everyday lives. She has earlier written on how children with congenital heart disease experience their everyday lives and social relationships.

Connie Susa, M.Ed., has been a pioneering parent leader in Rhode Island. She was the first parent of children with disabilities to train and mentor her peers for the Rhode Island Department of Education. She led the initiative to create the RI Parent Information Network when federal funds became available. For the RI Developmental Disabilities Council, Connie helped build a curriculum and materials at the University of Rhode Island to plan for the future of aging parents and their adult sons and daughters with developmental disabilities. She was Director of Child and Family Services for United Cerebral Palsy of Rhode Island. Connie has written and presented extensively on the inclusion of individuals with disabilities in education, employment, and community life. Along with other families, she established and presently coordinates Personal Lifetime Advocacy Networks of Rhode Island.

Mobin Tawakkul, M. Eng., is currently the Chair of Disability Needs & Awareness Working Group (DNA-WG) Committee for a U.S. non-profit organization called the Association of Muslim Health Professionals (AMHP). He received his bachelor's degree in chemical engineering and master's degree in pharmaceutical engineering from the University of Michigan in 2002 and 2003, respectively. His interests include investigating novel accessibility solutions available in American society that can educate and empower the American Muslim community to serve and assist those with disabilities.

Jane W. Turnbull-Humphries, M.Ed, NCC, is a doctoral student in rehabilitation counseling at Auburn University and a National Certified Counselor. She was honored with the 2007–2008 Wendy Baker Memorial Endowed Graduate Award given for demonstrating outstanding spirit, abilities, and values while working with students with disabilities. She has presented and participated in research in areas such as self-advocacy, autonomy, diversity, HIV/AIDS awareness, eating disorders, and posttraumatic stress disorder. Her current dissertation area of interest is the underutilization of group work in vocational rehabilitation settings.

Jo Violet, M.B., B.S. (Lond), D.C.H., M.R.C.Psych., is Consultant in Child and Adolescent Psychiatry, with an interest in psychotherapy. At the time of the research informing her chapter, she was working in an inner London Child and Adolescent Mental Health Service (CAMHS) affiliated with the Tavistock and Portman NHS Foundation Trust that specialized in disability and autism. Jo has an interest in the broad spectrum of disability and developmental disorders within children and has worked in child and adult psychotherapy. Her CAMHS service involvement included diagnostic work of children with suspected autism and psychotherapy with parents who had a child with a disability.

Jacqueline Remondet Wall, Ph.D., H.S.P.P., C.R.C., is an Associate Professor in the School of Psychological Sciences at the University of Indianapolis. Trained in rehabilitation and industrial-organizational psychology; much of her work has been consulting with organizations that provide human service, including developing methods of monitoring outcomes.

Mohammed Yousuf is currently the President and Founder of HelpHandicap Foundation. He is a certified aging-in-place specialist (CAPS) and an accessibility specialist. He is a co-chair of People with Disabilities Affinity Group and a member of Diversity Impact Forum. He received his bachelor's degree in electronics and communication engineering from Osmania University in 1988, master's degree in computer engineering from Wayne State University in 1992, and CAPS certification in 2006. He completed Harvard University's program in Universal Design, Fair Housing & ADA/ABA Guidelines in 2007.

Stephanie T. Zito is a doctoral student in special education at Auburn University. Her research interests include self-determination and peer mentoring for students with disabilities. She is a member of the Honor Society of Phi Kappa Phi and currently serves as Graduate Student Vice President for the Auburn chapter.